ROUTLEDGE LIBRARY EDITIONS:
ALCOHOL AND ALCOHOLISM

I0130928

Volume 8

ALCOHOLISM

ALCOHOLISM

New Knowledge and New Responses

Edited by
GRIFFITH EDWARDS
AND
MARCUS GRANT

Routledge
Taylor & Francis Group

LONDON AND NEW YORK

First published in 1977 by Croom Helm

This edition first published in 2024
by Routledge
4 Park Square, Milton Park, Abingdon, Oxon OX14 4RN

and by Routledge
605 Third Avenue, New York, NY 10158

Routledge is an imprint of the Taylor & Francis Group, an informa business

British Library Cataloguing in Publication Data
A catalogue record for this book is available from the British Library

ISBN: 978-1-032-59082-0 (Set)
ISBN: 978-1-032-60756-6 (Volume 8) (hbk)
ISBN: 978-1-032-60758-0 (Volume 8) (pbk)
ISBN: 978-1-003-46039-8 (Volume 8) (ebk)

DOI: 10.4324/9781003460398

Publisher's Note
The publisher has gone to great lengths to ensure the quality of this reprint but points out that some imperfections in the original copies may be apparent.

Disclaimer
The publisher has made every effort to trace copyright holders and would welcome correspondence from those they have been unable to trace.

ALCOHOLISM

New Knowledge and New Responses

Edited by
GRIFFITH EDWARDS and MARCUS GRANT

CROOM HELM LONDON

© 1977 Griffith Edwards and Marcus Grant

Croom Helm Ltd,
2-10 St John's Road, London SW11

British Library Cataloguing in Publication Data

Alcoholism.
  1. Alcoholism – Congresses
  I. Edwards, Griffith II. Grant, Marcus
  362.2'92   HV5009

ISBN 0-85664-479-X

Printed in Great Britain by Biddles Ltd, Guildford, Surrey

CONTENTS

Contents *(continued)*

Section III: Treatment and Education

PREFACES

From the President of The Royal College of Physicians, Sir Cyril Clarke

The Royal College of Physicians of London has always been much concerned with preventive aspects of medicine. When in 1726 it was 'appointed by the law of this Kingdom to take care of the health of His Majesty's subjects in London and within 7 miles circuit of the same', Dr Freind, the only MP Fellow, drew the attention of the House of Commons to 'the evil of the excessive drinking of spirituous liquors'. More recently, the College has thrown its weight against cigarette smoking, has endorsed the value of the fluoridation of water supplies and suggested measures to prevent coronary heart disease.

It therefore gives me, as President of the College, great pleasure to write one of the prefaces to the report of this outstanding symposium on the problems of alcoholism. The papers given cover ground common to physicians, psychiatrists, accident surgeons, physiologists and geneticists, with the aim of bringing workers in these disciplines closer together. The table of contents shows which particular problems were tackled, and the main emphasis is to give information about what to do when the diagnosis is established, whether the disorder presents as a medical or as a social question. The symposium also deals with the much more difficult dilemma of when it does not 'present' at all. It is likely that a considerable proportion of the population drinks too much for its optimum health but the people who do so often appear well and have no obvious medical or social problem. They are however already in a way dependent and should be aware that they are at risk because some added stress may tip the balance adversely.

It seems certain that the prevalence of alcoholism is rising in this country and the pattern of services needed to stem it and to make the public aware of its dangers is an important issue. What is also clear, however, is that whoever heads the team should know of the information contained in this book. I wish it well.

Cyril A. Clarke, KBE, MD, PRCP, FRS

From The President of The Royal College of Psychiatrists,
Professor Linford Rees

Alcoholism is acknowledged to be a seriously growing problem in many parts of the world. It is a complex disorder with psychiatric, physical, psychological and social aspects, having far reaching harmful effects on the family and society, as well as on physical and mental health of the alcoholic himself. It has been estimated that in England and Wales 11 out of every 1,000 in the adult population have a serious drink problem, and alcoholism is now a major cause of admission to psychiatric and general hospitals.

Alcoholism is a medico-social problem of such magnitude that this comprehensive volume, embodying advances in knowledge of causation, treatment and prevention, fills an urgent need.

The multifactorial nature of alcohol dependence necessitates multiplicity of disciplinary approaches for the study of both its aetiology and its diverse clinico-pathological manifestations. This is provided in the book by an up-to-date account of epidemiological, social, psychological, biological and genetic aspects of the disorder. Similarly, the varieties of physical harm resulting from alcoholism are authoritatively described as well as its impact on the family, home and work, and its role in accidents, crime and suicide. Modern advances in treatment are carefully assessed and how further improvements in therapy and rehabilitation can be achieved.

The recent alarming increase in the proportion of young people with serious alcoholic problems brings home the urgent need for effective preventive measures. The contributors have presented their material in a lively and interesting style, and the book will be read with interest and benefit by all those concerned with the care of this perplexing, distressing and disabling disorder.

W. Linford Rees, MD, FRCP, PRCPsych

INTRODUCTION

Griffith Edwards and Marcus Grant

'Delivery of health care' is a phrase much in vogue. Research carried out a few years ago in Camberwell showed, however, that among people identified by a community survey as having a serious drinking problem, not more than 22 per cent had been in contact with any appropriate help during the previous twelve months. So far as drinking problems are concerned, the delivery men have manifestly not been very successful.

Not only is health care failing to reach over 75 per cent of the potential customers, but the primary health team and the hospital services have here great difficulty in working out their respective roles. Communication between hospital and outside world over these tricky and often intensely worrying problems is all too seldom in terms of the real consultation or shared conference: bits of paper go to and fro.

There must also be concern as to how within the hospital service the psychiatrists on the one hand, and the physicians and surgeons on the other, are working together on alcohol problems. The larger truth perhaps is that for most of the time they simply do not work together. Too often they seem to go about things in a way which fragments the reality of the patient's needs. The linked problems are lack of knowledge, lack of confidence and lack of communication.

Such worries about the way in which alcohol problems are currently being met in this country are likely to be the stuff of rather dispirited and reiterative conversation whenever people specially interested in these matters talk over their experiences. There is an awareness of course that health response to people with drinking difficulties does not stand on its own, but that what is happening in this special sector is a reflection of the much wider business of general health and social service organisation.

What constructively is to be done, so that in the most practical terms we can be better assured that a forty year old woman living down the road and drinking three bottles of sherry a day, will meet up with someone who can initiate humane, technically competent and integrated help, before her liver is damaged, her children in care or she commits suicide? How are we to avoid all the delivery men severally just passing her by, or the hepatologist treating her liver, with her family

and her personal life being neglected? How alternatively are we to
ensure that the psychiatrist is not the only expert she sees, with the
physical aspects of her problems given inadequate attention? Is
someone going to help the family before the children are in care?
There is no one master stroke which can meet the question of 'what
to do'. The answer lies partly in terms of the slow business of
accumulating more knowledge, is partly the continuing task of
professional education, and lies also of course in the planning and
evolution of better services shaped in terms of all the growing
understandings.

Sometimes, though, one way to help things move forward a little
is to hold a conference which specially focuses on a problem. In
September 1976, a four-day meeting attended by senior doctors from
all parts of the United Kingdom was held at the Institute of Psychiatry.
Its feature was the declared intent of putting together evolving
scientific understanding, psychiatric and general medical concerns and
the perspectives of the doctor who works in the community. The
intention was then on the basis of such review to try to look practically
at the future of cooperative health care for the troubled drinker. The
insistence was that old professional barriers should be transcended. The
product of that lively meeting is this book.

The book is not though just a collection of the papers as they were
originally delivered at the Conference. In the light of the panels and
floor discussions, authors were invited, where appropriate, to carry
their thinking further and produce for this book papers which took
account of the debates. Rather than publishing transcripts of the actual
discussions, we believe that the best way to use the valuable
contributions made by so many discussants is to allow their thinking to
find its reflection in the revision of papers.

The papers which were delivered bore witness to the fact that there
have indeed been advances in understanding many aspects of drinking.
But it is equally clear that there are important gaps in knowledge. Basic
questions of nomenclature are still in confusion — not everyone can
agree even as to what is meant by 'alcoholism'. When it comes to
explaining abnormal drinking it is not as yet easy to put together
explanations at sociological, psychological and biological levels,
although this begins to look more hopeful. The role of fiscal and
control policies in preventing harm from drinking is a subject on which
views diverge. To talk of getting more people into treatment makes
little sense unless treatment can be shown to be effective, and as
assumptions as to the worth of traditional therapies are being

questioned.

The meeting certainly gave major and critical attention to show how better cooperation between professionals is to be achieved, and the shape of new services determined. The new patterns will have to build on the realities of what is available: with current NHS stringencies it is for some years going to be a matter of better deployment of existing resources, rather than lush new investment. Different parts of the country will find different answers and there is room for much variety in experiments.

And everyone is of course aware that a phrase like 'community based', or words like 'team' or 'cooperation' and 'multidisciplinary', all too easily become modish slogans while the woman still drinks her sherry behind the curtains. The September meeting, for those who attended, seemed to move understanding a little forward, and we hope that this book can serve the same purpose. But there is still a long way to go before the delivery system achieves the goal of reaching the majority of people in need, with help which works.

A Note on the Alcohol Education Centre

The Alcohol Education Centre (AEC) is an independent organisation whose function is to provide education and training for all those who work with the problems resulting from alcohol abuse. It runs a wide range of conferences, seminars and courses. Further information about its activities can be obtained from the Organiser, Alcohol Education Centre, The Maudsley Hospital, 99 Denmark Hill, London SE5.

Editors' Acknowledgements

The Conference on which this book is based and hence the content of the book itself, owes much to the time given to conference planning by Dr D.L. Davies and Dr Roger Williams. The organisation of the meeting was carried out by the staff of the AEC: particular thanks are due to Mr Mike Lewington and Mrs Kate Gosney. The typing of material for publication was largely undertaken by Mrs Julia Polglaze in the Addiction Research Unit, and we are grateful for her supreme skill and unfailing patience. The preparation of transcript material was undertaken by Mrs Lorna Webster. Art work was prepared by Mrs Patience MacGregor; the index was compiled by Dr David Hirst.

We particularly wish to acknowledge the generous financial support given by Lederle Laboratories, without whom this book could not have been produced.

SECTION I. SCIENTIFIC UNDERSTANDING

1 CIRRHOSIS AND ALCOHOL CONSUMPTION: AN EPIDEMIOLOGICAL PERSPECTIVE

Wolfgang Schmidt

This paper will briefly outline some epidemiological aspects of cirrhosis. Using this disease as a point of departure, the relationship between the magnitude of alcohol-related health and social problems in populations and the general level of alcohol consumption, will then be discussed.

Alcohol causes not only cirrhosis; it is also a factor in the aetiology of gastritis, pancreatitis, cardiomyopathy, peripheral neuropathy and toxic psychosis. Alcohol is definitely related to cancer of the mouth, pharynx, larynx and oesophagus, and is a major factor in suicide, assault and accidents (Schmidt & Popham, 1975). But this paper discusses cirrhosis because this disease has certain attributes which make it uniquely suitable as an index of the magnitude of alcohol problems generally. These attributes are: (1) it often has a fatal outcome and is a sufficiently common cause of death (Masse et al., 1976); (2) it is one of the leading causes of death among heavy drinkers (Schmidt & de Lint, 1972); (3) there is no doubt as to the substantial contribution of heavy alcohol use to total deaths from this cause (Schmidt, 1976); (4) the aetiological importance of long-term heavy alcohol intake has been established beyond doubt, and recent experimental work has convincingly shown that a direct hepatotoxic effect of alcohol is mainly responsible for the development of this disease (Israel et al., 1975; Rubin & Lieber, 1974); (5) from extensive follow-up studies, we know that the rate of death from cirrhosis among heavy drinkers is fairly stable over time (Schmidt, 1976); and (6) we also know that the rate of death from cirrhosis due to factors other than alcohol use has varied very little over the last twenty years in most Western countries (Jollife & Jellinek, 1942; Schmidt, 1976). Hence, such changes as we find in cirrhosis mortality can be attributed to changes in the number of chronic heavy users of alcoholic beverages. In other words, an increase in deaths from cirrhosis in a given year implies that some time in the not too distant past, the number of chronic heavy users of alcohol must have increased accordingly. Since consumption patterns

that are conducive to the development of cirrhosis also result in a very
wide range of other health and socio-economic problems, it is a
reasonable assumption that changes in cirrhosis mortality reflect
changes in all those problems that result from the chronic heavy use of
alcohol (Schmidt & Popham, 1975). The cirrhosis statistics that are
given in this paper are, therefore, intended to convey the trends in
chronic alcohol problems generally rather than in this disease only. The
statistics employed all refer to death from this cause, which is the
most accessible and reliable measure of the impact of cirrhosis.
Estimating the incidence or prevalence of cirrhosis in general
populations is not easy and has probably never been attempted. Data
from Canada and the USA will be used for illustration. The reason for
this choice is simply one of convenience.

Cirrhosis Mortality

Mortality rates from cirrhosis vary greatly from country to country.
As can be seen in Table 1, in a recent year, the rates of death from this
disease in Western countries have ranged from 5.7 to 57.2 per 100,000
of the adult population — a tenfold difference.

Table 1   Deaths attributed to cirrhosis per 100,000 population 25 years
of age and older in various countries

Country	Rate	Country	Rate
France	57.2	Hungary	20.7
Portugal	55.1	Belgium	20.5
Italy	52.1	Canada	19.6
Austria	49.1	Poland	17.2
West Germany	39.6	Denmark	16.2
Spain	38.3	Sweden	15.6
Romania	34.6	Bulgaria	10.5
United States	28.6	New Zealand	8.2
Czechoslovakia	28.1	Norway	7.6
Greece	26.8	Finland	7.5
Yugoslavia	25.2	Netherlands	7.4
Switzerland	24.6	Southern Ireland	7.0
Japan	21.8	United Kingdom	5.7

Source: The primary data were taken from the World Health Statistics Annual
(WHO 1973); the data for the USA and Belgium refer to 1971; for all other
countries to 1972.

Probably there exists no other chronic degenerative disease in the Western world that varies as widely in the rate of occurrence from country to country as cirrhosis. Rate differences among general populations of such magnitude usually indicate *a priori* the importance of environmental influences in the aetiology of the disease. The rate in the United Kingdom is the lowest in these series. Even if countries from other parts of the world are added to this comparison, including Eastern and Central European, and Central and South American countries, the United Kingdom retains its distinction of having one of the lowest known cirrhosis mortality rates. As will be discussed later, this position is somewhat anomalous.

Over the past two decades, cirrhosis mortality has been increasing at a steady and often rapid rate in most parts of the world. Table 2 provides indices of changes for the various countries.

Table 2 Average annual rates of change in cirrhosis death rates in various countries for the period 1959-71

Country	Rate of Change in Per Cent	
	Male	Female
Czechoslovakia	9.17	1.50
Sweden	7.50	2.67
Italy	7.08	4.67
Austria	6.00	3.67
Denmark	5.50	1.50
West Germany	5.50	3.00
Canada	5.17	4.08
United States	3.83	3.42
Belgium	2.58	3.25
Portugal	2.25	2.00
France	2.17	0.83
Norway	1.67	− 2.17
Finland	1.50	− 0.67
Netherlands	1.42	− 0.67
Northern Ireland	1.33	− 0.75
England and Wales	1.08	1.75
Switzerland	0.83	2.92
Southern Ireland	0.42	1.75

Source: Based on data in Masse *et al.*, 1976.

Evidently there was an increase in all countries in this series for males. The increases tended to be largest in countries which historically ranked high in the mortality from this disease. As a result of this trend, geographic differences in cirrhosis mortality have become more marked over the past ten to twenty years. This development is illustrated in Figure 1, which shows the correlation between cirrhosis mortality rates in the late 1950s and early 1970s in the same series of countries.

Figure 1 Male Age Standardized Mortality from Cirrhosis of the Liver in 18 Countries (see Table 2) Correlation 1959/1971. Based on data in Masse *et al.*, 1976.

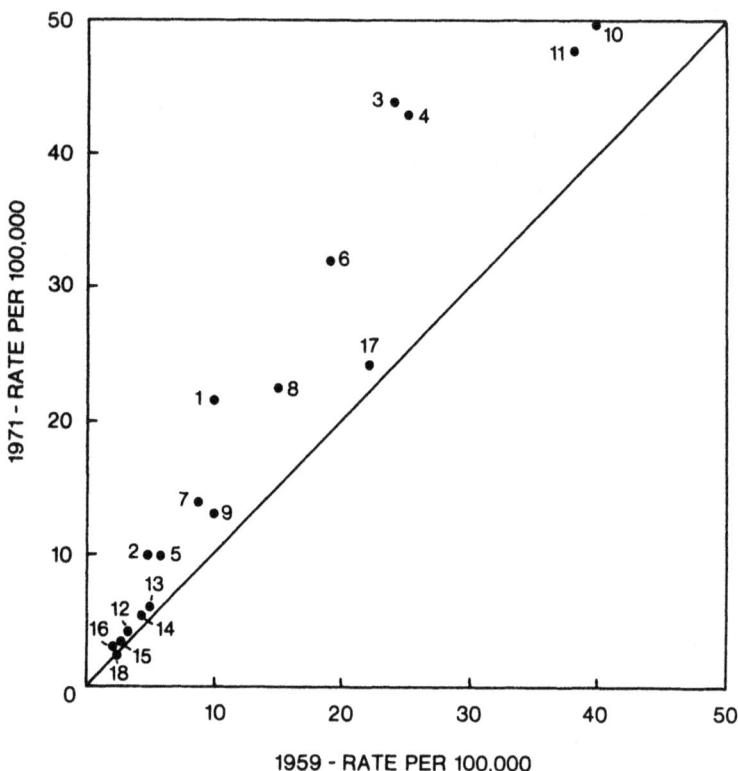

Evidently, all the dots on the scatter diagram are situated above the bisector, which implies an increase in all instances. Furthermore, the distances between the bisector and the dots tend to increase together with the rate of cirrhosis in the base year – which illustrates the point made before – namely, that the rate of increase was largest in countries which traditionally had much liver disease.

The rate of increase was generally greater in males than in females. As a consequence, the sex specific rates also tend to diverge through time. Table 3 illustrates the changes in the sex ratio that have occurred over the last thirty years.

Table 3   Ratio of male to female death rate from cirrhosis in the population 20 years of age and older, Canada and Ontario, 1946-74

Year	Canada	Ontario
	Sex Ratio	
1946 – 1950	1.77	1.67
1951 – 1955	1.74	1.78
1956 – 1960	1.95	1.84
1961 – 1965	1.89	1.75
1966 – 1970	1.92	1.84
1971 – 1974	2.15	2.16

Source: The primary data were taken from Vital Statistics (Statistics Canada Annual Reports, 1946-74); death rates are based on centred two-year moving averages.

These data refer to Canada, but similar changes have been observed in many parts of the world (WHO, 1946-73). If these ratios represent genuine long-term tendencies, we would predict that the existing preponderance of males among persons with cirrhosis will become even more pronounced in the future.

Cirrhosis death rates are sensitive to the age distribution. The rates are quite insignificant up to early adulthood, then rise continuously up to 65 years of age and decrease thereafter. Examples of the changes in the age-specific rates that have occurred over the post-war period are shown in Table 4.

The rise between 1950 and 1972 in Canada has been largest in the rates for ages 35 to 49 and smallest for those over 65 years. This

Table 4   Ratio of last to first year death rate from cirrhosis and
average annual rates of change in these death rates by age
and sex, Canada 1950-72

Age	Ratio			Rate of Change in %		
	Male	Female	Total	Male	Female	Total
20-34	1.80	1.58	1.71	3.63	2.27	3.24
35-49	4.01	2.76	3.52	13.72	8.00	11.45
50-64	2.70	2.23	2.49	7.73	5.60	6.76
65+	1.88	1.28	1.57	4.01	1.34	2.59

Source: The primary data were taken from Vital Statistics (Statistics Canada
Annual Reports, 1950-72); death rates are based on centred two-year moving
averages.

observation holds for all countries for which valid data are available. As
can be seen in Table 5, the increases in this age group are always
substantial and sometimes enormous.

As a consequence, the mean age of death has decreased in many
countries. For Ontario, this decrease was from 60.4 for the five-year
period 1946-50, to 56.9 for the five years 1970-74 (p < 0.01) (Schmidt,
1976). This trend becomes particularly relevant if the impact of the
disease is judged from the loss of life span or the reduction of working
life it causes. In this sense, the importance of a chronic or fatal disease
is inversely related to the age of its occurrence.

The place of cirrhosis among other causes of death can be expressed
in several ways. One is to calculate the relative frequency of death from
cirrhosis as a proportion of all deaths. Tables 6 and 7 respectively show
such calculations for Canada and the USA.

As can be seen, the relative frequency in the adult population has
increased enormously in these two jurisdictions. This inverse
relationship between general mortality and mortality from cirrhosis is
by no means restricted to North America, but is generally observed and
also holds for the United Kingdom — at least for the past twenty years
(WHO, 1950-1973; Masse *et al.*, 1976). Apparently, cirrhosis contributes
an ever increasing share to the general mortality.

Another way to illustrate the relative importance of cirrhosis in the
overall mortality of a country is to list the leading causes of death. Such
a tabulation is shown in Table 8 for the USA and two States of the
Union.

Table 5   Ratio of last to first year death rate from cirrhosis and average annual rate of change in these death rates for the age group 35 to 44 in selected countries, 1957-71

Country	Ratio		Rate of Change in %	
	Male	Female	Male	Female
Czechoslovakia	5.03	2.26	28.79	9.00
Sweden	2.38	3.89	9.86	20.64
Italy	2.85	1.91	13.21	6.50
Austria	3.13	3.36	15.21	16.86
Denmark	2.61	2.10	11.50	7.86
West Germany	2.91	2.32	13.64	9.43
Canada	2.12	1.42	8.00	3.00
United States	1.75	1.55	6.25	4.58
Belgium	1.91	1.39	7.00	3.00
Portugal	1.40	1.30	2.86	2.14
France	1.60	1.43	4.29	3.07
Norway	2.42	2.50	10.14	10.71
Finland	2.09	3.20	7.79	15.71
Switzerland	1.67	3.75	4.79	19.64

Source: Based on data in Masse *et al.,* 1976

Table 6   Deaths attributed to cirrhosis per 1,000 deaths from all causes in the population 25 years of age and older, Ontario, 1944-73

Year	Cirrhosis Ratio		
	Male	Female	Total
1944	4.95	3.34	4.20
1950	6.72	5.57	6.21
1955	8.33	5.42	7.07
1960	11.00	7.87	9.59
1965	11.68	8.13	10.16
1970	16.30	10.91	13.97
1973	21.77	13.05	17.91

Source: The primary data were taken from Vital Statistics (Province of Ontario Annual Reports, 1944-1973); cirrhosis deaths are based on centred two-year moving averages.

Table 7   Deaths attributed to cirrhosis per 1,000 deaths from all causes
for various age groups, USA 1946-72

Year	Cirrhosis Ratio		
	25 years and older	35 to 44	45 to 54
1946	8.8	17.3	16.6
1950	10.3	25.2	21.8
1955	12.2	34.8	30.0
1960	13.1	40.0	36.4
1965	14.7	49.1	42.9
1970	17.3	61.6	52.6
1972	17.7	65.5	52.6

Source: The primary data were taken from the Vital Statistics (US Government
Annual Reports, 1946-72), the Statistical Abstracts (US Bureau of the Census,
1946-72), and the United Nations Demographic Yearbook (United Nations,
1946-72); cirrhosis deaths are based on centred two-year moving averages.

Table 8   Ranks for leading causes of death in the population 25 to 64
years. United States 1950, 1973; New York State and
California, 1950, 1970

Cause of Death	Rank					
	United States		New York State		California	
	1950	1973	1950	1970	1950	1970
Diseases of Heart	1	1	1	1	1	1
Malignant Neoplasms	2	2	2	2	2	2
Cerebrovascular Diseases	3	4	3	4	4	5
Accidents	4	3	4	5	3	3
Influenza and Pneumonia	5	8	6	6	7	7
Suicide	6	6	7	9	5	6
Cirrhosis of Liver	(7	5)	(5	3)	(6	4)

Source: Primary data were taken from: Vital Statistics (US Government Annual
Reports, 1950, 1973); US Statistical Abstracts, the New York State Census,
and the State of California Census (US Bureau of the Census, 1950-1974).

Cirrhosis, which in 1950 had been the seventh leading cause of death for adults in the productive years of life, has become the fifth leading cause after heart disease, cancer, accidents and cerebrovascular diseases. Even more striking, in the States of New York and California, cirrhosis has become, respectively, the third and fourth leading cause in the population of this age range. In most countries for which valid data can be obtained, cirrhosis ranks now among the five leading causes of death for adults between 25 and 64 years of age – the productive years of life.

This high rank in the hierarchy of causes of death is also reflected in the comparison of the magnitude of rate increases among various causes shown in Table 9 (for Ontario), and Table 10 (for the USA).

For example, in Ontario, cirrhosis is now the most rapidly increasing cause of death in the population over 25 years of age, followed by cancer of the lung and bronchus, and suicide. In the USA, the order of these causes, with respect to rate of increase, is somewhat different. Lung cancer leads, cirrhosis assumes second place followed closely by homicide. It is of some interest that the third rank in this comparison is occupied by suicide in Canada and by homicide in the USA.

Again, this observation on relative magnitude of increase applies to most countries in the Western world (WHO, 1950, 1972). With rare exceptions, the first two ranks are held by cirrhosis and cancer of lung and bronchus. Apparently, the two causes of death in the adult population which have risen most rapidly are also potentially the most preventable diseases. Lung cancer is as closely related to smoking as cirrhosis is to drinking – both being behaviours we may term 'self-

Table 9 Rate of death per 100,000 population 25 years of age and older, ratio of last to first year death rate and annual rate of change in death rates from cirrhosis, lung cancer and suicide, Ontario, 1950, 1972

Cause of Death	Rate of Death		Ratio			Rate of Change in %		
	1950	1972	Male	Female	Total	Male	Female	Total
Cirrhosis	7.6	21.4	3.32	2.47	2.81	10.59	6.69	8.25
Cancer of Lung	19.2	51.0	2.63	3.20	2.65	7.44	10.53	7.53
Suicide	13.6	21.2	1.38	2.18	1.55	1.76	5.39	2.54

Source: The primary data were taken from Vital Statistics (Province of Ontario Annual Reports, 1950, 1972); death rates are based on centred two-year moving averages.

24   *Alcoholism: New Knowledge and New Responses*

Table 10 Rate of death per 100,000 population 25 years of age and
older, ratio of last to first year death rate and annual rate of
change in death rates from cirrhosis, cancer of the respiratory
organs and homicide, USA, 1950, 1972

Cause of Death	Rate of Death 1950	1972	Ratio Male	Female	Total	Rate of Change in % Male	Female	Total
Cirrhosis	15.1	28.4	1.95	1.86	1.88	4.34	3.92	4.00
Cancer of the Respiratory Organs	23.9	67.2	2.85	3.03	2.82	8.39	9.25	8.29
Homicide	7.0	12.1	1.85	1.53	1.73	3.85	2.42	3.31

Source: The primary data were taken from the Vital Statistics (US Government
Annual Reports, 1950, 1972), the Statistical Abstracts (US Bureau of the
Census, 1950, 1972), and the United Nations Demographic Yearbook (United
Nations, 1950, 1972); death rates are based on centred two-year moving
averages.

indulgent'. In this regard, a characteristic of mortality in the Western
world during the last twenty years has been lack of improvement and
even some increase in the general mortality of middle-aged men, in
contrast to the mortality of other segments of the population which
has shown improvement. The explanation for this trend lies largely in
the rapid increase of diseases related to alcohol and tobacco use which
have affected men of this age range more than any other group
(Schmidt & Popham, 1975).

Cirrhosis Mortality Rates and Per Capita Consumption

Let us now examine briefly evidence that relates temporal and spatial
variation in cirrhosis rates to variation in the rates of alcohol
consumption. The evidence concerning this question is very extensive
and here reference will be made only to a few key illustrations, to make
the point. For example, if we look once more at geographic
comparisons shown earlier: evidently international and regional
differences in mortality rates are very closely associated with
differences in the apparent *per capita* consumption of alcoholic
beverages (Figures 2,3 and 4).

Figure 2 Cirrhosis Mortality per 100,000 Population 25 Years of Age and Older and Alcohol Consumption Per Capita. Death rates for the USA and Belgium are 1971, all other death rates are for 1972 (World Health Statistics Annual, 1973). Consumption figures are the 1968-70 average (Sulkunen, 1976).

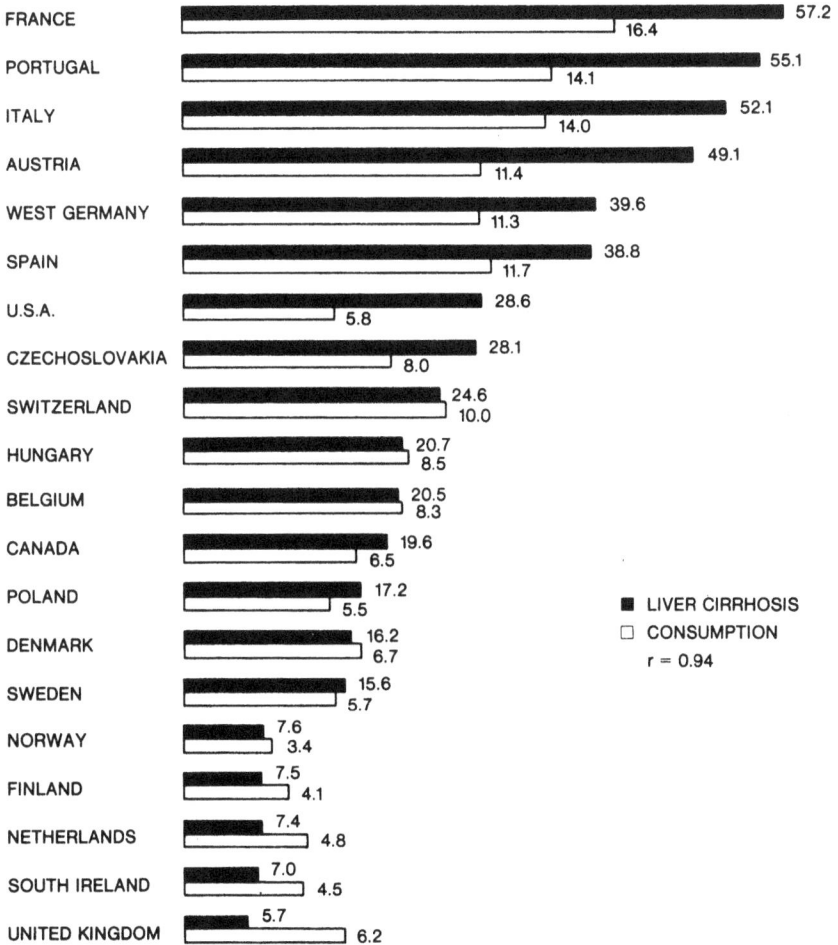

Country	Liver Cirrhosis	Consumption
FRANCE	57.2	16.4
PORTUGAL	55.1	14.1
ITALY	52.1	14.0
AUSTRIA	49.1	11.4
WEST GERMANY	39.6	11.3
SPAIN	38.8	11.7
U.S.A.	28.6	5.8
CZECHOSLOVAKIA	28.1	8.0
SWITZERLAND	24.6	10.0
HUNGARY	20.7	8.5
BELGIUM	20.5	8.3
CANADA	19.6	6.5
POLAND	17.2	5.5
DENMARK	16.2	6.7
SWEDEN	15.6	5.7
NORWAY	7.6	3.4
FINLAND	7.5	4.1
NETHERLANDS	7.4	4.8
SOUTH IRELAND	7.0	4.5
UNITED KINGDOM	5.7	6.2

■ LIVER CIRRHOSIS
□ CONSUMPTION
r = 0.94

Figure 3 Cirrhosis Mortality Per 100,000 Population 25 Years of Age and Older
and Alcohol Consumption Per Capita 15 Years of Age and Older, Provinces
of Canada, 1971. Sources: Vital Statistics and The Control and Sale of
Alcoholic Beverages in Canada (Statistics Canada Annual Reports, 1971).

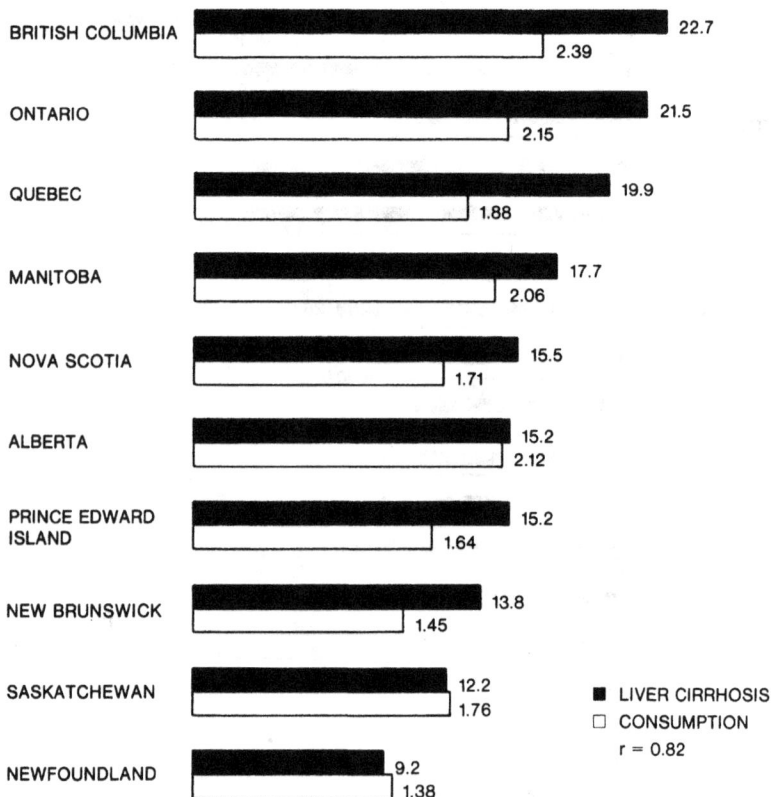

Province	Liver Cirrhosis	Consumption
BRITISH COLUMBIA	22.7	2.39
ONTARIO	21.5	2.15
QUEBEC	19.9	1.88
MANITOBA	17.7	2.06
NOVA SCOTIA	15.5	1.71
ALBERTA	15.2	2.12
PRINCE EDWARD ISLAND	15.2	1.64
NEW BRUNSWICK	13.8	1.45
SASKATCHEWAN	12.2	1.76
NEWFOUNDLAND	9.2	1.38

■ LIVER CIRRHOSIS
□ CONSUMPTION
r = 0.82

Figure 4 The Regression of Cirrhosis Mortality on Wine Consumption in the
Eastern United States, 1950. Based on data in Schmidt and Bronetto, 1962.

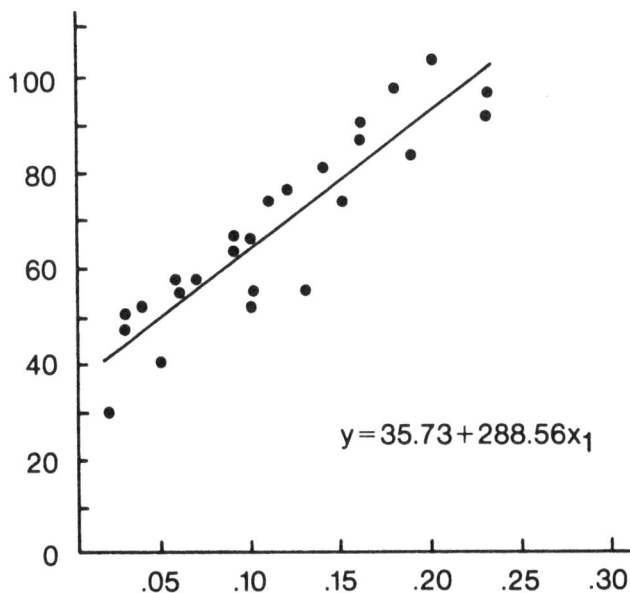

$$y = 35.73 + 288.56x_1$$

High coefficients of correlation are also obtained in temporal series as
shown for Ontario (Figure 5)

Associations of the type shown here have been confirmed by a long
series of empirical investigations involving many regional and temporal
comparisons. The picture that emerged is consistent: the rate of death
from cirrhosis rises and falls with the level of alcohol consumption in
general populations (Schmidt & Popham, 1975).

An objection to the inference that these correlations reflect a
cause-effect relationship is that the temporal series shown here, as well
as most of those reported in the literature, involve gradual and
unidirectional trends which do not permit us to distinguish spurious
correlations. It is generally accepted that abrupt and decisive changes
in the independent variable involving shifts in both directions, provide
a better opportunity to test such associations. Such instances have
occurred during and shortly after the First World War in several
countries due to severe reductions in the supply of alcohol. These

Figure 5 Cirrhosis Mortality Per 100,000 Population 20 Years of Age and Older
and Alcohol Consumption Per Capita, Population 15 Years of Age and Older,
Ontario 1928-1972. Sources: Vital Statistics (Statistics Canada and Province
of Ontario Annual Reports, 1928-72).

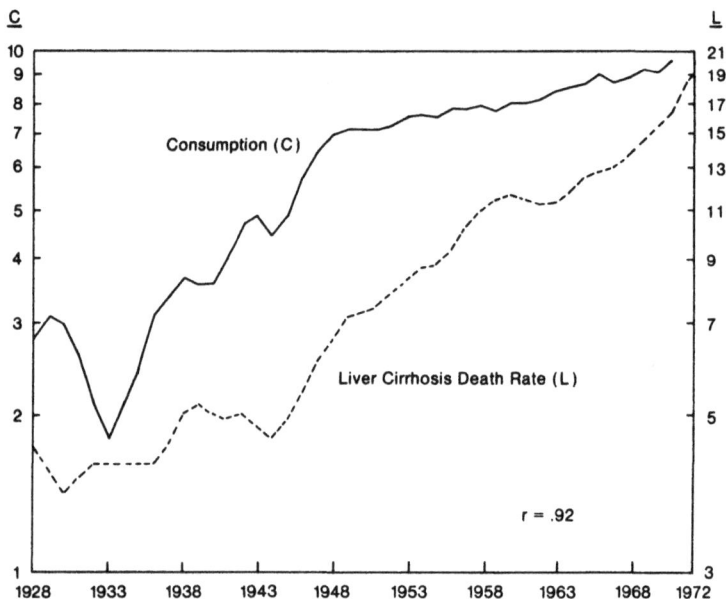

reductions were always accompanied by a remarkably rapid and very
substantial drop in the cirrhosis death rates (Schmidt & Popham, 1975).

Events of this nature can be thought of as natural experiments in
epidemiology. The typical scenario involves a community that is
subjected to a disturbance that produces a drastic change in its exposure
to risk. The links between this alteration in exposure and associated
changes in disease manifestations are then explored.

In liver disease, the classical natural experiment occurred in France
during the Second World War. During this period, the French were
subjected to drastic restrictions in the supply and availability of
alcohol — particularly of wine. Figure 6 illustrates the dramatic effect
of the reduction in alcohol consumption on cirrhosis mortality, and
the very rapid resumption of the pre-war trends when alcohol became
again freely available.

Figure 6   Cirrhosis Mortality Rates: Paris 1907-56. Based on data in Ledermann, 1964.

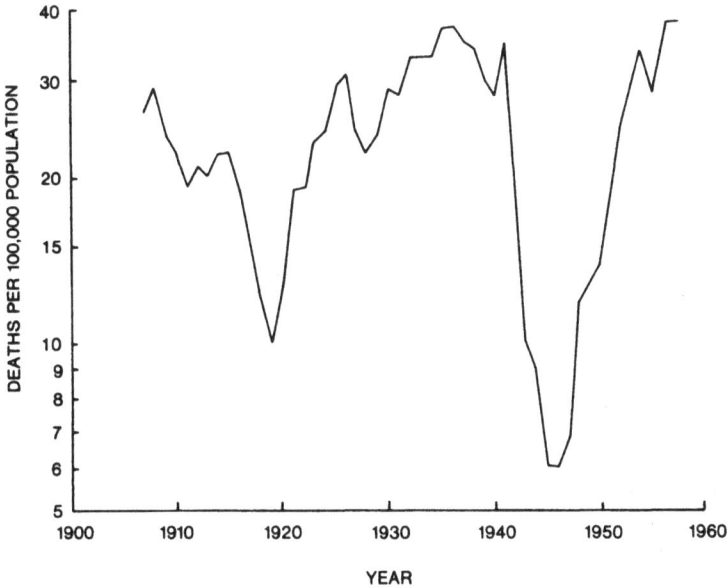

These data are often questioned on two grounds:

(1)   It is argued that wartime mortality statistics in an occupied country are notoriously unreliable and therefore that the apparent reductions in mortality may be due to reporting artefacts. The answer to this objection has been provided by French medical schools who pointed out that, during the war period, it was difficult to find cases of cirrhosis to demonstrate to students while the wards had been flooded with such cases prior to the war (Masse *et al.*, 1976).

(2)   These data have also been questioned on the grounds that deaths from chronic disease would not be expected to drop so suddenly when the aetiological agent became less accessible. However, it has been pointed out that such sharp changes in cirrhosis mortality are not inconsistent with the clinical source of the disease. Often the cirrhotic process can be halted by abstinence

and conversely a previously established liver pathology can be reactivated in a short time when drinking is resumed. (Terris, 1967.)

Our earlier observation on the age and sex distribution of these deaths is also consistent with the hypothesis that variation in alcohol consumption rates explains variation in cirrhosis death rates. Adult males have higher death rates and higher alcohol consumption rates than adult females. On the other hand, up to age 25 there are no consistent sex differences in mortality.

The data shown in Table 11 also indicates that, in this age group, the rates for both sexes and the sex ratios have remained quite stable over the past thirty years. This is due to the fact that mortality from cirrhosis among infants, children and young adults is caused by factors other than alcohol use. Apparently these factors have varied very little over time.

Table 11   Deaths attributed to cirrhosis per 100,000 population under age 25, Ontario, 1944-74

Year	Rate of Death		
	Males	Females	Total
1944-49	.21	.18	.19
1950-54	.24	.18	.21
1955-59	.26	.23	.25
1960-64	.24	.28	.26
1965-69	.22	.18	.20
1970-74	.13	.12	.13

Source: The primary data were taken from Vital Statistics (Province of Ontario Annual Reports, 1944-74).

Figures 7 and 8 illustrate two further points.

The first is that the United Kingdom, which appeared to have resisted the epidemic of alcoholic liver disease for some time, has recently also been affected. Although the increases are small compared with some of the other countries for which valid data are available, the

Figure 7 Cirrhosis Mortality Per Capita 25 Years of Age and Older and Alcohol Consumption Per Capita 15 Years of Age and Older, United Kingdom, 1954-73. Sources: Produktschap voor Gestilleerde Dranken, 1954-73; United Nations Demographic Yearbook, 1970; World Health Statistics Annual, 1953-73; and personal correspondence with Central Statistical Office, London, England, 1976.

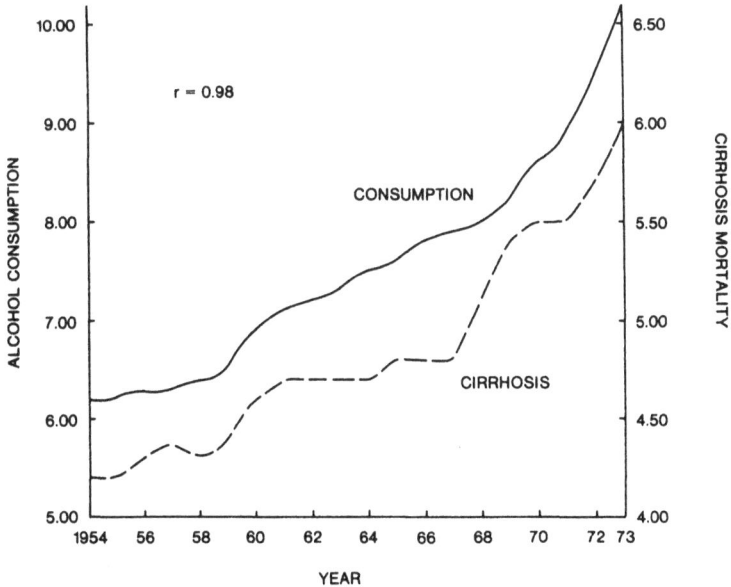

signs are unmistakable. The acceleration in these rates in the United Kingdom in the 1970s is similar to that of Ontario during the 1950s (Figure 9).

The explanation for this apparent time lag in the behaviour of the United Kingdom rates is not fully understood and I am currently planning some research on this question.

The second point that is well illustrated on the graph for Ontario concerns the very close association between changes in the death rate and changes in the general level of consumption of alcoholic beverages in the population at large. It should be emphasised that the principal function of the correlations which have been shown is not to add support to the vast clinical experience and experimental evidence which has established the association between cirrhosis and alcohol use beyond dispute: rather it is to demonstrate a relationship between *per capita*

Figure 8 Regression of Cirrhosis Mortality Per Capita 25 Years of Age and
Older on Alcohol Consumption Per Capita 15 Years of Age and Older,
United Kingdom, 1954-73. Data base same as Figure 7.

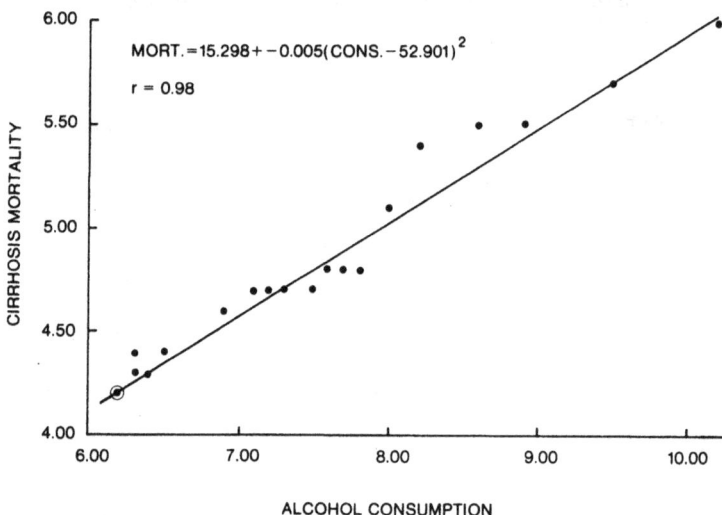

$$MORT. = 15.298 + -0.005(CONS. - 52.901)^2$$

$$r = 0.98$$

consumption and the incidence of this disease, or, to put it differently,
to demonstrate that the level of consumption in the population at large
has a bearing on the prevalence of users of cirrhogenic quantities.

Since consumption patterns that are conducive to the development
of cirrhosis also result in a very wide range of other health and social
problems, we may state that the overall level of use has a bearing on
the magnitude of alcohol problems in society, or, in more statistical
terms, that the extent of excessive use of alcohol in society is a
function of the overall level of use in the population at large. This
conclusion has been the subject of much debate. Some have argued
that this is a naïve interpretation of statistical evidence (de Lint, 1971),
others have categorically denied that the level of consumption in a
group has anything to do with the rate of excessive use (Bales, 1946;
Ullman, 1958). The reason for these objections appears to have been
the absence of any logically necessary connection between total
consumption and the prevalence of heavy use (Bruun *et al.*, 1975).

It will become evident in this paper that a clarification of this issue
is crucial to a discussion of the prevention of alcohol problems. The
pertinent data will therefore briefly be reviewed.

Figure 9 The Regression of Cirrhosis Mortality Per Capita 20 Years of Age and Older on Alcohol Consumption Per Capita 15 Years of Age and Older, Ontario 1932-73 and Estimates of the Proportion of Alcoholic Cirrhosis. Sources: Vital Statistics (Province of Ontario Annual Reports, 1932-73) and The Control and Sale of Alcoholic Beverages in Canada (Canada Statistics Annual Reports, 1932-73).

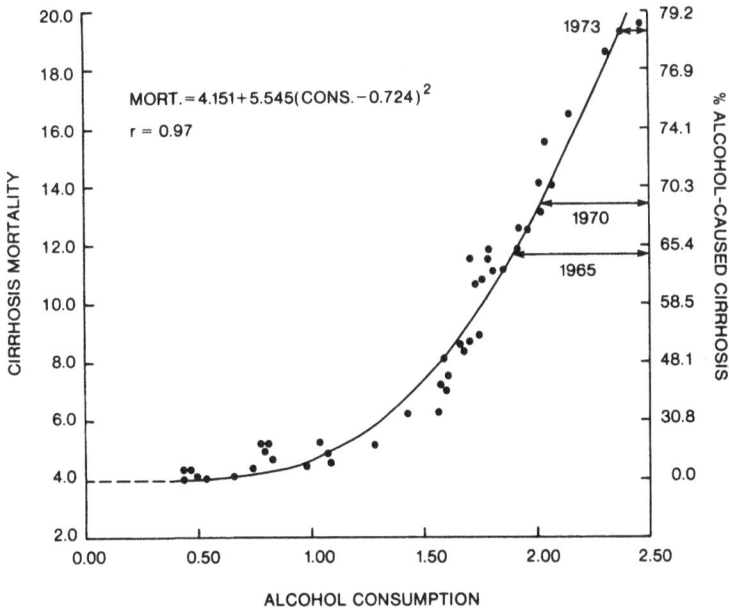

$$MORT. = 4.151 + 5.545(CONS. - 0.724)^2$$
$$r = 0.97$$

Distribution of Alcohol Consumption

Individual alcohol consumption covers a wide range of doses from an occasional drink taken to mark a special occasion to the sometimes lethal quantities consumed by alcoholics. Theoretically, these individual levels may be distributed over the full range in many different ways. For example, a relatively high level of general consumption may not necessarily imply a high prevalence of heavy users and conversely a lower *per capita* consumption would not preclude the existence of higher rates of alcoholism. Similarly, increases in general consumption may imply that alcohol is more widely, or regularly enjoyed by social drinkers or an increase in the prevalence of heavy drinkers, or both. In short, the level of consumption in the population at large, by itself, does not tell us how the drinkers of various quantities are distributed over the full range of possible consumption levels. In statistical terms the question raised here refers to the nature of the relationship between the mean consumption of a population and the proportion of the population consuming excessive amounts.

Ledermann — a French mathematician — was the first to examine this question systematically (Ledermann, 1956). He obtained distributions of drinkers according to their average daily quantities of consumption from data that were available in the literature. Although these data referred to populations with quite different consumption means, he found that consumption distributions he obtained had certain characteristics in common. Firstly, they were highly skewed curves. This finding was not unexpected. It has been known for some time from drinking surveys, case-finding studies of heavy drinkers and from the application of indirect methods for the estimation of the prevalence of alcoholism that the proportion of heavy drinkers in general populations tends to be relatively small and that a large majority are moderate drinkers. Hence, one would have expected a considerable concentration of drinkers at the moderate levels and a sharp decline in their numbers as the quantities tend towards the excessive. Figure 10 illustrates, in a stylised form, the shape of such a distribution.*

Figure 10 Theoretical Distribution of Drinkers According to Their Annual Consumption of Alcoholic Beverages. Based on data in Ledermann, 1956.

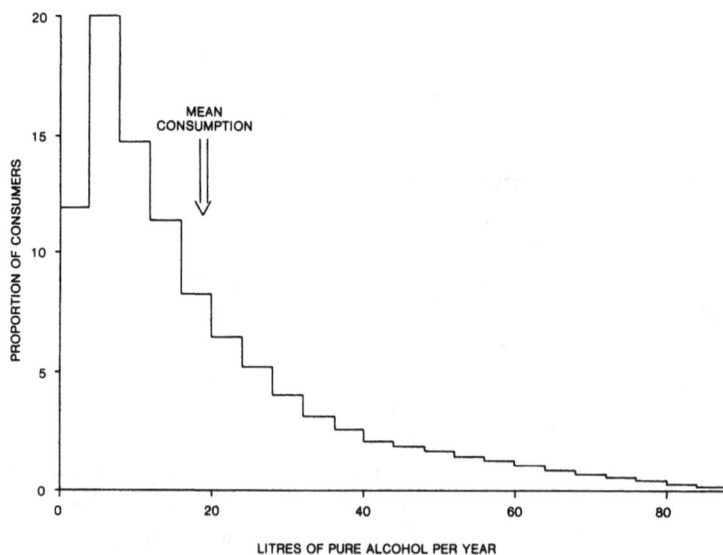

* The graph approximates the distribution of consumption of male drinkers in Ontario in 1972 (m 17.5 litres of absolute alcohol).

A distribution of this type is described statistically by two parameters – namely, the mean and a measure of dispersion. Hence, the frequency of drinkers at any point, or above a certain point of the consumption range depends on these two measures. Neither of these alone is a sufficient determinant. The next question to ask, then, is: under what conditions would one expect the proportion of heavy drinkers to vary in the same direction as the mean? Evidently the answer must be related to the measure of dispersion. For example, a change in the latter may counterbalance a change in the mean so that an increase in overall consumption may have no effect on the proportion of heavy drinkers.

It is against this background that the second of Ledermann's observations must be considered. He found that the measure of dispersion of the several distributions he examined differed very little. (The measure of dispersion in these instances was the standard deviation of the logarithms of consumption.) This absence of major variation in the measure provides the empirical basis for the conclusion that the overall consumption in a population is a determinant of the rate of heavy use. The implication is clear: when the total consumption in a country increases, the prevalence of heavy users is likely to increase as well. This relationship is illustrated in Figure 11.

The mechanism responsible for this apparent invariance in the distribution pattern is not fully understood but we have some information which permits a sketching of the processes that are probably involved. Ledermann pointed out that, in surveys, drinkers tend to explain their pattern of consumption with reference to the consumption of others. He felt, therefore, that drinking could be thought of as 'other oriented behaviour' and that a form of social contagion seems to be responsible for the interrelatedness of the frequencies with which certain consumption levels occur. He also referred to a *boule de neige* effect which implies a process by which each drinker's consumption influences and is influenced by the level of consumption of other drinkers. The aggregate of these influences may then be thought of as the alcohol sentiment or the level of acceptance of alcohol use in a population and this level of acceptance in turn affects again the level of use of the individual drinker.

Skog (Bruun *et al.*, 1975) illustrates the process of contagion as follows:

Mr X, who drinks in moderation, for some reason increases his consumption of alcohol by 25 per cent, as compared to last year. Like most of his friends, Mr X is a social drinker, Because he now

Figure 11 Variation in the Proportion of Heavy Drinkers as a Function of Per Capita Consumption as Found by Empirical Methods. Heavy Drinkers — average daily consumption of 20 cl. and over of pure alcohol. Source: Ledermann, 1964.

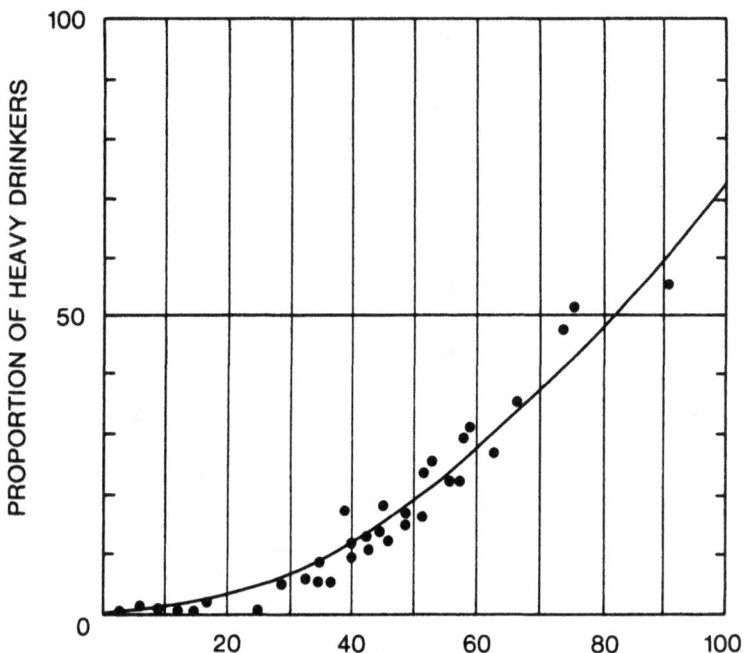

PER CAPITA CONSUMPTION IN LITRES OF PURE ALCOHOL

drinks more frequently than a year ago, the probability of his friends being offered a drink when they visit him is correspondingly increased, so that his friends' consumption level is also raised. As this process continues, Mr X's friends may come to feel obliged to serve him a drink on his return visit. And so it goes on; a rising consumption affects the drinking habits of every consumer with the semblance of a spreading wave.

Mr Y too, is likely to be influenced by a change in his friends' drinking habits. Thought not exactly a heavy consumer, Mr Y drinks at a level well above that of his companions. Given more opportunities to drink, Mr Y will probably do so, and this tendency may be reinforced by the dependence-producing potential of alcohol. Eventually, Mr Y crosses over to the side of heavy use.

The point which this quotation seeks to illustrate is that an increase in the consumption of 'normal' drinkers may induce changes in the drinking habits of near-heavy drinkers which may in turn lead to an increase in the prevalence of heavy users. The example describes how new habits may spread, but it does not explain why Mr X increased his consumption in the first place, nor does it indicate possible reasons for increases in consumption in the population at large. To answer these questions, we have to examine social, cultural and economic conditions.

The Diffusion of Drinking Habits

Of relevance here is the diffusion of new drinking habits by which is understood an exposure to and an eventual adoption of new drinking styles. Many circumstances can be identified that may foster this process. Increased foreign travel exposes many to different drinking patterns; inventive advertising depicts alcohol use in a variety of new drinking situations; alcohol products with innovative use values are being introduced by the industry; films and television facilitate the dissemination of foreign drinking customs, and international trade often uses consumption models from other cultures in bidding for customers (Sulkunen, 1976). The resulting diversification of consumption habits usually leads to an increase in the overall consumption, since newly-acquired drinking patterns do not replace older, traditional patterns, rather they are added to them (Makela, 1975).

A consequence of the diffusion of drinking customs is the integration of alcohol use into social occasions that were formerly not associated with alcohol use. Drinking under these circumstances tends to become an everyday occurrence rather than an event that marks a special occasion. This intrusion of alcohol into routine social life is often thought of as 'civilised drinking', implying that it is a less problematic habit than more sporadic drinking patterns.

The cumulative growth that has resulted from the adoption of new drinking styles led to higher overall levels of use by opening up to all drinkers – the heavy and light drinkers – new, socially acceptable drinking opportunities (Sulkunen, 1976). These developments were facilitated by increasing affluence over the recent past.

In the course of this review, trends in cirrhosis mortality have been described. The significance of these deaths as indices of the rate of excessive alcohol use and as evidence of a serious and growing public health problem have been emphasised. We have considered the constancy of population consumption distributions and have concluded that, under these circumstances, the relative frequency of high level consumers depends upon the mean per drinker consumption in a population. Hence, factors which alter total consumption may be expected to alter the magnitude of alcohol-related damage.

Models of Prevention

It remains to examine how compatible the various schools of thought on the prevention of alcohol problems are with this conclusion. One school is based on the disease concept of alcoholism. In accordance with this concept, alcohol consumption of heavy drinkers or alcoholics is considered to be symptomatic of a distinct disorder and the problem is thought to be drunkenness — not drinking, and alcoholism — not alcohol. A sociological formulation of this view reads as follows: An alcoholic 'is no more a drinker than a kleptomaniac is a customer or a pyromaniac is a campfire girl. Alcoholics may consume alcohol. They do not drink.' (Bacon, 1958.) This position has always been favoured by the distilled beverage industry and was recently formulated very succinctly in a submission to government by the Association of Canadian Distillers (1973): 'Alcohol and alcoholism are two entirely different subjects — while alcoholism is a major health problem, alcohol is not. Just as sugar is not the cause of diabetes, alcohol is not the cause of alcoholism.' This statement implies that factors which may influence the consumption level of social drinkers will have no effect on the pathological drinker and vice versa. Evidently, in this view, the problem is located entirely in the person which renders total consumption in the population at large an irrelevant statistic from a preventive point of view. Such preventive strategies as are supported by the proponents of this school are intended to reduce the acute problems of drunkenness and impairment.

A second approach takes as a point of departure the observation that, in some European countries where alcohol is used regularly with meals and is an integral part of everyday activities, drunkenness and other types of dangerous drinking are uncommon. Accordingly, it is felt that prevention could be achieved by encouraging drinking as an incidental part of routine activities (Plaut, 1967). To facilitate such integrative drinking, this school proposed to promote — through education and suitable legislation — customs such as use of wine with meals and generally raise the acceptance of alcohol use in society. To achieve such acceptance, it has also been suggested that restrictions on advertising of alcoholic beverages be removed, the legal drinking age lowered, and alcoholic beverages introduced at an early age. Generally, restrictions are thought to be impediments to the adoption of healthy drinking styles and, therefore, undesirable (Plaut, 1967).

Clearly the preventive strategies formulated by the proponents of this school of thought also are not compatible with the earlier observations that the general level of consumption has a bearing on the prevalence of excessive users. It will be recalled that recent tendencies towards integrative drinking have been identified among the factors leading to increased *per capita* consumption. Given the relationship between the latter and rates of excessive use, one would predict that facilitating alcohol use in the manner implied by the integration school would not only fail to prevent alcohol problems but might, in fact, contribute to a rise in such problems. In this regard, recent experiences in Finland provide an interesting example. There, the frequency of drinking occasions had been fairly low compared with most other Western countries, but when drinking did occur, it often resulted in intoxication. This pattern of infrequent but concentrated consumption was often accompanied by violent behaviour (Kiviranta, 1974). To minimise these harmful effects, new laws were passed whose aims were to facilitate integrative drinking styles. It was thought that the tendency of concentrated drinking would be counteracted if alcohol were to become more readily accessible than had hitherto been the case. The new legislation had a very remarkable effect on the overall level of consumption as is shown in Figure 12.

On the basis of earlier discussion concerning the relationship between the mean and the prevalence of heavy use, a proportionate rise in the frequency of heavy use would have been expected. This has, in fact, occurred. Surveys conducted before and after the changes in the control laws showed, for example, that the number of drinking occasions on which drinkers reached intoxicating blood alcohol levels increased by about 25 per cent (Bruun *et al.*, 1975). Although it is conceivable that the change of the law succeeded in one of its aims – namely, to increase the number of problem-free drinking occasions – this increase was not, as it had been hoped, at the expense of heavy drinking occasions. Rather, the overall increase that occurred affected drinking at all levels of use with a particularly marked effect on the rate of heavy use.

Fallacies of the Integration Theory of Prevention

The fallacy of the integration theory of prevention can be traced largely to the erroneous interpretation of cross-cultural observations. Of particular relevance in this respect are two assertions: the first is that, in countries such as Italy, where drinking is largely confined to meals,

Figure 12 Per Capita Consumption of Alcohol in Finland, 1964-73, in Litres of Pure Alcohol by Type of Beverage. Source: Bruun *et al.*, 1975.

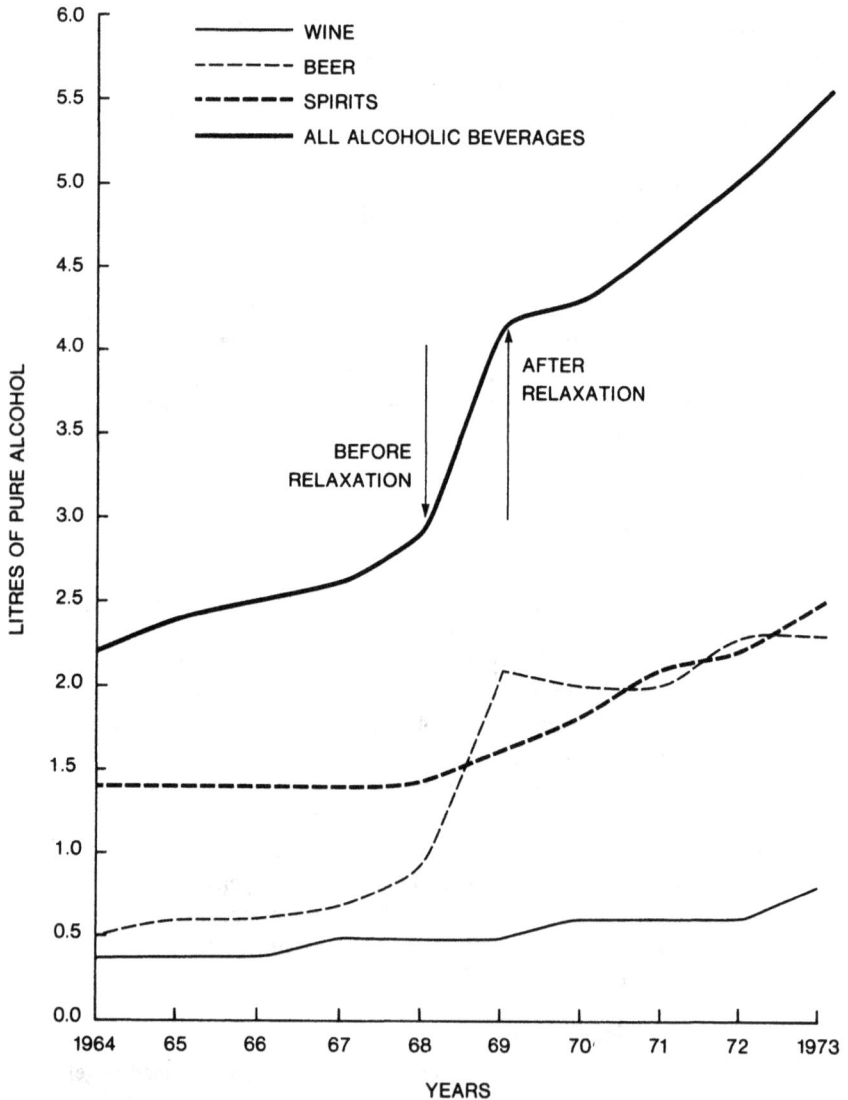

the rates of alcohol problems are low (Plaut, 1967). On re-examination
of the survey statistics and other data which led to this statement, it
became clear that this conclusion was not warranted. First, alcohol use
in this country is by no means restricted to mealtimes. On the contrary,
it is an incidental part of many occasions. In this regard, it is relevant
that, where alcohol use has a regular dietary function, drinking also
tends to be an integral part of many other activities, including work
and recreation. A consequence of these drinking practices is a high level
of overall consumption and a predictably high level of problems related
to chronic heavy use. In the case of Italy, this expectation is confirmed
by available statistics. Not only is the rate of death from cirrhosis high
in this country – it is among the highest known – but so are the rates
of alcoholism and acute problems such as alcohol-related industrial and
traffic accidents (Bonfiglio, 1963; Ledermann, 1956, 1964).

The second assertion concerns the effect of temperance sentiments
on the occurrence of alcohol problems. Mäkelä (1972) re-examined one
key study which arrived at the conclusion that negative attitudes
towards drinking in a person's childhood home are likely to add to the
social complications attending his use of alcohol later in life. As an
extension of this finding, it has been argued that cultural patterns which
foster alcohol use as a natural part of growing up are less likely to
generate alcohol problems in adult life. In the study in question,
alcohol-using male students of three religious groups – Jewish,
Episcopalian and Methodist – were compared. The Methodist Church
represents the total abstinence position. The Episcopal Church and the
Jewish faith sanction drinking. Mäkelä did not find support for the
conclusion the investigators reached. In fact, when all subjects in the
comparison were taken into account, including those who did not use
alcohol, which the investigators neglected to do, a quite different
picture emerged: social complications caused by drinking were more
common among the Episcopalians than the Methodists. These findings
do not, therefore, show that negative attitudes toward drinking in a
person's childhood home increase the likelihood of drinking problems
later in life; in fact, they suggest the opposite.

These assertions deserve careful scrutiny because they have
considerably influenced thinking on the prevention of alcohol problems.
Although they were erroneous, they nevertheless contributed
importantly to the formulation of the so-called integration theory of
prevention which found its most articulate expression in the writings
of North American social scientists (Plaut, 1967). But this theory was
also enthusiastically embraced by the alcoholic beverage industry; it

affected the communications on alcohol problems in the media, and influenced legislators and educators in the alcohol field. This popularity among groups representing such diverse interests is not surprising. The implication that the overall volume of consumption in the population at large is an insignificant statistic from a public health point of view is clearly an attractive one for the industry. The possibility the theory afforded of relaxing restrictions on the availability of alcohol came at an opportune time for governments. Public sentiment in many countries was thought to favour a more liberal approach and the theory apparently provided scientific sanction for it. This happy coincidence of what appeared to be politically opportune and scientifically sound, contributed importantly to the trend of liberalisation of control laws that has occurred over the past two decades in many jurisdictions.

However, the discrepancies between the theory and events in the real world could not be ignored indefinitely. Researchers from Italy and France – the two countries most widely quoted for their integrated and civilised drinking habits – were not convinced that all was well in their respective countries. They produced revealing statistics on the adverse consequences of so-called 'civilised drinking styles' (Bonfiglio, 1963; Bresard, 1969; Ledermann, 1964). Researchers in North America directed attention to the close relationship between cirrhosis mortality and the overall level of alcohol use in society. The significance of this association was clear: the prevalence of drinkers of cirrhogenic quantities – in other words, the rate of heavy drinkers – is intimately tied to the level of consumption in the population at large. The work on the nature of the distribution of alcohol use provided additional support for this relationship and first indications concerning the mechanisms responsible for the dependence of rates of alcohol problems on the overall consumption.

By now, the conclusion that a change in the consumption level of the population at large has a bearing on the health of the people is well substantiated and no longer disputed.

Controls as Preventive Strategies

One result of these developments is a renewed interest in alcohol control policies as preventive strategies. Controls tend to focus on the population at large rather than on individuals – a focus which is consistent with the above conclusion.

The potential usefulness of the many diverse restrictions through which control can be exercised has recently been examined in great detail (Bruun *et al.*, 1975; Popham, Schmidt & de Lint, 1976). The conclusions reached can be summarised as follows: there is strong evidence that whenever beverage alcohol becomes more readily available because of a relaxation in control laws, levels of consumption and rates of alcohol problems tend to increase. Furthermore, alcoholic beverages tend to behave in the consumer market like many other commodities, so that their consumption is affected by their price level.

Forecasting of Consumption

This review began with a description of recent trends in the magnitude of alcohol problems and it has been shown that the trends were intimately associated with changes in the consumption level.

In conclusion, we may ask what the future holds with respect to alcohol use. There exist many methods to forecast the demand of a commodity but, by and large, they are based on the interpretation of statistical data of past movements of relevant variables. The factors known to have a bearing on the demand of alcoholic beverages are: (1) personal disposable income; (2) real price of the beverages in question and prices of related commodities that serve as substitutes or complements; and (3) changes in taste as reflected in trends in beverage preference (Bruun *et al.*, 1975; Lau, 1975). Recently we have developed a set of forecasting equations which performed well over a historical sample period (1956-72) as shown in Figure 13. The dotted line form 1972 to 1984 represents a forecast of the demand which utilises these equations and projections of the afore-mentioned three variables as generated by a National Forecast Service (1975).

The forecast depicted in the graph indicates that the consumption per adult in Canada will continue to increase at roughly the same rate of growth experienced during the period 1956 to 1972 with minor variations from year to year. Over the entire forecast period, consumption is seen to reach 3.95 gallons per adult which represents a 73 per cent increase over the level of 1972. Malignac (1971) has examined similar forecasts for the countries of the European Economic Community. He reported that the EEC planners use the current alcohol consumption level of France as an estimate of future potential sales in other member countries.

Earlier in this paper, it was shown that the relationship between *per capita* consumption and the prevalence of heavy drinkers is parabolic, i.e. changes in the rate of heavy drinkers will, on the average, be proportional to the square of the increase in *per capita* consumption (Figure 11). Accordingly, we would expect that the rate of heavy users will increase greatly over the next ten to twenty years. Obviously forecasts rely, to a large extent, on historical data. No matter how sophisticated the methods used, there is always the possibility that new factors may

Figure 13 Predicted and Actual Canadian Consumption of Alcoholic Beverages in Gallons of Absolute Alcohol Per Adult. Source: Lau, 1976.

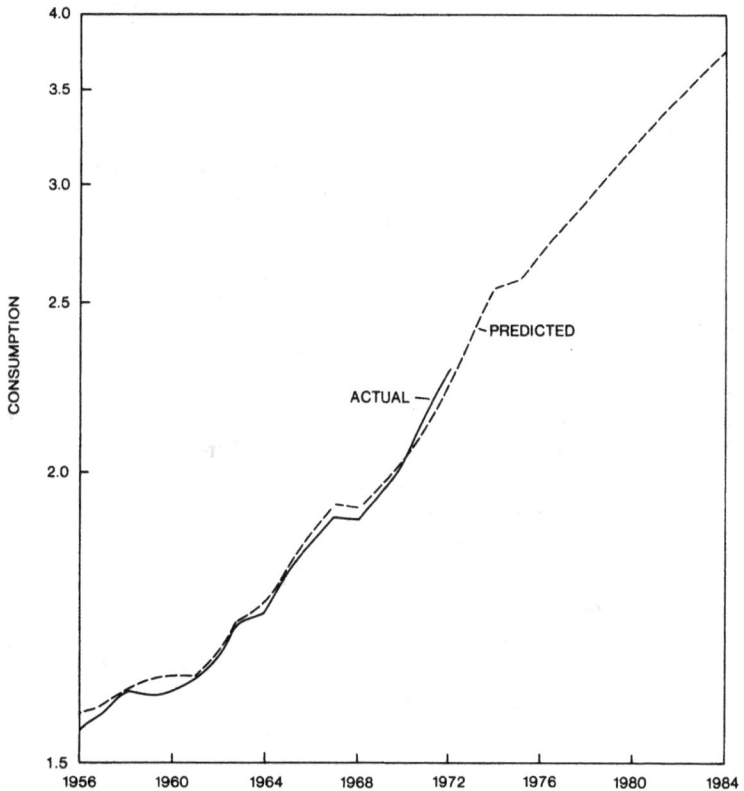

come into play that could affect consumption one way or the other. However, econometric analysis has generally proved very successful in making predictions and it may well be that, in the absence of a concerted effort of prevention, the predicted levels of alcohol use will actually occur. For such a programme of prevention to be effective, controls will have to play a significant part. On this, one can quote Edwards' (1971) views:

> The reason why a person drinks abnormally is connected with both his personality and with his environment; his drinking will, in fact, result from an interaction of the two, so that, for example,

an anxious person living where alcohol is cheap and attitudes to drinking are permissive will be more likely to become an excessive drinker than an anxious person who finds alcohol more difficult to obtain and attitudes less approving. Since we are not able to manipulate personality and produce a race with no neuroses, the only realistic method of exerting a benign influence on the prevalence of chronic alcohol problems is by control of environmental conditions of drinking and it is the availability element that remains the prime candidate for control.

References

Association of Canadian Distillers, 1973. Submission to the Government of Ontario.

Bacon, S.D. (1958). Alcoholics Do Not Drink. In: Understanding Alcoholism. S.D. Bacon (ed.). Philadelphia: Annals of the American Academy of Political and Social Science, vol.315, pp.55-64.

Bales, R.F. (1946). Cultural differences in rates of alcoholism. Quart. J. Stud. Alc. 6: 480-99.

Bonfiglio, G. (1963). Alcoholism in Italy. Brit. J. Addict. 59: 3-10.

Brésard, M. (1969). Alcoolisme et conscience collective. Revue d'Alcoolisme 15(2): 81-96.

Bruun, K., Edwards, G., Lumio, M., Mäkelä, K., Pan, L., Popham, R.E., Room, R., Schmidt, W., Skog, O.-J., Sulkunen, P. and Osterberg, E. (1975). Alcohol Control Policies in Public Health Perspective. Helsinki: Finnish Foundation for Alcohol Studies.

Central Statistical Office, London, England (1976). Personal correspondence.

de Lint, J.E.E. (1971). Alcohol Use in Canadian Society. In: Critical Issues in Canadian Society. C.L. Boydell, C.F. Grindstaff and P.C. Whitehead (eds.). Toronto: Holt, Rinehart and Winston, pp.490-9.

Edwards, G. (1971). Public health implications of liquor control. The Lancet, 424-5, August 21.

Israel, Y., Kalant, H., Orrego, H., Khanna, J.M., Videla, L. and Phillip, J.M. (1975). Experimental alcohol-induced hepatic necrosis: Suppression by propylthiouracil. Proc. Nat. Acad. Sci. 72(3): 1137-41.

Jolliffe, N. and Jellinek, E.M. (1942). Vitamin deficiencies and liver cirrhosis in alcoholism. VII. Cirrhosis of the liver. Quart. J. Stud. Alc. 2: 544-83.

Kiviranta, P. (1974). Alcoholism Syndrome in Finland. Helsinki: Finnish Foundation for Alcohol Studies.

Lau, H.-H. (1975). Cost of Alcoholic Beverages in Canada as a Determinant of Alcohol Consumption. In: Research Advances in Alcohol and Drug Problems, vol.II. R.J. Gibbins et al., (eds.). New York: John Wiley and Sons.

Lau, H.-H. (1976). Forecasting of Canadian Consumption of Alcoholic Beverages. Addiction Research Foundation Substudy No.758. (Mimeograph.)

Ledermann, S. (1956). Alcool, Alcoolisme, Alcoolisation. Données Scientifiques de Caractère Physiologique Économique et Social. Institut National d'Etudes Démographiques, Travaux et Documents, Cahier No.29. Paris: Presses Universitaires de France.

Ledermann, S. (1964). Alcool, Alcoolisme, Alcoolisation. Mortalité, Morbidité,

Accidents du Travail. Institut National d'Etudes Démographiques, Travaux
   et Documents, Cahier No.41. Paris: Presses Universitaires de France.
Mäkelä, K. (1972). Consumption Level and Cultural Drinking Patterns as
   Determinants of Alcohol Problems. Paper presented at the 30th International
   Congress on Alcoholism and Drug Dependence, Amsterdam.
Mäkelä, K. (1975). Consumption level and cultural drinking patterns as
   determinants of alcohol problems. J. of Drug Issues, Fall Issue.
Malignac, G. (1971). Le Marche Commun et la Lutte Contre l'Alcoolisme. Paper
   presented at the 17th International Institute on the Prevention and Treatment
   of Alcoholism, Berlin.
Masse, L., Juillan, J.M. and Chisloup, A. (1976). Trends in mortality from
   cirrhosis of the liver, 1950-1971. World Hlth Stat. Rep. 29(1): 40-67.
National Forecast Service (1975). Candide Model 1.1. Ottawa: Informetrica
   Limited, July 11.
Plaut, T.F.A. (Prepared by) (1967). Alcohol Problems: A Report to the Nation
   by the Cooperative Commission on the Study of Alcoholism. New York:
   Oxford University Press.
Popham, R.E., Schmidt, W. and de Lint, J.E.E. (1976). The Effects of Legal
   Restraint on Drinking. In: The Biology of Alcoholism, vol.IV: Social
   Biology. B. Kissin and H. Begleiter (eds.). New York: Plenum Publishing
   Corporation, pp.579-625.
Produktschap voor Gedistilleerde Dranken, 1954-1973. Hoeveel Alcoholhoudende
   Dranken Worden er in de Wereld Gedronken? Schiedam, Nederland.
Province of Ontario Annual Reports (n.d.). Vital Statistics. Toronto: Queen's
   Printer.
Rubin, E. and Lieber, C.S. (1974). Fatty liver, alcoholic hepatitis and cirrhosis
   produced by alcohol in primates. N. Engl. J. Med. 290(3): 128-35.
Schmidt, W. (1976). The Epidemiology of Cirrhosis of the Liver: A Statistical
   Analysis of Mortality Data. In: Proceedings of the 3rd International
   Symposium 'Alcohol and the Liver'. Toronto: Canadian Hepatic Association,
   in press.
Schmidt, W. and Bronetto, J. (1962). Death from liver cirrhosis and specific
   alcohol beverage consumption. Amer. J. Publ. Hlth. 52(9): 1473-82.
Schmidt, W. and de Lint, J.E.E. (1972). Causes of death of alcoholics. Quart. J.
   Stud. Alc. 33(1): 171-85.
Schmidt, W. and Popham, R.E. (1975). Heavy alcohol consumption and physical
   health problems: A review of the epidemiological evidence. Drug and Alc.
   Depend. (Lausanne) 1: 27-50.
Statistics Canada Annual Reports (n.d.). The Control and Sale of Alcoholic
   Beverages in Canada. Ottawa: Queen's Printer and Controller of Stationery.
Sulkunen, P. (1976). Drinking Patterns and the Level of Alcohol Consumption:
   An Overview. In: Research Advances in Alcohol and Drug Problems, vol.III.
   Y. Israel et al. (eds.). New York: John Wiley and Sons, pp.223-81.
Terris, M. (1967). Epidemiology of cirrhosis of the liver: National mortality data.
   Amer. J. Publ. Hlth.57: 2076-88.
Ullman, A.D. (1958). Sociocultural Backgrounds of Alcoholism. In:
   Understanding Alcoholism. S.D. Bacon (ed.). Philadelphia: Annals of the
   Amer. Acad. of Polit. and Soc. Sci., vol.315, pp.48-54.
United Nations (n.d.). U.N. Demographic Yearbook. New York: UN Publishing
   Service.
United States Bureau of the Census (n.d.). Census Populations by State.
   Washington, D.C.: US Government Printing Office.
United States Bureau of the Census (n.d.). Statistical Abstracts of the USA
   Washington, D.C.: US Government Printing Office.

United States Government Annual Reports (n.d.). Vital Statistics of the USA
Washington, D.C.: US Government Printing Office.
World Health Organization (n.d.). World Health Statistics Annual, vol.1
Geneva, Switzerland: WHO Office of Publications.

2 THREE THEMES IN THE EPIDEMIOLOGY OF ALCOHOLISM

Norman Kreitman

The aim of this paper is to promote discussion of certain problematic topics in the epidemiology of alcohol abuse. Since there is *no* aspect of the subject which stands forward as notably free of ambiguities and as the field is such a large one, some selection is clearly necessary. Those wishing a more comprehensive view may consult the general review by Edwards (1973) on the substantive issues in the epidemiology of alcoholism, and the admirable review of methodological problems by Room (1975).

Three themes will be touched upon, each in all conscience large enough to merit a book of its own. These are the consumption of alcohol in the general population, estimations of the prevalence of alcoholism, and more briefly, the assessment of alcohol-related problems.

The Consumption of Alcohol in the General Population

The days when the study of drinking of the general population was held to be irrelevant for students of alcoholism have long passed, and for good or ill the topic is now of central interest. The literature is considerable, and contains a lot of figures. It might be useful to consider just what these numbers denote, and how they relate to each other. To obtain a comprehensive picture of normal drinking patterns, several components have to be linked together.

The Total Amount of Alcohol Consumed in a Population in a Unit Period of Time

The principal source of such data is the Revenue Departments of the government, and since they have a financial incentive to be accurate the figures may be more trustworthy than is sometimes true of other official statistics. In many countries, data are produced annually concerning the volume and type of all legally produced alcoholic beverages. Some of these of course are exported, but details are also available for exports and imports.

This is a promising start, but three problems arise. Firstly, it is assumed that production of alcohol which is illicit or otherwise unreported is of negligible volume. This is probably true for the United Kingdom, although sales of brewing kits for both beers and wines need to be watched. But it is certainly not true for other countries, such as Ireland or France. Secondly, it cannot be uncritically assumed that all beverage alcohol produced within the nation is in fact consumed. In Italy and France, for example, considerable quantities of cheap wine are used in glut years as industrial fuel. Lastly, any economist would point out that estimates of total consumption should make allowance for changes in the magnitude of stocks of liquor before and after the period of study. No such adjustments have ever been attempted by alcohologists.

The point will repeatedly be made here that the essence of the epidemiological method is comparison. The first two sources of error of the three just noted, will clearly weaken the cogency of international comparisons. Indeed, while such comparisons may be useful in the study of physical disorders, they are notoriously treacherous in virtually all psychiatric and social enquiries. Decades of controversy have been required to clarify whether, for example, suicide rates can legitimately be compared between nations, and opinion is still far from uniform. Secular trends *within* nations are more dependable. However, the third point noted above suggests that existing methods of estimation could well be refined.

The Population at Risk

The size of the total population in a nation is readily ascertained from the national census, but the use of the total population figure can be profoundly misleading. Not only is the inclusion of women, who everywhere consume less than men, of dubious validity, but in certain areas such as South America, the proportion of the population under 15 may in some instances approximate to 50 per cent, yet very few are drinkers. The inclusion of women and children in the denominator thus renders the mean of rather bizarre significance.

The more appropriate figure is the total number of people who actually consume alcohol, but to determine what that value is it is necessary to estimate the number of non-drinkers. The definition of an abstainer (or 'very light' drinker) is as difficult and uncertain a task as that of defining an alcoholic, and estimates will be exquisitely sensitive to the details of the definition and the intensity of search. In the United Kingdom it appears that total abstainers and very infrequent drinkers represent something in the region of 10 per cent of the adult population. However, this figure is unlikely to be true

uniformly across the country; often temperance movements or
disapproving minorities of other kinds are most prominent precisely
in areas where heavy drinking is rife. Thus even if figures of quantity
of alcohol consumed in different regions were available, any mean
derived from a national estimate of abstainers would be highly
problematic.

Thus both the numerator and the denominator required to express
mean consumption have substantial margins of uncertainty. How far
the errors are mutually cancelling is anybody's guess. Analogous
problems arise in many other areas of psychiatric epidemiology, but
for most purposes some degree of uncertainty can be accepted. The
problem of alcohol consumption is made much more difficult, however,
if one of the purposes of deriving such figures is to relate them to
models based on the lognormal distribution. For this curve it can be
shown that for the range of values usually cited, inflation of the mean
by a factor of x leads to an inflation of the tail of the curve above a
given critical level of x^2. Thus small errors carry formidable penalties.

The Distribution of Consumption

The principal method for ascertaining the distribution of alcohol
consumption across a general population is by survey methods. Their
use raises a series of questions, of which the most salient is that of
under-reporting. Pernanen (1974) for example concludes that surveys
elicit only between 20 per cent and 70 per cent of the consumption
known from other sources to occur in the population. The reasons for
under-reporting are complex, but the point to be noted is the
likelihood that under-reporting is selectively biased, with heavy drinkers
(Popham, 1970) and alcoholics (Bailey *et al.,* 1965) under-declaring
their intake to a greater extent than more moderate consumers. The
implication is that the lognormal curve already mentioned may reflect
the distribution of truthfulness rather than that of alcohol consumption.

A uniform bias would still leave intact the possibility of comparison
between groups, but it appears that in addition to the under-reporting
by heavy consumers there is a further differential effect by social class,
with the middle class being less honest than the working class. Social
class comparisons, while probably basic to an understanding of alcohol-
related problems, must therefore be viewed with extreme
circumspection.

In passing it might be noted that the use of *median* values would in
principle be less subject to bias by selective under-reporting, and would
be preferable in between-group comparisons than the mean, which is in

any case an unsatisfactory statistic for asymmetrical distributions. Medians appear never to have been seriously considered in alcohol research; perhaps they should be examined more closely.

Cursory mention might be made of three other techniques that have been employed to supplement or replace survey methods. Family expenditure surveys are one such. However, they exclude the important subgroup of people, possibly conspicuously heavy drinkers, who do not live in families. They are maintained by housewives, who often do not know how much their husbands spend on drink. They yield national estimates of alcohol consumption, which, according to the responsible government departments, account for only 60 per cent of the quantity known to be consumed. They refer to expenditure by a group of people rather than by individuals. Lastly, they make no allowance for the different cost of alcohol in different parts of the country. They are clearly of limited value. It is true that the data they yield appear to correlate moderately well with what is known of temporal trends or is suspected regarding regional variation and social class differences, but they can scarcely be trusted as a primary source of information.

Another and rather unusual method is the analysis of sales data in situations where the purchaser's name has by law to be recorded. This approach has been exploited in an ingenious Canadian study (de Lint and Schmidt, 1968), but despite its originality it remains the case that purchasing and consuming are not necessarily carried out by the same individual. Moreover, the primary data will rarely be available.

Finally, there is the intriguing possibility of using direct observation of alcohol consumption. Much, perhaps most, alcohol consumption occurs in public (Dight, 1976), at least in Scotland, and hence is in principle accessible to measurement. Techniques of observation have been developed which appear to be reasonably reliable and we may well see them being employed perhaps in conjunction with orthodox surveys.

Methods and Questions

This brief review of the types of data relating to general population consumption has been pursued without much consideration of the kinds of questions they could be used to answer. This strategy has been deliberate. Methodology and hypotheses stand in a dialectical relationship to one another. The difficulties already reviewed imply that there is a distinct limit to the range and type of questions about alcoholism that can be raised at the present time.

Nevertheless, one can say something about the issues which at least in theory centre on the distribution of consumption in the general population. Certainly it is not enough to state, as do some authorities and government agencies, that the data are intrinsically interesting. No data are intrinsically interesting; they gain life only if addressed to some question, though of course they may contribute to the more precise definition of the problem.

It appears that there are three general preoccupations, not always clearly enunciated, underlying much of the work in this area. The first is the issue as to whether the normal consumption pattern is distributed bimodally or unimodally. If we inspect the high consumption tail of the distributions so far reported in the literature, they appear to be smooth, showing a decreasing number of individuals consuming an increasing quantity of alcohol, with no apparent break in the line. If this is so, then 'alcoholics' must be considered as individuals who at least with respect to alcohol consumption simply form one end of a distribution curve. Conversely, an abrupt break in the line, especially if it were an upward deflection, would suggest that a group of individuals were being observed who differed qualitatively from the rest of the population. Such a discontinuity has been demonstrated with respect to the lower tail of the IQ curve and has been of immense importance in furthering our understanding of mental defect.

A second question, or set of questions, concerns the relationship between consumption on the one hand and alcohol-related problems or alcoholism on the other. It is essential that this relationship should be clarified in the general population, rather than as shown in such atypical groups as clinic populations, agency referrals and the like. In defining any such relationship it may well be necessary to refine the consumption half of the equation by specifying, for example, the effects of different types of beverage or of patterns of drinking.

The third set of considerations comprise the issues that relate to public policy. Dependent upon answers to the preceding question (concerning the precise relationship between consumption and problems) it may or may not be possible to offer advice on the public health aspects of alcoholism. The need to do so is perhaps heightened by the very limited therapeutic success which appears to be possible with present treatment methods. It is not always the case that prevention is better than cure, but when there is little or no cure available then any prevention must be considered desirable.

These three sets of questions are — and in my view should be — at the forefront of epidemiological research programmes throughout the world. This emphasis appears to be entirely justified, but it is worth recalling yet again that definitive answers will not be obtained until a great deal more effort has gone into the methodology.

Alcoholism

It has been well said that the epidemiologist's primary concern with alcoholism is to escape from the field before his reputation is hopelessly tarnished. Those too foolhardy to accept this sage advice come to realise that they are being presented not with one, but with two distinct sets of questions.

The first problem or set of problems is posed by clinicians. In their hospitals they are confronted by a group of patients who display the varied pattern of psychological and physical characteristics which make up the clinical syndrome termed alcoholism. That there is substantial uncertainty as to just what those characteristics may be, and an urgent necessity for a more modern and precise description of this group need not detain us at present. The clinician in effect says to the epidemiologist, sometimes in terms of considerable exasperation; how many people are there in the community *like this?* Where are they concentrated, what are their features in the preclinical phase of the disorder, what size and type of services are required for their treatment, and so on down the list of questions.

To this the stock epidemiological response is, 'Tell me your definition of a case and I will then try to find some operational equivalent which will be sufficiently close to your clinical description to serve for practical purposes.' At this point an impasse is reached. The clinician is assuming that people either are or are not alcoholics, and that there exist discontinuous criteria for their designation. If this were so, as it might be so for, say, nuclear schizophrenia, and is for pregnancy, then the traditional techniques of epidemiology could be deployed and the sacred first step — so beloved of the textbooks — namely the definition of a 'case' could be achieved. But the bulk of the evidence suggests that the more appropriate analogy might be with hypertension (rather than with coronary thrombosis) or with osteoporosis (rather than with pathological fracture). Clinical descriptions of alcoholism indicate that the main criteria are continuously distributed, and any estimate of rates must therefore depend on the cut-off points which at present can only be arbitrary. Indeed, the whole concept of prevalence might itself be misleading, as Ingham and Miller (1976) have argued in connection with neurosis.

Meanwhile the social scientist is pacing about in the wings, restless and impatient. He comments that what is important is the mass of disability, violent behaviour, broken marriages and social deterioration attributable to alcohol. He speedily follows this by indicating that the proportion of individuals affected by these disasters who might be 'clinical alcoholics' whatever that may mean, is small, and that attempts to delineate them are at best boring and at worst betoken a parochial, irresponsible frivolity in the face of a major social problem. Mutterings may be heard of medical empires and an attack may follow on the 'medical model' espoused by leading physicians round about 1890. Maintaining his composure, the epidemiologist may opt for either of two strategies. He may quit the field, believing that the questions are too fluid to be answered. This is rather like a boxer complaining that his opponent will not stand still to be hit. The alternative is to grasp the nettle, to realise that epidemiology is itself a social science if it is anything. Behaviours like delinquency, suicide and parasuicide have been much researched, and in principle the same could be done for 'problems' associated with alcohol. But if he embraces this orientation the investigator will not be contributing data at the end of the day about 'alcoholics', and clinicians and health administrators may well be exasperated at the absence of the kind of information they expect for other disorders.

These alternatives have of course been somewhat caricatured and in reality both types of approach can be combined (though rarely within the same study). For present purposes, however, it might be useful if we consider them separately.

The Prevalence of Alcoholism

Indirect methods: The ideal situation for the use of these techniques is (a) to have available data based on unequivocal criteria, which is (b) routinely recorded, and (c) has a constant relationship to the phenomenon under study. Needless to say such a fortuitous combination is very rare. The history of the Jellinek formula and the reasons for its retraction illustrate some of the difficulties. Cirrhosis is the marker that has been more commonly used, but suicide, road accidents and mortality ratios of various kinds have also been employed. All pose similar problems concerning the intermediate ratio, i.e. that between the prevalance of the marker and alcoholism. It is often difficult to estimate accurately, and cannot be assumed to be uniform across time or between population subgroups. Cirrhosis, diet and social class may have complex interactions with alcohol consumption, as may even primary symptoms such as delirium tremens. Between-group comparisons are thus hazardous.

The Study of High Risk Groups

It is now possible to draw up a substantial list of risk factors for alcoholism (e.g. Wilkins, 1974) which may serve both as valuable aids to clinical practice and as a screening device in the first stage of a survey. This may be a rewarding approach provided all individuals in the high risk group can then be individually examined, but any estimate derived by this strategy must of course be critically dependent upon the availability of risk factors applicable across the whole social spectrum. Thus industrial accidents may help identify alcoholism among machine operators but not among company directors; the latter would require their own 'indicators' and if these are less easily available, comparison of the two social groups would be biased.

Recorded Mortality and Morbidity

Death certification applies only to the dead, and we do not yet know if mortality relative to morbidity is consistent across groups such as, for example, occupational categories. Nevertheless given the range of mortality ratios, which for cirrhosis is an astounding twenty-fold difference between the highest and lowest occupational groups, there is clearly matter here for closer scrutiny.

Hospital morbidity data must as always reflect the structure of local health services and the serial filtration that occurs at each level of referral, together with variations in diagnostic criteria. The latter will be less serious with the more extreme variants of alcoholism, such as encepalopathy, or even DTs, but such features apply of course only to a minority of the cases generally termed alcoholics. The need for the redescription of the alcohol dependence syndrome in operational terms has already been noted.

Population Surveys

Anyone embarking on a survey of a random sample of the general population will have to accept that the number of 'clinical alcoholics' he can identify is likely to be small, even if he has major resources available. The problem of case definition has also been touched on, and Clark (1966) has demonstrated how very susceptible such surveys are to relatively minor changes in the definition of a 'case'. The WHO definition is remarkable for having been derived by consensus, yet having virtually no one prepared to defend it. In the present state of the art it is necessary for the investigator to spell out his own criteria, and here we may note a certain irony: surveys are undertaken in order to overcome the selective referrals and conceptual stereotypes of agencies such as AA, the police or medical services, yet the instruments used in most surveys are very much of the type 'Have you been in trouble with the police?', 'Have you ever attended AA?', 'Has your doctor ever told you?', etc. The procedure may not be totally irrational, however, since presumably an individual labelled by a number of different agencies is likely to have the characteristics which the investigator is interested in, but the situation is distinctly odd. As with other forms of stigmatised behaviour, denial by respondents is common, as was noted in conjunction with high consumption. It is again worth stressing that the dangers are not so much simple under-estimation as selective under-reporting.

Tangential Measures
Finally there is a host of more peripheral indices which have commonly been used. These include arrests for various kinds of drink-related problems, hospital admission figures and the like. Perhaps the most comprehensive use of such data was the Macrae Report (1965). The most that could be concluded was that in some very general sense alcoholism was probably increasing in Scotland. This was sufficient for the purposes of the Report but could scarcely be said to bring much precision to the issue.

The Questions
Data on the prevalence of alcoholism – its distribution in time, space and by types of person – could be put to all the uses classically served by epidemiology. These are too familiar to require rehearsal here. But is alcohol a continuous or discontinuous entity, and either way, by what criteria should it be recognised? However, to identify a problem as one of theory is no invitation to armchair speculation. The most efficient position for thinking to some purpose is on one's feet.

Alcohol-Related Problems
We noted earlier that the concept of alcoholism tends to bifurcate into a clinical syndrome on the one hand, and a more diffuse notion of problematic behaviours and personal difficulties on the other. There are almost certainly vastly more individuals who would be identified as problem drinkers according to the latter criterion than could be designated as alcoholics, and perhaps for this reason 'problems' figure more prominently in population-based studies. Yet paradoxically the notion of a 'problem' seems to have been left unadorned by the

blessings of analysis. Even such a distinguished and experienced
investigator as Knupfer (1972), is content to write:

> If a person chooses to spend a lot of his time in a state of
> intoxication, who is to say that that is a problem? My position is
> that if either he thinks it is a problem or his wife does, or his boss
> does, or he gets arrested for drunkenness, then it is a problem. I
> also reserve the right to decide that it is a problem, even without
> those conditions, if he drinks, say, a fifth of whisky a day.

Such fluidity is self-defeating. We can neither agree nor disagree with
the inclusion of any particular 'problem' while the concept remains so
elastic (as well as tautologous).

With this vital first stage at such an unsatisfactory state, it is not
surprising that a veritable cascade of difficulties descend as soon as we
attempt to probe any further. Many of these have been admirably
reviewed by Room (1975), and repetition here would be superfluous.
By and large they are homologous with those already noted in
connection with population consumption and alcoholism, but have the
further dimension of difficulty in that many of the items counted as
problems appear to be reflections of a social context as much as the
behaviour of the individual. This being so it is almost meaningless to
compare problems in different social contexts, since that context has
itself entered into the definition of the problem. Such confusion of
dependent and independent variables is the most potent ground for
dissatisfaction with the present state of knowledge.

All the same, it may be precisely in such ill-defined areas that
epidemiology may have the most to contribute. Undoubtedly
psychological equilibrium and social function is impaired in many
individuals by their use of alcohol. The task then becomes to specify
and measure those dislocations. To do so implies coming to intellectual
grips with the social, as well as the psychological and perhaps somatic
processes involved. Such an exercise carries epidemiology straight to
the centre of social psychiatry but that is where it properly belongs.
Of course, this means that any epidemiologist unwilling to learn to
think sociologically and to collaborate wherever possible with
sociological colleagues had better go off and learn another trade.

Conclusions

It has not been possible here to consider such complex topics as the
relationship of alcohol to violence or suicide, or the organisation of

services concerned with alcohol problems. What has emerged rather is the suggestion that the most fundamental issues constitute an interconnected triad. They are the distribution of normal alcohol consumption practices in the general population, the prevalence of clinical alcoholism and the analysis and measurement of alcohol-related disabilities. Each poses formidable methodological complexities, and it may well be that the next decade will be largely occupied with their solution rather than with producing answers to the substantive questions. It may also be that further experience in wrestling with these difficulties may quite legitimately lead to a re-formulation of the problems themselves; the scientist has no more justification for posing unanswerable questions than an artist has in conjecturing works of art in a non-existent medium.

These notes of caution should in no way be taken to imply that the endeavour is not eminently worthwhile. The programme of work ahead of us can be discerned with reasonable clarity, and given the necessary men, money and enthusiasm, the gains may prove to be substantial. Our thinking about other forms of drug abuse, including opiate addiction, has been revolutionised by comprehensive epidemiological studies, and it may well be that a similar harvest awaits us in the epidemiology of alcoholism.

References

Bailey, M., Haberman, P. and Sheinberg, J. (1965). The epidemiology of alcoholism in an urban residential area. Quart. J. Stud. Alc. 26: 19-40.

Clark, W. (1966). Operational definition of drinking problems and associated prevalence rates. Quart. J. Stud. Alc. 27: 648-68.

Dight, S. (1976). Scottish Drinking Habits: A survey carried out for the Scottish Home and Health Department. OPCS Social Survey Division, HMSO.

Edwards, G. (1973). Epidemiology applied to alcoholism: a review and examination of purposes. Quart. J. Stud. Alc. 34: 28-56.

Finnish Foundation for Alcohol Studies (1975). Alcohol control policies in public health perspective.

Ingham, J. and Miller, P. (1976). The concept of prevalence applied to psychiatric disorders and symptoms. Psycholog. Med. 6: 217-25.

Knupfer, G. (1972), in: Life History Research in Psychopathology, vol.2, p.257. Roff, Robins and Pollack (eds.). Univ. Minnesota Press.

Macrae, E.K.M. (1965). Alcoholics: Health services for their treatment and rehabilitation. Report of Sub-Committee of the Standing Medical Advisory Committee, Scottish Home and Health Department.

de Lint, J. and Schmidt, W. (1968). The distribution of alcohol consumption in Ontario. Quart. J. Stud. Alc. 29: 968-73.

Pernanen, K. (1974). Validity of survey data on alcohol use. Alcohol and Drug Problems I: 355-74.

Popham, R.E. (1970). Indirect methods of alcoholism prevalence estimation: A critical evaluation. In Alcohol and Alcoholism. Popham, R. (ed.). Toronto University Press.

Room, R. (1975). The measurement and distribution of drinking patterns and problems in general population. WHO paper OMH/C/75.5.

Wilkins, R.H. (1974). The Hidden Alcoholic in General Practice. London: Paul Elek (Scientific Books) Ltd.

3 FACTORS INFLUENCING ALCOHOL CONSUMPTION

David Robinson

Introduction

This chapter is about drinking and about the prevention of alcoholism. As such it is about an ordinary everyday activity, on the one hand, and about the prevention of one of the major health and social problems of our time, on the other. The ordinariness of the everyday activity can be judged by the fact that roughly four out of five adults in England will have had an alcoholic drink of some kind within the past month. The magnitude of the health and social problems are elaborated elsewhere in this volume.

Given the very broad scope of this chapter, I am going to concentrate, for the most part, on a small number of core themes beginning with a brief discussion of the place of alcohol in everyday life, going on to suggest that the consumption of alcohol is surprisingly little studied, to outline certain models of alcoholism prevention and, finally, to look at some of the 'factors' which it has been suggested could be manipulated in order to influence alcohol consumption. In addition, however, certain broader contextual issues will be indicated which need to be considered if any progress is to be made in preventing, or making less likely the development of, alcohol-related problems.

Alcohol and Everyday Life

As the contributions to this volume show, the relationship between man and alcohol is of interest to us not only at the level of bodily process. While the chemical properties of alcohol provide a necessary base, the behavioural concomitants of drinking alcohol depend as much on ideas of what alcohol does to a person as they do on complex biochemical processes. For 'when a man lifts a cup', write MacAndrew and Edgerton (1970),

> . . .it is not only the kind of drink that is in it, the amount he is likely to take, and the circumstances under which he will do the drinking that are specified in advance for him, but also whether the contents of the cup will cheer or stupify, whether they will induce affection or aggression, guilt or unalloyed pleasure. These and many

other cultural definitions attach to the drink even before it touches the lips.

And, of course, intimately related to ideas about the *effects* of alcohol are ideas about the place of drinking in relation to other activities. From the earliest recorded times alcohol has been used as an integral part of significant social occasions; in religious ritual; in rites of passage from birth to funeral; in public happenings; in feasts and meetings; in magic and in medicine.

But a recurrent feature of the literature on alcohol and drinking is the conflict between its beneficial and its harmful effects. For example, the earliest Indian literary sources, the Vedic hymns, give detailed accounts of the use of Sura in sacrificial ritual but roundly condemn drinking outside the ritual occasions as likely to lead to quarrels and mislead men from the path of virtue. In the Old Testament, wine is specified in Numbers for use as a libation in the temple service. 'The wine for the proper drink-offering shall be a quarter of hin to each ram; you are to pour out this strong drink in the holy place as an offering to the Lord.' (28:7) By contrast several passages in the Book of Proverbs warn against wine's dangers. In the New Testament wine is mentioned as a festive drink, as a medicament and as a supreme symbol, but again there are many references to inappropriate drinking: 'Likewise must the deacons be grave, not double tongued, not given to much wine' (1 Timothy 3:8).

The field studies of social anthropologists show how cultural practices, in relation to drink, range from total rejection to avid immersion. The *form* of drinking is usually quite explicitly stipulated, including the kind of drink that can be used, the amount and rate of intake, the time and place of drinking, the accompanying ritual, the sex and age of the drinker, and the whole range of behaviour proper to drinking. The *meanings* of drinking, however, its relation to other aspects of the culture and society, are usually more implicit.

At the extremes, though, the meanings are relatively clear. For example, among the Kofyar of Northern Nigeria, 'people make, drink, talk and think about beer', and, as Netting (1965) puts it, 'certainly believe that man's way to God is with beer in hand'. But in contrast to those who consider alcohol to be essential and blessed are the people who regard it as dispensable or destructive. The Hopi and other Pueblo Indian tribes of the American Southwest, for example, so abhorred the use of alcohol, and felt that it threatened their way of life, that they successfully banned it from their settlements for many years.

But one of the shortcomings of much of the anthropological literature which mentions drinking is that it tends to give vivid descriptions of orgiastic drinking sprees, exciting but untypical, while ignoring the prosaic and everyday routines in terms of which most people actually do their drinking. Heath, however, in his classic, and rightly much reprinted, study of the Bolivian Camba (1958) gives a detailed account of many aspects of *everyday* drinking practices including: the type of alcohol which is drunk, mostly pure cane alcohol which 'is probably the most potent alcoholic drink in customary usage anywhere in the world' − 80 per cent pure alcohol; the cost of alcohol and its method of production and sale; the occasions on which alcohol is drunk,' only during fiestas, but these are not infrequent'; the context in which drinking takes place, 'only within a social context, solitary drinking is inconceivable to the Camba'; and the common drinking rituals. He then goes on to describe the Camba attitudes toward drink; their comportment when drunk, 'hangovers and hallucinations are unknown among these people. . .A farmhand will "snap out of" intoxication abruptly when the call to breakfast is sounded after a fiesta', and to suggest, in summary: '. . .that alcohol plays a predominantly integrative role in Camba society, where drinking is an elaborately ritualised group activity and alcoholism is unknown'.

Using material from many field studies, such as Heath's, there have been attempts to identify the *function* of alcohol in particular sets of societies, or even for *all* societies. And obviously the identification of the part which alcohol plays in a society could have clear implications for the prevention of problems related to its consumption. Horton (1943), for example, examined the files of the Cross-cultural Survey in the Institute of Human Relations at Yale and extracted information on drinking behaviour, based on the degree of insobriety commonly reached by adult male drinkers, and related it to various indicators of subsistence anxiety. All this, together with the manipulation of other supporting data, led Horton to conclude that the primary function of alcoholic beverages in *any* society is the reduction of anxiety. Unfortunately, the preventive policy implications of such a 'discovery' are, at best, obscure.

Given the wealth of anthropological, literary and historical work bearing on alcohol consumption it is not surprising that cultural variations in drinking practices, such as those mentioned earlier, are well documented. There has been rather less effort, however, to pick out the *similarities* in drinking practices across cultures. Nevertheless it is almost universally reported that drinking is considered more suitable for men than for women and that it is a *social* rather than a solitary activity, but done much more in the society of age mates and peers than with elders or in the family circle.

Among other regularities are that drinking is more often considered appropriate for those who grapple with the external environment than for those whose task it is to carry on and maintain a society's internal activities. This distinction was symbolised in ancient India by the difference between the god Indra, the scourge of enemies, the thunderer, the roisterer, the heavy drinker, and Varuna, the sober guardian of order and morality. In ancient Greece, the worship of Dionysius could transport the worshipper into an extraordinary, even frenzied, state; that of Apollo encouraged only social morality. Drinking was a prominent feature of the Dionysian rites but not at Apollonian ceremonies.

In general, warriors and shamans are more likely to use alcohol with cultural approval than are judges and priests. A priest is generally the conserver of tradition, the guide and exemplar for his fellows in precise replication of ritual in ways that please the gods. Drinking rarely goes with the priestly performance of ritual, except in symbolic usage, as in the Mass. But a shaman, who has personal relations with the supernatural, must directly encounter potent forces beyond ordinary society. Drinking is rarely considered to interfere with this function.

When the fate of many hinges on the action of a single person, that person is usually not permitted to drink before performing the critical activity. The high priests of the Old Testament were particularly forbidden to drink 'wine or strong drink' when discharging their priestly duties in the Sanctuary. Airline pilots today are forbidden to drink for a number of hours before flying as well as during the flight. The notable exception is French pilots who have wine with their in-flight meals; but then alcohol is defined as food by the French!

A ban on alcohol is usually imposed when it is considered dangerous to heighten the emotions of large numbers of people who gather together at the same occasion. There is an inscription dating from the year 5 BC near the stadium at Delphi which forbids the carrying of wine into the stadium on pain of a five drachma fine. There is a move now to have alcohol banned from soccer grounds; it has already been banned at Twickenham for the coming season in an attempt to curb rugger hooliganism.

So, if we were to find a society in which women must drink more than men, in which drinking must be done alone or in the company of one's mentors and dependents, or in which the upholders of dogma, whether theological or political, are expected to drink more heavily than do others, we should know that we have encountered a society basically different from others so far reported upon.

Alcohol Consumption

But all this talk of cross-cultural similarities and differences, anthropological field material, Vedic hymns, Greek Gods and the beer freaks of Northern Nigeria must not blind us to the fact that we know remarkably little about patterns of alcohol consumption. The question of who drinks what, when and where may seem pretty simple-minded. But it is not a simple question to answer, as anyone who has, for example, attempted to conduct a general population drinking survey will readily acknowledge (Robinson, 1976). At a personal level, how many of us could give an account, even 90 per cent accurate, of how much, of what we've drunk with whom, where, in the past week, or three days, or even yesterday, or this morning?

In a way this general lack of attention to everyday drinking behaviour is understandable. For given that there are limited resources of money, facilities and time, both therapists and researchers can usually claim to have more immediately pressing matters to attend to. If it is not the pleas of patients it is the pleas of their families and friends. If it is not the reorganization of services it is changes in the liquor licensing laws, or the setting up of detoxification centres, or the introduction of new laws concerned with drinking and driving, or the need to stress the importance of 'the alcoholism problem' to government departments, professional colleagues, oneself or the general public. In short, there are enough social, political, personal, legal, medical and administrative 'problems' caused by, or closely associated with, the consumption of alcohol for the description of everyday drinking behaviour to be considered as, at best, a peripheral matter.

But what are the problems? Who defines them in what situations for what purposes? These are not mere sociologists' quibbles but part of a whole set of issues which are too little considered by those who study, treat or are in some way involved with alcoholics. For people do not just suddenly become alcoholics any more than they just suddenly become ill (Robinson, 1971). The process of becoming an alcoholic begins by someone making a link between everyday drinking and the development of some problem. That link may be based on the quantity which the person consumes, or their behaviour after consuming a certain amount, or their behaviour in other related contexts, or on the importance which they appear to give to alcohol in terms of finance, time or precedence over the other commitments such as family, marriage or work. And we must not forget that all these links are being made by particular people who occupy positions with more or less formal, professional or administrative power *vis-à-vis* the person who is deemed to have 'a problem'. So any attempt to understand why particular people get into the position of being a problem — in this case an alcoholic — must be informed by an appreciation of their social-structural position. This means that we do not just take organisations or professions or laws to be things out there, agreed and static while people change and somehow develop problems. People in organisations, or in their relations with professionals, or in response to or because of laws, are being defined as having problems. Not only that but the organisations, professions and laws may actually increase their likelihood of developing them (Robinson, 1972).

But all this having been said, the one thing which links all these considerations together in the case of alcohol-related problems is that neglected issue — everyday drinking behaviour. In his introduction to Cahalan and associates' book *American Drinking Practices* (1969), Seldon Bacon identifies its importance in this way:

> . . .there are studies and books and pamphlets, there are conferences and national organisations and films, there are newspaper reports and laws and hand-books on procedures. . .One is concerned with disease, another with accidents, a third with sales control, a fourth with criminal justice. One is based on biochemistry, another on personality, a third on political art or science and a fourth on community organisation and public health. [This book centres] attention on the phenomenon central to all these approaches and central to all the problems no matter what their form, no matter what discipline or language is employed: namely man using alcoholic beverages. . .All too frequently, this core, this essential and crucial precondition to *all* questions and answers, has been forgotten.

Prevention

It is clear, from what has been said so far, that it would be difficult to identify *any* aspect of everyday social life which does not, in some way, influence the form, regularity or quantity of alcohol consumption. This, of course, in relation to prevention tells us everything and, thus, nothing; since those who are concerned with prevention don't *merely* want explanations of why the world is as it is — however sophisticated or elegant such theories may be — they want descriptions and explanations which contain 'factors with handles on'. In this particular field they want factors related to the consumption of alcohol, or the development of alcohol-related problems, which they can manipulate — because prevention is about manipulation, and successful manipulation, of course, is something which needs political clout since prevention-of-problem manipulation is merely some people deciding to do things which they consider will be a good thing for other people.

Increasing attention is currently being given to legislative measures, such as those concerned with public inebriates or drunken drivers, which focus on specific sections of the drinking population, or on legislation aimed at whole communities which is intended to make less likely the development of alcohol problems through the regulation of the amount or character of alcohol consumption. The principal measures are those which control the number of places in which alcoholic beverages may be purchased, the type and location of outlets, the age at which persons may consume and purchase alcoholic beverage, the hours and days of sale, differential taxation and price control and state control of production.

Models of Prevention

The arguments advanced for and against the efficacy of any or all these control measures are many and various. However, as Popham, Schmidt and de Lint (1974) have recently pointed out, three 'models of prevention', appear to underpin a great deal of the research, controversy and policy proposals. These are, in brief:

1. *The Bimodal Model:* according to which heavy alcohol consumption of problem drinkers and alcoholics is considered to be symptomatic of some disorder peculiar to them. Therefore, by implication, the distribution of consumption in a population will be bimodal in character, and factors which may cause a change in the consumption level of normal drinkers will have little or no effect on that of pathological drinkers. Accordingly, legal measures which seek to control the prevalence of alcoholism by restraining overall consumption are held to be misdirected and ineffective. . .
2. *The Integration Model:* in terms of which it is believed that to eradicate or even substantially reduce the prevalence of alcoholism would require fundamental changes in the social and mental health status of the population. However, it is also

believed that more problems result from the mysticism associated with alcohol, and the guilt attendant upon its use than would occur if drinking were an integrated part of everyday life. . .Thus it is argued that young people should be introduced to alcoholic beverages at an early age so that they may learn to drink moderately, and come to regard the activity as of no greater significance than eating. Restrictive control measures are seen both as reinforces of an unhealthy ambivalence towards drinking, and as impediments to the adoption of healthy drinking styles. . .

3. *The Single Distribution Model:* whose proponents argue that the frequency distribution of alcohol consumption per drinker in any given population is continuous, unimodal and positively skewed. . . the variance is constant and only the mean differs from one group to another. Under these circumstances, the relative frequency of high level consumers. . .depends upon the mean per drinker consumption in a population, and factors which alter the latter may be expected to alter the former. Since the same distribution is found to obtain in populations which differ greatly in attitudes towards drinking, beverage preferences, drinking customs, and the educational and legal measures employed to combat the problems of alcohol, it is concluded that there is as yet no way to modify the prevalence of heavy consumers without altering the average consumption of other drinkers.

The weight of argument among the international experts of alcoholism field seems currently to favour Model 3; the simple conclusion that relaxing the legal controls on alcohol availability and consumption 'leads to an increase in consumption, and an increase in consumption adds to the complications'. In the light of the Prohibition experience in the United States, and other examples of drastic controls on liquor availability, it is clear that highly restrictive controls on accessibility *do* lead to lower consumption and a reduction in certain major alcohol problems. However, as mentioned earlier, tight control needs political clout and is only likely to be achieved if there is substantial public support − while the controls themselves are apt to involve costs which may be seen to outweigh their benefits. Such costs include resentment of the system by those who consider themselves non-drinkers, an increase in the production of illicit liquor, certain difficulties of law enforcement, the loss of tax revenues and the reduction in the personal and social enjoyment which alcohol consumption so clearly provides for large sections of the population.

This again demonstrates the importance of the question of who benefits from alcoholism, or at least the question of who benefits from maintaining the conditions in which alcoholism is able to develop. Here the issue is one of large-scale socio-legal policy: the balancing of costs and benefits or rather the balancing of one set of costs against another set of costs. If we want to understand why the policies are as they are then we must ask such questions as which pressure groups and factions are pushing for which kinds of controls over which kinds of activities, and why?

The possibility of certain costs resulting from drastic controls is often invoked as a reason for rejecting *any* form of restraint in alcohol production, availability or consumption. However, increased attention is currently being given to the possibility of gradual overall consumption control. A recent WHO working party on *Alcohol Control Policy in Public Health Perspective* outlined its position as follows (Bruun *et al.*, 1975):

> Provision of appropriate treatment and rehabilitation services is vital, but with a health problem of such large dimensions, and one where response to treatment is by no means always certain, it is clear that the institution of effective preventive policies should receive urgent public health attention. . .The most helpful lead which has emerged in recent years. . .is the notion that the rate of any alcohol-related problem in a population is related to the *per capita* level of alcohol consumption in that population, with the corollary that any measures which diminish total alcohol consumption will decrease the alcoholism rate. It therefore becomes relevant to public health to identify factors potentially within society's grasp — [factors with handles on] which may influence overall consumption rates, for the manipulation of these factors might form a basis for the practical public health approach now urgently required.

Griffith Edwards (1971) put it rather more clearly and succinctly:

> Since we are not able to manipulate personality and produce a race with no neurosis, the only realistic method of exerting a benign influence on the prevalence of alcohol addiction is by control of the environmental conditions of drinking, and it is the availability element that remains the prime candidate for control.

Alcohol Control Strategies

I now want to look very briefly at some of the particular preventive strategies which have been suggested, along with some which have actually been tried. It is necessary to consider strategies, rather than *a* strategy, because of course, there is no one-shot way of preventing the development of alcohol-related problems, other than by getting rid of alcohol which is politically impossible and, as we have seen, creates as many problems as it solves. Morris Chafetz (1974), the ex-Director of the American National Institute on Alcohol Abuse and Alcoholism recently stressed the need for a multi-pronged preventive approach. 'The alcoholic condition', he said

. . .is the product of many factors: genetic, biological, social and psychological, each interacting in different ways in different individuals. It is my view that when [a problem] . . .results from multiple causes, it is not sensible to seek a 'magic bullet'. . . Rather, the approach to prevention should delineate its multiple causes and then attempt to minimize their destructive effects.

He went on to point up some strategic failures: 'We have tried Prohibition, and it failed. We have tried campaign slogans, and they failed. We have tried educational programs based on fear, and *they* have failed.'

By and large, there are two main classes of measures which have been proposed. The first, broadly socio-cultural, and the second, related to the distribution of consumption. The socio-cultural proposals are based on the research which has attempted to explain different rates of alcoholism among a variety of social and cultural groups. After reviewing a great deal of this literature Blacker (1966) concluded that:

. . .in any group or society in which drinking customs, values and sanctions. . .are well established, known and agreed upon by all, consistent with the rest of the culture, and are characterised by prescriptions for moderate drinking and prescriptions against excessive drinking, the rate of alcoholism will be low.

This kind of thinking dominated the 1950s and clearly underpinned reports such as that of the *Cooperative Commission on the Study of Alcoholism* (Plaut, 1967) which suggested that what was needed, in order to stem the rising tide of alcoholism, was a set of 'national drinking norms' to replace the diverse, fragmented and frequently contradictory set of norms that currently exist relative to alcohol use, since the current condition was felt to foster ambiguity, anxiety and confusion over what proper drinking practices ought to be. Not all 'socio-cultural' proposals combined such arrogance and naïveté. Some, such as those which Wilkinson put forward in his book *The Prevention of Drinking Problems: legal control and cultural influences* (1970), were more modest and more possible, even if not more desirable. He argued that drinking problems can be reduced by encouraging people to develop healthy drinking practices such as drinking wine with meals, and, in particular, by *integrating* the use of alcoholic beverages into a wide variety of social situations, such as sporting events, and by encouraging 'cheery taverns' where people would go to meet their friends rather than simply to drink.

A similar 'integration' philosophy lay behind the proposals of the Clayson (HMSO, 1973) and Erroll (HMSO, 1974) reports on Liquor Licensing, which will be discussed again briefly later. It also lies behind the Glasgow study, by Davies and Stacey (1972), of 'children and alcohol'. Their report concludes:

> . . .that children begin to learn about alcohol early in life, even before primary school. By age 6 a majority recognise the behavioural manifestations of drunkenness, and many are capable of identifying some alcoholic drinks by smell alone; they also perceive people in different roles to like alcohol in different degrees. By the age of 8 most children have attained a mastery of the concept of alcohol and in general the rate at which children acquire a broad understanding in this sphere was greater than anticipated.

On the basis of this and similar work there has been a fair amount of pressure recently to make it respectable to give drink to one's young children in order that, from an early age, they may grow up to see drinking as part of family or group activity, to be taken-for-granted rather than be something special, and in general to demystify the whole drinking experience. In an ideal world, this would be fine. Unfortunately many parents are far too confused and guilty about their own drinking, as the Davies and Stacey study also shows, to transmit anything to their children beyond their own ambivalence. Those who understand this point and yet still put forward a socio-cultural approach are forced to propose some kind of 'educative' campaign. Chafetz (1974), for example, who admitted that most campaigns and

educational programmes had been a complete failure was forced, by the
logic of his own socio-cultural position, to propose 'an educational
campaign'. 'I believe', he said,

> . . .that our educational institutions should provide theoretical
> information about alcohol and its use. This didactic material should
> be provided in the hygiene curricula of schools, with emphasis on
> the benefits, as well as the deficits, of alcohol. It should show how
> different the response will be when drink is consumed with food
> and while sitting in a relaxed atmosphere, in contrast to drinking
> without food and in tense circumstances; how the use of alcohol
> imparts meaningful experience when partaken of with another,
> while a drink alone is as uncommunicative as talking to oneself;
> and how intoxication is sickness and not strength. . .By providing
> educational information within a didactic setting and by integrating
> drinking experience with family use, immunization against
> unhealthy, irresponsible drinking behaviour can be provided as a
> bulwark against alcoholism.

This is the usual resting place of the socio-cultural approach: incredibly
well-intentioned pious statements of hope, with little or no guides to
action.

But does everyone want to control alcoholism anyway? Who are the
people, in other words, who are getting something out of alcoholism?
This is a reasonable, too little asked, but important and researchable
question. Because it is clearly the case that if all the alcoholics in the
world suddenly 'got better' overnight there would be an awful lot of
unhappy people around: including, for example, those families which
like, for a variety of reasons, to keep one of their members ill; those
professors of psychiatry who like their consultative power in relation
to government departments; those specialists of various kinds who
have carved out alcoholism as their area of expertise; research
sociologists who like to have their mortgages paid in return for giving
easy-to-come-by opinions about alcohol-related problems; large sections
of the general public who are reassured by seeing someone worse off
than themselves; comedians, cartoonists and concerned young
playwrights who would lose one of their hand-me-down topics; and
many more. And what about alcoholics themselves, what are they
getting out of their alcoholism? We must not slip into the position of
assuming that alcoholics, their intimates, professionals and members
of the wide public are all dedicated to the swiftest possible solving of

all alcohol related problems. A socio-cultural approach to prevention can only work if it is based on a *realistic* assessment of society and culture: a simple point which is rarely appreciated, or if appreciated rarely acted on.

Distribution of Consumption Approach

As outlined earlier, prevention proposals related to the distribution of consumption are based on a body of research which suggests that the popular distinction between 'normal drinkers' and 'alcoholics' can not be made on the basis of consumption alone since, graphically speaking, the distribution of consumption does not produce a large number of people clustered at the low consumption end of the distribution (normal drinkers) and a hiccup at the high end of the distribution caused by the smaller number of high consumers. Rather the distribution of consumption curve is unimodal, smooth and without discontinuities and, further, has a general character which appears to be stable across levels of overall consumption, and everyday drinking patterns and practices.

The major focus of those who want to reduce overall consumption has been the availability factor, and the most popular proposal has been to manipulate the price of the commodity. Seeley (1960), for example, estimated that tripling the price of drinks would produce a significant decrease in *per capita* consumption and cirrhosis of the liver. Rather more sophisticated schemes, in which the price of alcohol would be index-linked to rates of disposable income, have also been suggested. But have changes in policy which affect availability actually had any impact on overall consumption rates and, more important, on the rate of alcohol-related problems? Wolfgang Schmidt discusses the relationship between consumption and cirrhosis, elsewhere in this volume.

Effects of Controls

Anyone looking for conclusive evidence on the effectiveness of particular control policies will soon be disappointed. For although alcohol control measures are frequently modified in many parts of the world it is very difficult to assess their effect. First, most changes tend to be small. Sweeping and dramatic changes are extremely rare. Second, some changes in social control measures have followed significant changes in social behaviour so it is almost impossible to tease out the relative weights of the many simultaneous changes. Third, alcohol policy changes are often part of a packet of changes so it is again impossible to decide which change produced which effect. Nevertheless, Whitehead (1975) has recently looked at the effects of two sets of changes in alcohol control measures, both liberalising: the increased availability of certain types of alcoholic beverages in Finland and the lowering of the legal drinking age in many parts of the United States and Canada.

Alcohol control policies in Finland have traditionally favoured beverages with a low alcohol content. In 1969, restrictions on the distribution of medium strength beer were lifted. Whereas previously such purchases could be made only from stores operated by the state monopoly they were, in 1969, released from unrestricted retail distribution. In addition, retail liquor stores were permitted in rural communities for the first time.

These changes resulted in a swift and marked increase in the consumption of alcoholic beverages. During 1969, alcohol consumption increased by 49 per cent over its 1968 level. Most of this increase was in the form of medium beer which the new law had made more available. According to Mäkelä (1972):

... beer accounted for the bulk of the increase, and the proportion of beer in the total consumption of alcoholic beverages grew substantially. In the following years, however... the consumption of strong drinks increased at the same rate as before. It therefore appears... [that] the release of medium beer from market restrictions raised total consumption to a new level — but not at the expense of 'hard' liquors, the rate of increase of which was not affected.

On the basis of survey data dealing with periods both before and after the change in the law, Mäkelä (1970) concludes that the more liberal system of distribution did not foster more temperate patterns of consumption, but rather led to an increase in the number of drinking occasions and the average level of consumption. Basically, new drinking practices (e.g. beer with meals) were *added* to the former ones rather than becoming a substitute for them. The Finnish case provides a clear example of what can happen to the level of consumption when alcoholic beverages are made more available.

Liquor Licensing
In recent years a good deal of attention has been given to one particular kind of control over consumption — liquor licensing laws.

During the early 1970s, for example, several states and provinces in the United States and Canada reduced the age for legal purchase and consumption, usually from 21 to 18 but in some instances 21 to 19. Those who favoured this liberalisation argued, like Erroll on this side of the Atlantic (but not Clayson), that such changes are unlikely to lead to an increase in alcohol-related problems because many young people already drink even though they are under the legal age. Surveys revealing that most people who will ever use alcoholic beverages have already done so by the time they reach the minimum age are cited to support this view. In essence, the position is that a change in the drinking age simply makes licit a previously illicit form of behaviour.

Two main types of study have thrown light on this proposition. The first dealing with the effect of the changed legal drinking age on level of consumption and the second looking at legal age changes and level of alcohol-related problems, road accidents in particular. Wolfgang Schmidt and his colleagues (1974) at the Addiction Research Foundation in Ontario, using time-series data on sales of alcoholic beverages found that the reduction in the minimum age contributed to a substantial increase in the level of consumption among 18 to 20 year olds and that the extra drinking was done on public premises. As to road crashes, several studies have looked at the effect of lowering the drinking age on the rate of alcohol-related road crashes in which young drivers were involved. These studies focus on different jurisdictions, examine somewhat different periods of time and use different methodologies to study the questions at hand, but the conclusions from these studies are similar: that the reduction of drinking age has led to higher rates of alcohol-related collisions and associated damage (Cucchiaro *et al.*, 1974; Williams *et al.*, 1974; Zylman, 1974).

The Erroll Committee's proposal to reduce the legal age for on-consumption from 18 to 17 in this country has, of course, received fairly short shrift from the British Government. In fact, none of the committee's 100 or so recommendations have been acted on, not even the very sensible minor ones which would have simplified and made less anomalous certain aspects of the licensing system. For example, under the present system a liquor licence is granted to an individual in respect of particular premises. Thus two unrelated sets of features are considered together, rather like an individual only being able to get a driving licence to drive one particular car which in turn is taxed only for that particular driver. Accordingly, the Committee, very sensibly, proposed a new procedure with two separate licences. However, 'perfectly sensible' proposals like that have not been taken up by the

Home Office under either Conservative or Labour administrations because neither is willing to be identified with the main body of proposals which, as a whole, would significantly relax controls over alcohol consumption.

When the then Home Secretary, Mr Maudling, appointed the Erroll Committee in 1970 he clearly imagined that the question of liquor licensing would merely set off the same old tired debate between the trade, on the one hand, and the temperance organisations, on the other, with the general public — tongues hanging out — somewhere in the background. In the event, of course, the medical profession produced the strongest evidence while most of the liquor trade organisations wanted to maintain the *status quo;* and when the report was published in 1972 the 'heavy' press, the 'popular' press, the professional, police, medical and legal press, and the general public were all against the Committee's proposals to relax controls (Robinson, 1974). In fact the members of the Erroll Committee appeared to be almost the only group of people in England and Wales who didn't understand the implications of the relationships between alcohol consumption, alcohol problems and everyday social life. If they *did* understand them then we can only agree with a leader in the *Lancet* which characterised the Erroll report as one of 'almost rollicking irresponsibility'.

Conclusion

To concentrate merely on the 'drinker and his illness' is readily agreed, these days, to be insufficient if one is trying to understand, prevent or alleviate alcohol-related problems. In practice, however, this ready agreement and the often heard calls for the alcoholic to be considered 'in his social environment' or 'in the community' rarely results in anything more than a cursory nod in the direction of 'the family' before getting down to, in some way, changing 'the drinker'.

In this chapter I have tried to indicate some of the social issues which need to be seriously addressed by anyone who wants to understand alcoholism. These include questions of definition; who defines which people for what purposes as having some alcohol-related problem — and who has the problem anyway; the drinker, his intimates, or some under group? At the level of policy we want to know how policy is formed, in response to what kind of pressure from which groups, for what purposes and on the basis of what evidence. As for treatment we need a much clearer idea, for example, about how professional attitudes and practice in relation to alcoholics develop and change; about the relationships between professional, voluntary

and other lay helpers; and about why alcoholism is such a low status
specialty within medicine and what implications this has for those who
consider themselves or are considered by others to have some alcohol-
related problem. These are not just ethereal questions fit only for
sociologists' lunchtime seminars, but crucial matters to be considered
by anyone seriously interested in how alcohol-related problems develop,
and are experienced, handled and suffered. In addition, of course, we
must not lose sight of the substance at the heart of the whole concern,
alcohol. For however sophisticated our handling of rotten livers, our
development of integrated helping services, or our analyses of whether
or not alcoholism is a disease — whatever a disease is — the core activity
underpinning all our concerns will still be 'man consuming alcohol in
the course of his everyday life'. That is the context in which problems
arise, that is the context in which certain problems might be prevented,
and it is that context which this chapter has been concerned with.

References

Bacon, S. Introduction to Cahalan, D., Cisin, I. and Crosslay, M. (1969). American
    Drinking Practices: a national study of drinking behavior and attitudes. New
    Jersey: Rutgers Centre of Alcohol Studies, New Brunswick.
Blacker, E. (1966). Socio-cultural factors in alcoholism. International Psychiatry
    Clinics 3(2):51.
Bruun, K. *et al.* (1975). Alcohol Control Policies: in public health perspective.
    vol.25. Helsinki: Finnish Foundation of Alcohol Studies.
Chafetz, M.E. (1974). Prevention of alcoholism in the United States: utilizing
    cultural and educational forces. Preventive Medicine 3.
Cucchiaro, S., Ferreira, J. Jnr. and Sicherman, A. (1974). The effect of the 18
    years old drinking age on auto accidents (mimeo). Cambridge, Mass.:
    Operations Research Center, Massachusetts Institute of Technology.
    Williams A.F., Rich R.F., Zador P.L. and Robertson L.S. (1974). The legal
    minimum drinking age and fatal motor vehicle crashes. Paper to the 6th
    International Conference on Alcohol, Drugs and Traffic Safety. Toronto;
    and Zylman R. (1974). Fatal crashes among Michigan Youth following
    reduction of legal drinking age. Quart. J. Stud. Alc. 35:283.
Davies, J. and Stacey, B. (1972). Teenagers and Alcohol: a developmental study
    in Glasgow, vol.2. HMSO.
Edwards, G. (1971). Public health implications of liquor control. Lancet 424.
Heath, D.B. (1958). Drinking patterns of the Bolivian Camba. Quart. J. Stud.
    Alc. 19:491.
Horton, D. (1943). The functions of alcohol in primitive societies: a cross-
    cultural study. Quart. J. Stud. Alc. 199.
MacAndrew, C. and Edgerton, R.B. (1970). Drunken Comportment: a social
    explanation. London: Nelson.
Mäkela, K (1970). The frequency of drinking occasions according to consumed
    beverages and quantities before and after the new liquor laws.
    Alkoholipolitukka 35:246.

Mäkelä, K. (1972). Consumption level and cultural drinking patterns as
    determinants of alcohol problems. Paper to the 30th International Congress
    on Alcoholism and Drug Dependence. Amsterdam.
Netting, R. (1962). A West African Beer Complex. Cited in: Maudelbaum, D.C.
    (1965). Alcohol and culture. Current Anthropology 6:281.
Plaut, T.F.A. (1967). Alcohol Problems: a report to the nation. New York: The
    Cooperative Commission on the Study of Alcoholism. Oxford University Press.
Popham, P.E., Schmidt, W. and de Lint, J. (1974). The effects of legal restraint
    on drinking. In Biology of Alcoholism, vol.III, Kissin, B and Belgeiter, H.
    (eds.). New York. Social Biology, Plenum Press.
Report of the Departmental Committee on Liquor Licensing, 1972. HMSO
    Cmnd.5154, (The Erroll Report).
Report of the Departmental Committee on Scottish Licensing Law, 1973.
    HMSO Cmnd.5354, (The Clayson Report).
Robinson, D. (1971). The Process of Becoming Ill. London: Routledge and
    Kegan Paul.
Robinson, D. (1972). The alcohologist's addiction: some implications of having
    lost control over the disease concept of alcoholism. Quart. J. Stud. Alc.
    33:1128.
Robinson, D. (1974). The Erroll Report: key proposals and public reaction.
    Brit. J. Addict. 69:99.
Robinson, D. (1976). From Drinking to Alcoholism: a sociological commentary.
    London: John Wiley and Sons.
Seeley, J.R. (1960). Death by liver cirrhosis and the price of beverage alcohol.
    Canadian Medical Association Journal 83:1361.
Schmidt, W. and Kornaczewski, A. (1974). The effect of lowering the legal
    drinking age in Ontario on alcohol-related motor vehicle accidents. Paper to
    the 6th International Conference on Alcohol, Drugs and Traffic Safety.
    Toronto.
Schmidt, W. (1976). Cirrhosis and alcohol consumption. Paper to the conference
    on Alcoholism: advances in medical and psychiatric understanding. London:
    Institute of Psychiatry.
Whitehead, P.C. (1975). Effects of liberalising alcohol control measures.
    Addictive Behaviours: an international journal 1:3.
Wilkinson, R. (1970). The Prevention of Drinking Problems: alcohol control and
    cultural influences. New York: Oxford University Press.

4 THE ROLE OF LICENSING LAW IN LIMITING THE MISUSE OF ALCOHOL

Christopher Clayson

Introduction

Modern licensing law in Great Britain, more or less as we know it today, was enacted for England and Wales in 1902, and for Scotland in 1903. It was based on the proposition that by restricting the opportunities to purchase and consume, the misuse of alcohol could be diminished. The new law seemed for a time to be taking effect as judged by the reduced consumption of beer in England, and the smaller number of drunkenness offences. Apparently it was even more effective in the latter part of World War I when much harsher licensing restrictions were widely, if temporarily added: and it worked to best effect in the late twenties and early thirties. Consumption and misuse were alike at their lowest level in 1930 (Harrisson, 1943). But that, I suggest, was not due to wise licensing law. It was more probably due to poverty since 1930 was the depth of the great depression. Indeed, the situation was in some respects comparable with what was to happen in France a decade or so later, during the German occupation of World War II, when there was, for instance, a sharp drop in the incidence of cirrhosis of the liver.

However, in Great Britain the poverty passed, and in a generation was replaced by affluence. The consumption of alcohol steadily increased. Since 1960, with the public ability to spend an ever augmented proportion of disposable income on alcohol, consumption and misuse have risen to the highest level this century, or nearly so.

The Departmental Committees on Licensing Law, 1971-3

Confronted by this unhappy trend, one of the actions taken by the government was to appoint two Departmental Committees; one under Lord Erroll of Hale for England and Wales, and the other, under my chairmanship, for Scotland. The purpose of the committees was to advise whether any changes in licensing law would be appropriate in attempting to control a deteriorating situation. The reports were presented to Parliament in December 1972 (the Erroll Report) and August 1973 (the Clayson Report).

The committees were suitably impressed, though not, I think, misled, by the number and sometimes the weight of discordant testimonies. Various recommendations to the committees included the following:

1. Complete freedom to drink without restriction.
2. Complete abolition of the brewing and distilling industries.

These two extreme proposals were regarded as self-cancelling.

3. The reintroduction of the severe controls of World War I.
4. Central control of the availability and distribution of alcohol.

Both (3) and (4) would have required harsh measures which would have been neither politically acceptable nor socially desirable. Observing the name but eluding the efficacy of the law would have become a national pastime and would have probably promoted illegal distilling.

5. Maintenance of the present law on the ground that it would be better to persevere with the present ineffective practice rather than risk the perils which it was feared might attend rash innovations.

But if the great British public continues to increase its expenditure on alcohol by about £250 million annually, and continues to consume it within the present licensing restrictions, the inevitable result will be an increase in the social pressure to drink, and an aggravation of the very evils we seek to avoid.

6. Relaxation of the licensing law.

Having considered all these possibilities, and having sifted the evidence with care, the Departmental Committees decided, each in its own way in matters of detail, to advise Parliament to relax the law.

Reactions to the General Proposal

Reactions were predictable. Editorial comment in the *British Medical Journal* (1972, 1974, 1976) was generally guarded or unfavourable. We were said to be reporting more in the interests of the drinker and the convenience of the tourist than for the public health. One distinguished MP (Taylor, 1976) said that the country should not be dictated to by a small minority of people who wished to go continental in every aspect of their daily lives. He compared the British level of alcoholism with the more serious problem in France which he, and others, have attributed to the greater opportunities to purchase and consume in that country. But international comparisons are notoriously difficult. Of course there is more alcoholism in France than in Great Britain, but in making that comparison it should also be stressed that there are far fewer crimes of violence associated with alcohol in France than in Great Britain. International comparisons involve many variables, and can be misleading or even dangerous.

Comparison of Scotland with England and Wales

In examining the role of licensing, I suggest that the most valid comparison is between that part of Great Britain called Scotland, and that part of Great Britain called England and Wales. In such a comparison, the variables are relatively few. We are, after all, the same race or at least for a thousand years we have been a mixture of the same ancient races (apart from very recent additions). We have a common language, common tradition, culture and manners. We endure the same taxation of alcoholic liquor, and are subjected to the same campaign of witless advertisement. What is different, however, is licensing law, and it is interesting to study what has emerged over the years in the misuse of alcohol.

The expenditure per adult per week does not vary greatly between Scotland and England. The Annual Family Expenditure Survey Reports of the Central Statistical Office provide information which shows that the weekly cost of alcoholic drink per adult for the three years 1972-4 averaged 95p for the United Kingdom and 106p for Scotland. Certain Certain caveats must be recognised here. The estimates are only about three-fifths of what could be expected from the United Kingdom statistics of the Customs and Excise; and we cannot tell whether this under-recording varies as between Scotland and England. Again, random sampling variance means that in 1972, for instance, the estimate for Scotland was subject to a larger standard error (UK 0.03, Scotland 0.09). The problem of under-recording may have been solved in the Blennerhassett Report (1976), which gives the weekly per capita consumption in Scotland at £1.57 as against the average for the English Regions of £1.54 – an insignificant difference. Taken together with the data from the Central Statistical Office referred to above, I suggest we can conclude that the average weekly consumption of alcohol per capita is the same (or only slightly greater) in Scotland than in England.

But the facilities for consuming this liquor are significantly less in Scotland, since under the Scottish Licensing Law there are 17 per cent fewer permitted hours per week in which liquor can be purchased and consumed in licensed establishments, and there are no Sunday permitted hours in public houses at all. (The new provision in the 1976 Act will be referred to later.) Thus, with fewer facilities and equal consumption, the pressure to drink in licensed premises is higher in Scotland. This is not compensated for by drinking in the more relaxed atmosphere of home. On the contrary, evidence from the Office of Population Censuses and Surveys (OPCS) surveys, which was made available to the Departmental Committees, showed that — apart from the use made of licensed premises and their more restricted hours — only 36 per cent of Scottish regular drinkers also drank at home as against 42 per cent of English regular drinkers. Thus, with more restrictive licensing law in Scotland, there is greater social pressure to drink than in England: consequently there is greater misuse of alcohol. Hence the licensing law should be relaxed.

Let me elaborate this reasoning a little further. If, as has been suggested by those who oppose relaxation of licensing law — whether in Scotland or in England and Wales — greater opportunities to purchase and consume genuinely lead to more consumption, then by this time there should be much greater consumption in England and Wales than in Scotland. But as we have seen, this is not so. What little difference there may be is the other way round. Similarly, if greater opportunities to purchase and consume mean more alcoholism, then, after many years of more liberal licensing, there should be much more alcoholism in England and Wales than in Scotland. In fact, there is very much less in proportion to population. Again, if greater opportunities to purchase and consume result in more driving under the influence of drink, then such offences should be far more common in England and Wales than in Scotland. In fact, there are far fewer (about one third) in proportion to vehicles licensed.

Now this same argument applies to whatever index of the misuse of alcohol we care to study from simple drunkenness offences on the one hand to deaths from alcoholism or cirrhosis of the liver on the other. In every instance, the situation in Scotland where the licensing law is restrictive is far worse than in England where the law has long been more relaxed. I am convinced that it is the more restrictive licensing which Scotland has so long endured that is very largely responsible for the unhappy plight in which Scotland now finds itself.

Other Possible Factors

There have, of course, been other suggested explanations of this phenomenon. The *climate* has been blamed. The argument is that in the austere and frozen North, purposeful drinking, especially of spirits, is necessary to maintain the vigour of the race, in contradistinction to England, where the warmth of the climate disposes the minds of the natives to the more indolent and contemplative refreshment of beer and lager. This theory will not do, since experts tell us that it is just as easy to become addicted to beer and lager as to spirits. Then it is suggested that the position in Scotland is due to the Scottish habit of *mixing drinks,* particularly beer and whisky, which in terms of results gives an alcohol effect seen to be more than purely additive. This unfortunate practice is simply a manifestation of the Scot attempting to secure the maximum effect in the limited drinking time available to him.

The recent survey by Susan Dight (1975) on Scottish drinking habits shows — among many important observations — that 30 per cent of the alcohol consumed is consumed by 5 per cent of the drinkers, all men. I suggest that this is one more result of the pressure to drink. I know of no comparable figures for England and Wales but I would predict with great confidence that such data would show that in England and Wales the more relaxed licensing law has over the years given rise to a larger proportion of moderate drinkers and a smaller proportion of heavy drinkers than we find in Scotland.

Lastly, the *quality of Scottish public houses* is said to be partly to blame for Scottish drinking habits. The OPCS surveys, to which I have already referred, showed that in Great Britain 17 per cent of men did *not* take their wives into public houses whereas in Scotland the figure was 33 per cent. Similarly, in Great Britain 64 per cent of people found the public houses to be warm and friendly places, whereas in Scotland the figure was only 50 per cent. In Great Britain, 44 per cent of drinkers went to pubs, mainly for company: in Scotland the figure was 37 per cent. Since in surveys the reported figures for Great Britain included those for Scotland, the actual differences between England and Wales, and Scotland, must be even more marked than the figures indicate. One of the reasons for the better quality and atmosphere of the public houses in England is in my opinion the more relaxed English licensing law, with less emphasis on the pressure to drink.

In making these comments, I do not wish to imply that in my view the English are models of sobriety: I am explaining why the Scots are worse. The fundamental reason why in Great Britain as a whole the misuse of alcohol is increasing is that the British public has more money to spend. Just as in the 1930s the apparent success of liquor licensing was due to poverty, so in the 1970s its failure is due to affluence. In the last twelve years or so, there has been no change in licensing law. But increasing money supply has allowed the British public during that period to increase its average weekly per capita consumption from 9 units to 14.5 units of alcohol. If that is how the British public elects to spend its money, licensing law will not stop it, or even restrain it. As I have emphasised already, only very harsh licensing law could do that — or a recurrence of severe poverty. Under present conditions, however, the role of licensing law must change. What the law can and should do is to relax the pressure to drink and so mitigate some of its evils. Lord Erroll's committee showed how it should be done in England and Wales and my committee showed how it should be done in Scotland. The Scottish proposals have largely, but by no means entirely, been incorporated in the Licensing (Scotland) Act, 1976.

Proposals for Relaxation of Licensing Law

Although both Departmental Committees pressed for relaxation of the law, there were differences of principle and of detail between them. So far as *administration* is concerned, Lord Erroll's proposals were for liberalisation of the law based on the existing English practice of Licensing Justices. In Scotland, we proposed a lesser degree of liberalisation based on a new system of licensing. Briefly, this would entail three fundamental requirements:

1. The licensing authority will consist of elected representatives of the people, nominated by district councils from among their own number, but not responsible to the district council.

2. The licensing authority will be required to give written reasons for its decisions when asked to do so.

3. If these reasons appear to be wrong in law, or an altogether unreasonable exercise of discretion, there can be an appeal on stated grounds to a judge, namely, in Scotland, the Sheriff.

Such a system will impose a more thoughtful and balanced judgement on licensing boards, and the possibility of a final legal appeal will promote the careful objectivity which has sometimes been said to have been lacking in the past. In the fullness of time, the new licensing system will achieve a better distribution of improved licensed premises than we have now.

I do not propose to comment further on licensing administration, but rather to focus attention on the *social aspects of licensing*. We were concerned to see the law changed in such a way that the consumption of alcohol became more and more a relaxed part of some other social activity, and less and less an end in itself. To this end, we made the greater part of our recommendations, of which the following are illustrative examples.

Entertainment Licence

This would allow places licensed for public entertainment to apply for a liquor licence for the needs of patrons only. The licence would operate strictly within the new statute and by-laws. (Unlike the corresponding English proposal, the licensing authority would not have discretion to exempt the premises from permitted hours requirements.) This proposal has been incorporated in the new Licensing (Scotland) Act.

Residential Licence

This was to have provided in Scotland a facility which already exists in England and Wales. The proprietors of guest houses would have been able to supply, for example, liquor ancillary to a main meal for residents only. This proposal was not accepted by the government, apparently on the ground that a restricted hotel licence would meet the case. This would not, in fact, be appropriate, since the restricted hotel certificate is intended to provide for non-residents as well as residents, which is precisely what guest house proprietors do not want. I consider that a useful step — albeit a modest one — towards meeting our aims has been lost.

Family Drinking

The Departmental Committees saw much advantage in making proposals which they hoped would keep the family together, and would develop parental responsibility for introducing the young to the observation of the normal use of alcohol at home and in society, and in due course to the partaking of it.

We know from the work in the University of Strathclyde (Davies and Stacey, 1972) that it is the children from the strongly 'anti-drink' and strongly 'pro-drink' families who themselves find most difficulty in adjusting to alcohol when they meet it. We also know that among the Jewish people, who do introduce children to alcohol sensibly within the family circle, there is very little alcoholism. Evidence which came later from Susan Dight's survey showed that the importance we attached to establishing and developing the family influence was correct. For instance, at the present time, the great majority of Scotsmen who drink prefer to do so with other men rather than with their wives. In fact, the number of drinking occasions spent with their wives is less than one quarter of the total. Again, the great majority of young people who drink learned to do so not within the family circle, but with their own friends, commonly (as I observed in the course of our investigations) under less than ideal conditions. In this connection McKechnie *et al.* (in press) from the Alcohol Research and Treatment Group of the Crichton Royal Hospital, Dumfries, have concluded that more addictive than non-addictive drinkers had their first drinks in the company of persons outside the family.

We believed that children should be introduced to alcohol within the family, not as some exciting experiment, but as part of the normal process of growing up. In addition, the Departmental Committees proposed two new measures, namely the Refreshment Licence and the Public House Children's Certificate.

The Refreshment Licence

This is provided for in the Scottish Act. The establishments concerned have been referred to in Parliament and press as 'cafe-pubs'. This is an unfortunate term since they will not in any sense be pubs. They will have no bar, and only table service. They will be, however, a type of cafe in which the family can sit down together, and have their snacks and refreshments. Where the refreshments include alcoholic liquor, all the licensing law will apply with limited permitted hours, and the prohibition of the sale of alcohol to persons under 18 years of age.

The Public House Children's Certificate

The idea of this addition to the public house licence was that where the establishment met certain prescribed standards and the licensee was willing, the grant of a children's certificate would allow the family to enter the premises for refreshment. The children, as in the case of the refreshment licence, could not partake of alcohol till they were old enough.

This proposed development was rejected by the government. Health ministers had been informed by the Advisory Committee on Alcoholism (1975) that the number of public houses with the accommodation and clientele to make such a venture a success would be limited. At the present time, the committee is right. The then Secretary of State for Scotland (Ross, 1975) was more forthright in his repudiation of the proposition, which he said was not in accordance with 'present Scottish

drinking practices and attitudes to drink'. But we were not planning
on the basis of present drinking practice, but rather for the rest of this
century and beyond. According to the law of averages, there will not
be repeats of the major reviews which Lord Erroll undertook for
England and Wales and which I undertook for Scotland, for thirty
years. Long before then – if we are to have more relaxed and civilised
drinking – there must come a time of social advance when parents
with children can go into suitable public houses for this purpose. At
the present time, only a few pubs in Scotland could meet these
conditions, but from my investigations I am satisfied that, given
legislative support, improvement would have been rapid. Unhappily,
that situation will not now arise, since the necessary provision has been
excluded from the Act.

The Permitted Hours

We recommended an optional increase of 31.8 per cent in the permitted
hours in Scotland. If fully taken up, this would have afforded
significant relaxation in the social pressure to drink. The Act is less
generous. Even when public houses are granted permitted hours for
Sunday (for which special application and consideration will be
required), the total extension, if fully utilised, would only represent an
increase of 12.4 per cent. I fear this may not achieve any significant
progress in reducing pressure to drink. It may just meet the demands of
increasing consumption.

The Future

A new law, however justified the change, cannot suddenly transform
the habits of the times. People enquire 'When will the new Act diminish
alcoholism?' The answer is 'I do not know.' Licensing law of itself –
even if all our recommendations had been accepted – cannot do this
since other factors are involved, namely taxation and health education.
I have not discussed taxation because it was not in my remit.

Health education, however, is closely linked to licensing law and in
the long run may well be more important. But education needs
enlightened licensing, rather than the restrictive form we have had for
so long. The Scottish Health Education Unit – not a body dedicated to
the promotion of alcoholism – supports my committee's proposals
fully, and wishes more of them had been enacted.

The old idea, embodied in the licensing provision of 1902-3, that
the misuse of alcohol could be diminished by restricting opportunities
to purchase and consume, may have been valid in the days when

disposable incomes were very modest. But it is certainly not valid today when disposable incomes are large and increasingly spent on alcohol. The role of licensing has changed. Its role now is to mitigate the evils we all see by reducing the pressure to drink; by improving the quality of leisure; by discouraging drinking as an end in itself; and by encouraging moderate drinking as part of some other social activity. The new Scottish legislation will, from an administrative point of view, discard much that was obsolete and promote much that is wise in the practice of licensing; but, in view of its limitations, will not have the full social impact on drinking habits for which we had hoped.

References

Advisory Committee on Alcoholism (February, 1976). Report to Health Ministers.
British Medical Journal, Editorial. (1972), II, 625; (1974), I, 132; (1976), I, 359.
Central Statistical Office: Family Expenditure Surveys. (1972, 1973, 1974). London: HMSO.
Davies, J. and Stacey, B. (1972). Teenagers and Alcohol. London: HMSO.
Department of the Environment. (1976). Drinking and Driving (The Blennerhassett Report). London: HMSO.
Dight, S. (1976). Scottish Drinking Habits. London: HMSO.
Harrisson, T.H. (1943). The Pub and the People. London: Victor Gollancz.
McKechnie, R.J., Cameron, D., Cameron, I.A. and Drewery, J. British J. Addict. (in press).
Report of the Departmental Committee on Liquor Licensing (1972). (The Erroll Report). Cmnd.5154, London: HMSO.
Report of Departmental Committee on Scottish Licensing Law. (1973). (The Clayson Report). Cmnd.5354, London: HMSO.
Ross, W. Hansard. 15 April 1975, col.15.
Taylor, T. Hansard. 1 July 1976, col.813-14; 27 July 1976, col.428-9.

5 ALCOHOLISM: WHAT PSYCHOLOGY OFFERS

Jim Orford

Introduction: Borrowing from General Psychology

Behind the need for discussions about the treatment of alcoholism, about the need for prevention, lies a rather mysterious and paradoxical aspect of human behaviour; the repetitive use of a substance which appears to other people to be damaging to a person's life. We should expect to be able to look to the science of behaviour, to psychology, for some sort of understanding of this strange phenomenon. What this chapter will do, is to take the reader on a borrowing expedition through parts of psychology, to see what aspects are likely to have most relevance to alcoholism and alcohol dependence. Little will be said about specific alcoholism research; the focus will be much more on those parts of general psychology that seem most relevant and applicable, and for this no apology is offered. Progress in alcoholism research is sometimes held up by thinking of alcoholism only as a specialty. Figure 1 shows diagrammatically the topics that will be covered, and at the same time provides a rough outline of a psychological model of alcoholism.

Learning Mechanisms

The first topic is familiar territory, namely learning mechanisms in habit development. This area is covered much more fully by Cappell in his contribution to this volume, but here it is worth noting three features of operant, or reward and punishment, learning which are of particular relevance to the development of alcohol dependence. One is the *partial* nature of much reinforcement: it is not necessary for reinforcement to occur every time a particular response occurs. Second, it is *probabilities* that are involved. We are not talking about one response taking the place completely of another response, but rather about certain responses gradually becoming more probable and other responses less probable. Third, there is the *gradient of reinforcement,* a fact which may go quite a long way to explaining paradoxical behaviour: reward which follows immediately upon behaviour is more effective in shaping behaviour and making it more probable or less probable in the future, than is reinforcement that occurs later on. Behaviour may have both rewarding and punishing consequences, but

Figure 1 Psychological Factors and Alcoholism: A Summary

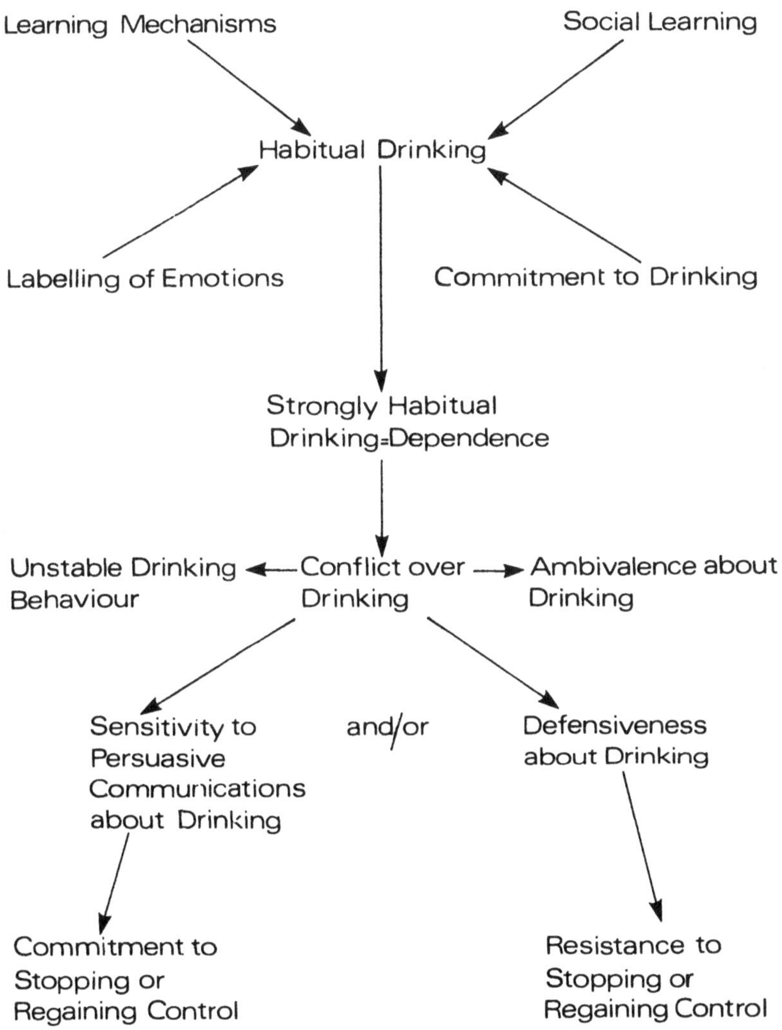

Learning Mechanisms   Social Learning

Habitual Drinking

Labelling of Emotions   Commitment to Drinking

Strongly Habitual
Drinking=Dependence

Unstable Drinking ◄── Conflict over ──► Ambivalence about
Behaviour   Drinking   Drinking

Sensitivity to   and/or   Defensiveness
Persuasive   about Drinking
Communications
about Drinking

Commitment to   Resistance to
Stopping or   Stopping or
Regaining Control   Regaining Control

it is the immediate consequences that are most important.

Hence the often insidious nature of the development of alcoholism, is understandable in terms of some very basic laws of learning. In the light of these facts it is not surprising that some people should become progressively more and more involved in a form of behaviour that has self-damaging consequences. The role of classical conditioning should not be neglected either. The repeated association of the many visual, auditory, tactile and olfactory stimuli which surround drinking occasions must result in chains or complexes of stimuli with much attached conditioned meaning for the individual.

Social Learning

These mechanisms of habit formation say little about some of the social processes whereby habits can become instilled in human beings. They say nothing, for example, about the power of imitation to produce changes in behaviour, or about the power of conformity. Consider for instance the experiments by Asch (1956) showing the compelling way in which having a number of other people say that something is right when the evidence of your own eyes suggests that it is wrong, can affect your behaviour. Subjects made few'mistakes when being asked to perform a perception task on their own, but if they were asked to do it in the company of six or seven other people who gave the wrong response, then a high proportion of subjects were likely to conform to the response given by the rest of the group. Experiments by Stanley Milgram (1963) expand the same theme. Subjects were induced to give what they thought were powerful electric shocks to other people, on the basis that the experimenter had said this was a safe procedure, that he was in charge and that no harm would come to the victim; this, despite the fact that the experiment was set up in a way that made the subject believe that these were powerful electric shocks, and despite the people receiving the shocks making some indications that the shocks were extremely painful.

These are just two amongst many experimental demonstrations of the great power of social conformity. Their application to drinking behaviour must be obvious: we are all subject to a variety of pressures to consume alcoholic drinks, and some people are more subject to these pressures than others depending upon such factors as the region in which they live and the nature of their social group. So there are a number of processes that involve habit formation and all of them can be highly relevant to the formation of drinking habits. William James said, in his *Principles of Psychology*, in 1891: 'We must make automatic and habitual as early as possible as many useful actions as we can and guard against the growing into ways that are likely to be disadvantageous to us as we should guard against the plague.' More recently someone who has been involved in research into alcoholism (Reinert, 1968) has said 'Never underestimate the strength of a habit.' That is an important statement; we tend to think that habits are just habits, not things that can be as compelling as alcohol dependence seems to be. There are, though, processes here which normally serve the interests of man, but which can, if the circumstances are right, prove to be harmful to man; and alcohol dependence is one example.

Cognitive Factors and Emotion

There are some other psychological processes that might be important in becoming someone who is alcohol dependent. Work by Stanley Schacter (1964) on the importance of cognitive factors in emotion deserves note. His theory, which has now become very popular, is that an emotional state is a function of two things: physiological arousal of some kind and the cognitive interpretation of the circumstances in which you are physically aroused. One of his experiments, which was particularly influential in the development of this theory, involved injecting subjects with adrenalin, and then providing the subjects with opportunities for different cognitive interpretations of the resulting physiological state. No one was told that he had had adrenalin; they were all told that they had an injection of some vitamin preparation. Some subjects were prepared for the effects of adrenalin by being told that the side-effects of the drug they had been given included increased breathing, flushing, increased heart-rate, etc. (i.e. the effects of adrenalin). Other people were not accurately warned: they were either told that nothing would happen, or they were deliberately misled and told that they would have side-effects that in fact did not occur. Schacter's prediction, which was borne out by the results, was that when subjects had an explanation of their physiological state provided for them (being told correctly what the results of the injection would be), then they would be able to attribute their physiological state to the injection, and would not need to explain their state in terms of emotion. In other words, they would turn out to be very much less emotional, both in their behaviour and in how they described themselves, than the people who had no such explanation provided for their altered physiological state. The other more intriguing part of their experiment consisted of actually providing people with quite different social circumstances in which they might interpret their physiological state.

One involved anger, the other euphoria and in both cases the emotion was aroused by having another 'subject', in fact a 'stooge', behave in an euphoric or angry fashion. The euphoric 'subject' started to tear up paper and throw it around the room, make paper planes and generally act the fool. In the other case the real subject and the stooge 'subject' were given questionnaires to fill in which were highly personal and rather frustrating, and the stooge got appropriately annoyed and finally tore up the questionnaires and left the room. In these two cases, despite the same physiological arousal from the drug, the 'anger' subjects acted and described themselves as angry and the 'euphoric' subjects acted and described themselves as euphoric.

Now the relevance of this to alcohol dependence has to do with the labelling or mis-labelling of arousal. There is perhaps no direct evidence for this assertion, but arguing from a solid basis of theory and findings in general psychology, when a habit has developed (such as a strong habit of drinking), then a process is going to arise in which physiological states are more often labelled in some drink-specific way. Whereas most of us describe ourselves from time to time as bored, tense, depressed, sad and so on, it might be expected that someone who has a strong habit of drinking is going to label some of these emotions as 'needing a drink' or something similar. The stronger the habit of drinking, the more salient or 'pre-potent' the drinking act amongst all possible actions, the more likely that emotional arousal will be interpreted in terms of need, desire or craving for alcohol. The picture becomes much more complicated for the drinker who suffers physiological withdrawal symptoms when not drinking. An extra source of arousal, for which drinking may really bring physiological relief, is then added to the existing range of sources of arousal.

Commitment

Then there is the work on commitment by Jack and Mary Brehm and others in the United States (Zimbardo, 1969) that suggests that committing yourself to something (as indeed the alcoholic may be committed to drinking, or as the ex-alcoholic or the teetotaller may be committed to not drinking) actually alters motivation. Not just the other way round — that motivation affects one's commitment as attitude affects behaviour — but rather that making a commitment to behaviour actually acts back upon and increases motivation. In one of the experiments by the Brehms they had subjects come to an experiment having fasted or having gone without water for a number of hours. They were then asked if, for the sake of the experiment, they would commit themselves to a further eight hours of hunger or thirst, and they were able to show that subjects who voluntarily committed themselves in this way then actually described themselves as less hungry or less thirsty. Not only that, but using a more direct measure of their motivation, they were able to show that when there was an opportunity to order food for later on, voluntary commitment to further hunger resulted in ordering less food. Subjects who committed themselves to a further period without liquid, when told that they could now have something to drink, in actual fact drank less. So we have here direct behavioural measures of motivation having been changed by commitment. There are also experiments by J. Brehm in which he was able to show that physiology was altered by commitment. He used plasma-free fatty acids as an indication of hunger and he was able to show that a voluntary commitment to further hours of hunger actually reduced the level of this physiological index.

This work on commitment is again potentially highly relevant to the study of alcoholism, because the notion of commitment is central to the idea of dependence as a psychological state. Dependence may be thought of as a complex state combining repetitive appetitive or consuming behaviour, emotional attachment to stimuli associated with this behaviour and a cognitive commitment to the behaviour. The cognitive element of this triadic state (behaviour, emotion and cognition) is as important as the others, and work cited above shows how influential it can be upon even physiological aspects of function.

Conflict and Loss of Control

One may think of the resulting state that the dependent person finds himself in as a state of conflict, depicted by a 'pay-off decision matrix' which represents the decision dilemma. Figure 2 is a hypothetical illustration with four examples of the pros and cons of continued drinking or stopping drinking, for someone in this position. Janis (1968) has thought about smoking dependence in a very similar way and has drawn up what he calls a 'balance sheet' for the addictive smoker, a balance of reasons for stopping smoking, reasons for carrying on smoking, reasons for altering smoking behaviour, reasons for altering to filter-tipped cigarettes, altering to cigars, etc.

One of the classic experiments on conflict had to do with rats who were rewarded with food at one end of an alleyway (the goal) and then, on a later occasion, were given electric shocks in the same place, so that they were thrown into what is called an 'approach-avoidance conflict'. The assumption, borne out by much research, was that the approach

Figure 2 The Decision Dilemma for the Excessive Drinker

PAY-OFF DECISION MATRIX.

	IF DISCONTINUE USE	IF CONTINUE USE
EXAMPLE OF A POSITIVE OUTCOME	Respect from non-users	Relief of anxiety
EXAMPLE OF A NEGATIVE OUTCOME	Disrespect from users	Premature death

motivation and the avoidance motivation got stronger as the goal was reached, but that the avoidance motivation increased more steeply. Hence the resultant motivation was in favour of avoidance near the goal and was in favour of approach further from the goal. So the animal was in some sort of stable equilibrium: if you put the animal in the runway near the goal, avoidance was stronger than approach, and it would run back to the equilibrium point: if you put the animal in the runway well away from the goal, then approach was stronger than avoidance, and it would run towards the equilibrium point. Now it has been suggested, and for sound reasons, that in some forms of alcoholism one may have approach-avoidance conflict which is of the opposite sort — one in which the approach gradient is in fact steeper than the avoidance gradient (Astin, 1962; Heilizer, 1964). If that is the case, the result is unstable equilibrium — the approach motivation is stronger than avoidance near the goal, whereas avoidance motivation is stronger than appraoch further from it. So you have the position in which a person will remain away from the goal so long as he does not approach the equilibrium point of no return. But if something pushes him beyond that point, then approach is more powerful, and you have something analogous to the 'loss of control' phenomenon which is talked about so frequently in alcoholism work.

In fact, the theme of loss of control is now considered to have been a bit overplayed — the idea that an alcohol dependent person is totally out of control with regard to alcohol. A great deal of work has now established that in fact most alcoholics are to some degree in control. There is an experiment — and this is about the only experiment which will be quoted here which is specifically an alcohol experiment — carried out by Marlatt and his colleagues (1973). Alcoholics on the one hand, and so called social drinkers on the other, were given either tonic alone or vodka and tonic. Half of each group were told that they were getting tonic alone and half of each group were told that they were getting vodka and tonic. So there were four possible experimental combinations, and eight groups in all (four groups of alcoholics and four groups of social drinkers). The figures in Table 1 are the average amounts of alcohol consumed by subjects in a free-drinking situation, after they had been given the priming dose of either tonic alone or vodka and tonic and having been told it was one or the other. The results indicate — and in fact an analysis of variance showed quite clearly — that being an alcoholic versus being a social drinker made a lot of difference to how much a subject drank, in any condition. It did not matter what he was given in that priming dose or what he was told he had in the priming dose; if he was an alcoholic, he tended to drink more than if he was a social drinker. Another important factor was what subjects were told was in that priming dose: those who were told that they were getting vodka with their tonic in their first drink went on to drink more than the others. Of the three experimental factors, the one that was *not* important was what was actually in that first drink: whether subjects in fact had vodka in their first drink made no difference. This is just one piece of research that illustrates the importance of expectation, or of the cognitive interpretaton of what is going on, rather than of the pharmacological properties of the first drink.

Another much more naturalistic study of loss of control and alcoholism, is one by Paredes and his colleagues (1973), in which some alcoholic patients, receiving treatment, were given alcohol under circumstances in which they could have gone on to drink more if they had so wanted. In fact relatively few did, and whether or not they did made no subsequent difference to whether they stayed or did not stay in the treatment programme. Furthermore, an increasing number of studies show that many alcoholic patients who receive treatment subsequently take up a pattern of drinking which is not alcoholic on

Table 1 Average beverage consumption, by different groups in the
experiment by Marlatt *et al.* (1973). Fluid ounces.

Actually given	Alcoholics Told		Social Drinkers Told	
	Tonic only	Vodka and Tonic	Tonic only	Vodka and Tonic
Tonic only	10.94	23.87	9.31	14.62
Vodka and Tonic	10.25	22.13	5.94	14.44

the one hand, and is not totally abstinent on the other hand, but
involves some form of limited drinking. Some of these studies reported
unplanned limited drinking, that is studies of treatment in which
everybody was advised to abstain but none the less some subsequently
went on to limited drinking (e.g. Orford *et al.,* 1976). There are also a
number of studies where limited drinking has actually been planned for,
and subjects have been advised to limit their drinking and have been
taken through a training programme to do just that (e.g. Sobell and
Sobell, 1973). These treatment studies throw some light on the
mechanisms of control and the process of loss of control in alcoholism,
and show that our former, relatively simple, concepts about total loss
of control in alcoholics are not quite right, and that the matter is indeed
a lot more subtle than that.

Dissonance, Defensiveness and Attitude Change

One of the implications of a person being in a state of conflict has to do
with the associated personal discomfort which social psychologists call
cognitive dissonance. This is supposedly an uncomfortable state of mind
in which a person holds simultaneous and conflicting thoughts or
cognitions — the cognition that one is behaving or has behaved in a
particular way, and the cognition that this is not the right and proper
way to behave, or that it is a way that is potentially damaging to health
or social relationships. The theory goes on — and again there is much
supportive experimental evidence now — that motivation arises to
reduce this discomforting state. Amongst the mechanisms for reducing
a state of dissonance are a number of disagreeable, defensive behaviours

that seem to accompany alcoholism. Alcoholics are notorious for denial, rationalisation, inconsistency and ambivalence. These are some of the things that have made alcoholics unpopular patients, but it is useful to think of these apparently disagreeable behaviours as part of the alcohol dependence process, and as part of the effort to reduce this discomforting state of cognitive dissonance that arises when one's behaviour is clearly in conflict with one's knowledge of what should be appropriate behaviour for oneself.

In terms of attitude change, it might be supposed that dependent people would be particularly sensitive, one way or the other (either particularly attracted to or particularly averse to) persuasive communications on the subject of their dependence. Janis, for example, went on to talk about people who were in a balance or conflict and who had good reasons for carrying on, but also good reasons for stopping a particular form of behaviour, being particularly interested in messages about their behaviour. People might look out for information about different ways of smoking, might be particularly interested in league tables of tar and nicotine content for example, in order to find some way in which they could reduce their dissonance. In fact there is quite a lot of work on attitude change suggesting that people who are committed to a particular form of behaviour may also have some motivation to avoid relevant information about changing this behaviour. An interesting piece of work on car seat belts, for example, showed that people for whom the wearing of seat belts was most relevant (the most frequent car users) were the least persuaded by fear-arousing communications on the subject (Berkowitz and Cottingham, 1960). There has also been a lot of work on the impact of fear-arousing communications about the importance of adequate dental care, showing that certain sorts of people are not responsive. For example, people who are in other ways anxious and people who generally avoid disturbing information find it particularly difficult to accommodate fear-arousing communications on this topic.

So the conflict surrounding drinking for the dependent drinker can lead either to greater interest in changing, or to greater defensiveness and resistance to changing. As those who treat alcohol dependence know, both attitudes can exist almost simultaneously in the same person, or one may follow the other suddenly and unpredictably. Indeed this is perhaps the central dilemma of alcoholism prevention and treatment; the difficulty of predicting when change will occur or when resistance will occur.

Personality

Finally a word about individual psychological differences. On the basis of psychological factors, it is going to be extremely difficult to predict who is going to be most susceptible. It may well be that one individual is particularly susceptible to some form of pharmacological or social reinforcement from drinking. For example this person may particularly appreciate the socially disinhibiting effects of alcohol, and on those grounds would appear to us to be susceptible. However, this same person may have grown up in a social milieu which provides fairly strict training in drinking habits and such a person would, on those grounds, be relatively unsusceptible. The point which is being made is that we have a multitude of factors operating here, and it is going to be extremely difficult to say who is going to be the most susceptible. For this reason the search for an alcoholic personality or an alcoholic type has become less and less popular in recent years, and no one now expects to find one type of alcoholic personality.

In fact if we look at the few research reports that are satisfactory in the sense of having a longitudinal perspective – in other words studies that have really found out something about people when they were youngsters and have followed them up until such a time when they might or might not have developed alcoholism – we find that there is some evidence in favour of there being a high risk group of people. These are young men who are described by other people as being relatively unrestrained, unresponsive to authority, impulsive and aggressive. Particularly if such a person has an alcoholic father or a father who is deviant in some other way, this type of person appears to carry something of a higher risk than others. But this conclusion is based on only a limited amount of research activity by Lee Robins (1966), the McCords (1960) and Jones (1968), and all had limitations of sample or method.

Not only are individual differences important in developing habitual behaviour, but there must also be individual differences in reactions to conflict, in the adoption of defences about drinking, and in the process of stopping or regaining control. An 'alcoholic' is someone who has not only developed strongly habitual drinking behaviour, but is also someone who has not yet reacted to the conflict involved by becoming a teetotaller or by making a drastic reduction in consumption. Hence any explanation of his presence in the alcoholic population must take into consideration the bearing of individual personality differences upon all the processes shown in Figure 1. In this light, it is even less surprising that simple personality explanations of alcoholism have failed to explain very much.

So much for a meandering journey through some areas of general psychology. The purpose of this chapter is to convince the reader that much which is to be found in the science of behaviour may be drawn on to help the understanding of alcoholism. It has not been the intention to spell out in detail every possible application, but rather to point to the rich fund of possible borrowings, and to leave it to the specialist on alcoholism to work out how best he himself may borrow.

References

Asch, S.E. (1956). Studies of Independence and Conformity. A Minority of One Against a Unanimous Majority. Psychological Monographs. vol.70, part 9: 416.

Astin, A.W. (1962). Bad habits and social deviation: a proposed revision in conflict theory. J. of Clin. Psychol. 18: 227-31.

Berkowitz, L. and Cottingham, D.R. (1960). The interest value and relevance of fear arousing communications. J. of Abnor. and Soc. Psychol. 60: 37-43.

Heilizer, F. (1964). Conflict models, alcohol, and drinking patterns. J. of Psychol. 57: 457-73.

James, W. (1891). Principles of Psychology. London: Macmillan.

Janis, I.L. and Mann, L. (1968). A Conflict Theory Approach to Attitude Change and Decision-Making. In: Psychological Foundations of Attitudes. A.C. Greenwald, T.C. Brock and T.M. Ostrom (eds.). New York: Academic Press.

Jones, M.C. (1968). Personality correlates and antecedents of drinking patterns in adult males. J. of Consul. and Clin. Psychol. 32: 2-12.

Marlatt, G.A., Demming, B. and Reid, J.D. (1973). Loss of control drinking in alcoholics: an experimental analogue. J. of Abnor. Psychol. 81: 233-41.

Mc Cord, W. and McCord, J. (1960). The Origins of Alcoholism. Stanford: Stanford University Press.

Milgram, S. (1963). Behavioural study of obedience. J. of Abnor. and Soc. Psychol. 67: 371-8.

Orford, J., Oppenheimer, E. and Edwards, G. (1976). Abstinence or control: the outcome for excessive drinkers two years after consultation. Behav. Res. and Ther. 14: 409-18.

Paredes, A., Hood, W.R., Seymour, H. and Gollob, M. (1973). Loss of control in alcoholism: an investigation into the hypothesis, with experimental findings. Quart. J. Stud. Alc. 34: 1146-61.

Reinert, R.E. (1968). Alcoholism as a bad habit. Bulletin of the Menninger Clinic (Topeka, Kansas), vol. 32.

Robins, L.N. (1966). Deviant Children Grown Up: A Sociological and Psychiatric Study of Sociopathic Personality. Baltimore: Williams and Wilkins.

Schacter, S. (1964). The Interaction of Cognitive and Physiological Determinants of Emotional State. In: Advances in Experimental Social Psychology. L. Berkowitz (ed.). vol.1. New York: Academic Press.

Sobell, M.B. and Sobell, L.C. (1973). Individualized Behavior Therapy for Alcoholics. Behav. Ther. 4: 49-72.

Zimbardo, P.G. (ed.) (1969). The Cognitive Control of Motivation: The Consequences of Choice and Dissonance. Glenview, Illinois, Scott, Foresmans.

6 BEHAVIOURAL ANALYSIS OF ALCOHOLISM

Howard Cappell

Introduction

To suggest without qualification that one can provide a behavioural analysis of alcoholism would be immodest. Although behavioural analysis is a comparatively straightforward enterprise, alcoholism is an extraordinarily complex phenomenon. Each of many disciplines has developed its own conceptual and practical approach to alcoholism; perhaps no other health problem has ever been subject to such a variety of attempts at understanding and amelioration.

Although the term 'alcoholism' will be used throughout this chapter, one hesitates to define it from a behavioural perspective because to do so would presume to exclude perfectly acceptable alternatives that differ in emphasis, such as a medical definition. Instead, the chapter will begin with the conservative premise that it is both possible and profitable to conceive of elements of alcoholism as behaviour, and hence subject to analysis in much the same terms as any behaviour.

The essential strategy of behavioural analysis is to isolate a phenomenon of interest into objectively observable and measurable components. Only in this way can the phenomenon be characterised descriptively, and only in this way is it possible to ascertain with some confidence the effect of an intervention. An aspect of alcoholism that is particularly suited to such an analysis is drinking behaviour *per se*. Drinking is a discrete and observable behaviour; it is not difficult to define, and with the help of technology its occurrence can even be determined retrospectively. We can readily measure important aspects of drinking such as its frequency, distribution over time and amount consumed. Because of the quantifiability of drinking, we can make comparisons within and between individuals and populations. And perhaps most importantly, we have a firm basis for determining whether or not a particular operation has any effect on drinking behaviour.

Finally, it should be added that this discussion will cover only a particular version of a behavioural approach. It does not consider attempts to study alcoholic behaviours other than drinking, and it concentrates upon an operant analysis. The latter emphasises a functional analysis of the relationship between emitted behaviour and its consequences. This is to be distinguished from behavioural approaches to the treatment of alcoholism rooted in the tradition of Pavlovian conditioning, of which attempts to condition an aversion to alcohol directly are an example.

Beginnings of a Behavioural Approach

Prior to the 1960s, there was virtually no research in which the drinking behaviour of alcoholics was directly observed. In the absence of such research, one could do little but speculate on the determinants of this crucial aspect of alcoholism, relying on hunches, anecdotes and the self-report of alcoholics. Remedy for this empirical deficiency was initiated in the seminal work of Mello, Mendelson and their colleagues and collaborators, beginning with work that first appeared in 1964 (Mendelson, 1964). Subsequent research by these investigators (e.g. Mello and Mendelson, 1971; 1972) provided a descriptive account of heavy drinking and many of its consequences in alcoholic men. This research gave impetus to other behaviourally oriented researchers through its attack on concepts such as 'craving' and 'loss of control' (see Mello, 1975 for a review), and by its testament to the merits of a relatively dispassionate empirical approach. Central to this effort was the development of an operant model of alcoholic drinking in which subjects could acquire alcohol contingent upon the performance of a simple and quantifiable response. This early operant work yielded important results. In one study (Mello and Mendelson, 1972), the introduction of a work requirement for acquiring alcohol was found to have a profound impact on the pattern and consequences of drinking behaviour. Moreover, the manipulation of the amount of work required to obtain a unit amount of alcohol also had a controlling effect on the amount of alcohol acquired (Mello, McNamee and Mendelson, 1968); increasing the work requirement suppressed drinking, a finding that has been independently confirmed (Bigelow and Liebson, 1972). Although these manipulations were quite elementary, the import of such studies was considerable in suggesting where to look for sources of control over drinking behaviour: might it not be more profitable to scrutinise the environment of the alcoholic, rather than his intra-psychic life, in the search for effective interventions?

Further Exploitation of Operant Techniques

With the self-administration of alcohol established as a behaviour amenable to objective measurement and to some extent manipulable, it was not long before experimenters began systematically to assess the effects of various behavioural interventions on alcoholic drinking. One important aspect of this effort has been Nathan's extensive work (e.g. Nathan, O'Brien and Lowenstein, 1971) on the relationship between alcohol consumption, affect and interpersonal behaviour in alcoholics. Somewhat more germane to the present discussion is the growing body of knowledge on interventions of a behavioural nature derived directly from general principles that were established independently of alcoholism research *per se*. All of these studies have employed as subjects persons diagnosed as alcoholics with an extensive history of drinking, and all were conducted in the controlled environment of a hospital research ward.

In one such study (Cohen *et al.*, 1971a) an attempt was made to determine whether the occurrence of abstinence was subject to experimentally applied contingencies. Subjects were free to drink up to twenty-four ounces of spirits at three-day intervals. On the days during which drinking was permitted, the experimenters determined the financial threshold required to generate abstinent behaviour. Although the monetary utility of drinking varied among individuals, for each of four subjects it was possible to strike a price for which abstinence could be purchased. This ranged from $7.00 to $20.00 for a day of abstinence; of course, there is no telling what inflation has done to the absolute price of abstinence during the last six years. The cost of abstinence was subject to modification; it went up if subjects consumed 10 ounces of spirits prior to price negotiation, or if payment was delayed several days beyond the subjects' discharge of their part of the contingency agreement. However, the essential effectiveness of the contingency was not undermined.

Other studies have established the efficacy of different operant procedures in controlling drinking. One such procedure was used not to establish abstinence but 'controlled drinking' among alcoholics (Cohen *et al.*, 1971b). When the experimental contingency was in effect, a subject who exceeded his daily ration of 5 ounces of alcohol was consigned twenty-four hours or more to an environment devoid of social contact and recreational opportunities, and permitted to eat only pureed food. This contingency was remarkably effective in maintaining an intake level that did not exceed 5 ounces of alcohol; moreover, drinking increased dramatically when the contingency was removed.

Such a procedure is somewhat draconian, and it is important to note that a less dramatic consequence of drinking can be effective in suppressing it. Bigelow *et al.* (1974) allowed alcoholics to consume up to twenty-four drinks per day under various conditions. When no contingency was in effect, the subjects drank virtually all that was available. However, when a consequence of taking a drink was confinement for ten or fifteen minutes in a small isolation booth, drinking could be suppressed to half its baseline level. Griffiths *et al.* (1974) extended these results to show that contingent physical isolation and confinement were not necessary to achieve a comparable suppression of drinking, but that a short period of restriction on social interaction with staff and other residents of the ward was sufficient.

The available laboratory studies constitute compelling demonstrations of the vulnerability of excessive drinking to contingency control. But they are subject to the obvious criticism that the laboratory situation may not provide an adequate model for the complexities of the 'real world'. However, there is one notable example of an attempt to apply operant principles to the treatment of alcoholism in a field situation (Hunt and Azrin, 1973). The subjects were sixteen alcoholics assigned on a matched basis to experimental and control conditions. The Community-Reinforcement programme applied to those in the experimental group was 'designed to rearrange the vocational, family and social reinforcers of the alcoholic such that time-out from these reinforcers would occur if they began to drink'. The reinforcers involved access to support and counselling with regard to employment, legal assistance, family counselling, vocational and social counselling. The control group was not included in this programme of considerable support. As it turned out, there was little opportunity to apply the contingency of loss of reinforcements as was done in the laboratory studies – drinking in the experimental group occurred too rarely for this to be necessary. Compared to controls the experimental subjects were drinking much less, suffered less from unemployment, spent less time absent from home, and less time in institutions at a six-month following.

These results are very impressive, but although they offer some comfort to proponents of an operant approach, they are not without flaw. The major problem is in determining whether the experimental group did so much better because the reinforcers were made *contingent,* or simply because they were made *available* regardless of their conditional status. Clearly, the experimental group received vastly more support than the controls regardless of the conditional nature of the support. None the less, Hunt and Azrin's data provide some support for the promise of an operant approach in a non-laboratory setting.

To summarise: this handful of behavioural studies represents a beginning more than a definitive conclusion. Operant procedures are clearly effective in tightly controlled environments, and may have promise in somewhat less constrained situations as well. But perhaps the most important feature of this nascent line of behavioural research is to show that alcoholism is amenable to study by rigorous scientific methods applied to humans.

Behavioural Analysis: Aetiology versus Strategy

The version of behavioural analysis that I have briefly outlined can be construed in different ways. Behavioural principles may be offered as a causal scientific account for many aspects of human activity, including excessive drinking (aetiology); alternatively, or additionally, they may be construed as a basis for suggesting procedures that can be applied to promote or suppress particular behaviours (strategy). An aetiological account might argue that the *origin* of behaviour is to be sought in the reinforcement history of organisms, and that deviant behaviour is supported by its reinforcing consequences. But interestingly, most proponents of behavioural analysis spend little time dwelling on the question of the aetiology of alcoholism. This is not to say that the principles are weak or inapplicable or that the issue is unimportant, but only that the general issue of causality does not claim a high priority in the scheme of behavioural analysis as it is currently constituted. In the case of alcoholism, the primary focus is on how drinking behaviour is currently maintained in individual cases, and on how the environment may be rearranged to promote changes in drinking. Such a strategy may be applied granting any assumption about the aetiology of drinking. For example, even if the origin of excessive drinking is biological, a behavioural approach may still provide interventions that are effective in controlling it. Indeed, it has been argued (Sobell and Sobell, 1975) that an excess of conceptual analysis concerning the causes of alcoholism may be unproductive or even damaging given our present state of factual knowledge.

To some readers such a stance may seem positively reactionary, but the reaction may be a healthy one. Consider, for example, the behavioural approach that was adopted in the search for an aetiology of alcoholism based on the model of behaviour that prevailed during the 1950s and still has adherents today. This approach (Cappell, 1975) has been referred to as the Tension Reduction Theory of alcoholism (TRT). The essential idea of this approach is that much behaviour is acquired and expressed in the service of maintaining psychological homeostasis. In this view, behaviour is learned and emitted to the extent that it redresses some motivational imbalance in the organism, namely a state of tension that is aversive if not removed. The consumption of alcohol was thus seen as a mechanism for managing tension from a variety of sources (cf. Conger, 1956). It was assumed that alcohol effectively reduces tension, and moreover that rats and people would learn to drink alcohol, in some cases to excess, because of this reinforcing property. This was an approach that emphasised aetiology over strategy. Many predictions could be derived about the situations in which drinking should occur, and in fact many predictions were tested using rigorous scientific methodology. Yet the success of this enterprise was not enviable, and the commitment to this highly plausible theory of aetiology probably outlived its empirical justification to a considerable degree (Cappell, 1975). Moreover, the TRT was not notably productive of suggestions for effective interventions to suppress drinking.

None of this argues against theories of aetiology and the benefits they can generate, particularly if they are correct. What is being said is that a somewhat less conceptually constrained analysis of behaviour may be preferable to an aetiological orientation at the present time.

Operant behavioural analysis as strategy is utterly empirical. It is an amalgam of a few simple assumptions (e.g. behaviour is governed by its consequences) and methodological biases (e.g. behaviour that cannot be precisely defined and measured is essentially refractory to objective analysis). Even a brief description of the research that has sprung from this orientation attests to its considerable potential. The question is not whether the approach is meritorious in principle – clearly it is. Rather, the issue is whether the environment of the problem drinker can be manipulated in a way that is at once effective in controlling drinking and within the bounds of feasibility and social acceptability.

References

Bigelow, G. and Liebson, I. (1972). Cost factors controlling alcoholic drinking. Psychol. Rec. 22: 305-14.

Bigelow, G., Liebson, I. and Griffiths, R. (1974). Alcohol drinking: suppression by a brief time-out procedure. Behav. Res. Ther. 12: 107-15.

Cappell, H. (1975). An evaluation of tension models of alcohol consumption. In: Research Advances in Alcohol and Drug Problems. R.J. Gibbens *et al.* (eds.). New York: Wiley and Sons, vol.2, pp.117-209.

Cohen, M., Liebson, I., Faillace, L. and Speers, W. (1971a). Alcoholism: controlled drinking and incentives for abstinence. Psychol. Rep. 28: 575-80.

Cohen, M., Liebson, I., Faillace, L. and Allen, R. (1971b). Moderate drinking by chronic alcoholics: a schedule-dependent phenomenon. J. nerv. ment. Dis. 153: 434-44.

Conger, J.J. (1956). Alcoholism: theory, problem, and challenge. II. Reinforcement theory and the dynamics of alcoholism. Quart. J. Stud. Alc. 17: 296-305.

Griffiths, R., Bigelow, G. and Liebson, I. (1974). Suppression of ethanol self-administration in alcoholics by contingent time-out from social interactions. Behav. Res. Ther. 12: 327-34.

Hunt, G.M. and Azrin, N.H. (1973). The community-reinforcement approach to alcoholism. Behav. Res. Ther. 11: 91-104.

Mello, N.K. (1975). A semantic aspect of alcoholism. In: Biological and Behavioural Approaches to Drug Dependence. H. Cappell and A.E. LeBlanc (eds.). Toronto: Addiction Research Foundation, pp.73-87.

Mello, N.K., McNamee, H.B. and Mendelson, J.H. (1968). Drinking patterns of chronic alcoholics: Gambling and motivation for alcohol. In J.O. Cole (ed.). Clinical Research in Alcoholism. Psychiatric Research Report No.24. Washington D.C.: American Psychiatric Association, pp.83-118.

Mello, N.K. and Mendelson, J.H. (1971). A quantitative analysis of drinking patterns in alcoholics. Arch. gen. Psychiat. 25: 527-38.

Mello, N.K. and Mendelson, J.H. (1972). Drinking patterns during work-contingent and non-contingent alcohol acquisition. Psychosom. Med. 34: 139-64.

Mendelson, J.H. (ed.) (1964). Experimentally induced chronic intoxication and withdrawal in alcoholics. Quart. J. Stud. Alc. Suppl. No.2.

Nathan, P.E., O'Brien, J.S. and Lowenstein, L.M. (1971). Operant studies of chronic alcoholism: Interaction of alcohol and alcoholics. In: Biological Aspects of Alcohol. M.K. Roach *et al.* (eds.). Austin: University of Texas Press, pp.341-70.

Sobell, M.B. and Sobell, L.C. (1975). The need for realism, relevance and operational assumptions in the study of substance dependence. In: Biological and Behavioural Approaches to Drug Dependence. H. Cappell and A.E. LeBlanc (eds.). Toronto: Addiction Research Foundation, pp.133-67.

7 THE BIOLOGICAL BASIS OF ALCOHOLISM: SOME RECENT EXPERIMENTAL EVIDENCE

J.M. Littleton

Ethanol is a non-specific depressant of the central nervous system. The reasons for its depressant effects on the brain are unknown, but it shares properties with the general anaesthetics which suggest it may have a direct action on neuronal cell membranes (Kalant, 1975). Ethanol interacts with many metabolic processes in brain, and has been shown to influence the metabolism of many central neurotransmitter substances (Littleton, 1975; Egana and Rodrigo, 1974). The relation of these changes to its central depressant and euphoriant effects are also unknown.

Ethanol, once consumed, is rapidly absorbed from the stomach and small intestine and quickly enters the brain from the blood stream. The onset of its central effects are therefore swift and determined by factors controlling absorption, for example, concentration of ethanol in the beverage, presence of other substances in the stomach and so on. The duration of action of ethanol is limited mainly by the rate of metabolism of ethanol in the liver. Here, ethanol is broken down at a constant rate, probably mainly by alcohol dehydrogenase, to acetaldehyde (Brentzel and Hesse, 1975). This primary metabolite is of considerable interest because it is in many ways more toxic and more potent than ethanol itself (Holtzman and Schneider, 1974). Little acetaldehyde leaves the liver, most of it is oxidised to acetate and is utilised as such, some is metabolised by other pathways of unknown significance, and a small amount enters the circulation to augment that formed by extra-hepatic metabolism of ethanol (Majchrowicz, 1975).

The prolonged consumption of ethanol leads to a state of tolerance. This initially can be partly attributed to a more rapid metabolism of the drug (Griffiths *et al.*, 1974). Subsequent liver damage may obscure this aspect of tolerance. Pharmacological or cellular tolerance is also a feature of prolonged ethanol consumption. In this state the cells of the nervous system appear to adapt in some way to the presence of ethanol, so that normal function is possible, even when high concentrations of ethanol are maintained. Still further consumption of ethanol may lead to the stage of ethanol dependence where normal function of the central nervous system is impossible in the absence of ethanol (Griffiths *et al.*, 1974).

Ethanol dependence is a recognisable clinical entity and, like most forms of dependence, psychological and physical aspects of the condition can be distinguished (Edwards and Gross, 1976). In both cases identification of the state of dependence rests on the observation of a withdrawal syndrome in the absence, or relative absence, of the drug. Thus, psychological dependence is shown by anxiety, irritability and strong desire for ethanol when the drug is withdrawn; physical dependence is characterised by tremor, autonomic signs and sometimes convulsions on withdrawal (Victor, 1970).

At first glance ethanol dependence seems a relatively simple subject for study. There is a well-defined disease agent, ethanol; a quantifiable sub-acute stage of the disease, tolerance to ethanol; and a straightforward test of the presence of the disease, the physical and psychological withdrawal syndrome. Despite this relative simplicity, the biochemical and biological bases of ethanol dependence are still not well understood. The main reason is one common to many intractable problems in medical and psychiatric research, the lack of an adequate animal model. Clearly, ethanol dependence is a pathological condition unique to man, and should be studied in man whenever possible. Equally clearly, the basic pathology is likely to reside in the brain; there are very few measurements which are possible ethically or technically on the brain of the living human subject. Similarly, investigation of biological factors predisposing to ethanol dependence in man, is for example, sex, age or race, are greatly complicated by social, religious and economic factors which limit availability of ethanol, or acceptability of ethanol intake. One would wish to formulate and test hypotheses of ethanol dependence in laboratory animals, but the prerequisite – unequivocal demonstration of ethanol dependence itself in a laboratory animal – has been surprisingly difficult to obtain.

One major problem of the induction of ethanol dependence in laboratory animals is that they metabolise ethanol much more rapidly than does man. In consequence, a much greater quantity of ethanol needs to be consumed by animals to maintain blood ethanol concentrations in the range where ethanol dependence results. Ways around these difficulties have been found which rely on the forced administration of ethanol to laboratory animals. Some involve repeated administration of ethanol by stomach tube (Hammond and Schneider, 1973); some replace up to 40 per cent of dietary calories by ethanol in a liquid diet (Freund, 1969). Our own method produces high blood ethanol concentrations by forcing rats or mice to breathe ethanol vapour (Griffiths *et al.*, 1973a). When groups of mice are exposed to ethanol vapour so that blood ethanol concentrations are maintained between 1 and 4 mg.ml.$^{-1}$ for periods of a week or ten days, ethanol dependence results. Withdrawal of ethanol is characterised by excitement, bordering on panic; a great increase in voluntary ethanol consumption if ethanol is made available for drinking; and by tremors, pilo-erection and convulsions (Littleton, 1975). These animal models, although far from perfect, therefore seem to illustrate aspects of both psychological and physical dependence. Their use over the last five years has at last begun to yield some clues to the biochemical bases of ethanol dependence.

It was stated above that ethanol is metabolised in the body to acetaldehyde, a compound which is both more potent as a central depressant and is more toxic than ethanol. It is standard pharmacological practice, when faced with a situation like this, to consider the possibility that some effects of the drug, i.e. ethanol, may be due to the action of its metabolite, in this case, acetaldehyde. It seems unlikely that the very small amounts of acetaldehyde found in the brain after a single dose of ethanol could account for the acute central depressant effects observed. However, the possibility exists that prolonged administration of ethanol might lead to a build-up of acetaldehyde in the brain which could lead to tolerance and dependence — on acetaldehyde rather than on ethanol. Alternatively, the small concentration of acetaldehyde present in the circulation during chronic ethanol consumption might lead to toxic effects which predisposed the individual to ethanol dependence (for discussion see Truitt, 1970).

There is a very simple way to test whether acetaldehyde is the cause of ethanol dependence. If the administration of acetaldehyde alone mimics ethanol dependence, then the possibility exists. If we could show that administration of ethanol in a way in which it was not metabolised to acetaldehyde did not produce dependence, then the evidence would be overwhelming. The first experiment was easy. We simply forced mice to breathe acetaldehyde vapour in a concentration designed to give the same blood acetaldehyde concentrations that would be achieved in ethanol administration. The animals exhibited 'acetaldehyde dependence', showing a withdrawal syndrome very similar to that of ethanol dependence (Ortiz *et al.*, 1974). The second experiment has so far proved impossible. We have attempted to administer inhibitors of alcohol dehydrogenase together with ethanol to prevent the formation of acetaldehyde, but the drugs available are not effective enough, or specific enough to allow interpretation of the results (Littleton *et al.*, 1974). From our experiments, therefore, all we can say is that acetaldehyde produced from ethanol *could* be the cause of ethanol dependence. Maybe we should talk of 'acetaldehydism' rather than alcoholism.

There have been several studies of the metabolism of ethanol by alcoholics. Presumably many if not all these subjects were ethanol dependent. Several studies have suggested that alcoholics have higher concentrations of acetaldehyde, in blood or in breath, than normal subjects after a standard ethanol dose (Korsten *et al.*, 1975; Freund and O'Hollaren, 1965). Interpretation is difficult. Did these subjects initially have a different metabolism of ethanol so that they produced more acetaldehyde, which made them dependent, or was it their chronic consumption of ethanol which altered their metabolism of the drug, so that they now produce more acetaldehyde? We do not know, but there are hopes of experiments that we are now carrying out in which we pre-test individual animals for acetaldehyde production and then attempt to relate this to subsequent ethanol dependence susceptibility.

There is little doubt therefore that acetaldehyde plays some part in ethanol dependence, but whether this is a main role, and whether acetaldehyde measurements will ever be of value in predicting the individual at risk of ethanol dependence remain to be seen.

We do not know the mechanism of the acute depressant effect of ethanol, although indirect evidence suggests that it may be a direct physical effect on neuronal cell membranes. Since adaptation, or cellular tolerance, to the depressant effects of ethanol seems to be a prerequisite for ethanol dependence, it is logical to look at the level of the membrane for the fundamental basis of dependence. The mechanism of the adaptation of cell membranes to ethanol is unknown, but evidence from lower organisms suggests that animals can actually change the lipid composition of their membranes in the continued presence of ethanol (Ingram, 1976). This has the effect of restoring normal membrane function, even while the ethanol is still present. This is cellular tolerance. If the organism found it difficult to return to its original membrane lipid composition, then it would be unable to function properly in the absence of ethanol. This would be a form of ethanol dependence. Now, ethanol does affect lipid metabolism in higher animals and man (Lieber *et al.*, 1975) but this has never been studied in relation to dependence. We have recently obtained results which strongly suggest that a general reduction in fatty acid utilisation accompanies the induction of physical dependence. If we can show that this prevents re-adaptation of membrane lipids in response to ethanol withdrawal, then we may have come close to establishing the fundamental cellular basis of ethanol dependence. This possibility will briefly be returned to later when discussing the toxic effects of ethanol associated with dependence.

Much neuropharmacology over the past twenty years has attempted to explain drug action in the central nervous system in terms of effects on specific central neurotransmitter systems. For example, the properties of major tranquillisers are often regarded as being due primarily to central dopamine receptor blockade (Snyder, 1976). In many cases this approach has led to a useful if gross oversimplification of the varied biochemical effects of centrally acting drugs. Not surprisingly the same approach has been applied to ethanol dependence, and has provided some insight into the neurotransmitter systems involved in dependence and in the withdrawal syndrome.

The monoamine neurotransmitters were among the first to be studied (Griffiths *et al.,* 1973b; Post and Sun, 1973). It was logical to investigate these, as they were suspected of involvement in anxiety and mood changes, all common in ethanol dependence. In addition, ethanol shares a route of metabolism with the amines (via the respective aldehydes (Walsh *et al.,* 1970)) and has also been suggested to have direct physical effects on postsynaptic amine receptors. Experiments on ethanol dependent animals have shown an increase in catecholaminergic activity in brain when compared to controls (Pohorecky, 1974). Catecholamine turnover in the central nervous system continues at a high rate during the early period of withdrawal, but probably falls thereafter. Catecholamine receptors show a reduced sensitivity to catecholamines in dependent animals, and this persists into the withdrawal syndrome (Israel *et al.,* 1972). When specific drugs are used to influence catecholamine neurones it can be shown that these changes are important for the expression of the withdrawal syndrome (Goldstein, 1973; Griffiths *et al.,* 1974). In particular, ethanol withdrawal excitement, tremor and convulsions seem to be related to changes in brain catecholamine metabolism. Some similar changes have been reported in brain 5-hydroxytryptamine metabolism (Pohorecky *et al.,* 1974), but these may be of lesser importance.

In man, the excretion of urinary catecholamines has been measured in alcoholics during a drinking bout, and during the subsequent physical withdrawal syndrome. The results are surprisingly similar to those reported in animals. Urinary catecholamine excretion is raised during drinking, and shows a further rise during withdrawal which correlates with the severity of the withdrawal syndrome (Feldstein, 1971). It must be remembered that these results are complicated by the presence of catecholamine metabolites from the periphery, and their origin is not only the central nervous system.

Other neurotransmitters in the brain have been measured during the induction of ethanol dependence in laboratory animals. Acetylcholine concentrations are said to change, so that low concentrations are found in dependent animals (Hunt and Dalton, 1976). This reduction does not persist into the withdrawal syndrome. As a general rule in neuropharmacology acetylcholine concentrations appear to 'follow' states of consciousness or arousal rather than provoke them. It would be foolish, however, to disregard cholinergic neurones in attempting to find the neurotransmitter basis of ethanol dependence and withdrawal.

We have measured the concentrations of free amino acids in brain in ethanol dependent animals (Griffiths and Littleton, 1974). Many of these amino acids are thought to have a neurotransmitter function as well as playing roles in other aspects of brain metabolism. Our research suggests to us that the amino acids which may be of particular importance in the expression of the withdrawal syndrome are gamma-aminobutyric acid (GABA), proline and aspartate. Many other amino acids also appear to be altered in ethanol dependence but this, of course, may simply reflect the enormous metabolic upheavals which are the consequence of coping with the high concentration of ethanol. Interestingly, some of the amino acids in which concentration changes are observed are those which are the precursors of the monoamine neurotransmitters discussed earlier. We do not yet know whether these changes play any part in the observed alteration in monoamine metabolism.

Many other neurotransmitters undoubtedly exist in the brain, and it is probable that ethanol will be shown to have some effect on many, if not all, of them. Recent attention has been focused on the peptide neurotransmitters, and research into the basis of morphine dependence has been greatly accelerated by the discovery of enkephalin (Hughes *et al.*, 1975). This peptide binds to morphine receptors in the brain, and appears to be a naturally occurring analgesic in some central nervous pathways. Its discovery has obvious implications for all states of euphoria and drug dependence. In this context, it is worth mentioning that ethanol and morphine psychological dependence share many characteristics (Littleton, 1975). Recent theories of ethanol dependence have suggested that morphine-like derivatives of acetaldehyde and catecholamine metabolites might occur during chronic administration (Davis and Walsh, 1970). This is not far-fetched. Compounds of this type, of which the major class are the tetrahydroisoquinolines, have been recovered from the urine of patients receiving L-DOPA who have been given ethanol (Sandier *et al.*, 1973). So far it has not proved possible to isolate tetrahydroisoquinolines from ethanol dependent animals receiving ethanol alone, or from body fluids of alcoholics. The possibility that these metabolites are produced at some site and play a role in ethanol dependence must not be ignored.

Finally, in this section on the biochemical basis of ethanol dependence, mention should be made of the possible role of toxic effects of ethanol in instituting the dependent state. Ethanol and acetaldehyde are both capable of producing structural and functional damage to cellular components. In particular mitochondria seem to be relatively susceptible to damage (Cederbaum and Rubin, 1975). Not surprisingly, much of this damage occurs in the liver and may be related to the production of acetaldehyde in this organ. Clear evidence of liver dysfunction in chronic ethanol administration is shown by the enormous accumulation of triglycerides in liver which occurs after several days of ethanol administration to laboratory animals. If we study the onset of this aspect of liver dysfunction we find it closely parallels the severity of the withdrawal syndrome (Abu-Murad *et al.*, 1976). Drugs which increase the degree of liver damage, such as carbon tetrachloride, seem to increase the severity of ethanol withdrawal whereas others, which prevent hepatic triglyceride accumulation, reduce the intensity of the subsequent withdrawal syndrome (unpublished results).

There are, of course, several ways in which a disturbance of liver function could affect the severity of the ethanol withdrawal syndrome. Hepatic gluconeogenesis is depressed by chronic ethanol administration and this may be an important factor determining brain metabolism in the absence of ethanol. We have explored the possibility that ethanol-induced hepatic damage, like that produced by other drugs (Knott and Curzon, 1975), leads to a large increase in plasma and brain tyrosine, tryptophan and phenylalanine. If this occurred, it would contribute to the changes in monoamine neurotransmitters observed, since these amino acids are the precursors of the monoamines. As yet, the evidence is equivocal (unpublished results); some animals show these changes, others do not. If hepatic changes do lead to alteration in plasma amino acid concentrations during induction of ethanol dependence, it seems unlikely that this is the main reason for ethanol dependence occurring in all animals.

Recently, we have become more interested in the general disorder of lipid metabolism which is reflected by this accumulation of triglycerides in liver. The reason does not appear to be because of increased synthesis of triglycerides or fatty acids; rather it seems that once triglycerides have been synthesised the fatty acid groups from them cannot be utilised. Thus, triglycerides do not accumulate only in the liver; plasma hypertriglyceridaemia and accumulation in other organs also occurs (unpublished results). If this is an inhibition of fatty acid utilisation it may be of great importance in understanding the cellular basis of ethanol dependence. Cells need fatty acids to alter membrane characteristics in response to new stimuli. If chronic ethanol administration prevents this ability, this may explain why a withdrawal syndrome occurs on removal of ethanol. Clearly, if we could understand this disorder more fully we may be able to prevent its occurrence, and perhaps reduce susceptibility to ethanol dependence.

In summary, ethanol dependence susceptibility seems to be related to three main factors:

1. The metabolism of ethanol and acetaldehyde. It may be suggested that the greater the amount of acetaldehyde produced, or not rapidly metabolised, the greater the susceptibility to dependence.

2. The induction of cellular or pharmacological tolerance seems to be necessary for the induction of dependence.

3. A basic inability to adapt to the absence of ethanol. This could be a disorder of lipid metabolism, related to triglyceride accumulation in liver. This change shows a close association with dependence.

The expression of the ethanol withdrawal syndrome seems to be mediated by several pathways and neurotransmitter systems in the brain. The catecholamines appear to be of particular importance. Other toxic effects of ethanol may play a role in determining the severity of the withdrawal syndrome.

Biological factors which we have studied in animals in relation to susceptibility to ethanol dependence include age, sex, genetic complement, diet and environment. All can be shown to have an effect on either susceptibility to dependence, or on severity of the withdrawal syndrome, which can be explained by biochemical differences within the preceding scheme. The biochemical approach to alcoholism which we employ uses the differences provided by these biological factors further to explore the basic nature of ethanol dependence and the ethanol withdrawal syndrome.

References

Abu-Murad, C., Griffiths, P.J. and Littleton, J.M. (1976). Catecholamine metabolism and the role of liver dysfunction in the induction of ethanol dependence. Br. J. Pharmac. 56: 377P-8P.

Brentzel, H.J. and Hesse, S. (1975). Significant pathways of hepatic ethanol metabolism. Fed. Proc. 34: 2075.

Cederbaum, A. and Rubin, E. (1975). Molecular injury to mitochondria produced by ethanol and acetaldehyde. Fed. Proc. 34: 2045.

Davis, V.E. and Walsh, M.J. (1970). Alcohol, amines and alkaloids: a possible basis for alcohol addiction. Science. 167: 1005-1007.

Edwards, G. and Gross, M.M. (1976). Alcohol dependence: provisional description of a clinical syndrome. Br. Med. J. 1: 1058-61.

Egana, E. and Rodrigo, R. (1974). Some biochemical effects of ethanol on the central nervous system. Int. J. Neurol. 9: 143-55.

Feldstein, A. (1971). Effect of ethanol on neurohumoural amine metabolism. In: The Biology of Alcoholism. B. Kissin and H. Begleiter (eds.). Press New York London, vol.1, pp.127-60.

Freund, G. (1969). Alcohol withdrawal syndrome in mice. Ach Neurol. 21: 315.

Freund, G. and O'Hollaren, P. (1965). Acetaldehyde concentrations in alveolar air following a standard dose of ethanol in man. J. Lipid Res. 6: 471-7.

Goldstein, D.B. (1973). Alcohol withdrawal reactions in mice: effects of drugs that modify neurotransmission. J. Pharmac. Exp. Ther. 186: 1-9.

Griffiths, P.J., Littleton, J.M. and Ortiz, A. (1973a). A method for the induction of dependence in ethanol in mice. Br. J. Pharmac. 47: 669P-70P.

Griffiths, P.J. Littleton, J.M. and Ortiz, A. (1973b). Evidence for a role for brain monoamines in ethanol dependence. Br. J. Pharmac. 48: 354P.

Griffiths, P.J., Littleton, J.M. and Ortiz, A. (1974). Changes in monoamine concentrations in mouse brain associated with ethanol dependence and withdrawal. Br. J. Pharmac. 50: 489-98.

Griffiths, P.J. and Littleton, J.M. (1977). Concentrations of free amino acids in brains of mice during the induction of physical dependence on ethanol and during the withdrawal syndrome. Br. J. Exp. Path. 58: 19-27.

Hammond, M.D. and Schneider, C. (1973). Behavioural changes induced in mice following termination of ethanol administration. Br. J. Pharmac. 47: 667P.

Hotzman, S.G. and Schneider, F.H. (1974). Comparison of acetaldehyde and ethanol depression of motor activity in mice. Life Sci. 14: 1243-50.

Hughes, J., Smith., T.W., Kosterlitz, H.W., Fothergill, L.A., Morgan, B.A. and Morris, H.R. (1975). Identification of two related pentapeptides from the brain with potent opiate agonist activity. Nature 358: 577-9.

Hunt, W.A. and Dalton, T.K. (1976). Regional brain acetylcholine levels in rats acutely treated with ethanol or rendered ethanol-dependent. Brain Res. 109: 628-31.

Ingram, L.O. (1976). Adaptation of membrane lipids to alcohols. J. Bacteriol. 125: 670-8.

Israel, M.A. (1972). Changes in activity and hormonal sensitivity of brain adenyl cyclase following chronic ethanol administration. Experientia 28: 1322-3.

Kalant, H. (1975). Direct effects of ethanol on the nervous system. Fed. Proc. 34: 1930-41.

Knott, P.J. and Curzon, G. (1975). Tryptophan and tyrosine disposition and brain tryptophan metabolism in acute carbon tetrachloride poisoning. Biochem. Pharmac. 24: 963-6.

Korstein, M.A. Matsuzaki, S., Feinman, L. and Lieber, C.S. (1975). High blood acetaldehyde levels after ethanol administration in alcoholics. New Eng. J. Med. 292: 368-89.

Lieber, C.S., Teschka, R., Hasamura, Y. and De Carli, L.M. (1975). Differences in hepatic and metabolic changes after acute and chronic alcohol consumption. Fed. Pr c. 34: 2060.

Littleton, J.M. (1975). The experimental approach to alcoholism. Br. J. Addict. 70: 99-122.

Littleton, J.M. Griffiths, P.J. and Ortiz, A. (1974). The induction of ethanol dependence and the ethanol withdrawal syndrome. The effects of pyrazole. J. Pharm. Pharmac. 26: 81-91.

Majchrowicz, E. (1975). Effect of peripheral ethanol metabolism on the central nervous system. Fed. Proc. 34: 1948-52.

Ortiz, A., Griffiths, P.J., Littleton, J.M. (1974). A comparison of the effects of chronic administration of ethanol and acetaldehyde to mice; evidence for a role of acetaldehyde in ethanol dependence. J. Pharm. Pharmac. 26: 249-60.

Pohorecky, L.A. (1974). Effects of ethanol on central and peripheral noradrenergic neurons. J. Pharmac. Exp. Ther. 189: 380-91.

Pohorecky, L.A., Jaffe, L.S. and Berkeley, H.A. (1974). Effects of ethanol on serotonergic neurons in the rats brain. Res. Commun. Chem. Path. Pharmac. 8: 1-11.

Post, M.E. and Sun, A.Y. (1973). The effect of chronic ethanol administration on the levels of catecholamines in different regions of the rat brain. Res. Commun. Chem. Path. Pharmac. 6: 887-94.

Sandler, M., Carter, S.B., Hunter, K.R., Stern, G.M. (1973). Tetrahydroisoquinoline alkaloids in VIVO metabolites of L-DOPA in man. Nature 241: 439-43.

Snyder, S.H. (1976). The dopamine hypothesis of schizophrenia; focus on the dopamine receptor. Am. J. Psychiatry 133: 197-202.

Truitt, E.B., Jr. (1970). Is there a biochemical lesion in the disease of alcoholism? Ohio St. Med. J. 66: 681-3.

Victor, M. (1970). The alcohol withdrawal syndrome; theory and practice. Postgrad. Med. 4: 68-72.

Walsh, M.J. Truitt, E.B., Jr and Davis, V.E. (1970). Acetaldehyde mediation in the mechanism of ethanol-induced changes in norepinephrine metabolism. Molec. Pharmac. 6: 416-24.

8 GENETICS AND ALCOHOLISM

James Shields

'It might be thought that the investigation of alcoholism along genetical lines would be a forlorn task.' Thus Slater and Cowie (1971) opened the section on alcoholism in their book *The Genetics of Mental Disorders*. As others had done, they pointed to the enormous group differences in the proclivity to alcoholism which cannot be accounted for by genetics — differences in alcohol consumption between countries, social classes and occupations. They made the important point that in groups where heavy drinking is common, addicts will tend to be less deviant in personality than in groups where alcohol consumption is low.

To the problems in investigating the genetics of alcoholism we may add the very heterogeneous reasons for drinking, and (not peculiar to genetic studies) the difficulties of defining and ascertaining alcoholism. If it is hard to get a patient to admit his drinking problem, how much harder will it be to obtain accurate information about his relatives. Denial of any genetic influence in alcoholism is therefore perhaps more understandable than in schizophrenia or intelligence.

On the other hand, the very fact that it is known that an individual must imbibe ethanol before he can suffer from alcoholism permits a pharmacogenetic approach to the necessary environmental agent. This is more than can be said for schizophrenia or intelligence. In pharmacogenetics one searches for individual genetic differences in response to the drug and endeavours to elucidate the mechanisms, by means of animal models where appropriate. In this respect, genetic studies of alcoholism might be thought to hold particular promise.

This review will attempt to summarise the current status of genetic studies in alcoholism, first dealing briefly with animal work, human pharmacogenetics and the possible influence of known genes on the predisposition to alcoholism. Such work does not do away with the need for good clinical genetic studies. The review will go on to refer to family studies on the relationship between alcoholism and other psychiatric disorders, and on the incidence of drinking problems in the families of alcoholics; and of course to studies of twins, and to recent reports on the adopted-away children of alcoholics. The genetics of alcohol consumption in animals and man has recently been well reviewed by Kalervo Eriksson (1975) of Helsinki.

Animal Studies

It has been repeatedly demonstrated in experimental studies that inbred strains of rats and mice differ in their preference for, or avoidance of, alcohol. Moreover, by selective breeding of heterogeneous rat populations, strains have been specifically selected for drinking or avoiding alcohol. In these strains differences have been found in the ability to metabolise acetaldehyde. The drinker strains tend to have the higher ALDH activity. Eriksson points out that rodents can manifest many of the characteristics of human alcoholism, 'such as drinking to intoxication voluntarily, showing dependence upon alcohol, and demonstrating a willingness to work for alcohol and a strong motivation to get it'. Strains of mice have been bred for their susceptibility to withdrawal symptoms. While such studies suggest that there may be genetic variability in the response to alcohol in man too, estimates of heritability (or the proportion of the total variance due to genetic variability), calculated from animal studies, obviously cannot be expected to apply to any particular human population.

Human Pharmacogenetics

Human populations have been found to differ in their reaction to alcohol for reasons that are not purely cultural. Wolff (1973), for instance, found that Koreans, Chinese and Japanese became flushed more often than Caucasians after small oral doses of alcohol. This difference occurred even when the alcohol was administered shortly after birth. He speculated that these unpleasant effects of alcohol were under genetic control and contributed, along with other social factors, to the relatively abstemious drinking habits of most Mongoloid people. It would be as though they had an inbuilt antabuse system. Furthermore, there are differences between populations in the relative frequency of the genetic variants of the enzyme alcohol dehydrogenase. The form known as 'atypical' ADH in the West is the commonest in Japan. Ethanol is oxidised to acetaldehyde — a poisonous substance — by the ADH enzymes. Eriksson considers that the different genetic variants might affect the levels of acetaldehyde in the blood after taking alcohol. Stamatoyannopoulos, Chen and Fukui (1975) noted that the frequency of 'atypical' ADH in the Japanese was about 85 per cent, and this was also their reported frequency of alcohol sensitivity. The authors suggested a causative relationship between the two phenomena. However, this hypothesis has not yet been put to the test of seeing whether the traits are closely enough associated in the same individuals.

There are also said to be ethnic differences in the rate of elimination of ethanol from the blood. Fenna *et al.* (1971) found that Eskimos and some American Indians took longer than Caucasians to sober up, and they attributed this to differences in the rate of metabolism. Their study has been criticised by Lieber (1972), however. Two small studies of normal Caucasian twins (Vessell, 1972; Forsander and Eriksson, 1974) found ethanol elimination rates to be under a considerable degree of genetic control; heritability was estimated as being between 80 and 90 per cent. The promise, and some of the problems, of the pharmacogenetic approach to alcoholism have been outlined by Omenn (1975).

Marker Genes

Reference was made above to the hypothesis that the ADH genetic polymorphism may contribute positively or negatively to the predisposition to alcoholism. Are there any other known genes which might do so, even to a small extent? The association with colour blindness, which is reported from time to time (e.g. Cruz-Coke and Varela, 1965), is not generally confirmed. The colour vision defect of some alcoholics suffering from cirrhosis was found to have been acquired by heavy drinking; it could no longer be found after treatment (Reid *et al.*, 1968; Smith, 1972). Moreover, there is no support for sex-linked inheritance in alcoholism, which would be implied if there were a strong association or close genetic linkage with colour blindness.

A more promising lead may be the reported association between alcoholism and non-secretion of the ABH blood group substances in the saliva. This was first noted by Camps and Dodd in 1967. Two years later they confirmed their findings in an enlarged sample of 1,000 alcoholics, and showed they could not be accounted for by the part of the country from which the patients came (Camps, Dodd and Lincoln, 1969). The association was again confirmed by Swinson and Madden (1973) in Liverpool. While the amount of A, B or H substance secreted in the saliva may be influenced by other factors, the secretor versus non-secretor distinction is regarded by Race and Sanger (1975) as a clear genetic marker. That it is an artefact of drinking seems rather unlikely. The biggest problem about the reported association is that the excess of non-secretors is entirely accounted for by persons of blood group A. Of blood group A alcoholics, 47 per cent were non-secretors — about twice as many as would be expected. This apparent interaction effect of the *A* and *Non-secretor* alleles is unexpected. Swinson and Madden point to the need for sibship studies or a prospective study of people of known blood groups and secretor status before they become alcoholic. But at present this may be the nearest we can approach to an association between a marker gene and alcohol addiction, analogous to the association between blood group O and duodenal ulcer, now very well established though still not fully understood (*BMJ* Editorial, 1976).

It should not be forgotten here that genetic factors may be implicated in the complications of alcoholism, such as liver damage, and particularly its progression to cirrhosis. There is recent evidence from immune response studies which support this suggestion (Bailey *et al.,* 1976).

Family Studies

It is widely agreed that people of many different personality types and suffering from a wide variety of psychiatric disturbances become alcoholic. Is there any genetic connection between alcoholism and other psychiatric disorders? Or is alcoholism merely a complication, caused by stress, that can occur in almost any disorder? As in suicide and hysteria, perhaps, are any genetic factors in alcoholism quite non-specific, depending entirely on the nature of the genetic component (if any) of the particular disorder underlying the heavy drinking — depression, personality disorders or whatever?

From time to time family studies have reported a raised rate of alcoholism in the relatives of patients suffering from other conditions, and vice versa. Some of the reported associations must be briefly mentioned. First as regards schizophrenia: in Zurich, Manfred Bleuler (1972) reported an alcoholism rate of 24 per cent for the fathers of schizophrenics; in Sweden, Lindelius (1970) found alcoholism in 16 per cent of the parents; and in Newcastle-on-Tyne, Stephens *et al.* (1975) recently found that 16 per cent of the fathers and brothers of schizophrenics were heavy drinkers — about twice the rate found in their control group. On the other hand, there are no reports of a raised incidence of schizophrenia in the relatives of alcoholics. Alcoholic hallucinosis has sometimes been regarded as genetically related to schizophrenia. But from the work of Benedetti (1952), Scott (1967) and Schuckit and Winokur (1971), this seems unlikely, since no significant excess of schizophrenia was found in the relatives. It seems that it should be grouped with the symptomatic schizophrenia-like psychoses. In our Maudsley twin study the non-alcoholic identical twin of a woman with a schizophrenic-like alcoholic hallucinosis showed neurotic rather than schizoid characteristics (Gottesman and Shields, 1972, Case MZ9A).

As regards the affective disorders, Slater (1938) investigated the parents of manic depressives and found 10.7 per cent of the fathers to be alcoholic. Winokur (1974) finds an excess of alcoholism and sociopathy in the male relatives of depressives, but unlike Slater (see Shields, 1975, for a re-analysis of Slater's data) he finds it in only the unipolar and not the bipolar disorders, and it is restricted to cases of early onset. Alcoholism was reported in about 12 per cent of the fathers of depressives with an onset before the age of forty. Winokur regards alcoholism and sociopathy as belonging to what he calls 'depression spectrum disease'. His work on the families of alcoholics will be mentioned below.

Stenstedt (1952) found no excess of alcoholics in the families of manic depressives. Angst (1966) calculated a 22.6 per cent risk of alcoholism for the fathers of his endogenous depressive probands. This was similar to the rate reported for the fathers of neurotics in a comparable study. The rates for the brothers and sons were only 4.2 and 2.8 per cent. Angst considered there was no support for the view that alcoholism should be regarded as a masked form of depression.

In their studies of alcoholics, Åmark (1951) and Bleuler (1955) found only an insignificant increase of manic depressive disorders in the families, but Åmark reported an excess of psychogenic psychoses, mostly of a depressive nature, in parents and sibs.

George Winokur and his colleagues at St Louis and Iowa have developed many hypotheses — not always confirmed — about the existence of distinct disease entities within the depressions and other psychiatric disorders. They have speculated about possible genetic mechanisms, such as X-linked genes. In particular, they have considered the possible relation between alcoholism, primary depression and the sociopathic disorders. Their most recent work on alcoholism (Winokur *et al.,* 1970, 1971) is based on alcoholics, with or without another psychiatric diagnosis, collected in St Louis. A special effort was made to include female alcoholic probands, previously little studied genetically. The 259 probands included 103 women. About a third of the first-degree relatives were systematically interviewed. The rate of alcoholism in relatives was rather higher than that reported in other studies, being around 35 per cent (rather than 20 per cent) for various groups of male relatives. It was rarely above 9 per cent in female relatives. Many of the mothers, sisters and daughters, however, had depression. When alcoholism and depression were considered together, morbidity rates in the two sexes were approximately equal. There was little support for the team's previous hypothesis of three distinct types of alcoholism – primary, depressive and sociopathic (Schuckit *et al.*, 1969). In all three clinical groups, similar percentages of relatives had alcoholism or depression. The authors now favour the view that males and females differ in the way they express the same disorder, the males mostly by alcoholism, the females by depression (perhaps some of the latter had the St Louis Blues!). As already mentioned, Winokur's group have reported complementary findings when starting with unipolar depressive probands.

When the families of the female and male alcoholic probands were compared by Winokur in the St Louis study, the risks were not appreciably raised for the families of the females, contrary to expectation. Reich, Winokur and Mullaney (1975a) have analysed the data by means of the multiple threshold model (Reich, Cloninger and Guze, 1975b). This assumes that females have a higher threshold for becoming alcoholics; it takes more of the multifactorial causes of the disorder for them to become affected than it does for males. Reich *et al.* found both male and female alcoholism to be familial disorders, based on the same genotypes. But the rates in the male relatives of male patients were too high to be entirely accounted for by the additive effects of family genes, shared family environment and a different threshold for the two sexes. They concluded that the large sex effect in alcoholism was mostly due to social, non-familial environmental factors, including features of the environment peculiar to the individual. As we shall see later, there is some support from twin and adoption studies for the importance of environmental factors other than those particular ones shared by members of the same household.

All investigators agree about the mixture of psychopathic-like personality disorders and alcoholism in families. For example, alcoholism is part of Schulsinger's (1972) 'psychopathic spectrum': it was found more often in the biological relatives of psychopathic adoptees than in those of control adoptees or in the adoptive families. Hyperactive children (Morrison and Stewart, 1971; Cantwell, 1972) and women with 'St Louis' hysteria or Briquet's syndrome (Arkonac and Guze, 1963), have also been reported as having a raised rate of alcoholism in their families. Åmark, Bleuler and, among others, Winokur, find a raised incidence of personality disturbances in the relatives of alcoholics. Åmark's rate of 15 per cent for psychopathy among parents and sibs is fairly typical. It should be remembered that a high proportion of alcoholics that come to psychiatric attention have personality disorders themselves.

In a study of Swedish adoptees, Bohman (personal communication) has provisionally reported some of his findings. Adoptees whose biological fathers were alcoholic but not criminal had a raised rate of alcohol abuse and of crime, while this was not true of adoptees whose biological fathers were criminal but had no record of alcohol abuse. This suggests the existence of genetic influence on instability of personality, and (at least among parents whose children are placed for adoption) that these are more frequently present in alcoholics than in criminals whose behaviour does not come to the attention of bodies like the Swedish Temperance Boards.

If there are polygenic influences on the predisposition to alcoholism, they are almost certainly intertwined with those affecting personality. To get a line on whether any of the polygenes predispose to alcoholism as such, we need to look at the family studies more closely.

Åmark permits us to compare the influence of an alcoholic with that of a psychopathic parent on the sibs of alcoholic probands. Parental abnormalities of both types increased the rate of both types of disorder, compared with the situation when both parents were classified as normal; but alcoholic parents who were not also psychopathic increased the rate of alcoholism in sibs more than did psychopathic parents who were not also alcoholic. This suggests some specificity in the transmission of alcoholism. In the small group of nineteen families with a proband suffering from periodic bouts of alcoholism, there was an alcoholism rate of 32 per cent in the brothers – nearly half of it of the same type – and the psychopathy rate was not significantly higher than when both parents were normal. Here, at least, Åmark thought hereditary factors might play an essential role.

The family studies from Sweden, Switzerland and the USA agree in finding very much higher rates of alcoholism in the parents and sibs of alcoholics than those thought most appropriate for the general population. For first-degree male relatives typical risks were somewhat over 20 per cent in the earlier European studies, compared with something like 3.4 per cent for the general population (Fremming, 1951). In recent American work (Reich *et al.,* 1975a) rates were higher all round: 36 per cent for male relatives, compared with 11.4 per cent in the corresponding white male population.

One cannot of course conclude from this that genetic factors are the cause of the difference. One reason for caution is the high rate often reported for relatives genetically one degree less close than parents and sibs and on average sharing only 25 per cent, not 50 per cent, of their genes with the proband. Genetic theories predict much lower risks for second-degree than first-degree relatives. Yet Bleuler in his New York study reported a 15 per cent alcoholism rate in uncles and aunts. In St Louis Schuckit *et al.* (1972) found a rate of 31 per cent in half-brothers, compared with 32 per cent in full brothers. In Sweden, Kaij and Dock (1975) found that grandsons of alcoholics had had at least one registration for alcohol abuse as frequently as had the brothers; in the 45-55 age group the frequency was 43 per cent. These high rates in second-degree relatives could be explained partly but not entirely on genetical lines if there were a very high rate of assortative mating. In his New York study of alcoholism, Bleuler reported that 29 per cent of the spouses of his probands were alcoholic; and similarly, according to Angst, 29 per cent of the daughters of Swiss alcoholics marry alcoholic husbands.

This suggests the importance of the family or social milieu. For further evidence about the existence of genetic influences and the importance or otherwise of family environmental factors such as being brought up by an alcoholic parent, we need to turn to twin and adoption studies. The classical twin method endeavours to hold the family environment constant by studying twins brought up together and compares genetically identical with genetically dissimilar twins to find out whether the genes do make any difference. The study of twins reared apart, and strategies using adopted or fostered children, compare groups similar genetically but brought up in different family environments.

Twin Studies

Three population-based twin studies in Finland (Partanen *et al.*, 1966) and Sweden (Kaij, 1960; Jonsson and Nilsson, 1968) have compared drinking habits in MZ and DZ pairs and found evidence of a genetic influence. In Partanen's study of 902 male pairs in Finland, aged 28-37, the frequency of drinking and the amount drunk at a session both showed a moderate degree of heritability ($h^2 = 0.39$ and 0.36 respectively); non-twin brothers were no less alike than DZ twins. No correlation between drinking habits and personality traits was detected. But, except at younger ages, the factor labelled 'Out of Control' showed no significant tendency for MZs to be more alike than DZs ($h^2 = 0.14$).

Kaij studied 214 Swedish pairs where one or both of the twins had appeared at least once on the register of alcohol abusers. Their mean age was 37 (range 19-63). He classified drinking habits into five grades, from 0-4, ranging from total abstainer (in some of the co-twins) to chronic alcoholism. Table 1 shows that both MZ and DZ pairs were more alike than expected by chance, and that significantly more MZs than DZs fell into the same class, 53 per cent as compared with 28 per

Table 1 Swedish male twins (Kaij, 1960)

	Same drinking classification (Grades 0 - 4)	Expected by chance
MZ	31 out of 58 (53%)	14.50
DZ	39 out of 138 (28%)	29.44
	Both twins chronic alcoholics (Grade 4)	MZ:DZ Difference (X^2 Yates)
MZ	10 out of 14 (71%)	
DZ	10 out of 31 (32%)	$p < .05$
	Both twins heavy abusers or chronic alcoholics (Grades 3 or 4)	
MZ	19 out of 27 (70%)	
DZ	20 out of 61 (32%)	$p < .01$

cent. In pairs where at least one twin was a heavy abuser (Grade 3) or a chronic alcoholic, 70 per cent of 27 MZ pairs and 32 per cent of 61 DZ pairs were concordant, which is significant at the 1 per cent level. The same rates were obtained in respect of Grade 4 alcoholism.

It could be argued that the greater similarity of MZ than DZ pairs in drinking habits is due to the greater environmental similarities of the former. However, such information as there is on MZ twins brought up apart does not support this. There are five such pairs where at least one twin was a heavy drinker — three from Kaij's study and two from my separated twins (Shields, 1962). In four of them the twins were similar in drinking habits. MZ twins do not have to be brought up in identical environments for them to be alike. But this is hardly a trump card in the heredity-environment game. For example, in the author's pair Sm 15 where both twins were chronic alcoholics, both had been brought up in the same cider-drinking village, Ben by his mother and Ron by his maternal grandmother. At the age of 52 they still live there, though they do not go drinking together. All that can be said is that the fact that Ben was breast-fed and Ron not, and that Ron was brought up in a more harmonious, better disciplined home than Ben, did not have any influence on their drinking habits. In Kaij's discordant MZ or ?MZ pair 31, both twins were brought up by a father or grandfather who was a heavy drinker. No clear reason can be gleaned from the case history as to why only one of them became a chronic alcoholic after the age of thirty and the other is a normal Grade 1 drinker. Shared early family environment does not appear to be the critical factor in twin studies.

In our series of some 700 adult twins who have attended the Maudsley Hospital during a period of 28 years we have only had 22 who were diagnosed as suffering from alcoholism (Shields, unpublished data). Some of them were birds of passage who may perhaps have come once to the Emergency Clinic before returning to Wales or Ireland. In five of these pairs we have no information about zygosity or concordance. Among those where we have information there is possible concordance for alcoholism in only one possibly MZ pair, where the patient returned to Canada. In none of the other 6 MZ or 10 DZ pairs was the second twin discovered to have been alcoholic, though one of the MZ partners was a heavy social drinker; but in both groups – MZ and DZ–several co-twins had other, psychiatric or personality disorders, mostly of a neurotic kind rather than unipolar depression. This psychiatric series, if one can generalise from these provisional results, therefore supports Partanen's view that 'Out of Control' drinking is not under genetic control, and is contrary to Kaij's more extensive findings. But the discordance brings out the point that early family environment of the kind that is shared by all sibs, and even that shared by MZ twins, is not the critical factor in addiction. The reasons for the discordance are difficult to pinpoint, and vary from person to person. Often, as in the case of alcoholic hallucinosis mentioned earlier, it was hard to see what combination of personality factors and circumstances in their late adolescence led the one twin rather than the other to overstep the point at which she could control her drinking and to start the vicious circle. In a male MZ pair the one twin's heavy drinking appears to have started during a mild state of anxiety and depression. His co-twin has described similar feelings of anxiety, and has lost work on this account, but he has not been a heavy drinker. The attitude of the spouses may have contributed to the difference. In a third pair, pre-existing personality differences and choice of occupation (journalism) seem the most plausible explanation for the less aggressive twin's addiction.

Adoption Studies

In principle, a major advantage of the study of adoptees and similar strategies is that they can point to environmental factors which could prevent the development of a disorder such as alcoholism. The early study by Anne Roe and Barbara Burks (Roe, 1944; Roe, Burks and Mittelmann, 1945) suggested that a favourable foster home environment could have a protective effect. None of the 36 children of alcoholic parentage were known to be alcoholic at a mean age of 31, and only 3 used alcohol regularly. Unfortunately, there was no information about the drinking habits in seven cases. On the other hand, 10 of the children of alcoholics, compared with only 2 of 25 controls, had been in 'serious trouble' during adolescence, including trouble over drinking. However, the findings cannot be interpreted in a genetic direction, since mean age of placement of the children in the alcoholic group was 5½ years, significantly later than that of the control group.

Akin to the adoption strategy is the method using half-sibs employed by Schuckit, Goodwin and Winokur (1972). They studied 164 half-sibs of 69 alcoholics from a poor district in St Louis, where the prevalence of heavy drinking may have been high. Some of the half-sibs had an alcoholic biological parent, others not. Some were reared by an alcoholic parent or step-parent, others not (Table 2). The frequency of alcoholism in the half-sibs was found to be associated with the nature of the biological parentage rather than with the presence or absence of an alcoholic in the home. As mentioned earlier, the lack of difference between the half- and full-sib rates in this study makes any simple genetic explanation difficult. The findings might equally be thought to point to the general social environment in an alcoholic subculture.

But later on, adoption studies seemed to show that social conditions of this kind are not critical, at least in Denmark. (This was Åmark's conclusion in Sweden, too.) The two papers by Donald Goodwin and his Danish and American colleagues (Goodwin *et al.*, 1973, 1974) are based on the pool of all 5,500 Copenhagen, non-familial adoptees, 1924-47, originally assembled for schizophrenia research by Rosenthal, Kety, Wender and Schulsinger (see Rosenthal and Kety, 1968; Mednick *et al.*, 1974). The attempt is made here to summarise their results in a single table (Table 3).

Table 2 Incidence of alcoholism in half-sibs of alcoholics under different conditions of biological parentage and upbringing (data of Schuckit *et al.*, 1972)

	Biological Parent Alcoholic	
	Yes	No
Brought up by Alcoholic Parent or Step-parent		
	Proportion of Alcoholics:	
Yes	11/24 = 46%	2/14 = 14%
No	11/22 = 50%	9/104 = 8%

Table 3 Copenhagen adoption study of alcoholism (data of Goodwin *et al.*, 1973, 1974)

	Biological parent not hospitalised for alcoholism		Biological parent hospitalised for alcoholism	
	(1)	(2)	(3)	(4)
	Adoptee controls for (2)	Adopted Sons Total Studied	Adopted Sons, Sub-Group with Non-adopted Brothers (4) for comparison	Non-adopted Sons
	N = 78	N = 55	N = 20	N = 30
	%	%	%	%
Married, never divorced	74	62	70	60
Any psychiatric treatment	24	40	35	27
Any psychiatric hospitalisation	3	15	15	17
Treated for drinking	1	9	15	13
Ever alcoholic	5	18	25	17

All differences between (1) and (2) and none between (3) and (4) were statistically significant.

In the first paper, they studied fifty-five males, adopted within the first six weeks and established from the Psychiatric Register as having had a hospitalised alcoholic biological parent (column (2)). Their mean age was thirty. They compared them with a mixed group of seventy-eight adoptees (column (1)). Fifty of the latter had no biological parent in the Psychiatric Register, and twenty-eight had one parent who had been in mental hospital but not for alcoholism or schizophrenia. In the second paper Goodwin *et al.* selected those twenty of the fifty-five sons of alcoholics of column (2) where there were brothers or half-brothers who had been brought up in the same home as the alcoholic parent (column (3)). There were thirty such non-adopted sons for comparison (column (4)). The assessment of the sons was based on structured interviews by a Danish psychiatrist who did not know the parentage of the subjects. To qualify as alcoholic according to the Goodwin and Winokur criteria, a subject had to be a 'heavy' drinker and have problems in at least three of four groups. One of these groups includes blackouts and withdrawal symptoms, another loss of control and morning drinking. The foster home experiences of the index and control adoptees (columns (2) and (1) were found to have been similar. The adoptive parents of the index group had no more psychopathology, alcoholic or other, than the control group.

As can be seen in the bottom row of the table, the salient findings are that adopted-away sons of hospitalised alcoholics are significantly more often alcoholic than control adoptees (18 per cent vs. 5 per cent, columns (2) and (1)) and are no less often alcoholic than their non-adopted brothers reared with an alcoholic parent (25 per cent vs. 17 per cent, columns (3) and (4)). These rates are similar to those reported in the European literature. The index adoptees were more often divorced than the controls, but it was remarkable that the rates of psychiatric disturbance other than those related to alcohol problems were similar in the two groups. One would have expected more personality disorder and perhaps more depression in the index group if it is the link with these disorders that accounts for any genetic influence in alcoholism. (It is perhaps a pity that the authors did not obtain larger control groups and report the findings when the biological parents were normal separately from those where one parent had been hospitalised for depression or character disorder. They stated there was no significant difference between the two control groups and combined them.)

The findings therefore support the theory that rather specific genetic factors are involved in alcoholism; they do not lend support to theories about the direct environmental influence of parental alcoholism or social conditions generally — adoptive homes are relatively stable. The second of the Goodwin papers (Goodwin *et al.*, 1974) is of further interest in showing that the highest rate of alcoholism occurred in the sons of alcoholics who had four or more hospitalisations for the disorder (Table 4). These five parents accounted for half of the ten alcoholic sons found. As in Åmark's study, this raises the possibility that periodic bout drinking may be the type in which genetic influences are greatest and most specific. The Danish adoption studies on alcoholism continue.*

---

* Goodwin *et al.* (1975) state that '10 of 14 alcoholic adoptees had biological parents who were alcoholic, with no known alcoholism among the biological parents of non-alcoholics'. This, however, was a consequence of the way the adoptees were selected. They were the combined index and control adoptees of Goodwin *et al.* (1973).

Table 4 Severity of alcoholism in parents and frequency in sons
(data of Goodwin *et al.*, 1974)

No. of hospitalisations of alcoholic parents		Frequency of alcoholism in sons	
1	(8 parents)	2/22	(9%)
2-3	(6 parents)	3/15	(20%)
4-	(5 parents)	5/13	(38%)
Total		10/50	(20%)

Same trend in 20 adopted and 30 non-adopted sons.

Difference between sons of fathers with 1 and 4 or more hospitalisations significant at 0.05 level

Discussion

So much for the present state of the art. Where does the evidence lead us? If a reader were to be presented with a neat package of all the answers, he would rightly be sceptical. The genetics of alcohol addiction is not as simple as that. Certainly alcoholism would appear to have all the hallmarks of a disorder in which genetic factors are implicated. As we have seen, the genetic hypothesis is supported by evidence from animal studies, pharmacogenetics, family studies, twins and adoptees. But there are uncertainties and inconsistencies in the data, not all of which can be demonstrably accounted for by weaknesses in individual studies, different terminology or varying population prevalences of heavy drinking. Geneticists have interpreted the data in different ways. Obviously all admit environmental influences to some extent, although Goodwin *et al.* (1974) tend to think their evidence contradicts 'the oft-repeated assertion that alcoholism results from the interaction of multiple causes — social, psychological, biological, etc.', at least so far as the severe forms of alcoholism are concerned. There is no monogenic theory of alcoholism. To some extent everyone admits to multiple and heterogeneous aetiology. The claim that these causes can include genetic influences will not convince everyone, it must be freely admitted. It is difficult to know what evidence would.

Animal models are more appropriate here than they are in schizophrenia or manic depressive psychosis, but they might nevertheless be thought to have only limited relevance to drinking problems in man. Human pharmacogenetics may provide more promise for the future than agreed conclusions about the causes of alcohol addiction. But despite their limitations, these methods are used for their strong points, and Littleton's paper in the present volume has indicated some of them. The high alcoholism rates among second-degree relatives in some studies seem to point to the importance of the social environment rather than that of the genes, though adoption studies do not support this view. Reich's analysis, however, indicates that social factors have much to do with the sex difference in alcoholism.

Contrary to what might have been expected, the presence of an alcoholic parent in the home, whatever problems this creates, does not seem to be a specific cause of alcoholism − or if it is, one would have to argue that it also has the effect of driving some of the children to teetotalism. The increased risk for the sib of an alcoholic when the father is affected may then be largely genetic in origin.

People take to drink for different reasons. Perhaps some do so on the basis of a schizoid or endogenous depressive constitution; and Kaij has suggested that organic deterioration can sometimes be a cause rather than a consequence of heavy drinking. There is a disagreement about the closeness of the relation between alcoholism and the endogenous affective disorders generally. Probably alcohol problems rest more often on personality disorders, neurotic or psychopathic, than on a psychotic or borderline psychotic basis. There is growing evidence for a genetic contribution to personality and its disorders from various other twin studies and from adoption studies on criminality (Hutchings and Mednick, 1974) and psychopathy (Schulsinger, 1972). However, there is no agreed evidence that one particular type of deviant personality is more predisposed to addiction than another.

From the specific twin studies on alcohol consumption there is agreement that the amount drunk is influenced to some extent by genetic factors, but there are inconsistent findings concerning chronic alcoholism where pharmacogenetic and family studies might have led one to expect genetic factors to play the biggest part. The older Swedish studies by Åmark and Kaij which suggested this were good ones. They involved extensive interviewing, and the authors had access to the register of abusers of alcohol; and there is further support from the new Danish adoption studies.

It may seem somewhat paradoxical that the adoption studies, by failing to show the importance of the seemingly most likely environmental causes, have confirmed the probable role of genetic factors, while it is the twin studies that have highlighted the varied, multiple and chancy environmental causes of drinking problems −

causes which can arise at different stages of life. If one were to rely on the Maudsley twin study alone, one might be inclined to take a view about alcoholism similar to that taken by Slater (1961) about the genetics of 'hysteria' — that it is a symptom without genetic basis that can occur in a variety of disorders. But on balance recent developments suggest that the genetic investigation of alcoholism has become more encouraging than when it was looked at by Slater and Cowie five years ago. Probably genetic factors of different kinds are involved, including some biological influences on the metabolism of ethanol, as well as the more indirect influences on personality mentioned earlier. The pharmacogenetic approach and the recent adoption studies therefore lead one to hope that in the next few years work on genetic lines will lead to further understanding of alcoholism and why one man's drink is another man's poison.

Summary

Animal work, pharmacogenetics, the influences of single genes, the association with other psychiatric disorders, family studies, twin studies and adoption studies: these topics have all been reviewed in relation to alcoholism. Despite many uncertainties and inconsistencies, there is growing evidence — admittedly not satisfactory to everyone — that genetic factors, some general, others perhaps relatively specific, are probably involved (along with others) in the development of alcoholism in man.

References

Åmark, C. (1951). A study in alcoholism. Acta Psychiatrica et Neurologica Scandinavica. Supplement 70.

Angst, J. (1966). Zur Ätiologie und nosologie endogener depressiver psychosen. Monographien aus dem Gesamtgebiete der Neurologie und Psychiatrie 112. Berlin: Springer-Verlag.

Arkonac, O. and Guze, S.B. (1963). A family study of hysteria. New England Journal of Medicine 268: 239-42.

Bailey, R.J., Krasner, N., Eddleston, A.L.W.F., Williams, R., Tee, D.E.H., Doniach, D., Kennedy, L.A. and Batchelor, J.R. (1976). Histocompatibility antigens, autoantibodies, and immunoglobulins, in alcoholic liver disease. British Medical Journal 2: 727-9.

Benedetti, G. (1952). Die Alkoholhalluzinosen. Stuttgart: Thieme.

Bleuler, M. (1955). Familial and personal background of chronic alcoholics. In: Etiology of Chronic Alcoholism. O Dietholm (ed.). Springfield, Ill: Thomas, pp.110-66.

Bleuler, M. (1972). Die schizophrenen Geistesstörungen im Lichte langjahriger Kranken- und Familiengeschichten. Stuttgart: Thieme.

Genetics and Alcoholism   133

British Medical Journal (1976). Editorial: an ulcer in the family. British Medical
    Journal 2: 444.
Camps, F.E. and Dodd, B.E. (1967). Increase in the incidence of non-secretors
    of ABH blood group substances among alcoholic patients. British Medical
    Journal 1: 30-1.
Camps, F.E., Dodd, B.E. and Lincoln, P.J. (1969). Frequencies of secretors and
    non-secretors of ABH group substances among 1,000 alcoholic patients.
    British Medical Journal. 4: 457.
Cantwell, D.P. (1972). Psychiatric illness in the families of hyperactive children.
    Archives of General Psychiatry. 27: 414-17.
Cruz-Coke, R. and Varela, A. (1965). Colour blindness and alcohol addiction.
    Lancet 2: 1348.
Eriksson, K. (1975). Alcohol imbibition and behaviour: a comparative genetic
    approach. In: Psychopharmacogenetics, B.E. Eleftheriou (ed.). New York:
    Plenum Publishing, pp.127-68.
Fenna, D., Schaefer, O., Mix, L. and Gilbert, J.A.L. (1971). Ethanol metabolism
    in various racial groups. Canadian Medical Association Journal. 105: 472-5.
Forsander, O. and Eriksson, K. (1974). Förekommer det etnologiska skillnader
    i alkoholens ämnesomsättningen. Alkoholpolitik 37 (cited by Eriksson, 1975).
Fremming, K.H. (1951). The expectation of mental infirmity in a sample of the
    Danish population. Eugenics Society Occasional Paper No.7. London: Cassell.
Goodwin, D.W., Schulsinger, F., Hermansen, L., Guze, S.B. and Winokur, G.
    (1973). Alcohol problems in adoptees raised apart from alcoholic biological
    parents. Archives of General Psychiatry 28: 238-43.
Goodwin, D.W., Schulsinger, F., Hermansen, L., Guze, S.B. and Winokur, G.
    (1975). Alcoholism and the hyperactive child syndrome. Journal of Nervous
    and Mental Disease 160: 349-53.
Goodwin, D.W., Schulsinger, F., Møller, N., Hermansen, L., Winokur, G. and
    Guze, S.B. (1974). Drinking problems in adopted and non-adopted sons of
    alcoholics. Archives of General Psychiatry. 31: 164-9.
Gottesman, I.I. and Shields, J. (1972). Schizophrenia and Genetics: A Twin
    Study Vantage Point. New York: Academic Press.
Hutchings, B. and Mednick, S.A. (1974). Registered criminality in the adoptive
    and biological parents of registered male adoptees. In: Genetics, Environment
    and Psychopathology, S.A. Mednick, F. Schulsinger, J. Higgins and B. Bell
    (eds.). Amsterdam, Oxford, North Holland, New York: American Elsevier,
    pp.215-27.
Jonsson, E. and Nilsson, T. (1968). Alkoholkonsumtion hos monozygota och
    dizygota tvillingpar. Nordisk Hygienisk Tidskrift. 49: 21-5.
Kaij, L. (1960). Alcoholism in Twins. Stockholm: Almqvist and Wiksell.
Kaij, L. and Dock, J. (1975). Grandsons of alcoholics. Archives of General
    Psychiatry. 32: 1379-81.
Lieber, C.S. (1972). Metabolism of ethanol and alcoholism: racial and acquired
    factors. Annals of Internal Medicine. 76: 326-7.
Lindelius, R. (ed.) (1970). A study of schizophrenia. Acta Psychiatrica
    Scandinavica. Supplement 216.
Mednick, S.A., Schulsinger, F., Higgins, J. and Bell, B. (eds.) (1974). Genetics,
    Environment and Psychopathology. Amsterdam, Oxford, North Holland,
    New York: American Elsevier.
Morrison, J.R. and Stewart, M.A. (1971). A family study of the hyperactive
    child syndrome. Biological Psychiatry. 3: 189-95.
Omenn, G.S. (1975). Alcoholism, a pharmacogenetic disorder. In: Genetics and
    Psychopharmacology. J. Mendlewicz (ed.). Basel, New York: Karger, pp.12-22.
Partanen, J., Bruun, K. and Markkanen, T. (1966). Inheritance of Drinking

134   *Alcoholism: New Knowledge and New Responses*

Behaviour. Helsinki: The Finnish Foundation for Alcohol Studies.
Race, R.R. and Sanger, R. (1975). Blood Groups in Man. 6th ed. Oxford: Blackwell.
Reich, T., Winokur, G. and Mullaney, J. (1975a). The transmission of alcohol. In: Genetics Research in Psychiatry, R.R. Fieve, D. Rosenthal and H. Brill (eds.). Baltimore and London: John Hopkins University Press, pp.259-71.
Reich, T., Cloninger, C.R. and Guze, S.B. (1975b). The multifactorial model of disease transmission: I. Description of the model and its use in psychiatry. British Journal of Psychiatry. 127: 1-10.
Reid, N.C.R.W., Brunt, P.W., Bias, W.B., Maddrey, W.C., Alonso, B.A. and Iber, F.L. (1968). Genetic characteristics and cirrhosis: a controlled study of 200 patients. British Medical Journal. 2: 463-65.
Roe, A. (1944). The adult adjustment of children of alcoholic parents raised in foster-homes. Quarterly Journal of Studies on Alcohol. 5: 378-93.
Roe, A. Burks, B.S. and Mittelmann, B. (1945). Adult adjustment of foster-children of alcoholic and psychotic parentage and the influence of the foster-home. Memoirs of the Section on Alcohol Studies, Yale University, No.3. Quarterly Journal of Studies on Alcohol, New Haven.
Rosenthal, D. and Kety, S.S. (eds.) (1968). The Transmission of Schizophrenia, Oxford: Pergamon.
Schuckit, M.A., Goodwin, D.A. and Winokur, G. (1972). A study of alcoholism in half-siblings. American Journal of Psychiatry. 128: 1132-36.
Schulsinger, F. (1972). Psychopathy: heredity and environment. International Journal of Mental Health. 1: 190-206.
Scott, D.F. (1967). Alcoholic hallucinosis – an aetiological study. British Journal of Addiction. 62: 113-25.
Shields, J. (1962). Monozygotic Twins Brought up Apart and Brought up Together. London: Oxford University Press.
Shields, J. (1975). Some recent developments in psychiatric genetics. Archiv für Psychiatrie und Nervenkrankheiten. 220: 347-60.
Slater, E. (1938). Zur Erbpathologie des manisch-depressiven Irreseins. Die Eltern und Kinder von Manisch-Depressiven. Zeitschrift für die gesamte Neurologie und Psychiatrie. 163: 1-47.
Slater, E. (1961). The thirty-fifth Maudsley lecture: 'Hysteria 311'. Journal of Mental Science. 107: 359-81.
Slater, E. and Cowie, V. (1971). The Genetics of Mental Disorders. London: Oxford University Press.
Smith, J.W. (1972). Color vision in alcoholics. Annals of the New York Academy of Sciences. 197: 143-7.
Stamatoyannopoulos, G., Chen, S.-H and Fukui. M. (1975). Liver alcohol dehydrogenase in Japanese: High population frequency of atypical form and its possible role in alcohol sensitivity. American Journal of Human Genetics. 27: 789-96.
Stenstedt, A. (1952). A study in manic depressive psychosis: clinical, social and genetic investigations. Acta Psychiatrica et Neurologica Scandinavica. Supplement 79.
Stephens, D.A., Atkinson, M.W., Kay, D.W.K., Roth, M. and Garside, R.F. (1975). Psychiatric morbidity in parents and sibs of schizophrenics and non-schizophrenics. British Journal of Psychiatry. 127: 97-108.
Swinson, R.P. and Madden, J.S. (1973). ABO blood groups and ABH substance secretion in alcoholics. Quarterly Journal of Studies in Alcohol. 34: 64-70.
Vesell, E.S. (1972). Ethanol metabolism: regulation by genetic factors in normal volunteers under a controlled environment and the effect of chronic ethanol administration. Annals of New York Academy of Science. 197: 79-88.

Winokur, G., Reich, T., Rimmer, J. and Pitts, F.N., Jnr. (1970). Alcoholism. III. Diagnosis and familial psychiatric illness in 259 alcoholic probands. Archives of General Psychiatry. 23: 104-11.

Winokur, G., Rimmer, J. and Reich, T. (1971). Alcoholism. IV. Is there more than one type of alcoholism? British Journal of Psychiatry. 118: 525-31.

Winokur, G. (1974). The division of depressive illness into depression spectrum disease and pure depressive disease. International Pharmacopsychiatry. 9: 5-13.

Wolff, P.H. (1973). Vasomotor sensitivity to alcohol in diverse mongoloid populations. American Journal of Human Genetics. 25: 193-9.

9 THE ALCOHOL DEPENDENCE SYNDROME: USEFULNESS OF AN IDEA

Griffith Edwards

One of the major advances in alcohol studies over recent years has been concerned with analysis of alcohol consumption statistics. The original work was by Ledermann (1956). A chapter in this volume, by Schmidt, touches on some of the central issues, and there have been a number of other recent reviews (Bruun *et al.*, 1975; de Lint, 1976; Sulkunen, 1976). One of the conclusions is that, empirically the alcohol consumption distribution of a population is unimodal, rather than bimodal. The inference is that 'alcoholics' are not a species standing on their own, but a segment of the population defined only by a cutting point on a continuum. The concept of alcoholism as an entity seems therefore to take a knock (de Lint, 1971).

The idea that alcoholism is a discrete entity has also been undermined by a second major line of advance — the survey investigation of population drinking practices. What in this instance has emerged is that many people who are in trouble with their drinking, if interviewed some time later are no longer experiencing this type of trouble (Room, 1975; Clark, 1976). People move in and out of troubled drinking. The sociological view also emphasises that what counts as trouble depends on the eye of the beholder and the arbitrariness of definition. It can be argued that troubled drinking behaviour does not reside in the individual but results from the interaction between the individual and his environment (Clark, 1975): change the job, find new friends, grow a little older, ameliorate the marital interaction, and the trouble may fade away.

Yet a third line of research which has undermined old certainties is in the literature on 'return to normal drinking'. Davies (1962) challenged the accepted wisdom and showed that a not insignificant proportion of patients who had been diagnosed as suffering from alcoholism, returned to controlled drinking. This area of research has recently been reviewed by Litman (1977), and the idea 'once an alcoholic, always an alcoholic' no longer appears to hold. Follow-up studies where abstinence has been the goal, treatment studies which take controlled drinking rather than abstinence as the goal, experimental ward investigations which show that the alcoholic's drinking is highly amenable to the influence of environmental cues, all point in the same direction.

In the face of such a seeming mass of evidence coming from at least three directions, to retain the notion of a specific syndrome of alcohol dependence might seem obdurate. The evidence need not however be read as conflicting in any way with the idea of a syndrome, as it will be developed here. This chapter will explore the usefulness of that idea for clinical practice and for research, and in the final section consideration will directly be given to how the seemingly conflicting evidences and views may be reconciled. It must though be heavily emphasised that an idea is being explored rather than a fixed position taken. The available evidence simply does not allow dogmatism.

The Syndrome: Assumptions

The Meaning to be Given to the Word 'Syndrome'

By *syndrome* is meant an observable coincidence of phenomena. Not all the phenomena need always be present, or present in the same degree. A syndrome is a clinical and intuitive cluster. No assumptions need be made at the empirical stage as to the causal nexus, as to why these phenomena cluster in such fashion, as to 'the pathology'. The obvious challenge however is to get beyond the stage of observation to that of explanation.

Whether a *syndrome* is a *disease,* is largely semantic. The position that is taken here is that the validation of a syndrome rests only on empirical observation, while the decision as to whether that syndrome is a disease rests either on further elucidation of the pathological mechanisms involved, or alternatively on a decision which is culturally and politically determined, or on both (Edwards, 1970).

The Syndrome of Alcohol Dependence is not All-or-none

This statement is seen as being of crucial importance. We are not dealing with a monolithic entity where the question is whether 'it' is absolutely there, or absolutely not there. The position which is being taken is different from the traditional clinical approach which invites only the question whether a patient has or has not crossed a vital borderline — whether his condition is that of a 'problem drinker', or whether he has progressed to 'alcoholism'. If dependence is translated into psychological terms and seen as a drive state, the syndrome is a set of markers which allows identification of heightened drive state; familiarity with the possible variation in the intensity of the elements in the syndrome allows identification of degrees of heightened drive state. The idea of gradation has traditionally found some expression in the idea of phases of alcoholism (Jellinek, 1946), although that term seems to confuse the notion of career or socially determined secondary consequences, with that of the march of a pathological process.

In any culture where alcohol is an accepted recreational drug, dependence on alcohol is in a statistical sense a normal condition – most people will have some degree of drive toward seeking alcohol actuated by a variety of external or internal cues. The graph which would result if distribution of drive state were charted out for a population is conjectural, but it seems possible that toward the right end there would be a long low upper tail, representing the zone where people manifesting the dependence syndrome would be found. The syndrome implies not only a statistically abnormal degree of dependence, but the existence of abnormal drinking cues (drinking to relieve or avoid withdrawal symptoms): the intensity of those cues again is not all-or-none.

The Syndrome is Best Conceived as a Psycho-Physiological Disorder

Traditionally a distinction has been made between psychological (or psychic) dependence and physical dependence (Eddy *et al.*, 1965). Inherent in what has been said above is the idea that psychological dependence on alcohol is no more an inevitable abnormality than dependence on 'motor-cars, smart clothes, antiques, animals, people, sport, hobbies, work, clubs, gardening, playing cards, gambling, music, television, sweet foods, books, newspapers, trees and open spaces, holidays, political and religious activities' (Russell, 1976). Physiological dependence as evidenced by substance-specific disturbances on drug withdrawal on the other hand, is an abnormal condition. The idea of the syndrome as now developed is of an abnormal degree of psychological dependence, accompanied by evidence of physiological dependence. The raised psychological dependence has probably been to an important extent generated by the learning processes resulting from repeated relief or avoidance of withdrawal symptoms by further drinking (Wikler, 1961). The old dichotomy between psychological and physical dependence still has some usefulness (although to employ the same word in two senses invites confusion). So far as the dependence syndrome is concerned, what one observes is however best described as a *psycho-physiological disorder*, and understanding of the condition would be hampered by adherence to the old compartmentalisation.

The Syndrome is Always Environmentally and Personally Coloured

The syndrome may look different in France and in Utah. In France there is no necessity to hide the bottle, and alcohol is so readily accepted as a beverage that anyone who wants to drink more than his friends in the café, simply does so. His compulsion need not be a crippling social disability, nor bring with it the stigma of social disgrace. He has a cheap brandy on the way to work, and the café serves liquor at the appropriate hour. In Jellinek's terms he is a delta alcoholic, and shows 'inability to abstain' (Jellinek, 1960). Transfer that same man to a state in the USA where the sentiment is predominantly dry, and the environment will set him different problems if he continues to drink. He must then be ashamed of his drinking, he will have to impoverish his family to maintain his consumption, he will not be able to schedule his drinking so easily in terms of a regularly controlled habit – very easily his drinking will take on the colouring of 'loss of control', so that in Jellinek's terms he is then a gamma alcoholic. If pressures are such that he can only drink intermittently, he would be designated an epsilon alcoholic. Equally, social class within one country may be as potent an influence on drinking as differences across borders (Edwards *et al.,* 1972).

But with the cultural determinants, personal determinants also interact. The man who is uncontrolled in many of his dealings may be likely, if he develops the syndrome, to be true to his propensities. In Anglo-Saxon literature the 'psychopathic' alcoholic is a familiar stereotype (Williams, 1967): the patient who has poor impulse control, is likely to drink in a peaky and uncontrolled manner. On the other hand, the person who has a well integrated personality and who is generally responsive to social controls, is likely to do his best to avoid rubbing up society the wrong way when he becomes highly alcohol dependent. Different people when highly dependent may still also be seeking different experiences from alcohol, and the person who continues to look for euphoria as opposed simply to avoiding withdrawal, may drink in what appears to be an uncontrolled fashion, although his style is in fact purposive: some data on patterns of heroin use are relevant here (McAuliffe and Gordon, 1974).

What is being argued is that rather than promulgating a series of *species* of alcoholism as was inherent in Jellinek's formulation, we should recognise the one core syndrome and then look at the many different ways in which *pathoplastic* factors (Edwards, 1974), will shape and colour the presentation of this syndrome. This position is not merely academic, but bears directly on the daily business of the clinic. We need to see not 'cases' of alcohol dependence, but people whose experience can only be comprehended if we make the attempt to understand their environment and their being. This is more demanding than tidying the matter up in terms of reified sub-species, but a better investment.

Degrees of Alcohol Dependence, and Alcohol-Related Disabilities, Must be Distinguished

The much quoted WHO (1952) definition of alcoholism reads as follows:

> Alcoholics are those excessive drinkers whose dependence on alcohol has attained such a degree that it shows a noticeable mental disturbance or interference with their bodily or mental health, their interpersonal relations and their smooth social and economic functioning, or who show the prodromal signs of such development.

Over a number of years this definition served a purpose, not least by sharpening debate and inviting disagreement (Seeley, 1959; Keller, 1962).

A fundamental criticism of this definition however is that it confuses the notions of *dependence*, with that of *disability*. It is possible for a person to be in some degree dependent on alcohol while having sustained no interference with physical or mental health, or social or economic function. Similarly, it is eminently possible for a drinker to be in no way abnormally dependent on alcohol, but to have sustained major disabilities in several dimensions of his life. Benjamin, for instance, in a chapter in this volume, draws attention to the fact that alcohol related pancreatitis (a serious disability by any reckoning), may often result from a casual binge rather than from sustained drinking.

An attempt to separate out the co-varying happenings of *dependence* on the one hand, and *disability* on the other (often related, but not necessarily very closely), is therefore due. A recent report by a WHO scientific group (Edwards *et al.*, 1976), has proposed that (i) the dependence syndrome should be defined in terms of psycho-physiological dimensions which are not confused with the secondary consequences of dependence, and (ii) *alcohol-related disabilities* should be separately identified. It is accepted that around the individual's dependence syndrome, a clustering of alcohol-related disabilities will then usually be recognisable.

But disabilities can exist without the syndrome, and there must not be too exclusive focus of social concern on the drinker who has developed the syndrome. In many countries the dependence syndrome (or 'the disease of alcoholism') is in fact the predominant official concern. Perhaps a medical dominance in the right to define what counts as a problem, rather than a true reading of the nature and extent of damages, weights this emphasis in the USA and Britain. In other countries, such as France, the traditional concern is more with the relationship between quantities drunk and probability of stated disabilities being incurred (Péquignot, 1976). National habits and sensitivities deserve to be respected and often have functional value in particular national settings, but it is to be hoped that an approach which allows the importance both of dependence and of disabilities can invite and allow a greater openness of international understanding. Perhaps the entrenchment of different professional disciplines causes similar problems – the physician and the sociologist certainly need to cultivate a generous curiosity as to the nature of each other's realities in alcohol studies.

The Syndrome is Provisional

There is a research background which can be drawn on in considering aspects of this proposed syndrome. There are, for instance, many detailed descriptions of biological aspects of the withdrawal state, and there has been important work on behavioural aspects of dependent drinking: here the state of the art is well represented in two recent symposia proceedings (Gross, 1973; 1975). The bulk of exact information relates largely to observations made in experimental settings, which as usual have all the advantages of precision and control, but attendant limitations. Relatively little work seems to have been done on the phenomenology of abnormal drinking, as that behaviour actually takes place over time, and in the natural social settings. A series of papers have applied multivariate techniques to pools of information gained from patients' reports of symptomatology (Horn and Wanberg, 1969; Wanberg and Horn, 1970; Horn and Wanberg, 1970). Hershon (1977) has attempted to design sophisticated methods of obtaining data from patients, and has related dependence symptoms to drinking patterns.

For the present, clinical delineation of the dependence syndrome can certainly be aided by this background research literature, but to an extent the working model of this syndrome which the clinician is likely to find most useful is based on a synthesis of clinical experience – an attempt to sort out and put together what patients say, enlightened by research, but with many gaps and uncertainties in the scientific underpinning. What can be put forward is only a partly informed series of conjectures, but conjecture has its purpose if stated in sufficiently precise terms to allow testing and refutation.

The Recognition of the Syndrome

What then are the constituents of this proposed syndrome? The idea of a syndrome is for the clinician a working tool, but it is only of use to him if the description offered is commonsensical, and easily related to practice. A fairly detailed description of this syndrome with clinical amplification of the terms used, has been given by Edwards and Gross (1976), and by Edwards *et al.* (1976). No attempt will be made here to repeat those accounts in full, but the core elements will be described. Without labouring the point under each sub-heading, it should be assumed that every element of the syndrome may exist in degrees. The ordering of the elements as given below does not imply a temporal sequence of development.

Narrowing of drinking repertoire. As the individual moves progressively toward greater dependence, so his repertoire of drinking patterns (at first perhaps broadened), become increasingly narrowed. He tends to schedule his drinking in much the same way, day in and day out — weekends, for instance, no longer mean a variation in intake. For the practical business of taking the clinical history, it is essential to cultivate the skill of sympathetically eliciting from patients a live and detailed account of the way in which they are scheduling their drinking, and its variation. A clinical note such as 'usually drinks bottle of spirits-day' misses out vital information — *how* usually?

Salience of drink-seeking behaviour. An indirect means of gauging the degree of *drive* to drink, is the importance the individual attaches to satisfying this drive as gauged by its salience over other behaviours — the seeming disregard for adverse consequences, the neglect of responsibilities, the surrender of values and so on. Interpretation can of course only be made in the light of some awareness of the individual's personality and social responsiveness before his adjustment to life became overlaid with the drinking.

Increased tolerance to alcohol. Due largely to CNS tolerance to the effects of alcohol, the individual can drink large quantities without obviously getting drunk. Tolerance is of great importance to understanding the underlying psychophysiological processes of dependence, but as a practical clinical pointer it has its limitations. The way people behave when intoxicated is related to personality, and very much to cultural expectation (MacAndrew and Edgerton, 1969), more often perhaps than to degree of tolerance. Tolerance certainly can decline in later stages of the syndrome — the person 'gets easily drunk' — and this is a happening which may be very alarming for the patient concerned.

Repeated withdrawal symptoms. Alcohol withdrawal symptoms are typically experienced on waking, but with the highly dependent person careful questioning may reveal that he experiences sub-acute withdrawal during the day, or indeed wakes during the night disturbed by withdrawal symptoms. The range of possible symptoms is wide, and clinically the fact has to be borne in mind that none are specific to alcohol withdrawal — it is their appearance within the context of the syndrome's total picture which gives them meaning. Withdrawal symptoms which are clinically of particular use in gauging presence and degree of the syndrome include:

1. Affective disturbance. The patient will often find his own phrasing to describe the personal reality of this experience — 'frightened, ready to jump out of my skin, afraid of a knock on the door', 'like suicide', 'unable to face anything'; or at another extreme perhaps only 'tensed up, a bit of butterflies in the stomach'.

2. Tremor. Skilled clinical questioning may reveal the patient's awareness of some degree of tremulousness at a stage far short of 'the shakes'.

3. Nausea and retching. This is again a clinically useful diagnostic symptom within its context, despite its non-specificity. The patient may describe the experience as 'dry heaves' and there appears to be an element of pharyngeal hypersensitivity — an attempt to clean the teeth or just one gulp of a drink will immediately precipitate retching.

4. Sweating, and specially paroxysmal night sweating, is again a symptom which is often waiting to be elicited.

For working diagnostic purposes these non-specific and graded symptoms are usually of greater practical help than more dramatic and low frequency events, such as withdrawal fits or delirium tremens. The gradedness is in terms both of frequency and intensity of occurrence.

Relief-avoidance of withdrawal. The patient reports that he drinks with the *intention* of relieving withdrawal, and that the relief afforded is complete or near complete typically within thirty to forty-five minutes. He may also be aware that he is 'topping himself up' during the day so as to avoid withdrawal, or abort slight warning symptoms.

Subjective awareness of compulsion to drink. The compulsion which is here being talked about is often a worryingly real personal experience, though like so many important subjective experiences, difficult to phrase objectively. The patient may be ruminating on drinking in a manner more closely akin to obsessive experience than has been recognised – he may even have hit upon strategies of thought blocking. Premature introduction into the history-taking of orthodox terms such as craving or drink-centredness, or 'loss of control', may preclude the patient finding his own vivid and personally meaningful expression or anecdote. *Impairment of control* may though be an important experience – the patient knows that after a certain priming quantity of drink, he will strongly desire to go on drinking.

Reinstatement after abstinence. The patient with this syndrome who has been abstinent for seven to ten days will usually be experiencing no withdrawal symptoms (the possibility of a *chronic* withdrawal syndrome of different nature is beginning to receive attention). If however he drinks again beyond a certain threshold of frequency and quantity, the syndrome is likely to be reinstated. The rapidity of reinstatement seems often to be clinically related to the severity of the syndrome as independently judged by all the previous criteria.

Is There a Short-Cut to Diagnosis?

In this section seven constituents of the syndrome have been listed. To explore the patient's history under each of these headings in full detail is obviously time-consuming, but such detailed assessment might be seen as a necessary responsibility for the psychiatric team, as would be the full diagnostic work-up of any other complex condition. Is there however any abbreviated approach which could be used for screening, and be of special use perhaps to the general physician or the surgeon who will want to know how to recognise the condition? To give a confident answer to this question would be premature, and the development of a competent screening instrument would be a worthwhile technical task. But hazarding a guess, one might suspect that questioning on the following core triad would often be sufficient to make an initial diagnosis with some confidence:

1. The patient recognises that he is experiencing repeated alcohol withdrawal symptoms of any degree.

2. He recognises that he will on occasion or frequently, drink with the specific *purpose* of relieving these symptoms.

3. He recognises that such drinking will effectively and reliably provide relief within the expected short period.

Intelligent interpretation of the answers to these three questions should also provide some preliminary indication of *degree* of the syndrome's development.

The use of these three questions certainly cannot be a substitute for the fuller history, and that these questions constitute only a rough and ready approach to screening needs to be stressed. The choice of this particular set of questions might be mistaken for an overemphasis on the physical aspects of dependence, at the cost of psychological and social elements. Speculatively, these questions may have precision in their ability to elicit the evidence for the repeated *trials* in an operant learning process (drinking to relieve withdrawal), which may underly acquisition of the abnormal drive state.

The Clinical Usefulness of the Idea

A Shared Model of Understanding for Different Treatment Professions

Successful communication between referring agents and between different members of any treatment team can substantially contribute to the efficacy with which the needs of patients will be met — if terms are being used ambiguously and with the nature of their meaning so arcane that definition becomes the property only of the super-specialist, patients are likely to suffer in many ways. Some of these problems have been examined recently by Robinson (1976), and it seems probable that terms such as 'alcoholism' and 'alcoholic' are by now so lacking in precision as only to be passports to confusion.

The idea of the dependence syndrome might usefully remedy this confusion. Properly taught and explained (and there is a great backlog

of professional teaching to be done), different professions might here
find a rational basis for communication. Fully understood in its
implications, the idea might be expected to help forge understanding
between medical members of a treatment team and non-medical
members (such as the social worker or clinical psychologist), who may
be suspicious of the expansionism of medical explanation of human
problems, and the tendency to accord biological realities greater
precedence than psychological and social realities (despite denials). The
idea of the syndrome seeks to segment a psycho-physiological disorder
which is coloured by a host of psychological and socio-cultural factors
and only understood within those contexts; it is 'contracted' within
those contexts, and is lived with, and informally and formally reacted
to, only within those contexts. Furthermore with differentiation
between the syndrome and alcohol-related disabilities, the whole range
of those disabilities remains open to the widest contexts of
understanding. To give importance to the idea of the dependence
syndrome is not therefore to set up a monopoly of biological
understanding of abnormal drinking, or to foster a monolithic notion
of 'alcoholism' as a 'disease entity'.

A Shared Model of Understanding Between Clinician and Patient
On the basis of a community survey, Cartwright *et al.* (1975) have
gathered information on the way ordinary people at present handle
concepts of abnormal drinking, and it is clear that although there is
widespread token acceptance of 'alcoholism as a disease', there is at
the same time little depth of understanding as to what is meant by
this phrase. There is no functionally useful concept of alcoholism
latent within our society which can be called on, as available coinage
of understanding, when a patient and clinician encounter one another.
This is the point made so clearly by Rathod in his chapter in this book.
At each first-time encounter the coinage for mutual understanding is
therefore going to have to be minted.

The idea of the dependence syndrome may functionally serve this
purpose. The patient is not of course confronted with the bald
diagnostic statement, but first himself shares in the process of
constructing the detailed picture which moves toward the diagnosis.
The therapist can say 'what you have now told me, what we have
explored together seems to be this. . .', and the information can be
summarised and arrayed under the headings of the syndrome's
dimensions. With the facts agreed, the therapist must then sensitively
seek to give these facts their coherent meaning — 'I think these facts

add up to the picture of your having become *abnormally dependent* on alcohol, and we need to look at what those words mean. . .the implications for your health and for what you may now want to do.' The patient can see the therapist as having listened to him and as having engaged in a rational process of diagnosis with the reasoning explained. All this is very different from the sudden imposition by medical fiat of an arbitrary label, possibly fully understood in its implications by neither party (Edwards, 1968).

None of these communicative advantages follow automatically: this idea as any other is capable of being carelessly used, imposed and degraded in its meaning. But inherently it probably enshrines a sufficiently simple and explicit way of looking at things to be translated into common language, so as usefully to serve the brokerage of understanding which is the beginning of therapy.

A Basis for Negotiating Treatment Goals for Drinking

Questions relating to treatment goals have recently been reviewed at length by Pattison (1976). Treatment goals cannot be imposed on an unwilling patient. If however the goal is one which appears realistic to that patient himself, which can be seen as rationally related to the diagnosis rather than as punitive or controlling, which has in short been sensitively negotiated rather than abruptly announced, then that goal has some chance of being attained. The idea of dependence as a syndrome with graded intensities may guide the choice of goal in the following manner:

1. *If the syndrome is severe* as judged by the whole picture, then it is reasonable to tell the patient that his chances of returning to social drinking are slender (Orford and Edwards, 1977), unless he is receiving a treatment specially designed for 'unlearning' the dependence. His own experience of repeated failure to control his drinking will probably recommend the abstinence goal as one which makes sense — unless special behavioural treatments are being employed.

2. *If the syndrome is only minimally developed,* the patient giving for instance a history still of some variations in drinking pattern but occasional recent experience of mild but definite withdrawal symptoms, an occasional consequent eagerness for a drink at midday though retaining ability to postpone the first drink to an orthodox hour, and a report also that for periods of weeks he drinks

in a controlled fashion, then the likelihood of his attaining a social
drinking rather than an abstinence goal should be considered as very
possible. The question remains negotiable in the light of the patient's
progress. The loose and over-inclusive use of 'alcoholism' as a
diagnostic term might though result in abstinence being proposed
as the goal without proper discrimination between this type of case,
and one of greater syndrome severity. Diagnosis will be particularly
blurred if dependence and disabilities are confused, for the patient
with relatively mild psycho-physiological dependence may still have
lost his driving licence, broken his marriage or suffered from
pancreatitis.

3. *Intermediate degrees of the syndrome.* When the patient's condition
is not obviously of the syndrome's development towards one or
other extreme of severity (the large middle ground), the goal which
is to be set presents more difficulties. If negotiation rather than
imposition is to be the rule, in the light of all the limitations of
present knowledge, the clinician may believe that a conservative
approach is generally the most responsible, and that abstinence is
still normally the safest choice of goal.

To sum up the question of drinking goal choice, one might speculate
that the person who has not moved at all far to the right along the
curve of dependence severity and has evidence for the syndrome in
minimal degree, has a condition which is potentially threatening but
which can certainly regress: the person in the middle band is in a
dangerous position and quite likely to move further to the right unless
he stops drinking; while the person at the right hand end of the
distribution of dependence and with severe syndrome development,
has minimal chances of naturally moving to the left again, or of doing
so with the help of only routine treatments which do not aim to
dismantle the learning process.

*A Basis for Choosing an Appropriate Treatment Strategy for the
Drinking*

Given that the discrimination of degrees of the syndrome permits ideas
to be put forward as to what might be the attainable drinking goal for
a particular patient, it may then on the same basis be possible to discern
what treatment strategies are likely to be appropriate.

　　If the picture is of an extreme degree of dependence and thus
abstinence has been chosen as the goal, it is reasonable to do everything

to help the patient to become sober. It is then conventional to employ all orthodox strategies of psychotherapy, social adjustment and administration of deterrent drugs so as to consolidate and maintain sobriety, although the efficacy of this wide conventional approach is beginning to be questioned, and for this aspect of the treatment a more simple approach in terms of setting agreed goals and putting the demand more on the patient himself for their attainment, may often be sufficient (Edwards *et al.,* 1977; Orford and Edwards, 1977). But given that with the severe syndrome the consequence of relapse is likely to be rapid reinstatement (with all the attendant risks of super-added disabilities), it becomes obvious that any treatment strategies which either minimise the likelihood of relapse or rapidly interdict the relapse, are rationally indicated. The possibilities of designing therapies which focus specifically on relapse prevention have recently been discussed by Litman (1977), on the basis of research findings related to circumstances of relapse. It is also probable that with this severe degree of syndrome and the threats posed by likelihood of rapid reinstatement, newer developments in behavioural treatment will have a valuable place, if they can dismantle the dependence so that there is possibility of return to normal drinking. As Hodgson argues in his chapter on behavioural therapies, these methods would also be valuable if they partially treated the heightened dependence, so that the consequences of drinking would be less precipitously disastrous. Very much the same treatment consideration would apply to the intermediate spectrum of syndrome severity.

With definite but minimal evidence of the syndrome, treatment strategy has so far perhaps received too little thought. In the past it is probable that such patients have often either been inappropriately lumped in with more dependent subjects because discrimination has not been made in terms of degrees of dependence (with clinical judgement confused by degrees of disability), or such patients have simply been considered as not suitably severe cases for treatment – they have been administratively disposed of as 'problem drinkers' rather than 'real alcoholics'. They are, for instance, unlikely to fulfil the AA stereotype, or to affiliate with AA (Edwards *et al.,* 1967).

With such patients simple strategies aimed at social adjustment (a new job, amelioration of marital tensions), or psychotherapy which teaches new coping mechanisms, might be expected to lead to the syndrome regressing. There is a possibly important contrast here with the benefits of such general strategies for severe dependence, where similar approaches may be expected at best to lead to remission.

Patients with minimal syndrome development, themselves sometimes hit on strategies which are helpful — choosing a 'social drink' such as wine rather than spirits, setting themselves a definite upper limit, pacing the speed of their drinking against some other person or against the clock, not accepting drinks from friends at the bar. What is successful for them, may be the traditional recipe for disaster so far as the heavily dependent patient is concerned. Such patients are themselves hitting on informal behavioural techniques, and it might be expected that they have something to teach the behaviour therapist in terms of the design of more formal methods.

A close understanding of the subtleties of the dependence syndrome may also be clinically useful in monitoring the progress of minimally dependent patients. A distinction can then be made between regression in objective and subjective components of the syndrome. It is possible for a patient to be drinking in a manner which is overtly 'normal', whereas close questioning will reveal that his subjective relationship with alcohol is still far from normal — he wants to go on drinking, but with reluctance stops himself. Such a situation is not necessarily malign but may be very common during the first six or twelve months of a successful attempt to regain control. Intelligent monitoring of the syndrome's components should also give warning when dependence is in fact progressing, and some other goal of treatment has to be substituted.

Much that has been written in this section about the clinical usefulness of the idea of the syndrome, assumes the clinician's ability to recognise *degrees* of the syndrome's manifestations, and this is only acquired with experience — it is very much a learnt clinical skill, as say the ability to recognise the degree of a patient's depression. As with depression, there might be a possibility of developing rating scales to supplement clinical judgement.

Research Usefulness, and the Synthesis with Seemingly Contrary Evidence

In the opening section of this paper three lines of research were mentioned which, taken together, over recent years appear to have undermined the credibility of the simple notion of 'alcoholism' as a discrete and fixed entity. The three areas noted were the study of population alcohol consumption distributions, the survey evidence that drinkers move in and out of trouble experience, and the reports that clinically diagnosed alcoholics may either 'return to normal drinking' or show great malleability of drinking behaviour in response to experimental manipulation of cues or rewards.

Progress might however be made if rather than interpreting all this evidence as material opposed to the idea of a dependence syndrome, as *contrary evidence* which must be argued against by anyone who would seek to defend the validity of the syndrome idea, an attempt were made at synthesis of what are not necessarily to be taken as conflicting data.

Alcohol Consumption Distribution

The challenge here is to understand how the idea of the syndrome can be integrated with the evidence that consumption distribution is unimodal, rather than with a second small peak to the right.

Under this heading the first issue that should be confronted is whether the claimed evidence for unimodal distribution is convincing. To tackle this point adequately would require a detailed critique of the primary data sources on which the claim for unimodal distribution has been based. For present purposes it might simply be noted that any presumption that unimodality can be firmly established other than by large sample studies with very reliable data, is over-bold. And by no means all the data on which the claim rests are of unquestionable reliability. Heavier drinkers may be missing from samples because of a disproportionate likelihood of their being in prison or hospital. Where self-report is the basis, it should be remembered that there is some evidence that under-reporting may be greater among heavier drinkers (Pernanen, 1974). Whether such objections are only marginal, or of greater significance, requires further study.

But the more important issue under this first heading is in fact not whether present data on distribution are sufficiently conclusive to prove unimodality, but rather whether the unimodality question as usually posed is at all relevant to the essential argument. Distribution data of the type being considered are essentially static and cross-sectional: it is a flat picture of how a population is drinking at a given point in time, or a picture of behaviour summated for a rather narrow slice of time. Such distribution curves do not indicate dynamic distribution — the extent to which over time an individual changes his drinking habits. Static data with no time dimension cannot reveal whether there is a small sub-population at the upper end of the seemingly smooth curve, characterised by through-time (dynamic) likelihood of continuing to drink very heavily (or shifting to heavier but not to lighter drinking), with different probabilities for change in behaviour at lower levels on the curve. This argument may seem rather complex: putting matters in terms of a metaphor, we might not be able to distinguish between adult dwarves and normal children by a distribution curve of heights, but if we could bring in the dimension of *change* in height over time, the fact that there were two sub-populations would become apparent. Indeed, the matters that have to be examined under the next two sub-headings each deal in their way with questions of movement over time.

Survey Evidence and Movement in and out of Trouble

Once more, both the quality of the data and the essential nature of the argument have to be considered. As regards quality of data, the degree of sophistication to be found in drinking survey work is considerable, but it is of course unsafe to conclude that *all* that seems to be 'movement in and out' is true movement, as opposed to randomness produced by imperfect measurement and in particular subjects' denial. This type of survey is once again likely to under-contact the most seriously troubled drinkers.

As for the essential nature of the argument that has in this instance to be considered, the existence of a syndrome would of course in no way dictate that all people who have drink-related disabilities must continue over time to generate such disabilities. The distinction between syndrome and disability is logically crucial: in terms of the framework of ideas which has been proposed, many (or perhaps most) people with alcohol-related problems will not be suffering from the syndrome, and their freedom to move in and out of trouble will be influenced by personal factors and social forces. When higher levels of dependence enter into the equation, the 'mobility' is likely to be constrained but not of course absolutely constrained – a highly dependent person may still to a degree ameliorate his drinking or avoid troubles. If built into survey investigation, the idea of the dependence syndrome might well prove to have power in contributing to the explanation of why the drinking problems of some subjects regress and of others continue or worsen: the total explanation must certainly be psychological and social, as well as partly in terms of the consequences of dependence and its degrees (Clark, 1976). The possibilities of synthesis seem in no way forced.

'Return to Normal Drinking'

It is again no quibble to emphasise that quality of data has to be rigorously scrutinised – even where so-called independent information has been obtained from a wife, the wife may have been threatened and frightened into giving a report which is inaccurate. This contention should not be used prejudicially to dismiss important evidence which threatens orthodox assumptions, but neither would it be proper to dismiss the methodological question itself as of no importance. And not only do the data require scrutiny, but we need to be aware of the imprecision in the fundamental concept — 'normal drinking', 'controlled drinking' and 'social drinking' are all terms which are currently used interchangeably, but often with very loose operational definition. What is striking when the case series reports are examined, is how very incompletely the clinical profiles of patients loosely described as 'alcoholics' are often reported: it is frequently impossible to tell whether the patients concerned were alcohol-dependent, and degree of dependence is certainly something which can seldom be judged on published information. No one, however, claims that all 'alcoholics' return to normal drinking: the heuristic value of the idea of the dependence syndrome is that with clinical series (exactly as with survey populations), measures of the syndrome may contribute to explanations of varied natural history.

Those experimental ward studies which show the behaviour of drinkers as susceptible to experimental influences, certainly provide material directly relevant to the development of ideas on the nature of the dependence syndrome — they force an awareness that the person with this syndrome has not become exclusively motivated by his dependence and is still at the play of many forces. What has to be explored are the reasons for variation in cue responsiveness within the experimental population — presumably the quantification of degree of dependence might again contribute.

Comments have been made here on the dangers of too uncritically accepting the evidence which comes from certain important lines of research which represent a challenge to conventional medical views. Some of these methodological problems are discussed in greater detail by Kreitman in this volume. There should be no double standards, and it should immediately be admitted that evidence bearing on the validity of the syndrome and the many hypotheses which stem from the idea, is in some instances very incomplete, and perhaps in most instances unresearched. The value of the idea is the questions it invites, and the greatest wariness needs to be exercised against any tendency prematurely to take an idea as a fact.

Acknowledgements

For extremely useful comments on a preliminary draft of this paper, my thanks are due to Dr Herbert Blumberg, Dr Richard Eiser,

Dr Ray Hodgson, Dr Gloria Litman, Mr Howard Rankin, Mr Martin Raw, Mr Nigel Rawson, Dr Michael Russell, Mr Colin Taylor and Ms Clare Wilson. The ideas developed here owe much to discussions with colleagues on the WHO group of investigators on criteria for identifying and classifying disabilities related to alcohol consumption – in particular Professor Mark Keller, Dr Milton Gross, Mrs Joy Moser and Mr Robin Room. I am grateful to Mrs Julia Polglaze for unfailingly patient secretarial assistance.

References

Bruun, K., Edwards, G., Lumio, M., Makela, K., Osterberg, E., Pan, L., Popham, R.E., Room, R., Schmidt, W., Skog, O.-J and Sulkunen, P. (1975). Alcohol Control Policies in Public Health Perspective. Publication No.25. Helsinki: Finnish Foundation for Alcohol Studies.

Cartwright, A.K.J., Shaw, S.J. and Spratley, T.A. (1975). Designing a Comprehensive Community Response to Problems of Alcohol Abuse. Report by the Maudsley Alcoholism Pilot Project to DHSS. September, 1975.

Clark, W. (1975). Conceptions of alcoholism: consequences for research. Addict. Dis. 1: 395-430.

Clark, W.B. (1976). Loss of control, heavy drinking and drinking problems in a longitudinal study. J. Stud. Alcohol. 37: 1256-90.

Davies, D.L. (1962). Normal drinking in recovered alcoholics. Quart. J. Stud. Alc. 23: 94-104.

de Lint (1971). The status of alcoholism as a disease; a brief comment. Brit. J. Addict. 66: 108-9.

de Lint (1976). Epidemiological aspects of alcoholism. Int. J. Ment. Health. 5: 29-51.

Eddy, N.B. Halbach, H., Isbell, H. and Seevers, M.H. (1965). Drug dependence: its significance and characteristics. Bull. Wld. Hlth. Org. 32: 721-33.

Edwards, G. (1968). Patients with drinking problems. Brit. Med. J. 4: 435-7.

Edwards, G. (1970). The status of alcoholism as a disease. In: Modern Trends in Drug Dependence. R. Phillipson (ed.). London: Butterworths, chap.8.

Edwards, G. (1974). Drugs, drug dependence, and the concept of plasticity. Quart. J. Stud. Alc. 35: 176-95.

Edwards, G., Chandler, J. and Hensman, C. (1972). Drinking in a London suburb. I. Correlates of normal drinking. Quart. J. Stud. Alc. Suppl. 6: 69-93.

Edwards, G. and Gross, M.M. (1976). Alcohol dependence: provisional description of a clinical syndrome. Brit. Med. J. 1: 1058-61.

Edwards, G., Gross, M.M., Keller, M. and Moser, J. (eds.) (1976). Alcohol-related problems in the disability perspective. A summary of the consensus of the WHO group of investigators on criteria for identifying and classifying disabilities related to alcohol consumption. Quart. J. Stud. Alc. 9: 1360-82.

Edwards, G., Hensman, C., Hawker, A. and Williamson, V. (1967). Alcoholics Anonymous: the anatomy of a self-help group. Social Psychiatry. 1: 195-204.

Edwards, G., Orford, J., Egert, S., Guthrie, S., Hawker, A., Hensman, C., Mitcheson, M., Oppenheimer, E. and Taylor, C. (1977). Alcoholism: a controlled trial of 'treatment' and 'advice'. J. Stud. Alc. (in press).

Gross, M.M. (ed.) (1973). Alcohol Intoxication and Withdrawal. New York: Plenum.

Gross, M.M. (ed.) (1975). Alcohol Intoxication and Withdrawal. Experimental Studies II. New York: Plenum.

Hershon, H. (1977). Withdrawal Symptoms: Clinical Study of 100 Male Alcoholics. (unpublished).

Horn, J.L. and Wanberg, K.W. (1969). Symptom patterns related to excessive use of alcohol. Quart. J. Stud. Alc. 30: 35-58.

Horn, J.L. and Wanberg, K.W. (1970). Dimensions of perception of background and current situation of alcoholic patients. Quart. J. Stud. Alc. 31: 633 -58.

Jellinek, E.M. (1946). Phases in the drinking history of alcoholics. Analysis of a survey conducted by the official organ of Alcoholics Anonymous. Quart. J. Stud. Alc. 7: 1-88.

Jellinek, E.M. (1960). The Disease Concept of Alcoholism. New Haven: Hillhouse Press.

Keller, M. (1960). The Definition of Alcoholism. Quart. J. Stud. Alc. 21: 125-34.

Lederman, S. (1956). Alcool-Alçoolisme – Alcoolisation. Donées Scientifiques de Caractére Physiologique, Économique et Social. Institut National d'Etudes Demographiques, Cahier No.29. Presses universitaires de France.

Litman, G. (1977). Once an alcoholic, always an alcoholic: a review and critique: I. Experimental studies of intoxiation and controlled drinking as a by-product of treatment. (Addiction Research Unit Paper).

Litman, G.K. (1977). Once an alcoholic, always an alcoholic: II. Controlled drinking as the goal of treatment. (Addiction Research Unit Paper).

Litman, G.K. Eiser, J.R., Rawson, N.S.B., Rawson and A.N. Oppenheim (1977). Towards a Typology of Relapse, I. (In press: Drug and Alcohol Dependence).

McAuliffe, W.E. and Gordon, R.A. (1974). A test of Lindesmith's theory of addiction: the frequency of euphoria among long-term addicts. American Journal of Sociology. 4: 795-840.

MacAndrew, C. and Edgerton, R.B. (1969). Drunken Comportment: A Social Explanation. London: Nelson.

Orford, J. and Edwards, G. (1977). Alcoholism: A Comparison of Treatment and Advice. With a Study of Influence of Marriage. Maudsley Monograph.

Pattison, E.M. (1976). Non-abstinent drinking goals in the treatment of alcoholics. In: Recent Advances in Alcohol and Drug Problems. R.J. Gibbins, Y. Israel, H. Kalant, R.E. Popham, W. Schmidt and R.G. Smart (eds.). New York: Wiley, vol.3, chap.9.

Péquignot, G.-L. (1975). Substitutuion of an objective quantitative definition of 'Excess of Alcoholization' for the symptomatic definitions of alcoholism. Paper presented at Meeting of Investigators on Criteria for Identifying and Classifying Disabilities Related to Alcohol Consumption. Geneva: WHO.

Pernanen, K. (1974). Validity of survey data on alcohol use. In: Research Advances in Alcohol and Drug Problems, vol.1. R.H. Gibbins, Y. Israel, H. Kalant, R.E. Popham, W. Schmidt and R.G. Smart (eds.). New York: Wiley.

Robinson, D. (1976). From Drinking to Alcoholism: a Sociological Commentary. London: Wiley.

Room, R. (1975). The measurement and distribution of drinking patterns and problems in general populations. Paper presented at Meeting of Investigators on Criteria for Identifying and Classifying Disabilities Related to Alcohol Consumption. Geneva: WHO

Russell, M.A.H. (1976). What is dependence? In: Drugs and Drug Dependence. G. Edwards, M.A.H. Russell, D. Hawks and M. MacCafferty (eds.). Farnborough: Saxon House, chap.17.

Seeley, J.R. (1959). The WHO definition of alcoholism. Quart. J. Stud. Alc. 20: 352-6.

Sulkunen, P. (1976). Drinking patterns and the level of alcohol consumption: an international overview. In: Research Advances in Alcohol and Drug Problems. R.J. Gibbins, Y. Israel, H. Kalant, R.E. Popham, W. Schmidt and R.G. Smart (eds.). New York: Wiley, vol.3, chap.4.

Wanberg, K.W. and Horn, J.L. (1970). Alcoholism symptom patterns of men and women: a comparative study. Quart. J. Stud. Alc. 31: 40-61.

Wikler, A. (1961). On the Nature of Addiction and Habituation. Brit. J. Addict. 57: 73-9.

Williams, L. (1967). Alcoholism Explained. London: Evans Brothers.

World Health Organisation (1952). Expert Committee on Mental Health, Alcoholism Sub-committee, Second Report. Techn. Rep. Ser., No.48. Geneva: WHO.

SECTION II. THE VARIETIES OF HARM

10 ALCOHOLIC LIVER DISEASES – BASIC PATHOLOGY AND CLINICAL VARIANTS

Roger Williams and Michael Davis

One of the penalties of long-standing alcohol abuse is the development of liver damage and there is now ample evidence that the mortality rate from cirrhosis is between seven and thirteen times higher amongst alcoholics than those who do not drink to excess (Joliffe & Jellinek, 1941; Klatskin, 1961; Tashiro & Lipscomb, 1963; Gorwitz et al., 1970; Schmidt & de Lint, 1972; Schuckit & Gunderson, 1974; Gabriel, 1935; Nicholls et al., 1974). Epidemiological surveys from all over the world (Konar, 1957; Banerjera & Dasadhikary, 1963; Mukerjee et al., 1972; Aikat et al., 1974; Gigglberger, 1959; Gigglberger, 1968; Piesbergen & Jungermann, 1966; Lindner, 1975) have demonstrated that the average per capita consumption of alcohol in a population bears a direct relationship to the number of deaths from cirrhosis, and the striking fall in the cirrhosis mortality observed during the prohibition period in the United States (Martini & Bode, 1970) and also in association with war-enforced wine rationing in Paris (Péquignot, 1974), provided further evidence of a causal relationship between alcohol and chronic liver disease.

There is also convincing evidence from population studies that individuals with a high occupational exposure to alcohol are particularly prone to hepatic damage (Terris, 1967; de Lint & Schmidt, 1971). In a study of Austrian brewery workers who received a free daily allowance of four litres of beer (about 140g of alcohol), clinical and biochemical evidence of hepatic dysfunction was found in 26 per cent, an incidence nearly three times higher than in a group of workers from a nearby factory where free alcohol was not provided (Frank et al., 1967). In another survey of company employees in the USA the incidence of cirrhosis amongst those classified as problem drinkers was over twenty-eight times higher than in non-drinkers (Pell & D'Alonzo, 1968). In these latter studies most of the individuals were gainfully employed, emphasising the further important point that the development of severe alcoholic liver disease is not restricted to the socially incapacitated alcoholic.

In most parts of the world there has been a steady increase in the consumption of alcohol over the years and in parallel with this the importance of cirrhosis as a cause of death has also increased. This correlation was particularly well shown in the Canadian province of Ontario (Rankin *et al.*, 1975) where the average per capita consumption of alcohol rose from 1.77 litres in 1933 to 8.91 litres in 1967 (Figure 1). In association with this the cirrhosis mortality increased by nearly 350 per cent. In Great Britain national statistics have also documented a steady increase in the quantity of alcohol drunk over the past twenty years, and in particular over the last decade, and this has been paralleled by a rise in the incidence of alcoholic cirrhosis. A survey from Birmingham covering the years 1964-9 (Stone *et al.*, 1968) showed that 51 per cent of cases of cirrhosis were attributed to heavy drinking in contrast to 33 per cent for the period 1959-64 (Jain *et al.*, 1973), and in a more recent study from South London the proportion of alcoholics amongst cirrhotics had risen still further to 65 per cent (Hodgson & Thompson, 1976).

Patterns of Alcoholic Liver Injury

The toxic effects of alcohol on the liver can be broadly divided into three main types — fatty infiltration, alcoholic hepatitis and cirrhosis.

Fatty infiltration of the liver is the earliest lesion which can be detected and probably results from interference by alcohol with hepatic triglyceride metabolism (see chapter 11). Experimental studies have shown that fatty liver can develop in normal volunteers fed non-inebriating quantities of alcohol for a week or more (Lieber, 1967). Histologically large fat vacuoles are seen within hepatocytes, initially in the centrilobular area but involving the entire liver lobule in advanced cases. Rupture of liver cells can occur with coalescence to form fat cysts, and these may excite an inflammatory reaction leading to lipogranulomata. In some cases hepatic fibrosis is seen in association with fatty infiltration and occasionally this may be severe, involving the portal and centrilobular areas, but can always be distinguished from cirrhosis by the presence of an intact liver lobule. Clinically, patients with a fatty liver may be quite asymptomatic, although vague malaise and ill-defined right hypochondrial pain are often present. Occasional cases may be febrile. Hepatomegaly is almost invariably detectable but splenomegaly does not occur in uncomplicated fatty liver. Abnormalities in biochemical tests for liver function are generally mild but occasionally cholestatic jaundice may complicate the condition.

Figure 1 Relationship between per capita alcohol consumption and cirrhosis mortality in Ontario 1928-1967 (from Rankin *et al.,* 1975).

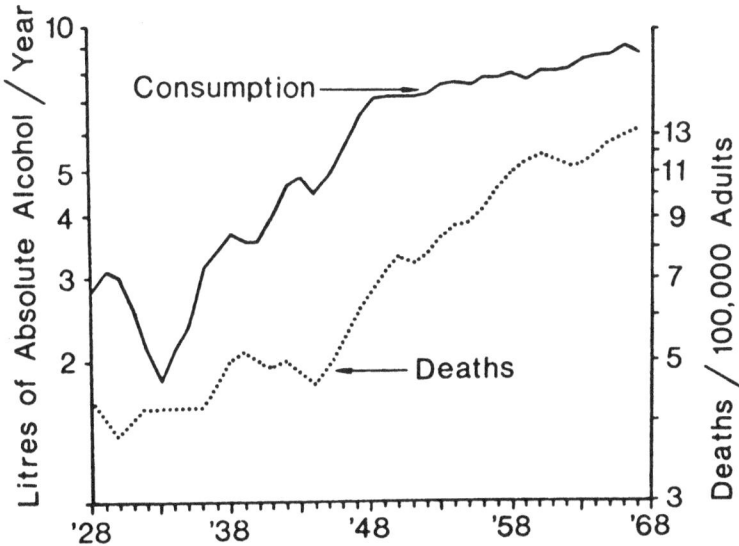

Uncomplicated fatty liver is generally considered to be a benign condition readily reversible when alcohol is withdrawn. However, deaths from fat embolism in association with this condition have been reported in American alcoholics, and negro women appear to be particularly susceptible (Kramer *et al.,* 1968).

Alcoholic hepatitis is characterised by necrosis of hepatocytes with inflammatory cell infiltration, and eosinophilic intracellular inclusions, known as alcoholic hyaline, are generally detectable in a proportion of liver cells (Lischner *et al.,* 1971). Fatty change is also generally superimposed on these changes. A variant of alcoholic hepatitis, characterised by a predominantly centrilobular distribution of necrosis which may lead to centrilobular fibrosis, is termed sclerosing central hyaline necrosis (Edmondson *et al.,* 1963).

Patients with alcoholic hepatitis classically present with fever, anorexia, malaise, upper abdominal pain and frequently become deeply jaundiced (Galambos, 1972a). Hepatomegaly and splenomegaly are not uncommonly found on clinical examination, and hepatic encephalopathy may complicate severe attacks. Patients with sclerosing central hyaline necrosis often show features of portal hypertension due to hepatic venous congestion, and in these cases ascites and oesophageal varices complicate the clinical picture and make the condition difficult to differentiate from severe decompensated cirrhosis. However, the severity of clinical illness varies widely and some patients may be asymptomatic despite histological evidence of alcoholic hepatitis. Biochemical tests of liver function are invariably abnormal in alcoholic hepatitis but the serum aspartate aminotransferase may be disproportionately low in relation to the degree of histological necrosis on liver biopsy. Mortality from alcoholic hepatitis has been reported at between 10 per cent and 30 per cent (Galambos, 1972a; Hardison & Lee, 1966) and deaths are generally associated with hepatic encephalopathy, severe infection and gastrointestinal bleeding. In a recent series from the Liver Unit at King's College Hospital, 13 per cent of patients died within a month of admission, but for cases of sclerosing central hyaline necrosis the figure was 31 per cent (Krasner *et al.*, 1977). The degree of abnormality in liver function tests provides some indication of the likely outcome, and in particular prothrombin time prolongation, which precludes liver biopsy, indicates a poor prognosis (Hardison & Lee, 1966; Porter *et al.*, 1971). The treatment of the condition is by general supportive measures and although corticosteroids have been tried their efficacy is unproven (Porter *et al.*, 1971; Helman *et al.*, 1971). Possible factors determining the development and progression of alcoholic hepatitis are discussed below.

Cirrhosis due to alcohol is classically micronodular in type with bands of fibrosis linking adjacent portal tracts and centrilobular areas to produce nodules of lobular size or smaller. However, with progression of the disease the cirrhosis becomes macronodular due to liver cell hyperplasia with regeneration nodules and the end result may be difficult to differentiate from cirrhosis due to other causes. The presence of marked fatty infiltration or a concomitant alcoholic hepatitis may aid the diagnosis but often these features are absent. Hyaline inclusions in the cirrhotic liver are not pathognomic with an alcoholic aetiology since they are also commonly found in primary biliary cirrhosis and hepatic Wilson's Disease (Scheuer, 1973).

A histological feature often seen in the liver biopsies of patients with alcoholic cirrhosis is iron overload. This occurs particularly commonly in men (Krasner *et al.*, 1977) and women are presumably protected to some extent by menstrual blood loss. Generally this abnormality is mild but sometimes so much iron is deposited in the liver that a diagnosis of haemochromatosis is suspected and indeed many patients with haemochromatosis have a history of heavy drinking (Finch & Finch, 1955; Powell, 1965). Recently, on the basis of family studies in patients with haemochromatosis (Bomford *et al.*, 1977) we have suggested that two genes are involved in the pathogenesis of the disease one giving rise to increased iron absorption, and the other to an enhanced avidity of tissues for iron storage. Since many alcoholic beverages contain large quantities of iron it seems likely that drinking could precipitate haemochromatosis in patients with both genetic abnormalities. Why less severe degrees of iron overload are seen in some alcoholics while others do not show this abnormality at all, must at present be a matter for speculation. One possibility, however, is that they possess one or other of the haemochromatosis associated genes which predispose them to hepatic iron overload when they drink.

Often when these diagnostic markers are absent, the grounds for making a diagnosis of alcoholic cirrhosis in a patient who happens to be a heavy drinker are no stronger than those of guilt by association. It is likely that a number of cases of cryptogenic cirrhosis are wrongly attributed to alcohol.

Relationship Between Alcohol Consumption and Cirrhosis

While epidemiological data leaves little doubt that alcoholism is associated with an increased risk of cirrhosis there is little information on how much alcohol can safely be drunk without risk of harm to the liver. On the basis of large scale population surveys in France, Péquignot (1971) has suggested that a regular daily intake of 80 g of alcohol or less (equivalent to about five pints of beer, or one third of a bottle of spirits) is relatively innocuous. When daily intake exceeds this figure the risk factor for the development of cirrhosis is increased five times, and more than 160 g daily is associated with a twenty-five-fold risk. While these figures may serve as a general overall guide, they are of little use in the individual patient, for susceptibility to the hepatoxic effects of alcohol appears to vary widely. Thus, in a French survey of patients with a clinical diagnosis of alcoholic cirrhosis, while 61 per cent admitted to a daily intake of at least 160 g of alcohol a significant proportion had drunk much less and in contrast a proportion had drunk equally heavily (Péquignot, 1971) (Table 1). In another survey from Scandinavia (Eghoje & Juhl, 1973) an attempt was made to correlate the duration of heavy drinking with the incidence of cirrhosis, and while the majority of patients had drunk at least 125 g

Table 1 Daily consumption in cirrhotic and non-cirrhotic patients
(from Péquignot *et al.*, 1964)

| | Daily alcohol intake (g) | | |
	<80	80-160	>160
Cirrhotics	5%	34%	61%
Non-cirrhotics	55%	36%	9%

of alcohol daily for ten years or more, a proportion had drunk less for a shorter period of time. Thus, although there is a rough correlation between the likelihood of cirrhosis developing and the quantity and duration of drinking, this correlation is by no means absolute.

Another aspect which is probably important in determining the clinical outcome is the pattern of drinking, and it appears that a regular steady intake of alcohol is far more deleterious to hepatic structure and function than sporadic 'binges'. In a survey of alcoholic patients with liver disease, Brunt *et al.* (1974) found that in patients with cirrhosis the majority drank heavily and regularly (Table 2), whereas an intermittent pattern of heavy drinking was far commoner amongst those with less severe abnormalities in hepatic histology. This correlates with the fact that in countries such as France and Italy, which have the highest mortality from alcoholic cirrhosis in the world, a steady daily consumption of alcohol is part of everyday life.

In the past, considerable emphasis has been placed on the possible role of associated malnutrition in the production of alcoholic liver injury. However, attention has recently been diverted away from these

Table 2 Drinking patterns in relation to severity of liver disease
(from Brunt *et al.*, 1964)

| Histological subtype | Drinking Patterns | | |
	Moderate %	Intermittent heavy %	Continuous heavy %
Fatty liver	8	60	32
Mild hepatitis	8	46	46
Severe hepatitis	0	35	65
Cirrhosis	13	45	42
Cirrhosis + hepatitis	5	49	46

factors by Lieber and his colleagues (Lieber *et al.*, 1975; Rubin & Lieber, 1974) who were able to produce alcoholic cirrhosis experimentally in the baboon despite feeding a nutritionally adequate diet. This is discussed further in chapter 11. There is also no evidence that the type of alcoholic beverage is important in determining whether cirrhosis will develop. Whenever a certain type of alcoholic drink has been particularly associated with cirrhosis, it has always been the most readily available, inexpensive or socially acceptable form of alcohol (Lelbach, 1976).

Relation Between Fatty Liver, Alcoholic Hepatitis and Cirrhosis

On the basis of numerous histological surveys amongst alcoholics, it has been estimated that only 30 per cent of heavy drinkers will develop alcoholic hepatitis and 10 per cent cirrhosis (Galambos, 1974). Indeed, although the majority of alcoholics have fatty changes on liver biopsy it has been repeatedly demonstrated that up to one third may have no demonstrable abnormality, and reversal of hepatic steatosis has been documented despite continuation of drinking (Christoffersen & Nielsen, 1971; Ugarte *et al.*, 1970; Leevy, 1968). The reason for this is not clear.

An unresolved issue is whether fatty infiltration of the liver can progress to cirrhosis without an intercurrent alcoholic hepatitis. Ultra-structural studies of hepatocytes in alcoholic fatty liver have demonstrated mitochondrial abnormalities which are identical to those seen in alcoholic hepatitis and cirrhosis (Lieber, 1975). Thus the effect of ethanol on the hepatocyte is likely to be more far-reaching than the functional metabolic abnormality which leads to fat accumulation. Certainly a number of patients present with established cirrhosis which has developed quietly and insidiously over the years with no frank episode of acute liver damage. However, this does not exclude the possibility of previous alcoholic hepatitis because, as previously discussed, the correlation between clinical symptoms and histological findings from liver biopsy may be poor.

The careful sequential histological studies of Galambos (1972a) leave no doubt that alcoholic hepatitis is a potentially pre-cirrhotic lesion. In a study of sixty-one patients with alcoholic hepatitis but no cirrhosis, reversal of the liver lesion was observed in six patients who abstained, whereas progression to cirrhosis occurred in twenty-three. While the majority of these patients had continued to drink, it is notable that two had become completely abstinent. In the remainder persistence of alcoholic hepatitis was observed with no progression to cirrhosis despite the fact that in many instances continued alcohol abuse could be documented. Thus, just as it is difficult to identify that minority of drinkers who are at risk from alcoholic hepatitis it is also difficult to predict, once the lesion is established, those who will progress to cirrhosis. Although careful clinical studies (Lelbach, 1975) have demonstrated a rough correlation between severity of histological liver disease and the duration and extent of alcohol abuse (Figure 2) there is very considerable overlap, suggesting that host factors are important in determining the degree of liver damage that will develop.

The mechanism of liver cell necrosis in acute alcoholic hepatitis is not well understood, but one possibility is that it is due to direct toxicity of alcohol or one of its metabolites. Acetaldehyde, a major

Figure 2 Relationship between quantity of alcohol consumed and duration of consumption to degree of liver damage in alcoholic patients Grade I — normal histology, II — fatty liver, III and IV — alcoholic hepatitis, V — cirrhosis (from Lelbach, 1975)

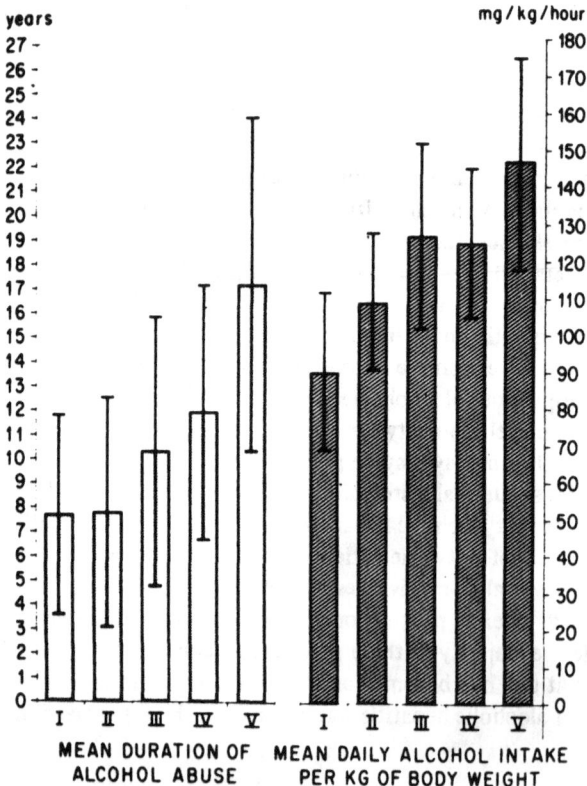

metabolite of ethanol, has been shown to exert toxic effects on many tissues (Walsh, 1971; Schreiber *et al.*, 1914; Cederbaum *et al.*, 1974) and recently it has been demonstrated that alcoholic patients with liver disease have higher than normal levels of acetaldehyde in the blood after an alcohol load (Korsten *et al.*, 1975). Individual variations in susceptibility to alcoholic hepatitis could thus be related to genetic or environmentally induced differences in the metabolism of ethanol via potentially toxic derivatives. Recently, however, considerable interest has focused on the possible role of immunological mechanisms in the pathogenesis and potentiation of acute alcoholic hepatitis. Using the leucocyte migration technique, Zetterman *et al.* (1976) have produced evidence that the lymphocytes of patients with acute alcoholic hepatitis are sensitised to extracts of alcoholic hyaline, and more recently they have reported the existence of circulating antibodies to alcoholic hyaline in the plasma of patients with this condition (Kanagasundaram & Leevy, 1976). These results are consistent with the hypothesis that alcohol or a metabolite disrupts hepatocellular metabolism which leads to the formation of alcoholic hyaline and alters the configuration of the hepatocyte membrane rendering it antigenically 'foreign'. In certain predisposed individuals this may stimulate a cell damaging immunological attack by lymphocytes. Susceptibility to alcoholic hepatitis would therefore be determined by individual differences in immune responsiveness as well as differences in ethanol metabolism. Progression of the lesion would be expected if the patient maintains the antigenic stimulus by continuing to drink, while conversely abstinence should be followed by resolution of the condition. Overall, observations of the clinical and histological course of alcoholic hepatitis are in keeping with this concept, but it cannot explain why a minority of individuals progress to cirrhosis despite abstinence (Galambos, 1972a; Brunt *et al.*, 1974; Galambos, 1972b).

Recently we have demonstrated that lymphocytes of patients with acute alcoholic hepatitis are cytotoxic to isolated hepatocytes (Cochrane *et al.*, 1977) (Figure 3), and that this cytotoxicity can be blocked by the addition of a purified liver-specific membrane protein. From this data it is clear that not only may an immune attack be directed against liver membrane antigens altered by alcohol, but in association with this there is a true autoimmune reaction against normal liver membrane proteins. In our patients cytotoxicity was no longer present following clinical and biochemical recovery from alcoholic hepatitis. It has yet to be shown that *in vitro* cytotoxicity is a true marker of hepatocellular necrosis *in vivo*, but if this is the case,

Figure 3 Lymphocyte cytotoxicity for isolated hepatocytes in patients with alcoholic hepatitis and other forms of alcoholic liver disease. The horizontal dotted line indicates the upper limit of the normal range (from Cochrane *et al.*, 1976)

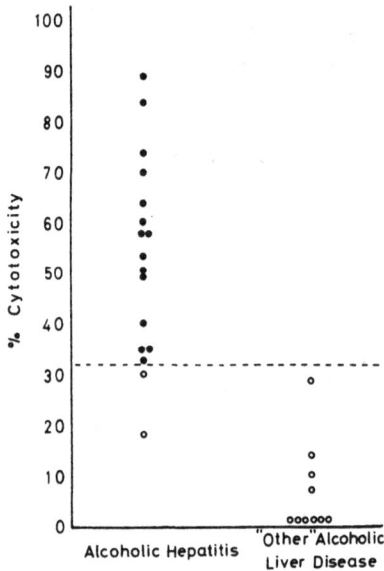

an inability to suppress this autoimmune response after the withdrawal of alcohol in predisposed individuals could explain why rarely there is progression to cirrhosis despite abstinence. Such a mechanism appears to be important in the pathogenesis of chronic active hepatitis (Eddleston & Williams, 1974), where there is considerable evidence that hepatic damage is perpetuated by an autoimmune attack on normal liver membrane proteins (Cochrane *et al.*, 1976).

Further support for the concept that immune reactions may be important in the development of alcoholic cirrhosis comes from recent observations that the incidence of serum autoantibodies is increased in patients with alcoholic hepatitis and cirrhosis (Cochrane *et al.*, 1977; Bailey *et al.*, 1976). Conversely, in patients with fatty change with or without fibrosis these abnormalities were not present. A further parallel between alcoholic cirrhosis and chronic active hepatitis is in the distribution of histocompatibility antigens in the two diseases, for in both there is an increase in frequency in HLA B8 and an absence of HLA A28 (Bailey *et al.*, 1976) (Table 3). We have suggested that the increase in frequency of HLA B8 in chronic active hepatitis is because this antigen is linked to genes which promote abnormally elevated and

Table 3 Incidence of the histocompatibility antigens HLA B8 and HLA A28 in patients with alcoholic liver disease and normal controls (From Bailey *et al.*, 1976)

	HLA A28	HLA B8
Controls	15%	25%
Alcoholic cirrhosis	0%**	45%*
Alcoholic no cirrhosis	10%	10%

* indicates P < 0.025, and ** P < 0.001

prolonged antibody responses (Galbraith *et al.*, 1974). In an alcoholic such markers would predispose to a particularly intense immune reaction against liver membrane antigens altered by ethanol and would, therefore, be expected to be particularly common in those who have progressed to cirrhosis. However, the association between alcoholic cirrhosis and the histocompatibility antigen HLA B8 is not as marked as in active chronic hepatitis where it is found in over 60 per cent of cases (Galbraith *et al.*, 1974). Nevertheless, the parallels between the two diseases provide persuasive evidence that immunological factors play some role in the pathogenesis of alcoholic cirrhosis. The proof of a causal relationship between all these *in vitro* markers of immunologically medicated cell damage, and the clinical and liver biopsy findings in patients will require a prolonged serial study.

Experimental evidence indicates that ethanol can stimulate hepatic collagen synthesis, and may also directly and indirectly inhibit hepatocellular regeneration (Leevy *et al.*, 1976). These two processes working together would clearly predispose towards the evolution of cirrhosis. Individual variations in the effect of ethanol on these metabolic functions would thus play a role in determining the outcome of alcoholic hepatitis in a drinker. Furthermore, Leevy *et al.* (1976) have suggested that the nutritional status of the patient, particularly with regard to folic acid and the B vitamin complex, are also important in determining the rate and extent of hepatic regeneration after alcoholic liver injury. While severe malnutrition is probably a more prominent feature in the American alcoholic than the patients seen in Great Britain the role of these factors requires further study.

Role of Sex in Determining Susceptibility to Alcoholic Liver Injury

In Great Britain, the overall increase in alcohol consumption over the past decade has been particularly marked amongst women (Litman, 1975), and this has been paralleled by a rise in the proportion of women presenting with alcohol related problems (Sclare, 1975). In a recent survey of patients presenting with alcohol-induced liver disease to the Liver Unit at King's College Hospital, we found that the proportion of females with severe alcoholic hepatitis or cirrhosis had risen markedly between the periods 1967-72 and 1973-5, and this change was even more dramatic for those under the age of fifty-five (Krasner *et al.*, 1977) (Table 4).

The suggestion that females may be particularly susceptible to alcohol-induced liver injury was first made in the 1940s (Spain, 1945) and observations from American, Australian and French studies (Schaffner & Popper, 1970; Wilkinson *et al.*, 1969; Lelbach, 1974; Galambos, 1972c; Péquingot, 1974) have supported this. Thus, in the USA, women, and in particular negro females (Lischner *et al.*, 1971) have a higher mortality from alcoholic hepatitis than males, and develop the disease at an earlier age, while Australian workers (Wilkinson *et al.*, 1969; Lelbach, 1974; Galambos, 1972c) found that women with cirrhosis had in general drunk less than their male counterparts and for a shorter period of time. The epidemiological studies of Péquingot *et al.* (1974) showed that while only 19 per cent of males with alcoholic cirrhosis had drunk less than 60 g alcohol daily, 63 per cent of cirrhotic females would admit to no more than this modest consumption.

Prompted by these findings we have recently analysed the histological patterns of alcoholic liver injury in male and female patients presenting to the Liver Unit at King's College Hospital between 1967 and 1975 (Krasner, 1977). This revealed that while there was a

Table 4 Changes in male:female ratio of patients with alcoholic liver disease presenting to a specialist referral unit (from Krasner *et al.*, 1977)

| | Male:Female ratio | |
	All patients	Patients under 55
1967-1972	3.4:1	4.5:1
1972-1975	2.3:1	2.1:1

significant male preponderance of mild hepatic lesions (fat $\pm$ fibrosis), a markedly higher proportion of females presented with cirrhosis and superimposed alcoholic hepatitis, and with central sclerosing hyaline necrosis (Table 5).

When the pattern of liver damage was analysed in relation to the ages of the patients (Table 6) it was found that the female preponderance of central sclerosing hyaline necrosis was confined to women under the age of fifty-five and particularly those under forty-five, where nearly one third of women in this age group showed this abnormality. By contrast, the overall incidence of inactive cirrhosis was significantly lower in women aged less than fifty-five than those in the older age group, and no cases of this lesion were found in women under the age of forty-five. In fact, the overall differences observed between males and females in the distribution of histological abnormalities were solely due to differences in women under the age of fifty-five, and over this age the pattern was identical to that in men.

Of the patients from whom a drinking history could be obtained, over 90 per cent of men admitted to a daily intake of at least 150 g alcohol, but only 65 per cent of women, despite the fact that overall they presented with more severe hepatic damage. Thus, it appears that in Great Britain, as in other parts of the world, women are particularly susceptible to severe alcoholic liver injury, and those in the younger age group seem to be especially at risk. Why this should be is not at present clear. One possibility is that drinking patterns of men and women may differ, with women drinking steadily throughout the day, while males may be more prone to sporadic bouts of heavy drinking

Table 5 Distribution of histological abnormalities in 215 males and 78 females with alcoholic liver disease presenting to a specialised referral unit (from Krasner *et al.*, 1977)

| | % with lesion | | |
	Males	Females	Significance of M/F Differences (p)
Fat $\pm$ fibrosis	21.9	7.7	< 0.005
Alcoholic hepatitis	12.6	15.4	NS
Sclerosing central hyaline necrosis	3.3	11.5	< 0.025
Inactive cirrhosis	24.2	19.2	NS
Cirrhosis + alcoholic hepatitis	32.5	44.9	≤ 0.01
Primary hepatocellular carcinoma	6.0	1.3	< 0.05

Table 6   Distribution of histological abnormalities in 169 males and
70 females with alcoholic hepatitis and cirrhosis, grouped
according to age (from Krasner *et al.*, 1977)

	% with lesion		
	Females		All males
	(n = 28)	(n = 42)	(n = 169)
	Age < 55 years	Age ≥ 55 years	
Alcoholic hepatitis	21.4	14.3	16.0
	NS	NS	
Central sclerosing hyaline necrosis	0	21.4	4.1
	p = 0.001	p < 0.0005	
Cirrhosis	35.7	11.9	30.8
	p < 0.01	p < 0.025	
Cirrhosis + hepatitis	46.9	52.3	41.4
	NS	NS	
Hepatoma	3.6	0	7.7
	NS	p = 0.006	

which are probably more hazardous to the liver (Brunt *et al.*, 1974).

It is also possible that the immunological factors discussed above in relation to the pathogenesis of alcoholic hepatitis and cirrhosis are more active in women than men. One finding in support of this is the fact that the incidence of serum autoantibodies was particularly high in women, particularly those with alcoholic hepatitis and superimposed cirrhosis (Table 7). Further evidence in support of an autoimmune aetiology is the fact that severe alcoholic hepatitis was found predominantly in women under the age of forty-five, who are also those principally affected by the autoimmune liver disease chronic active hepatitis (Sherlock, 1975). Furthermore, the tendency observed for alcoholic liver disease to become less active in older women is in keeping with the natural history of other autoimmune inflammatory conditions, which tend to 'burn out' after the menopause.

A proportion of our patients presented with a primary hepatocellular carcinoma. In all cases this was superimposed upon a cirrhotic liver, which had been known to exist for at least eight years. Malignant transformation is a well recognised complication of long-standing cirrhosis (Burdette, 1975), but it was interesting in our patients that this was almost completely restricted to males, all of

Table 7 Incidence of autoantibodies in males and females with alcoholic cirrhosis ± superimposed hepatitis (from Krasner *et al.*, 1977

	Patients		Normal population
	Males	Females	
Smooth muscle antibodies	23.4%	45.4%	1.9%
	$p < 0.05$		
Antinuclear antibodies	8.5%	31.8%	4.6%
	$p < 0.05$		

whom were over the age of fifty. The one female who presented with hepatoma was aged sixty-five. This striking male preponderance of hepatoma developing in a cirrhotic liver is in keeping with the observation of Krasner *et al.* (1976) that males are ten times more prone to develop a primary hepatocellular carcinoma on their cirrhotic livers than females, whatever the aetiology of their cirrhosis. The reason for this is not at present clear, but the well documented association between long-term treatment with anabolic steroids and the development of primary hepatocellular carcinoma (Editorial, 1973), suggests that the hormonal environment with testosterone and its derivatives may play an important role.

Effect of Abstinence on the Prognosis of Alcoholic Liver Disease

A number of studies have clearly demonstrated that abstention from alcohol significantly improves the long-term survival of patients with alcoholic cirrhosis (Brunt *et al.*, 1974; Sherlock *et al.*, 1971; Tygstrup & Juhl, 1971; Powell & Klatskin, 1968, and Table 8). In our patients, when cumulative survival was calculated by life table analysis, only 40 per cent of those who continued to drink survived, in contrast to 61 per cent of those who abstained (Figure 4). However, the long-term outlook for women, particularly those who continued to drink, was significantly worse than for men, both in terms of progression of alcoholic hepatitis to cirrhosis, and for life survival figures. Thus, nine women who showed alcoholic hepatitis alone on their first liver biopsy continued to drink, and of these seven developed cirrhosis. In contrast, progression to cirrhosis was observed in only one of the seven males presenting with this lesion who did not abstain. Furthermore, the mortality for women who continued to drink was significantly higher than for males. Only 30 per cent of women who did not abstain, and

Table 8 influence of abstinence on five-year survival in alcoholic liver disease

	% survival	
	Abstained	Continued drinking
Powell & Klatskin (1968)	63%	40.5%
Sherlock *et al.* (1971)	69%	34%
Tygstrup & Juhl (1971)	70%	44%
Brunt *et al.* (1974)	77%	48%

Figure 4 Effect of continuing or stopping drinking on cumulative survival from the time of presentation in 238 patients with alcoholic hepatitis or cirrhosis (from Krasner *et al.*, 1977)

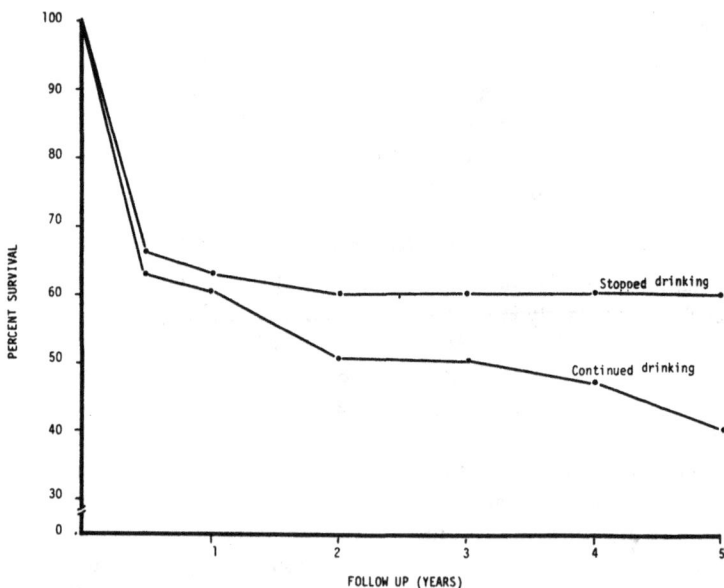

who survived their first hospital admission were alive at five years, in contrast to 72 per cent of men (Figure 5). Moreover, the average age of death for women (51.8 years) was almost eleven years younger than for men (62.5 years).

Even more disturbing, however, is the fact that women seem to benefit less from abstinence than men. In our series, all but one of the sixteen males who died, and in whom a drinking history was available, had continued to drink. In contrast, nearly half of the women who died claimed a significant period of abstinence. Thus, not only are women particularly susceptible to the more severe forms of alcoholic liver injury but their prognosis is worse than for men, whether or not they abstain. The higher incidence of autoimmune markers in our female patients suggests one possible explanation for these observations – namely that alcohol may trigger a particularly vigorous immune destruction of hepatocytes in women and that they are less able than men to suppress this reaction once alcohol is withdrawn.

Figure 5 Sex differences in cumulative survival for patients who survived three months after presentation and who continued to drink (from Krasner *et al.*, 1977)

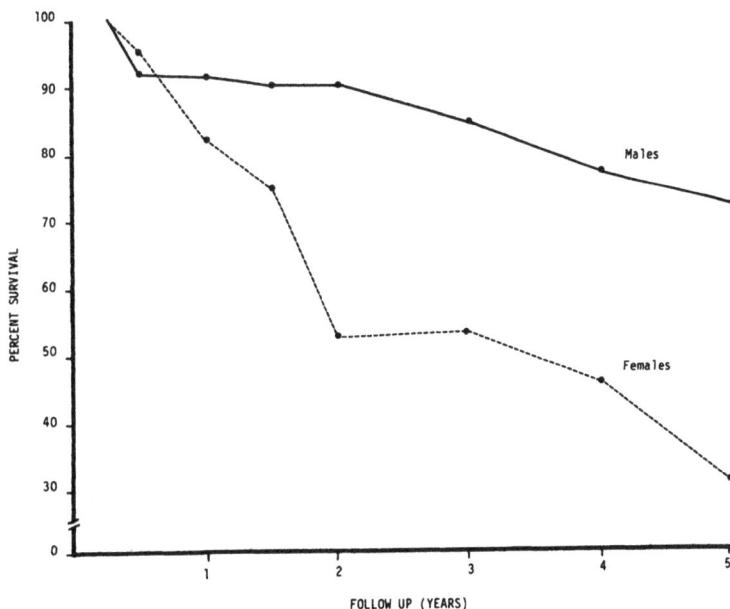

Certainly the fact that autoimmune liver disease is more common in females than in males would be in keeping with such an explanation, but in our present state of knowledge the hypothesis is at best tentative. Whilst every effort must be made to recognise alcohol abuse at an early stage and to encourage abstinence, these measures may still be inadequate to prevent the progression of liver disease in certain susceptible individuals, and particularly in women. If the management of patients with alcoholic liver disease is to be improved, there must be an improvement in our understanding of the factors which predispose to its development and progression.

References

Aikat, B.K., Ghosh, R.N., Chhutteni, P.N., and Dutta, D.V. Morphological features and Probable Mode of Evolution of Cirrhosis of the Liver in Adults in North India. Second Meeting of Liver Group, Varasani, India, 10 November 1974.

Bailey, R.J., Krasner, N., Eddleston, A.L.W.F., Williams, R., Tee, D.E.H., Doniach, D., Kennedy, L.A. and Batchelor, J.R. (1976). Histocompatibility antigens, autoantibodies and immunoglobulins in alcoholic liver disease. Brit. Med. J. 2: 727.

Banerjea, J.C. and Dasadhikary, C.R. (1963). Observations on hepatic cirrhosis, in the state of West Bengal. J. Assoc. Physicians India 11: 769.

Bomford, A., Eddleston, A.L.W.F., Kennedy, L.A. Batchelor, J.R. and Williams, R. (1977). Histocompatibility antigens as markers of abnormal iron metabolism in patients with idiopathic haemochromatosis and their relatives. Lancet 1: 327.

Brunt, P.W., Kew, M.C., Scheuer, P.J. and Sherlock, S. (1974). Studies in alcoholic liver disease in Britain. I. Clinical and pathological patterns related to natural history. Gut. 15:52.

Burdette, W.J. (1975). Neoplasms of the liver. In: Diseases of the Liver. L. Schiff (ed.). Philadelphia and Toronto: J.B. Lippincot Co., p.1057.

Cederbaum, A.I., Lieber, C.S., and Rubin, E. (1974). The effect of acetaldehyde on mitochondrial function. Arch. Biochem. Biophys. 161: 26.

Christoffersen, P. and Nielsen, K. (1971). The frequency of mallory bodies in liver biopsies from chronic alcoholics. Acta Path. Microbiol. Scand. A. 79: 274.

Cochrane, A.M.G., Moussouros, A., Portmann, B., McFarlane, I.G., Thomson, A.D., Eddleston, A.L.W.F. and Williams, R. (1977). Lymphocyte cytotoxicity for isolated hepatocytes in alcoholic liver disease. Gastroenterology (in press).

Cochrane, A.M.G., Moussouros, A., Thomson, A.D., Eddleston, A.L.W.F. and Williams, R. (1976). Antibody dependent cell-mediated (K-cell) cytotoxicity against isolated hepatocytes in chronic active hepatitis. Lancet 1: 441.

de Lint, J. and Schmidt, W. (1971). The epidemiology of alcoholism. In: Biological Basis of Alcoholism, Y. Israel and J. Mardones (eds.). New York: Wiley-Interscience, p.423.

Eddleston, A.L.W.F. and Williams, R. (1974). Inadequate antibody response to HBsAG or suppressor T-cell defect in development of active chronic hepatitis. Lancet 2: 1543.

Alcoholic Liver Diseases – Basic Pathology and Clinical Variants   175

Editorial (1973). Lancet 2: 1481.
Edmondson, H.A., Peters, R.L., Reynolds, T.B. and Kuzma, O.T. (1963).
Sclerosing hyalin necrosis of the liver in the chronic alcoholic. A recognizable
clinical syndrome. Ann. Intern. Med. 59: 646.
Eghoje, K.N. and Juhl, E. (1973). Factors determining liver damage in chronic
alcoholics. Scand. J. Gastroenterol. 8: 505.
Finch, S.C. and Finch, C.A. (1955). Idiopathic haemochromatosis: an iron
storage disease. Medicine 34: 381.
Frank, H., Heil, W. and Leodolter, I. (1967). Leber und bierkonsum;
vergleichende untersuchunger an 450 arbeitern. Much. Med. Wochenschr.
109: 892.
Gabriel, E. (1935). Uber die todesursachen bein alkoholikern. Z. Ges. Neurol.
Psychiatr. (Berlin) 153, 385.
Galambos, J.T. (1972a). Alcoholic hepatitis: its therapy and prognosis. In:
Progress in Liver Diseases, J. Popper and F. Schaffner (eds.).
New York: Grune and Stratton, vol.IV, p.567.
Galambos, J.T. (1972b). Natural history of alcoholic hepatitis. III. Histological
changes. Gastroenterology 63: 1026.
Galambos, J.T. (1972c). Alcoholic hepatitis: its therapy and prognosis. In:
Progress in Liver Diseases, H. Popper and F. Schaffner (eds.). New York:
Grune and Stratton, vol.IV, p.567.
Galambos, J.T. (1974). Alcoholic hepatitis.
In: The Liver and its Diseases, F. Schaffner, S. Sherlock and C. Leevy (eds.).
New York: International Medical Book Corporation, p.255.
Galbraith, R.M., Eddleston, A.L.W.F., Smith, M.G.M., Williams, R., McSween,
R.N.M., Watkinson, G., Dick, H., Kennedy, L.A. and Batchelor, J.R. (1974).
Histocompatibility antigens in active chronic hepatitis and primary biliary
cirrhosis. Brit. Med. J. 3: 604.
Galbraith, R.M., Eddleston, A.L.W.F., Williams, R., Webster, A.D.B. Pattison, J.,
Doniach, D., Kennedy, L.A. and Batchelor, J.R. (1974). Enhanced antibody
responses in active chronic hepatitis: relation to HLA-B8 and HLA-B12 and
porto-systemic shunting. Lancet 1: 930.
Gigglberger, H. (1959). Zur atiologie der launnec'schen cirrhose. Much. Med.
Wochenschr. 101: 853.
Gigglberger, H. (1968). Zur atiologie der lebercirrhose. Klinisch-statistische
untersuchungen an 400 kranken. Acta Hepatosplenol. 15: 415.
Gorwitz, K., Bahn, A., Warthen, F.J., and Cooper, M. (1970). Some
epidemiological data on alcoholism in Maryland. Quart. J. Stud. Alc. 31: 423.
Hardison, W.G. and Lee, F.I. (1966). Prognosis in acute liver disease of the
alcoholic patient. N. Eng. J. Med. 275: 61.
Helman, R.A., Temko, M.H., Nye, F.W. and Fallon, H.J. (1971). Alcoholic
hepatitis. Natural history and evaluation of prednisolene therapy. Ann.
Intern. Med. 74: 311.
Hodgson, H.J.F. and Thompson, R.P.H. (1976). Cirrhosis in south London.
Lancet ii: 118.
Jain, S., Paton, A. and Wansbrough-Jones, M.H. (1973). Cirrhosis in Birmingham.
Midl. Med. Rev. 9: 13.
Joliffe, N. and Jellinek, E.M. (1941). Vitamin deficiencies and liver cirrhosis
in alcoholism. Part VII: cirrhosis of the liver. Quart. J. Stud. Alc. 2: 544.
Kanagasundaram, N. and Leevy, C.M. (1976). Hepatic immune complexes in
alcoholic hepatitis. Gastroenterology 71: 914.
Klatskin, G. (1961). Alcohol and its relation to liver damage. Gastroenterology
41: 443.

176   *Alcoholism: New Knowledge and New Responses*

Konar, N.R. (1957). Observations on portal cirrhosis of the liver. With special reference to the diagnosis of early and late cases. J. Indian Med. Assoc. 28: 377.

Korsten, M.A., Matsuzaki, S., Feinman, L. and Lieber, C.S. (1975). High blood acetaldehyde levels after ethanol administration. N. Eng. J. Med. 292: 386.

Kramer, K., Kuller, L. and Fisher, R. (1968). The increasing mortality attributed to cirrhosis and fatty liver in Baltimore (1957-66). Ann. Intern. Med. 69: 273.

Krasner, N., Davis, M., Portmann, B. and Williams, R. (1977). The changing pattern of alcoholic liver disease in Great Britain – relationship to sex and immunological factors. Brit. Med. J. (in press).

Krasner, N., Johnson, P., Bomford, A., Eddleston, A.L.W.F. and Williams, R. (1976). Hepatoma in chronic liver disease. Gut 17: 390.

Leevy, C.M. (1968). Cirrhosis in alcoholics. Med. Clin. Amer. 52: 1445.

Leevy, C.M., Chen, T., Luisada-Opper, A., Kanagasundaram, N. and Zetterman, R. (1976). Liver disease of the alcoholic. In: Progress in Liver Diseases, H. Popper and F. Schaffner (eds.). New York: Grune and Stratton, vol.5, p.516.

Lelbach, W.K. (1974). Organic pathology related to volume and pattern of alcohol use. In: Research Advances in Alcohol and Drug Problems, R.J. Gibbins, Y. Israel, H. Kalant, R.E. Popham, W. Schmidt and R.G. Smart (eds.). New York: John Wiley and Sons, p.93.

Lelbach, W.K. (1975). Cirrhosis in the alcoholic and its relation to the volume of alcohol abuse. Ann. N.Y. Acad. Sci. 252: 85.

Lelbach, W.K. (1976). Epidemiology of alcoholic liver disease. In: Progress in Liver Diseases, H. Popper and F. Schaffner (eds.). New York: Grune and Stratton, vol.5, p.494.

Lieber, C.S. (1967). Chronic alcoholic hepatic injury in experimental animals and man. Biochemical pathways and nutritional factors. Fed. Proc. 26: 1443.

Lieber, C.S. (1975). Liver diseases and alcohol: fatty liver, alcoholic hepatitis, cirrhosis and their interrelationships. Ann. N.Y. Acad. Sci. 252: 63.

Lieber, C.S., DeCarli, L.M. and Rubin, E. (1975). Sequential production of fatty liver, hepatitis and cirrhosis in sub-human primates fed ethanol with adequate diets. Proc. Nat. Acad. Sci. USA. 72: 2.

Lindner, H. Indications as to the etiology of hepatic cirrhosis at the surface of the liver. International Symposium on Hepatic Cirrhosis, 4-5 April 1975, Wiesbaden, West Germany.

Lischner, M.W., Alexander, J.F. and Galambos, J.T. (1971). Natural history of alcoholic hepatitis. I. The acute disease. Amer. J. Dig. Dis. 16: 481.

Litman, G. (1975). Women and alcohol: facts and myths. New Behaviour, July: 126.

Martini, G.A. and Bode, C.H. (1970). Alcoholic cirrhosis and other toxic hepatopathies. In: The Epidemiology of Cirrhosis of the Liver, A. Engel and T. Larsson (eds.). Stockholm: Nordiska Bokhandelns Forlag, p.315.

Mukerjee, A.B. Dasgupta, M. and Sarkar, S.K. (1972). Hepatic cirrhosis in the tropics. J. Indian Med. Assoc. 59: 9.

Nicholls, P., Edwards, G. and Kyle, E. (1974). Alcoholics admitted to four hospitals in England. II General and cause-specific mortality. Quart. J. Stud. Alc. 35: 841.

Pell, S. and D'Alonzo, C.A. (1968). The prevalence of chronic diseases among problem drinkers. Arch. Environ. Health. 16: 679.

Péquignot, G. (1971). About the geographical aspects of cirrhosis. In: Alcohol and the Liver, W. Gerok, K. Sickinger, H.H. Hennekeuser (eds.). Stuttgart: F.K. Schattaeur, p.469.

Péquignot, G. (1974). Les problèmes nutritionnels de la société industrielle.

Vie Med. Can. Francais 3: 216

Péquignot, G., Chabert, C., Eydoux, H. and Courcoul, M.A. (1974). Increased risk of liver cirrhosis with intake of alcohol. Rev. Alcohol. 20: 191.

Piesbergen, H. and Jungermann, J. (1966). Zur Ätiologie und Pathogenese der Leberzirrhose. Z. Gastroenterol, 4: 345.

Porter, H.P., Simon, F.R., Pope, C.E., Volwiler, W. and Senster, L.F. (1971). Corticosteroid therapy in severe alcoholic hepatitis. A double-blind trial. N. Eng. J. Med. 284: 1350.

Powell, L.W. (1965). Iron storage in relatives of patients with haemochromatosis and in relatives of patients with alcoholic cirrhosis and haemosiderosis. Quart. J. Med. 34: 427.

Powell, W.J. Jr. and Klatskin, G. (1968). Duration of survival in patients with Laennec's cirrhosis. Am. J. Med. 44: 406.

Rankin, J.G., Schmidt, W., Popham, R.E. and de Lint, J. (1975). Epidemiology of alcoholic liver disease – insights and problems. In: Alcoholic Liver Pathology, J.M. Khanna, Y. Israel and H. Kalant (eds.). Toronto, Canada: Addiction Research Foundation, p.31.

Rubin, E. and Lieber, C.S. (1974). Fatty liver, alcoholic hepatitis and cirrhosis produced by alcohol in primates. New Eng. J. Med. 290: 128.

Schaffner, F. and Popper, H. (1970). Alcoholic hepatitis in the spectrum of ethanol-induced liver injury. Scand. J. Gastroent. (Suppl. 7) 5: 69.

Scheuer, P.J. (1973). Liver Biopsy Interpretation. London: Ballière Tindall.

Schmidt, W. and de Lint, J. (1972). Causes of death of alcoholics. Quart. J. Stud. Alc. 33: 171.

Schuckit, M.A. and Gunderson, E.K.E. (1974). Deaths among young alcoholics in the US Naval Service. Quart. J. Stud. Alc. 35: 856.

Schreiber, S.S., Oratz, M. and Rothschild M.A. (1974). Alcoholic cardiomyopathy II. The inhibition of cardiac microsomal protein synthesis by acetaldehyde. J. Mol. Cell Cardio. 6: 207.

Sclare, A.B. (1975). The woman alcoholic. J. Alcohol. 10: 134.

Sherlock, S. (1975) Chronic hepatitis. In: Diseases of the Liver and Biliary System. Oxford: Blackwell Scientific Publications, 5th ed., p.396.

Sherlock, S., Brunt, P. and Scheuer, P.J. (1971). Clinical and pathological aspects of alcoholic liver disease. In: Alcohol and the Liver, W. Gerok, K. Sickinger and H.H. Hennekeuser (eds.). Stuttgart: F.K. Schattauer, p.383.

Spain, D.M. (1945). Portal cirrhosis of the liver. A review of 250 necropsies with reference to sex differences. Amer. J. Clin. Path. 15: 215.

Stone, W.D. Islam, N.R.K. and Paton, A. (1968). The natural history of cirrhosis. Experience with an unselected group of patients. Q.J. Med. 37: 119.

Tashiro, M. and Lipscomb, W.R. (1963). Mortality experience of alcoholics. Quart. J. Stud. Alc. 24: 203.

Tygstrup, N. and Juhl, E. (1971). Copenhagen study group for liver diseases: the treatment of alcoholic cirrhosis; the effect of continued drinking and prednisone on survival. In: Alcohol and the Liver, W. Gerok, K. Sickinger, H.H. Hennekeuser (eds.). Stuttgart: F.K. Schattauer, p.519.

Ugarte, G., Iturriaga, H. and Insunza, I. (1970). Some effects of ethanol on normal and pathologic livers. In: Progress in Liver Diseases, H. Popper and F. Schaffner (eds.). New York: Grune and Stratton, vol.3, p.355.

Walsho, M.J. (1971). Role of acetaldehyde in the interactions of ethanol with neuroamines. In: Biological Aspects of Alcohol, M.K. Roach, W.N. McIsaac and P.J. Creaven (eds.). Texas: University of Texas Press, p.233.

Wilkinson, P., Santamaria, J.N. and Rankin, J.G. (1969). Epidemiology of alcoholic cirrhosis. Aust. Ann. Med. 18: 222.

Zetterman, R.K., Luisada-Opper, A and Leevy, C.M. (1976). Alcoholic hepatitis –

cell mediated immunological response to alcoholic hyalin. Gastroenterology 70: 382.

12 ALCOHOLIC LIVER DISEASES – NUTRITIONAL DEFICIENCY OR DIRECT TOXICITY?

Michael Davis

There has been controversy for many years as to whether liver disease in alcoholics can be prevented by the provision of a nutritious diet (Lieber, 1977; Hartroft, 1971). The concept that nutritional imbalance was important in its pathogenesis arose from the demonstration that certain dietary deficiency states can give rise to hepatic lesions, which resemble the early stages of alcoholic liver disease. Thus, protein-calorie malnutrition leads to fatty infiltration with hepatic fibrosis in both man (Waterlow and Weisz, 1956; Cook and Hutt, 1967) and primates (Ruebner et al., 1969; Patrick et al., 1973) and similar abnormalties develop in rats fed diets deficient in choline and other essential nutrients (Best et al., 1949; Hoffbauer and Zaki, 1965; Lucas and Ridout, 1967). These observations were extrapolated to alcoholic patients, who frequently show signs of advanced nutritional deficiency, due to their inability to afford food as well as alcohol (Leevy et al., 1975). However, most studies have involved the 'skid row' type of alcoholic, and this has probably led to an overestimation of the importance of dietary inadequacy in the pathogenesis of alcoholic liver disease. Certainly, severe hepatic damage can develop in well-nourished alcoholics (Lelbach, 1967).

Although superficially similar, the liver lesions associated with malnutrition differ in a number of ways from those produced by alcohol, providing further evidence against a primary role for nutritional imbalance in the pathogenesis of alcoholic liver disease. First, a number of experimental studies in primates with protein-calorie malnutrition have demonstrated that male animals are more prone to develop hepatic damage than females (Ruebner et al., 1969). In contrast, clinical and epidemiological studies in man would indicate that females are more susceptible to alcoholic liver disease than males (Péquignot et al., 1974; Williams and Davis, 1977). A further difference between nutritional and alcoholic liver disease is that, although severe fibrosis occurs in the former state (Iseri et al., 1966; Ramalingaswami, 1964), cirrhosis has never convincingly been demonstrated, and liver lesions are reversible on resumption of a normal diet (Ruebner et al., 1969). Similar considerations apply to the fatty infiltration and fibrosis

179

which frequently follows jejunoileal bypass operations for refractory obesity (Salmon and Reedyk, 1975; Soyer *et al.*, 1976; Drenick *et al.*, 1970), and although cases of cirrhosis have been reported after this procedure (Salmon and Reedyk, 1975; Peters and Reynolds, 1973), concomitant alcohol abuse has always been difficult to exclude. Moreover, the ultra-structural changes in the hepatocyte, which are seen in the earliest stages of alcoholic liver disease, with proliferation of the smooth endoplasmic reticulum, atrophy of the rough endoplasmic reticulum and mitochondrial abnormalities (Rubin and Lieber, 1968; Iseri *et al.*, 1966) are quite different from those observed in nutritional deficiency states (Ruebner *et al.*, 1969; Patrick *et al.*, 1973).

Choline deficiency in rats with hepatic steatosis and fibrosis can be exacerbated by concomitant administration of ethanol, probably via stimulation of the enzyme choline oxidase (Barak *et al.*, 1973). As a result, the quantity of choline available for formation of phospholipid from hepatic triglycerides is reduced, leading to an accumulation of triglycerides in the liver (Figure 1). However, susceptibility to choline deficiency appears to be related to the activity of hepatic choline oxidase (Hoffbauer and Zaki, 1965), and the importance of this mechanism in man is debatable, due to the almost complete absence of this enzyme in human liver (Sidransky and Farber, 1960). Because of the essential role of choline and other lipotrophic substances in the formation of phospholipids, a decrease in hepatic phospholipids (Ashworth *et al.*, 1961), and low levels of circulating lipoproteins (Oler and Lombardi, 1970) which are derived from them, are seen in association with experimentally induced deficiencies of these substances. A similar pattern is observed clinically in protein-calorie malnutrition (Waterlow and Alleyne, 1971). However, in alcoholic fatty liver increases in hepatic phospholipids (Lieber *et al.*, 1965) and circulating lipoproteins (Baraona and Lieber, 1970) are seen, emphasising again the difference between 'nutritional' and alcoholic liver disease.

It was the studies of Lieber and his colleagues which diverted emphasis away from nutritional factors as being of primary importance in the pathogenesis of alcoholic liver disease, and drew attention to the possibility of a direct hepatotoxic effect of ethanol. In a series of studies in normal and alcoholic volunteer human subjects (Lieber *et al.*, 1965; Lieber and Rubin, 1968; Rubin and Lieber, 1968), these workers were able to demonstrate that daily ingestion of the equivalent of one third to two thirds of a bottle of spirits led to the development of

Figure 1 Role of choline in hepatic lipid metabolism

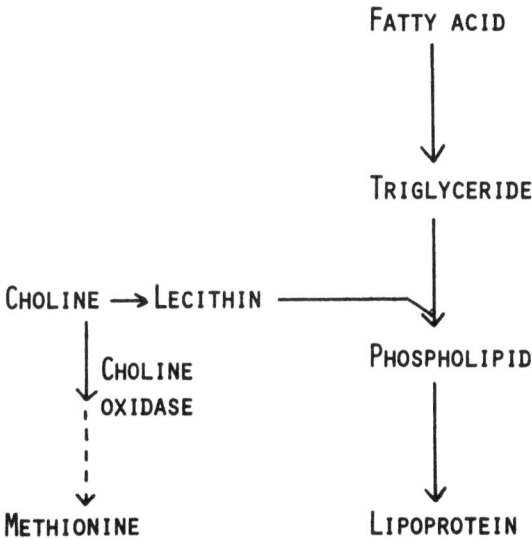

hepatic steatosis, despite a more than adequate dietary intake of protein and other essential nutrients. These changes were observed within one to two weeks of starting alcohol, and their severity increased with the quantity ingested. It is noteworthy that, despite the high total doses administered, blood levels of alcohol were almost uniformly of the order of 50 mg/ml., which is well below the legal driving limit for Great Britain.

However, fatty liver is a reversible lesion, and the question remained whether the more advanced stages of alcoholic liver disease (alcoholic hepatitis and cirrhosis) could also be attributed to alcohol toxicity rather than to a deficient diet. This led to the development of an animal model for alcoholic liver disease in the baboon. Animals were fed totally liquid diets containing more than adequate protein, fat and vitamin cofactors, but with 50 per cent of the total calories being supplied as alcohol. In this way, it was possible to reproduce the entire spectrum of alcoholic liver disease (Rubin and Lieber, 1974; Lieber *et al.*, 1975). All fifteen animals developed fatty infiltration of the liver, which increased in severity with the duration of alcohol intake. Most dramatic, however, was the evolution of alcoholic hepatitis, which was histologically indistinguishable from that seen in man, in five of the animals, with progression to florid cirrhosis within two to four years of starting the study.

Clearly, therefore, dietary factors alone cannot be the cause of alcoholic liver disease, and a direct toxic effect of alcohol seems likely. Possibly this is mediated via acetaldehyde, a product of ethanol metabolism which has been shown to adversely affect cellular metabolism in a number of ways, both in the liver and other organs (Walsh, 1971; Cederbaum *et al.*, 1974). In support of the acetaldehyde hypothesis is the demonstration that in alcoholics, blood levels of this metabolite after ingestion of alcohol are significantly higher than normal (Korsten *et al.*, 1975). In addition to direct toxicity, however, interest has recently developed in the possible role of immunological mechanisms in the pathogenesis of alcoholic hepatitis and cirrhosis. Using *in vitro* tests of cell-mediated immunity, lymphocytes from patients with alcoholic hepatitis have been shown to be sensitised to extracts of alcoholic hyaline (Zetterman *et al.*, 1976), and more recently to isolated liver cells (Cochrane *et al.*, 1977). It seems possible that alcohol or a metabolite might alter the structure of the liver cell membrane, thus triggering off an autoimmune reaction with destruction of hepatocytes. Further studies are clearly needed to determine the relationship between the direct toxic effects of alcohol and these immunological abnormalities.

Although nutritional imbalance may not play a primary role in the pathogenesis of alcoholic liver disease, these factors may be important in the potentiation of hepatic damage. Certainly clinical and experimental studies have shown that recovery from alcohol-induced liver disease is retarded if the diet is deficient in protein and other essential nutrients (Lieber *et al.*, 1969; Lieber, 1966; Phillips *et al.*, 1952), even if alcohol is withdrawn. Furthermore, although alcoholics may become malnourished as a result of poor dietary intake, due to economic factors, or to anorexia from gastritis, there is also evidence that alcohol may alter nutritional requirements. In this way, a diet which is adequate by conventional standards may become inadequate in the face of continuous heavy drinking. Ultra-structural studies have demonstrated a direct toxic effect of alcohol on the gastrointestinal mucosa (Rubin *et al.*, 1972), and malabsorption of xylose, fat, folic acid, vitamin B_{12} and thiamine have also been reported in alcoholics (Lindenbaum and Lieber, 1971; Roggin *et al.*, 1969; Mezey *et al.*, 1970; Tomasulo *et al.*, 1968; Thomson *et al.*, 1970; Halsted *et al.*, 1971). While fat malabsorption will obviously be exacerbated by pancreatic dysfunction, which is not infrequently seen in alcoholics, the role of direct alcohol toxicity in producing these intestinal abnormalities is uncertain since, except for vitamin B_{12} (Lindenbaum and Lieber, 1975), malabsorption could be corrected by feeding a nutritious diet despite continuing alcohol.

There is no doubt, however, that alcohol can cause malutilisation of dietary constituents, and perhaps the best documented example is the impaired handling of dietary lipid in alcoholics. Alcohol has been shown to decrease the oxidation of fatty acids (Barnes, 1965) while increasing hepatic lipogenesis (Lieber and Schmid, 1961) by blocking the metabolism of acetate via the tricarboxylic acid cycle (Figure 2). As a result fat accumulates in the liver. Thus, alcoholic patients show an imbalance between the quantity of dietary fat ingested and their capacity to metabolise lipid, the extent of hepatic steatosis being proportional to the quantity of fat in the diet (Lieber and Spritz, 1966; Lieber and De Carli, 1970). Furthermore, acute ingestion of large quantities of ethanol leads to mobilisation of fatty acids from tissues (Lieber *et al.*, 1965; Scheig and Isselbacher, 1965), putting an additional load on the liver. Of possible clinical relevance is the fact that medium chain triglycerides have been shown to be less susceptible than long chain triglycerides to alcohol-induced impairment of oxidation (Lieber *et al.*, 1967), and experimental administration of these substances has been shown to hasten the regression of alcoholic fatty liver.

Nutritional status with protein may be important in determining the rate and extent of hepatic regeneration after acute hepatocellular injury, and experimental observations that alcohol impairs hepatic protein synthesis in isolated perfused liver preparations (Kirsch *et al.*, 1973) may have important clinical implications. However, the effect of

Figure 2 Some effects of ethanol in hepatic lipid metabolism

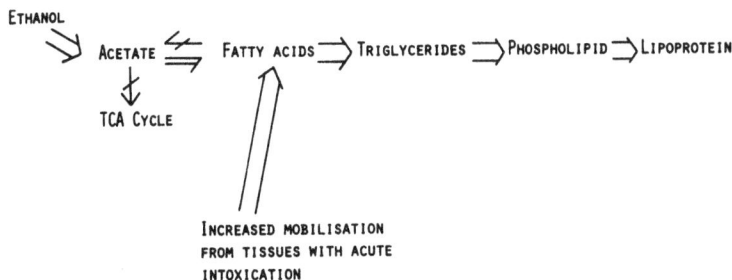

both acute and chronic alcohol ingestion on protein turnover in man is unknown.

Malutilisation of folic acid in alcoholics is suggested by the observation that macrocytosis occurs in a high proportion of these patients, despite normal levels of this vitamin in serum and erythrocytes (Wu *et al.*, 1974). Furthermore, alcohol appears to impair the liver's capacity to retain folic acid (Cherrick *et al.*, 1965; Sorrell *et al.*, 1974), and this, together with deficiencies of other vitamins and nutrients, may be important in limiting hepatic regeneration (Leevy *et al.*, 1975).

However, nutritional deficiencies in alcoholics with liver disease may be due more to hepatic dysfunction than to a direct effect of ethanol. In a recent survey of patients with cirrhosis, abnormally low plasma levels of pyridoxal phosphate, the biologically active form of vitamin B_6, were found in 71 per cent, but the incidence was no different in those with alcoholic and those with non-alcoholic liver disease (Labadarios *et al.*, 1977). Furthermore, regardless of aetiology, all these patients showed evidence of impaired utilisation of the vitamin, after intravenous supplementation in high doses. Overall, no significant changes were observed in plasma levels of pyridoxal phosphate after administration of pyridoxine hydrochloride, which is the commonly commercially available form of the vitamin. In contrast, a response was observed after pyridoxal phosphate itself was given, although this was markedly impaired compared with normal controls (Figure 3). The basis for this abnormal handling of vitamin B_6 appears to be increased degradation of pyridoxal phosphate, for the diminished response of these patients to supplementation was associated with an increased urinary excretion of its main metabolite, 4-pyridoxic acid. Thus, in alcoholics with liver disease, not only may the quantities of dietary constituents require adjustment, but also the forms in which they are supplied. Furthermore, in patients with severe acute hepatocellular necrosis, pyridoxal phosphate appears to be released from necrotic hepatocytes early in the course of the illness (Rossouw *et al.*, 1977), and this mechanism may contribute to deficiency in drinkers who develop acute alcoholic hepatitis.

Figure 3 The effect of intravenous pyridoxal phosphate on plasma concentrations of pyridoxal phosphate in normal controls and patients with cirrhosis

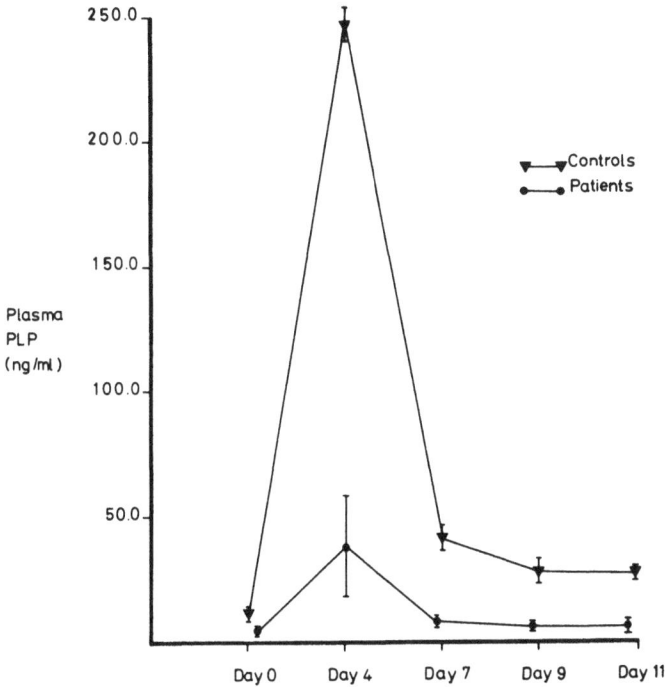

References

Ashworth, C.T. Wrightsman, F. and Buttram, V. (1961). Hepatic lipids; comparative study of effects of high-fat, choline-deficient, and high-cholesterol diets upon serum and hepatic lipids. Arch. Path. 72: 620.

Barak, A.J., Tuma, D.J. and Sorrell, M.F. (1973). Relationship of ethanol to choline metabolism in the liver: a review. Am. J. Clin. Nutr. 26: 1234

Baraona, E. and Lieber, C.S. (1970). Effects of chronic ethanol feeding on serum lipoprotein metabolism in the rat. J. Clin. Invest. 49: 769.

Barnes, E.W. (1965). Observations on the metabolism of alcohol in man. Brit. J. Nutr. 19: 485.

Best, C.H., Hartroft, W.S., Lucas, C.C. and Ridout, J.H. (1949). Liver damage produced by feeding alcohol or sugar and its prevention by choline. Brit. Med. J. 2: 1001.

Cederbaum, A.I., Lieber, C.S. and Rubin, E. (1974). The effect of acetaldehyde on mitochondrial function. Arch. Biochem. Biophys. 161: 26.

Cherrick, G.R., Baker, H., Frank, O. and Leevy, C.M. (1965). Observations on hepatic avidity for folate in Laennec's cirrhosis. J. Lab. Clin. Med. 66: 446.

Cochrane, A.M.G., Moussouros, A., Thomson, A.D., Portmann, B., Eddleston, A.L.W.F. and Williams, R. (1977) Lymphocyte cytotoxicity for isolated hepatocytes in alcoholic liver disease. Gastroenterology (in press).

Cook, G.C. and Hutt, M.S. (1967). The liver after Kwashiorkor, Brit. Med. J. 3: 454.

Drenick, E.J. Simmons, F. and Murphy, J.F. (1970). Effect on hepatic morphology of treatment of obesity by fasting, reducing diets and small-bowel bypass. N. Eng. J. Med. 282: 829.

Halstead, C.H., Robles, E.A. and Mezey, E. (1971). Decreased jejunal uptake of labelled folic acid (3H-PGA) in alcoholic patients. Roles of alcohol and nutrition. N. Engl. J. Med. 285: 701.

Hartroft, W.S. (1971). In: Alcohol and the Liver. New York: Schattauer Verlag, p.169.

Hoffbauer, F.W. and Zaki, F.G. (1965). Choline deficiency in baboon and rat compared. Arch. Path. 79: 364.

Kirsch, R.E., Frith, L. O'C., Stead, R.H. and Saunders, S.J. (1973). Effects of alcohol on albumin by the isolated perfused rat liver. Am. J. Clin. Nutr. 26: 1191.

Korsten, M.A., Matsuzaki, S., Feinman, L. and Lieber, C.S. (1975). High blood acetaldehyde levels after ethanol administration. N. Engl. J. Med. 292: 386.

Labadarios, D., Rossouw, J.E., McConnell, J.B., Davis, M. and Williams, R. (1977). Vitamin B_6 deficiency in chronic liver disease – evidence for increased degradation of pyridoxal-5-phosphate. Gut 18: 23.

Leevy, C.M., Zetterman, R. and Smith, F. (1975). Newer approaches to treatment of liver disease in the alcoholic. Ann. N.Y. Acad. Sci. 252: 135.

Lelbach, W.K. (1967). Leberschaden bei chronischem Alkoholismus. Ergebnisse einer klinischen, klinisch-chemischen und bioptischhistologischen Untersuchung an 526 Alkoholkranken wahrend der Entziehungskur in einer offenen Trinkerheilstatte. Acta Hepatosplen. 14: 9.

Lieber, C.S. (1966). Hepatic and metabolic effects of alcohol. Gastroenterology. 50: 119.

Lieber, C.S. (1977). Metabolic effects of alcohol on the liver. In: Metabolic Aspects of Alcoholism. Lieber, C.S., (ed.). Lancaster: MTP Press Ltd, p.31.

Lieber, C.S. and De Carli, L.M. (1970). Quantitative relationship between the amount of dietary fat and the severity of the alcoholic fatty liver. Amer. J. Clin. Nutr. 23: 474.

Lieber, C.S., De Carli, L.M. and Rubin, E. (1975). Sequential production of fatty liver, hepatitis, and cirrhosis in sub-human primates fed ethanol with adequate diets. Proc. Nat. Acad. Sci. USA 72: 437.

Lieber, C.S., Jones, D.P. and De Carli, L.M. (1965). Effects of prolonged ethanol intake: production of fatty liver despite adequate diets. J. Clin. Invest. 44: 1009.

Lieber, C.S., Lefevre, A., Spritz, N., Feinman, L. and De Carli, L. (1967). Difference in hepatic metabolism of long and medium chained fatty acids: the role of fatty acid chain length in the production of the alcoholic fatty liver. J. Clin. Invest. 46: 1451.

Lieber, C.S. and Rubin, E. (1968). Alcoholic fatty liver in man on a high protein and low fat diet. Amer. J. Med. 44: 200.

Lieber, C.S. and Schmid, R. (1961). The effect of ethanol on fatty acid metabolism: stimulation of hepatic fatty acid synthesis in vitro. J. Clin. Invest. 40: 394.

Lieber, C.S. and Spritz, N. (1966). Effects of prolonged ethanol intake in man: role of dietary adipose, and endogenously synthesised fatty acids in the pathogenesis of the alcoholic fatty liver. J. Clin. Invest. 45: 1400.

Lieber, C.S. Spritz, N. and De Carli, L.M. (1969). Fatty liver produced by dietary deficiencies: its pathogenesis and potentiation by ethanol. J. Lipid Res. 10:283.

Lindenbaum, J. and Lieber, C.S. (1971). Effects of ethanol on the blood, bone marrow and small intestine of man. In: Biological Aspécts of Alcohol, M.K. Roach, W.N. McIsaac and P.J. Creaven (eds.). Univ. Texas Press, p.27.

Lindenbaum, J. and Lieber, C.S. (1975). Effects of chronic ethanol administration on intestinal absorption in man in the absence of nutritional deficiency. Ann. N.Y. Acad. Sci. 252: 228.

Lucas, C.L. and Ridout, J.H. (1967). Fatty liver and lipotropic phenomena. Prog. Chemistry Fats and Other Lipids 10: 1.

Mezey, E., Jow, E., Slavin, R.E. and Tobon, F. (1970). Pancreatic function and intestinal absorption in chronic alcoholism. Gastroenterology 59: 657.

Oler, A. and Lombardi, B. (1970). Further studies on a defect in the intracellular transport and secretion of proteins by the liver of choline-deficient rats. J. Biol. Chem. 245: 1282.

Patrick, R.S., MacKay, A.M., Coward, D.G. and Whitehead, R.G. (1973). Experimental protein-energy malnutrition in baby baboons. 2. Liver pathology. Brit. J. Nutr. 30: 171.

Péquingot, G., Chambert, C., Eydoux, H. and Courcol, M.A. (1974). Augmentation de risque de cirrhose en fonction de la ration d'alcohol. Rev. Alc. 20: 191.

Peters, R.L. and Reynolds, T.B. (1973). Hepatic changes simulating alcoholic liver disease post-ileo-jejunal bypass. Gastroenterology. 65: 564 (abstract).

Phillips, G.B., Gabuzda, G.J. and Davidson, C.S. (1952). Comparative effects of a puried and an adequate diet on the course of fatty cirrhosis in the alcoholic. J. Clin. Invest. 31: 351.

Ramalingaswami, V. (1964). Perspectives in protein malnutrition. Nature. 201: 546.

Roggin, G.M., Iber, F.L., Kater, R.M.H. and Tabon, F. (1969). Malabsorption in the chronic alcoholic. John Hopkins Med. J. 125: 321.

Rossouw, J.E., Labadarios, D., McConnell, J.B., Davis, M. and Williams, R. (1977). Plasma pyridoxal phosphate levels in fulminant hepatic failure and the effects of parenteral supplementation. Scand. J. Gastroenterol. 12: 123.

Rubin, E. and Lieber, C.S. (1968). Alcohol induced hepatic injury in non-alcoholic volunteers. N. Eng. J. Med. 278: 869.

Rubin, E. and Lieber, C.S. (1974). Fatty liver, alcoholic hepatitis and cirrhosis produced by alcohol in primates. N. Eng. J. Med. 290: 128.

Rubin, E., Rybak, B.J., Lindenbaum, J., Gerson, C.D., Walker, G. and Lieber, C.S. (1972). Ultrastructural changes in the small intestine induced by ethanol. Gastroenterology. 63: 801.

Ruebner, B.H., Moore, J., Rutherford, R.B., Seligman, A.M., and Zuidema, G.D. (1969). Nutritional cirrhosis in rhesus monkeys: electron microscopy and histochemistry. Exp. Molec. Path. 11: 53.

Salmon, P.A. and Reedyk, L. (1975). Fatty metamorphosis in patients with jejunoileal bypass. Surg. Gyncol. & Obstet. 141: 75.

Schelg, R. and Isselbacher, K.J. (1965). Pathogenesis of ethanol induced fatty liver: III. In vivo and in vitro effects of ethanol on hepatic fatty acid metabolism. J. Lipid. Res. 6: 269.

Sidransky, H. and Farber, E. (1960). Liver choline oxidase activity in man and in several species of animals. Arch. Biochem. 87: 129.

Sorrell, M.F., Baker, H., Barak, A.J. and Frank, O. (1974). Release by ethanol of vitamins into rat liver perfusates. Am. J. Clin. Nutr. 27: 743.

Soyer, M.T., Ceballos, R. and Aldrete, J.S. (1976). Reversibility of service hepatic damage caused by jejunoileal bypass after re-establishment of normal intestinal continuity. Surgery 79: 601.

Thomson, A.D., Baker, H. and Leevy, C.M. (1970). Patterns of 35S-thiamine hydrochloride absorption in the malnourished alcoholic patient. J. Lab. Clin. Med. 76: 34.

Tomasulo, P.A., Kater, R.M.H. and Iber, F.L. (1968). Impairment of thiamine absorption in alcoholism. Amer. J. Clin. Nutr. 21: 1341.

Walsh, M.J. (1971). Role of acetaldehyde in the interactions of ethanol with neuroamines. In: Biological Aspects of Alcohol, M.K. Roach, W.N. McIsaac and P.J. Creaven (eds.). Univ. Texas Press, p.233.

Waterlow, J.C. and Alleyne, G.A. (1971). Protein malnutrition in children: advances in knowledge in the last ten years. Adv. Protein Chem. 25: 117.

Waterlow, J.L. and Weisz, T. (1956). The fat, protein and nucleic acid content of the liver in malnourished human infants. J. Clin. Invest. 35: 346.

Williams, R. and Davis, M. (1977). Alcoholic liver disease – basic pathology and clinical variants. In: Alcoholism: Advances in Medicine and Psychiatry. London: Croom Helm, p.157

Wu, A., Chanarin, I. and Levi, A.J. (1974). Macrocytosis of chronic alcoholism. Lancet 1: 829.

Zetterman, R.K., Luisorda-Opper, A., and Leevy, C.M. (1976). Alcoholic hepatitis – cell mediated immunological response to alcoholic hyaline. Gastroenterology 70: 312.

12 NEUROLOGICAL DISORDERS INDUCED BY ALCOHOL

C.D. Marsden

Introduction

Alcoholism can result in damage to virtually any part of the nervous system, and muscles too can be affected. Acute alcohol poisoning is too familiar to warrant further discussion, and its consequences as they affect the nervous system (fits, hypoglycaemia, head injury, anorexia, pressure palsies and so on), are well known. This short review will concentrate on the neurological consequences of chronic alcoholism.

The problem may be approached in two ways. In clinical practice patients present to neurologists with a variety of syndromes which, after due investigation, can be attributed to alcoholism (Table 1). However, the mechanism whereby alcoholics may develop such complications are many and varied (Table 2). An alcoholic may for example present in coma because he is drunk or hypoglycaemic, or because he has had a fit, or has developed a traumatic subdural haematoma, porto-systemic encephalopathy secondary to liver disease, or the Wernicke-Korsakoff psychosis. For practical purposes it is convenient to attempt to establish the major cause of an alcoholic's symptoms but, in fact, most alcoholics, by the time they present to neurologists, exhibit evidence of widespread nervous system damage. Thus, the patient presenting with a typical amnesic syndrome of Korsakoff, usually will have signs of cerebellar involvement and of a peripheral neuropathy. Accordingly, while it is diagnostically convenient to consider the various syndromes associated with alcoholism as discrete entities, these are usually the major manifestations of widespread nervous system damage. Why a given individual should present with a chronic progressive cerebellar syndrome, while another appears with a generalised peripheral neuropathy, is not clear; presumably the variation reflects the different metabolic consequences of alcoholism, and depends on such features as inherent vulnerability, type of alcohol intake, concurrent dietary deficiencies and other systemic effects of alcohol such as liver disease.

Muscle Disease (McArdle, 1974)

An acute alcoholic myopathy is a rare but striking illness. Following

189

Table 1 Neurological complications of alcoholism

Muscles	Acute alcoholic myopathy
	? Chronic myopathy
Peripheral Nerves	Pressure palsies (e.g. radial nerve)
	Generalised peripheral neuropathy
Central nervous system	Epilepsy
	Chronic cerebellar syndrome
	Central pontine myelinolysis
	Marchiafava-Bignami syndrome
	Amblyopia
	Wernicke-Korsakoff syndrome
	Dementia

Table 2 Mechanisms of neurological damage due to alcoholism

1. Direct alcohol poisoning	e.g. Acute myopathy
2. Secondary to vitamin deficiency	e.g. Wernicke-Korsakoff syndrome
3. Secondary to other metabolic consequences of alcoholism	e.g. Liver disease, hypoglycaemia, hyponatraemia
4. Secondary to trauma, anoxia, etc.	e.g. Head injury
5. Secondary to combinations of a variety of factors	e.g. Dementia

a prolonged debauch, the alcoholic presents with swollen, painful weak muscles and sometimes myoglobinuria as a result of acute muscle necrosis. Hyperkalaemia, renal damage and death have been reported. (Hypokalaemic weakness may occur in some alcoholics, but is painless and unaccompanied by myoglobinuria.) The acute muscle necrosis may be due to alcohol-induced poisoning of muscle phosphorylase. Acute alcoholic myopathy is reversible, recovering within two to three months of alcohol withdrawal.

Whether alcohol can cause a chronic myopathy is debatable. Although claimed to occur, the changes described may well have been secondary to peripheral nerve degeneration.

Peripheral Neuropathy (Victor, 1975)

Peripheral neuropathy develops, to a greater or lesser degree, in some 10 per cent of chronic alcoholics. It may vary in severity from an asymptomatic neuropathy manifest clinically as absent ankle jerks and diminished vibration sense in the legs, to a sub-acute severe neuropathy with marked weakness and sensory change. The legs are affected alone in some 70 per cent of cases; in the remaining 30 per cent the legs and the arms are affected. Both motor and sensory nerves are involved, but the autonomic nerves and cranial nerves usually are spared. Pain and muscle tenderness in the legs, or painful paraesthesiae ('burning feet') are common. Weakness, paraesthesiae and pain inevitably begin in the feet, and usually are slowly progressive, spreading up the legs to involve the arms in a minority of cases. The symptoms and signs are symmetrical in distribution, unless pressure palsies (e.g. a lateral popliteal nerve lesion or radial nerve lesion), are superadded. Such pressure palsies are common in alcoholics, both because of prolonged episodes of coma, and also because of the vulnerability of the already damaged nerves. Characteristically the cerebrospinal fluid is normal, and sensory and motor nerve conduction velocities are moderately slowed.

The pathogenesis of alcoholic peripheral neuropathy is not clear. Alcohol itself is unlikely to be the responsible toxin, for improvement of the neuropathy can occur by restoration of normal diet despite continued drinking; neuropathy does not occur in adequately nourished alcoholics. However, the exact nature of the dietary deficiency responsible has proved elusive.

There is a strong resemblance between alcoholic peripheral neuropathy on the one hand, and the many forms of nutritional neuropathy described under such terms as 'neuropathic beri beri', 'pellagra', 'Jamaican neuropathy' and 'the burning feet syndrome' in Second World War prisoners. Neuropathy occurs as a part of the illness in each of these conditions, in the setting of nutritional deficiency. The clinical and pathological features of such neuropathies are indistinguishable from those occurring in alcoholics. However, while beri beri is attributed to deficiency of vitamin B_1 (thiamine), and pellagra to deficiency of nicotinic acid, in those existing on polished rice and corn diets respectively, replacement of B_1 or nicotinic acid alone does not cure the neuropathies of beri beri or pellagra. Nor can the neuropathies of war victims, or other natural disasters be attributed to deficiency of a single vitamin. The general concept of all these nutritional neuropathies, and that of alcoholism, is that they are a consequence of multiple vitamin deficiencies, particularly those of the B complex. Alcoholic neuropathy responds slowly, over one or two years, to adequate dietary intake and multiple vitamin therapy, although final recovery may be incomplete. The protracted recovery is due to the long time needed for peripheral nerve regeneration.

Epilepsy

Fits are a symptom of an abnormal cerebral cortex, so can be caused by many of the consequences of alcoholism. Fits, of any type, may be precipitated in susceptible individuals by acute alcohol intoxication, by the hypoglycaemia it causes, or by alcohol withdrawal in the addict (as during delirium tremens). Such patients may not have a tendency to recurrent fits in the absence of alcohol. Other alcoholics may be epileptic in the sense that they exhibit fits even without the added complication of alcohol. Indeed, some epileptics are driven to alcohol as a refuge, despite its known capacity to induce fits. Finally, some alcoholics may have damaged their brain such as to establish a more or less permanent source of fits. Thus repeated anoxia, hypoglycaemia or head injury due to alcoholic episodes, may lead to cerebral cortical damage with resulting epilepsy. In practice, a fit in an alcoholic should be taken to indicate incipient or established brain damage.

Cerebellar Syndrome (Victor *et al.*, 1959)

In a relatively small number of alcoholics, the cerebellum appears to bear the brunt of the insult. Such middle-aged or elderly patients present with a sub-acute or chronic gait ataxia, with little or no involvement of the arms or speech. Nystagmus and tremor are unusual. This clinical picture is typical of midline cerebellar damage, and the pathological changes of Purkinje cell loss are most obvious in the anterior-superior vermis. Of such patients, 50 per cent exhibit other neurological evidence of alcoholism, such as peripheral neuropathy or the Wernicke-Korsakoff syndrome, but the symptoms and signs of these disorders are less conspicuous than those of the cerebellar involvement. The cerebrospinal fluid is usually normal, and air encephalopathy or CAT scanning reveals cerebellar cortical atrophy.

Such a cerebellar syndrome usually appears only in those who have consumed large quantities of alcohol for many years. Most (but not all) cases are undernourished, but unfortunately alcohol withdrawal and vitamin replacement usually no more than halts progression of the ataxia.

Central Pontine Myelinolysis (Adams *et al.,* 1959)

This rare and odd disorder usually is only diagnosed at autopsy, when a large single focus of dymyelination with axonal preservation is found in the pons. Such pathology is associated with an acute progressive brainstem lesion characterised by a pseudobulbar palsy and quadriplegia reminiscent of the picture of basilar artery thrombosis, and is rapidly fatal. The illness occurs in conditions associated with malnutrition other than alcoholism, but no specific vitamin deficiency has been identified, and no treatment is known.

Marchiafava-Bignami Disease (Jellinger & Weingarten, 1961)

Originally described in Italian red wine drinkers, this condition has now been recognised in other alcoholics, albeit rarely. The singular characteristic of the disease is demyelination of the corpus callosum. Such demyelination is similar to that seen in central pontine myelinolysis, and, as in the latter disease, no specific nutritional cause or treatment has been identified. The clinical picture is one of chronic progressive dementia, often with fits.

Alcoholic Amblyopia (Victor, 1963)

A small proportion of alcoholics develop bilateral progressive visual impairment, associated with characteristic central or centro-caecal scotoma and optic atrophy. A similar amblyopia may occur in nutritional neuropathies such as those common in prisoners of war. This suggests that alcoholic amblyopia is due to nutritional deficiency, and it does slowly recover with adequate nutrition and vitamin replacement. However, as with alcoholic neuropathy, no specific vitamin deficiency has been implicated. Furthermore, the clinical observation that alcoholic amblyopia occurs predominantly in smokers of rough tobacco has led to the hypothesis that cyanide intoxication (reversed by hydroxycobalamin, but not cyanocobalamin) may be involved.

The Wernicke-Korsakoff Syndrome (Victor *et al.,* 1971)

Of all the neurological complications of alcoholism, perhaps those described by Wernicke in 1881 and Korsakoff in 1887 are best known. Wernicke described three patients, two of whom were alcoholics, and the third a woman poisoned with sulphuric acid, who died rapidly after the onset of an organic confusional state accompanied by oculomotor abnormalities and ataxia. At autopsy, similar changes were found in all three cases, consisting of punctate haemorrhages in the grey matter around the third and fourth ventricles and the aqueduct. Six years later, Korsakoff drew attention to the characteristic memory deficit (amnesic syndrome) that so frequently accompanied alcoholic polyneuropathy. It is apparent that Wernicke recognised a cerebellar component in the illness that bears his name, while Korsakoff clearly identified a peripheral neuropathy with his amnesic syndrome. However, the close relationship between Wernicke's encephalopathy and Korsakoff's psychosis was not recognised by either author. In fact, the relationship has only recently been established beyond question.

Victor *et al.* (1971) in a classical monograph based on 245 cases of the Wernicke-Korsakoff syndrome (eighty-two of which came to autopsy) have concluded that Wernicke's encephalopathy and Korsakoff's psychosis are manifestations of a single disease. Of 186 patients presenting with Wernicke's encephalopathy who survived the acute illness, 84 per cent exhibited a typical Korsakoff's psychosis. Conversely, of 158 patients with a typical chronic Korsakoff's amnesic syndrome, 138 presented with a typical acute Wernicke's encephalopathy. Finally, the pathological changes in Wernicke's encephalopathy were similar in distribution, although severer in degree, to those of Korsakoff's psychosis.

The typical course of events is an initial acute or sub-acute illness consisting of an organic confusional state with oculomotor signs (nerve or gaze palsies and nystagmus) and ataxia – i.e. Wernicke's encephalopathy. Untreated, such patients lapse into coma and die. This acute illness is due to vitamin B_1 (thiamine) deficiency, and adequate replacement therapy rapidly clears the confusional state and ocular signs within a few days or weeks. If the acute illness is not too advanced, recovery may be complete. However, in 80 per cent or so of such cases, the confusion and eye signs resolve to unveil a syndrome of memory loss in the setting of clear consciousness – i.e. Korsakoff's syndrome. The latter is characterised by a loss of recent past memories and inability to form new memories, associated with other milder perceptual deficits and loss of initiative, and in some but not all cases confabulation. Such a chronic amnesic syndrome rarely responds to vitamin therapy. Thus the acute Wernicke's encephalopathy, which clears with vitamin B_1 replacement, is seen as the prelude to a chronic Korsakoff's amnesic syndrome, which is resistant to such treatment. The severity of the residual amnesic syndrome appears directly related to that of the preceding Wernicke's encephalopathy, and to the speed with which the latter is treated. Indeed, Wernicke's encephalopathy is a medical emergency, not only to prevent death, but also to avoid, or minimise, the ensuing disabling amnesic syndrome. Established alcoholics are well advised to take prophylactic vitamin B complex therapy to prevent the development of Wernicke's encephalopathy. Unfortunately, Wernicke's encephalopathy commonly is precipitated acutely in the alcoholic by intercurrent infection, a prolonged drinking bout or excessive glucose intake (which utilises thiamine), and may not be recognised rapidly in such clinical settings.

The Wernicke-Korsakoff syndrome also provides evidence to indicate that the neurological effects of alcoholism are widespread. Of Victor *et al.*'s 245 cases, some 80 per cent also exhibited evidence of cerebellar damage, and 80 per cent had signs of peripheral neuropathy; of those whose visual fields could be tested, 3 per cent had the characteristic findings of alcoholic amblyopia; of those who came to autopsy, 7 per cent had pathological evidence of central pontine myelinolysis.

Alcoholic Dementia (Ron, 1977)

Memory is but one aspect of human higher mental function. Personality, intellect, perception and cognition are other criteria that distinguish one individual from another. Dementia refers to a global loss of all such higher mental function. While a focal amnesic syndrome is well-established as a complication of alcoholism, whether a true dementia occurs has been a subject of controversy. However, there now seems little doubt but that a number of alcoholics do exhibit a progressive dementia, although its cause is uncertain.

Loss of cerebral cortical neurones has been demonstrated in some alcoholics at autopsy, while diffuse cerebral atrophy (manifest as cortical atrophy and ventricular enlargement) has been shown in life by air encephalography, and, more recently, by CAT scanning. Psychological testing has revealed true global dementia in some cases, or a pattern of frontal lobe deficit in a proportion of alcoholics with otherwise preserved higher mental function.

Thus, the evidence for dementia occurring in some alcoholics is fairly compelling, although how frequently it occurs is unknown. No single cause can be identified for alcoholic dementia. Many such patients were of obvious normal intellect and attainment prior to taking alcohol, so it is unlikely that the dementia antedated alcoholic abuse. Alcoholism predisposes to many potential insults that may cause diffuse brain damage, such as liver disease, anoxia, hypoglycaemia, malnutrition, head injury, fits, etc. All may combine additively to cause progressive dementia, quite apart from any role of alcohol itself as a direct neurotoxin.

Conclusions

The overall neurological consequences of alcoholism are diffuse nerve damage, affecting all parts of the peripheral and central nervous system. Although individual patients present with predominantly one problem, such as a peripheral neuropathy or a cerebellar syndrome, most will exhibit evidence of other neurological damage. What determines the emphasis in a given patient is unknown.

Most of the neurological disorders of alcoholism are related primarily to malnutrition, rather than the direct neurotoxic effects of alcohol. However, it is difficult to incriminate single vitamin deficiencies, as is the case in other 'nutritional neuropathies'. In addition, other consequences of alcoholism add other insults to the nervous system. Thus the neurological effects of chronic liver disease, hypoglycaemia and trauma may be apparent in some cases. Each patient's neurological problems are often of multifactorial origin. The frequency of obvious neurological disorders amongst alcoholics is difficult to establish, for only those with the more florid problems come to attention.

Finally, it is worth considering the role of brain damage associated with alcoholism as a possible factor in perpetrating the alcohol abuse. Thus, cerebral damage caused by alcoholism could lead to loss of control over alcohol intake, thereby generating a vicious circle.

References

Adams, R.D., Victor, M. and Mancall, E.L. (1959). Central pontine myelinolysis. Archives of Neurology and Psychiatry 81: 154-72.

Jellinger, K. and Weingarten, K. (1961). On the problem of Marchafava-Bignami syndrome. Wein Zeitschr. Nervenheilk. 18: 308-20.

McArdle, B. (1974). Metabolic and endocrine myopathies. In: Disorders of Voluntary Muscle, J.N. Walton (ed.). Edinburgh: Churchill Livingstone, pp.726-59.

Ron, M.A. (1977). Brain damage in chronic alcoholics. Psychological Medicine (in press).

Victor, M. (1963). Tobacco amblyopia. Archives of opthalmology 70: 313-18.

Victor, M. (1975). Polyneuropathy due to nutritional deficiency and alcoholism. In: Peripheral Neuropathy, P.J. Dyck, P.K. Thomas and E.H. Lambert (eds.). Philadelphia: W.B. Saunders, pp.1030-66.

Victor, M., Adams, R.D. and Collins, G.H. (1971). The Wernicke-Korsakoff Syndrome. Philadelphia: F.A. Davis.

Victor, M., Adams, R.D. and Mancall, E.L. (1959). A restricted form of
   cerebellar cortical degeneration occurring in alcoholic patients. Archives of
   Neurology 1: 579-688.

13 ALCOHOL AND THE PANCREAS

I.S. Benjamin, C.W. Imrie and L.H. Blumgart

The association between alcohol ingestion and inflammatory disease of the pancreas has been recognised for almost a century (Friedreich, 1878). Alcohol may cause both acute and chronic inflammation, and while clinicians have recently become more aware of this association, there has almost certainly been a true increase in the incidence of alcohol-related pancreatic disease, as one of the physical manifestations of the increasing problem of alcohol abuse in our society.

Several classifications of inflammatory disease of the pancreas have been proposed. One which has proved useful in clinical practice is to divide pancreatitis into (i) acute, (ii) recurrent acute, (iii) chronic relapsing, and (iv) chronic. Acute pancreatitis and recurrent acute pancreatitis are characterised by acute inflammation as a single episode or as repeated episodes respectively, following which the pancreas is presumed to return histologically and functionally to normal. In chronic relapsing and chronic pancreatitis, however, there is residual histological and functional damage, and a complete return to normal does not occur. Experience of the last two categories is limited in this country, and most reports originate from the United States or from France (Gambill, 1973; Mercadier et al., 1973). There is evidence to suggest, however, that chronic pancreatitis is increasing in the United Kingdom, and moreover, that there is an increasing incidence in females (James et al., 1974). The present paper reviews the mechanisms, clinical features and complications of alcohol associated acute pancreatitis. Data are drawn from retrospective and prospective studies carried out in the Glasgow Royal Infirmary (Imrie, 1974a; Imrie and Blumgart, 1975a&b; Imrie and Whyte, 1975).

Clinical Features

Table 1 indicates the common clinical features of acute pancreatitis. The disease usually presents as an acute abdominal emergency, from which abdominal pain is rarely absent and is usually accompanied by vomiting. Other epiphenomena, such as facial flushing in the absence of pyrexia, are seen with sufficient frequency to be helpful clinical pointers (Imrie, 1974b). Estimation of serum amylase during an acute attack usually provides the diagnosis, although in cases which present

Table 1 Clinical presentation of acute pancreatitis

	%
Vomiting	95
Sudden upper abdominal pain	85-90
Sudden onset pain: other sites	5
Gradual onset pain	2
No pain	2-5
Apyrexial with facial flushing	40

late the serum amylase may have returned to normal (70-300 IU/L). In
such cases estimation of urinary amylase proves useful, since this value
and the clearance of amylase from the serum remain elevated longer
than the level of amylase in the serum. The ratio of amylase clearance
to creatinine clearance is also elevated in the acute attack, and this
ratio (ACCR) may prove to be of value as a specific test for acute
pancreatitis (Warshaw & Fuller, 1975). Acute pancreatitis is a great
mimic, and may masquerade as a perforation or acute exacerbation
of a peptic ulcer, renal colic, acute appendicitis or myocardial infarction.
If the diagnosis is not to be missed, it is essential that these
investigations be performed on suspicion in all cases who present to
hospital with abdominal pain or vomiting.

Management

Deaths from acute pancreatitis are usually related to specific
complications, and our management of the acute attack, therefore,
now consists of a vigorous conservative approach aimed at preventing
such complications.

In the early phase the patient is acutely ill and may be shocked
with severe hypovolaemia, in part as a consequence of vomiting and
in part due to the release of vasoactive kinins, a condition for which
Trapnell has coined the term 'enzymic shock'. This phase of the
illness is managed by intravenous fluid therapy and nasogastric suction.
Urine output is carefully monitored and plasma electrolyte values
frequently checked. Severely ill patients may require several litres of
electrolyte solutions and plasma during the first twenty-four hours, and
at this time central venous pressure monitoring is helpful in selected
cases.

Acute renal failure is an early hazard, and carries a high mortality.
Hypovolaemia and hypotension are obvious causes, but additional

factors such as fibrin plugging of the renal glomerular capillaries (Gupta, 1971) or a specific renal vasopressor effect may also be important (Werner *et al.*, 1974). Urine output is, therefore, monitored carefully and if, despite adequate fluid replacement, oliguria occurs, diuretics are given. Peritoneal dialysis is indicated if acute renal failure becomes established, but there is also recent evidence for the specific value of peritoneal dialysis in cases of severe acute pancreatitis, even in the absence of acute renal failure (Ranson *et al.*, 1976).

Severe arterial hypoxia ($PaO_2 < 60$ mmHg) is found in 43 per cent of all patients with acute pancreatitis, often with few signs of respiratory embarrassment (Imrie *et al.*, 1976a). Arterial blood gas analysis is, therefore, performed in all patients with acute pancreatitis, and oxygen therapy should be instituted in those over the age of sixty, and in younger patients with a PaO_2 of less than 70 mmHg.

Following the first four days of illness, a careful watch is maintained for the development of pancreatic abscess or pseudocyst. The elevation of temperature frequently seen within the first twenty-four to forty-eight hours of an attack usually settles spontaneously. Persistent pyrexia after this time may be related to specific infective complications such as urinary tract or chest infections, but may herald the development of a pancreatic abscess, usually associated with leucocytosis and a tender mass in the upper abdomen. The indications for drainage of such an abscess must be carefully considered at this early stage, and differentiation from pseudocyst formation is important.

Development of a pancreatic pseudocyst may be suggested by persistent elevation of the serum amylase or urinary amylase clearance, and we have found ultrasound scanning of the abdomen helpful in identifying such cystic collections (Duncan *et al.*, 1976). Some pseudocysts resolve spontaneously, but 50 per cent ultimately require drainage, the preferred route being into or through an adjacent abdominal viscus.

Drug therapy in acute pancreatitis is limited largely to analgesia, and large doses of pethidine may be required. In cases of recurrent acute pancreatitis or in chronic pancreatitis with severe intractable pain, a careful watch must be maintained for opiate addiction, especially in alcoholic patients. Antibiotics are reserved for specific infective complications. Anticholinergics are not effective, and the value of specific drug therapy is as yet unproven. The protease inhibitor aprotinin (Trasylol) has been available for almost twenty years, but only one controlled trial has been reported (Trapnell *et al.*, 1974). This showed an improvement in the mortality rate in older patients treated with Trasylol, but mortality in the control groups was higher than that reported in uncontrolled studies (Imrie & Blumgart, 1975a&b; Imrie & Whyte, 1975), and the interpretation of the results is open to question. Double blind trials of Trasylol against placebo (Glasgow Royal Infirmary Trial) and Trasylol or glucagon against placebo (MRC Multi-Centre Trial) are now in progress and the final results are awaited. However, 120 cases have been admitted to the Glasgow Royal Infirmary Trasylol Trial over a period of two years, and there is no difference in mortality rate between the two treatment groups.

On the conservative régime outlined above most attacks of acute pancreatitis resolve within a week. Surgery in the acute phase is reserved for complications of the disease such as abscess or pseudocyst formation. All cases are investigated to identify aetiological factors, and biliary radiology forms an important part of this investigation. Those patients proven to have |biliary disease are admitted for appropriate biliary surgery, and recurrence of acute pancreatitis following operation is uncommon. Patients in whom alcohol consumption has resulted in pancreatitis tend to have recurrent attacks, and a proportion may proceed to chronic relapsing or chronic pancreatitis. Patients with chronic structural pancreatic damage may subsequently require surgery for intractable pain or for jaundice.

Incidence of Alcohol-Associated Pancreatitis

Table 2 shows the aetiological factors which may be associated with acute pancreatitis. It can be seen that disease of the biliary tract is present in a majority of cases, but that in Glasgow alcohol-associated pancreatitis accounts for 26 per cent of all cases admitted. There are several other less common causes, and only 7 per cent of cases are regarded as 'idiopathic', no demonstrable aetiology having been found (Imrie *et al.*, 1976a&b).

The incidence of alcoholic pancreatitis differs both nationally and locally. Table 3 shows a national 'league table' for the incidence of alcohol-associated pancreatitis. The United States heads the list, with more than two thirds of all cases in some areas of the country being of alcoholic aetiology. It is interesting to note that the incidence is different in urban and suburban populations, and there is also a great difference between charity and private institutions. The highest reported incidence of alcohol-associated pancreatitis occurs in areas where there is a high population of young working-class males with a heavy alcohol intake, served by city centre hospitals in South Africa, the USA and Scotland. The differences in incidence reported in the

Table 2 Aetiology of primary acute pancreatitis: 1971-6

58% Biliary Disease
24% Alcohol
11% Minor causes
Hyperlipoproteinaemia
Hyperparathyroidism
Hypothermia
Pancreatic-ampullary Ca.
Drugs
Viral infection
Worm infestation (SE Asia)
Scorpion bites (W Indies)
7% Idiopathic

Table 3 Acute pancreatitis. Percentage of alcoholic aetiology

USA	90% Howes *et al.*, 1975
	78% Ranson, 1974
	70% Gliedman *et al.*, 1970
	66% Lukash, 1967
S. Africa	59% Louw *et al.*, 1967
France	29% Berman *et al.*, 1961
Scotland	26% Imrie & Whyte, 1975
	23% Gillespie, 1973
England	12% Trapnell, 1972
	0% Pollock, 1959
Finland	10% Salmenkivi & Asp, 1972

Table 4 Acute pancreatitis. Percentage alcoholic aetiology:
England and Wales

1959	0% Pollock
1966	1% Trapnell
1972	12% Trapnell
1975	12% Bourke

United Kingdom are not surprising, since the drinking habits of the population of Glasgow (Imrie & Whyte, 1975) differ widely from those of the south of England (Trapnell, 1972). Indeed a similar incidence of alcohol-related acute pancreatitis has been reported from Edinburgh hospitals (Gillespie, 1973), and recent reports from England and Wales suggest a trend towards a higher incidence of alcohol-associated disease (Table 4).

The sex and age distribution of these cases is of interest. Between 1971 and 1974, 191 cases of acute pancreatitis were admitted to Glasgow Royal Infirmary, and of these forty-six were of alcoholic aetiology (24.1 per cent). Of the forty-six cases, forty-three were male (93.9 per cent) and three female. Among cases of alcoholic aetiology, all were aged under sixty years, while of those with biliary aetiology 47.5 per cent were aged under sixty and 52.5 per cent aged sixty years or over. A picture emerges of alcohol-associated pancreatitis as a disease predominantly of young males, and up to December 1976 we have yet to see a case of alcohol-associated pancreatitis in a male over the age of sixty.

Examination of more recent cases, however, reveals two further points. First, the incidence of alcohol-associated acute pancreatitis in females is increasing relative to that in males. Second, we are now seeing an increasing number of cases in younger adults and in teenagers. We have recently reported a case of alcohol-induced pancreatitis in a fifteen year old boy who had a regular high intake of alcohol (Thomson *et al.*, 1975). This increased incidence in young people and in females is in keeping with the changing pattern of alcohol consumption in our society in general.

Pathogenesis

The pathogenesis of alcohol-associated acute pancreatitis is uncertain, but is probably multifactorial. The main mechanisms which have been suggested are (i) duodenal reflux, (ii) sphincter spasm with increased pancreatic secretion, and (iii) transient hyperlipoproteinaemia.

Inflammation in the duodenum may splint the papilla of Vater, giving rise to reflux of duodenal contents into the pancreatic ducts. Proteolytic pancreatic enzymes activated by duodenal enterokinase then traverse the duct walls and enter the interstitial tissues of the pancreas giving rise to pancreatitis (McCutcheon, 1968).

Increased volume of secretion against a closed sphincter may produce pancreatitis. Alcohol increases gastrin and acid output by the stomach which in turn gives rise to an increased secretin level, producing a high volume bicarbonate-rich pancreatic secretion (Schapiro *et al.*, 1966). Circulating alcohol also increases pancreatic enzyme secretion (Lowenfels *et al.*, 1968). The presence of alcohol in the duodenum, however, increases tone at the sphincter of Oddi (Pirola & Davis, 1968; Walton *et al.*, 1965), and the increased volume of secretion against this closed sphincter causes ductal disruption and acute pancreatitis.

Cameron *et al.* (1975) have shown that alcohol consumption may be associated with high levels of triglycerides in the circulation – in effect a transient Type V hyperlipoproteinaemia. Local digestion of these triglycerides by pancreatic lipase produces increased local concentrations of free fatty acids, which in the absence of albumin binding are toxic to the pancreatic capillaries. This is an interesting recent hypothesis which may apply to a small group of patients.

No single form of ethyl alcohol has been specifically related to the production of acute pancreatitis. The relationship of less common forms of ingested alcohol, such as hair lacquer or methanol, to acute pancreatitis has not been determined.

Establishment of Alcoholic Aetiology

Patients are often reticent about alcohol consumption, and careful but direct questioning of both the patient and his relatives as to the patient's regular and recent intake of alcohol is essential. We have found it useful in quantifying intake to establish with the patient the amount of money spent on alcohol in one night or in one week, rather than attempting to assess the volume consumed. This questioning should be pursued in every case of pancreatitis, but it is also essential, of course, that full screening for other aetiological factors be carried out. It is especially important that full biliary radiology be performed, since patients consuming large quantities of alcohol may have acute pancreatitis as a result of biliary disease.

In our experience the majority of patients admitted with alcohol-associated pancreatitis are not true alcoholics, but are heavy 'binge' drinkers. The typical story is of a young male, in the habit of spending several pounds per week on alcohol, who has sudden onset of upper abdominal pain and vomiting twelve to thirty-six hours after a particularly heavy alcoholic spree.

Severity of Alcoholic Pancreatitis

In our prospective study carried out between 1971-4, 110 patients were admitted to Glasgow Royal Infirmary with acute pancreatitis related to biliary disease, and in these patients the mortality rate was

9.1 per cent. The mortality rate in forty-six cases of alcohol-related acute pancreatitis admitted during the same period was 8.7 per cent (Imrie & Blumgart, 1975a&b), despite the lower mean age in this group of patients. Major complications also occurred more commonly in this group, the incidence of pseudocyst formation being five times that of patients with biliary aetiology (Duncan *et al.*, 1976), and the incidence of abscess formation 2.5 times that of the biliary patients. Thus alcohol-associated acute pancreatitis, in comparison with biliary associated disease, carries an equal mortality rate and a higher complication rate in a younger population of patients.

The incidence of chronic pancreatitis is increasing in the United Kingdom (James *et al.*, 1974) and chronic alcohol abuse may proceed to a state of chronic pancreatitis with exocrine dysfunction with or without episodes of acute pancreatitis. Chronic pancreatitis has been found at post-mortem in one third of patients dying of medical complications of alcoholism, and pancreatic dysfunction was shown in fourteen out of thirty-two patients referred for treatment of alcoholism (Mezey *et al.*, 1970). Patients with chronic relapsing pancreatitis who stop drinking may achieve a remission of their symptoms, but we now treat surgically an increasing number of patients who continue to have intractable pain or develop obstructive jaundice.

Is an attack of acute pancreatitis an effective deterrent to the heavy drinker? Follow-up data are difficult to establish in this group, who are poor clinic attenders. We have found that only 10-12 per cent of patients with alcohol-associated acute pancreatitis stop drinking after a first or second attack, and these patients do so because they are frightened by the severity of their illness. In those who do not stop drinking, recurrent attacks are common, and alcohol on the breath is a frequent finding in these patients at afternoon follow-up clinic attendances.

A Worrying Problem

The problem of alcohol-related disease of the pancreas is one which is increasing in this country, and is in particular an increasing problem in young patients. The incidence of new cases of acute pancreatitis in the West of Scotland is at least 100 per million of population per annum, and of these almost a quarter are alcohol related. Alcohol-associated pancreatitis is a severe illness with a high incidence of major complications and the potential for chronicity. The severity of the disease makes the condition an important one since it may result in the death of a young patient during a single attack.

206   *Alcoholism: New Knowledge and New Responses*

References

Berman, L.G., Dunn, E and Straehley, C.J. Jr. (1961). Survey of pancreatitis –
Central New York Surgical Society. Gastroenterology 40: 94-108.
Bourke, J.B. (1975). Variation in annual incidence of primary acute pancreatitis
in Nottingham 1971-4. Lancet i: 967.
Cameron, J.L., Zuidema, G.D. and Margolis, S. (1975). A pathogenesis for
acute pancreatitis. Surgery 77: 754-63.
Duncan, J.G., Imrie, C.W. and Blumgart, L.H. (1976). Ultrasound in the
management of acute pancreatitis. Br. J. Radiol. 49: 858-62.
Friedreich, N. (1878). Disease of the pancreas. In: Cyclopaedia of the Practice
of Medicine, H.W. Ziemssen (ed.). New York: William Wood & Co., vol.VIII,
p.549.
Gambill, E.E. (1973). Pancreatitis. St Louis: C.V. Mosby Company.
Gillespie, W.J. (1973). Observations on acute pancreatitis, a retrospective clinical
study. Brit. J. Surg. 60: 63-5.
Gliedman, M.L., Bolooki, H. and Rosen, R.G. (1970). Acute pancreatitis. Curr.
Probl. Surg. 1-52 August.
Gupta, R.K. (1971). Immunohistochemical study of glomerular lesions in acute
pancreatitis. Arch. Pathol. 92: 267-72.
Howes, R., Zuidema, G.D. and Cameron, J.L. (1975). Evaluation of prohylactic
antibiotics in acute pancreatitis. J. Surg. Res. 18: 197-200.
Imrie, C.W. (1974a). Observations on acute pancreatitis. Br. J. Surg. 61: 539-44.
Imrie, C.W. (1974b). Facial flushing in acute pancreatitis. Lancet ii: 593.
Imrie, C.W. and Blumgart, L.H. (1975a). Acute pancreatitis. Lancet i: 453.
Imrie, C.W. and Blumgart, L.H. (1975b). Acute pancreatitis: a prospective study
on some factors in mortality. Bull. Soc. Internat. Chirurg. 6: 601-3.
Imrie, C.W., Allam, B.F. and Ferguson, J.C. (1976a). Hypocalcaemia of acute
pancreatitis: the effect of hypoalbuminaemia. Curr. Res. Med. Opinion 4:
101-16.
Imrie, C.W., Ferguson, J.C. and Sommerville, R.G. (1976b). Coxsackie and
mumpsvirus infection in a prospective study of acute pancreatitis. Gut.
18: 53-56.
Imrie, C.W. and Whyte, A.S. (1975). A prospective study of acute pancreatitis.
Br. J. Surg. 62: 490-4.
James, O., Agnew, J.E. and Bouchier, I.A.D. (1974). Chronic pancreatitis:
a changing picture? Brit. Med. J. 2: 34-9.
Louw, J.H., Marks, I.N. and Bank, S. (1967). The management of severe acute
pancreatitis. Postgrad. Med. J. 43: 31-44.
Lowenfels, A.B., Masih, B., Lee, T.C. and Rohman, M. (1968). Effect of
intravenous alcohol on the pancreas. Arch. Surg. 96: 440-41.
Lukash, W.M. (1967). Complications of acute pancreatitis. Unusual sequelae
in 100 cases. Arch. Surg. 98: 848-52.
McCutcheon, A.D. (1968). A fresh approach to the pathogenesis of pancreatitis.
Gut 9: 296-310.
Mercadier, M.P. Clot, J.P. and Russell, T.R. (1973). Chronic recurrent pancreatitis
and pancreatic pseudocysts. Curr. Probl. Surg. 1-47, July.
Mezey, E., Jow, E., Slavin, R.E. and Tobon, F. (1970). Pancreatic function and
intestinal absorption in chronic alcoholism. Gastroenterol. 59: 657-64.
Pirola, R.C. and Davis, A.F. (1968). Effects of ethyl alcohol on sphincteric
resistance at the choledochoduodenal junction in man. Gut 9: 557-60.
Pollock, A.V. (1959). Acute pancreatitis, analysis of 100 patients. Brit. Med. J.
1: 6-14.
Ranson, J.H.C., Rifkind, K.M., Roses, D.F., Fink, S.D., Eng, K. and Spencer, F.C.

(1974). Prognostic signs and the role of operative management in acute pancreatitis. Surg. Gyn. Obst. 139: 69-81.

Ranson, J.H.C., Rifkind, K.M. and Turner, J.W. (1976). Prognostic signs and non-operative peritoneal lavage in acute pancreatitis. Surg. Gyn. Obst. 143: 209-219.

Salmenkivi, K. and Asp, K. (1972). The aetiology and treatment of acute pancreatitis. Ann. Chir. Gynaecol. Fenn. 61: 281-3.

Schapiro, M.D.H., Wruble, L.D. and Britt, L.G. (1966). The possible mechanism of alcohol in the production of acute pancreatitis. Surgery 60: 1108-11.

Thomson, W.O., Imrie, C.W. and Joffe, S.N. (1975). Alcohol-associated pancreatitis in a 15 year old. Lancet 2: 1256.

Trapnell, J.E. (1966). The natural history and prognosis of acute pancreatitis. Ann. Roy. Coll. Surg. 38: 265-87.

Trapnell, J.E. (1972). The natural history and management of acute pancreatitis. Clin. Gastroenterol. 1: 147-66.

Trapnell, J.E. Rigby, C.C., Talbot, C.H. and Duncan, E.H.L. (1974). A controlled trial of Trasylol in the treatment of acute pancreatitis,. Brit. J. Surg. 61: 177-82.

Walton, B.E. Schapiro, H., Yeung, T. and Woodward, E.R. (1965). Effect of alcohol on pancreatic duct pressure. Amer. Surg. 31: 142-4.

Werner, M.H., Hayes, D.F., Lucas, C.E. and Rosenberg, I.K. (1974). Renal vasoconstriction in association with acute pancreatitis. Amer. J. Surg. 127: 185-90.

Warshaw, A.L. and Fuller, A.F. (1975). Specificity of increased renal clearance of amylase in diagnosis of acute pancreatitis. New Engl. J. Med. 292: 325-8.

14 ALCOHOL-INDUCED HYPOGLYCAEMIA AND ENDOCRINOPATHY

Vincent Marks

The syndrome of alcohol-induced hypoglycaemia is particularly important amongst the many alterations in metabolic and endocrine function produced by alcohol; not only because of its high mortality but also because of its possible contribution — when it occurs in a non-fatal form — to some of the long-term neurological and psychological disorders associated with chronic alcohol abuse.

Alcohol-induced hypoglycaemia was first observed by Brown and Harvey (1941) amongst illicit alcohol users in the USA. They, and most subsequent workers, considered that it might be due to hepatotoxicity from contaminants in the liquor rather than to alcohol itself (Tucker & Porter, 1942; Gadsden, Mellette & Miller, 1958). Not until twenty years later was it established, beyond doubt (Freinkel et al., 1963; Field et al., 1963; Marks & Medd, 1964) that pure alcohol alone is capable of producing severe and not infrequently fatal hypoglycaemia in susceptible subjects. Despite the fact that many hundreds of cases of alcohol-induced hypoglycaemia have been described in the literature, and doubtless many thousands more have gone unreported or undetected, the syndrome is still unknown to many whose job brings them into close contact with potential sufferers.

Fasting Hypoglycaemia

The best known and characterised type of alcohol-induced hypoglycaemia (Marks & Rose, 1965) is that which develops within six to thirty-six hours of the ingestion, by a previously malnourished or fasting individual, of a moderate to large amount of an alcohol-containing beverage providing 50-150 ml of pure ethanol, or more. This type of hypoglycaemia can be considered to be a variety of 'fasting' hypoglycaemia since — as will be explained later — the effect of alcohol in this situation is to produce accelerated starvation rather than to produce hypoglycaemia by pharmacological action. No age group is exempt from this type of alcohol-induced hypoglycaemia, but children are particularly susceptible to it. A disproportionately large number of references in the literature are to children and infants who, having gained access to the family cocktail cabinet, remained undiscovered until they had ingested a considerable amount of palatable but alcohol-rich liquor, such as sherry or port.

Patients are usually either stuporose or comatose when first seen by the doctor. The clinical features of acute neuroglycopenia such as a flushed, sweaty skin and tachycardia are generally completely absent. A history of recent alcohol ingestion can often be obtained from witnesses and the patient's breath may smell of drink although it seldom reeks of it. Nevertheless, the neurological symptoms may be mistakenly attributed to alcohol intoxication. Actual measurement of the blood alcohol concentration, however, more often reveals a value of less than 100 mg-100 ml than one above it (Madison, 1968). Hypothermia, with or without trismus, is common and may be the first clue to the presence of hypoglycaemia which can readily be confirmed, at the bedside, by measuring the blood glucose concentration with Dextrostix (Ames).

Diagnosis and Treatment

The blood glucose concentration in a patient with alcohol-induced hypoglycaemia is almost invariably below 40 mg-100 ml (2.2 mmol-litre) and often less than 30 mg-100 ml (1.5 mmol-litre). Lactic acidosis is common. Plasma insulin concentration is invariably low at the time of attack — and this might be useful, in retrospect, to help eliminate a diagnosis of hypoglycaemia due to insulinoma (Kahil *et al.*, 1964).

Clinically the distinction between alcohol-induced hypoglycaemia and coma due to alcoholic intoxication may be difficult if not impossible; indeed one cause of coma may merge insensibly and fatally into the other — hence the warning that 'tonight's hyperglycaemic inebriate may be tomorrow's hypoglycaemic corpse'.

Alcohol-induced hypoglycaemia, once diagnosed, can be treated by giving the stuporose but still conscious patient 25-30 g sugar by mouth; the comatose patient should be given the same amount of glucose intravenously. Intramuscular glucagon, which by liberating glucose from the liver is effective in relieving most other types of spontaneous and induced hypoglycaemia, is ineffective in alcohol-induced hypoglycaemia and is contraindicated.

Most of the reported cases have suffered only a single episode of alcohol-induced hypoglycaemia. Recurrent episodes are not uncommon, however (Tucker & Porter, 1942; Fredericks & Lazor, 1963; Freinkel *et al.*, 1963), and this can lead to confusion with other types of spontaneous hypoglycaemia. The most important clues to the correct diagnosis are an accurate history and blood alcohol, blood glucose and plasma insulin determinations, made on blood collected at the time of the hypoglycaemic episode. Provocative tests are of limited value as it may not be possible to reproduce the dietary conditions prevailing at the time of the original episode. Nevertheless, precipitation of an hypoglycaemic episode by the administration of 50-60 ml of alcohol after an overnight fast is strong suggestive evidence in favour of alcohol-induced hypoglycaemia (Marks & Medd, 1964; Freinkel & Arky, 1966; De Moura, Correia & Madiera, 1967).

Natural History

Spontaneous recovery from individual episodes of alcohol-induced hypoglycaemia is presumably the rule – even in the absence of specific treatment. Many deaths have, however, been reported from this condition even when hypoglycaemia was corrected immediately it was diagnosed. In the series of cases collected from the literature by Madison (1968), for example, a fatal outcome was recorded in 11 per cent of the adults and 25 per cent of the children, due presumably to irreversible brain damage.

In view of the known damaging effect of prolonged hypoglycaemia upon both central and peripheral nervous tissue (Marks & Rose, 1965), the possibility that at least some of the neurological consequences of chronic alcoholism are due to one or more unrecognised, but spontaneously recovering, episodes of alcohol-induced hypoglycaemia is worthy of serious consideration.

Pathogenesis

Alcohol-induced hypoglycaemia has been accepted, for the past decade or so, as due mainly, if not exclusively, to inhibition by alcohol of hepatic gluconeogenesis (Freinkel *et al.*, 1963; Field *et al.*, 1963). This is the process whereby glucose is manufactured in the liver from precursors such as glycerol, lactate, pyruvate and alanine which are brought to it in the bloodstream from peripheral tissues and which themselves lack the necessary synthetic enzymes to make glucose. Inhibition of hepatic gluconeogenesis persists for only as long as the alcohol concentration exceeds a certain minimal value. This is variable but is probably seldom less than 20 mg/100 ml. Alcohol has no effect on the release of glucose from the preformed glycogen stores of the liver – indeed in the alcohol naïve subjects large doses of alcohol may, through activation of the sympathetic nervous system, accelerate glycogenolysis and so lead to an acute rise in blood glucose concentration rather than to a fall (Marks & Chakraborty, 1973).

An important consequence of the lack of inhibition of alcohol on glycogenolysis is its failure to produce hypoglycaemia in the recently well-fed individual in whom liver glycogen stores are adequate to supply the body's need for glucose for as long as alcohol persists in the blood — or until another meal is taken. The relatively smaller glycogen storage capacity of the liver in children, compared with that of adults, and the greater reliance of children upon gluconeogenesis as a source of glucose after only a comparatively short period of fasting, explains their increased propensity to develop alcohol-induced hypoglycaemia. Previously malnourished adults and those who have gone without food for forty-eight to seventy-two hours also have diminished hepatic glycogen stores and are especially susceptible to alcohol-induced hypoglycaemia (Frienkel *et al.*, 1963).

Whilst inhibition of gluconeogenesis is adequate to explain the experimental production of hypoglycaemia in forty-eight to seventy-two-hour fasted normal volunteers, it is not, however, always adequate to explain the spontaneous occurrence of alcohol-induced hypoglycaemia in patients, many of whom, though possibly malnourished, are certainly not starving immediately prior to the onset of their attack. Evidence that additional factors, especially a derangement of endogenous glucocorticoid secretion, might play a part in the pathogenesis of some cases of alcohol-induced hypoglycaemia has come from a number of quarters, especially as adrenal insufficiency is a rare but important cause of hypoglycaemia even in the absence of alcohol. Arky and Frienkel (1966) established that healthy, previously well-nourished individuals, who invariably became hypoglycaemic when given alcohol after forty-eight to seventy-two hours without food, could be protected by prior treatment with exogenous glucocorticoids. Conversely, patients with either primary or secondary adrenocortical insufficiency are unusually susceptible to the hypoglycaemic properties of alcohol (Arky & Frienkel, 1964), and many of the published cases of alcohol-induced hypoglycaemia have been found, on detailed investigation, to be adrenocortical deficient.

In view of these observations we were fascinated to discover, during the course of an investigation into endocrinological function in patients admitted to an alcohol unit (Merry & Marks, 1973), that no less than 20 per cent of them had an abnormality of the hypothalamic-pituitary-adrenal (HPA) axis. In the majority of patients this took the form of an inability to increase plasma cortisol levels in response to insulin-induced hypoglycaemia, despite a perfectly normal response to exogenous ACTH, indicating a defect in the hypothalamic-pituitary part of the HPA axis rather than in the adrenal cortex itself. In the only subject who could be retested after six months abstinence from alcohol the abnormality of HPA detected when he was first seen had disappeared completely, suggesting that it was secondary to chronic alcohol abuse rather than its cause as others have suggested (Tintera & Lovell, 1949; Lovell & Tintera, 1951).

Steer and his colleagues (1969) drew attention to the high incidence of chronic alcoholism among patients reported to be suffering from the very rare syndrome of isolated ACTH deficiency, many of whom presented with alcohol-induced hypoglycaemia. The syndrome of isolated ACTH deficiency, when it occurs in children, is probably the consequence of an inborn error of metabolism involving ACTH synthesis but, in adults, is probably acquired. Our observations on HPA function in unselected chronic alcoholics suggest that at least some of the patients described as having selective ACTH deficiency are in fact suffering from abnormal HPA activity secondary to chronic alcoholism. It follows from this that alcohol may contribute to the development of hypoglycaemia by two distinct mechanisms; indirectly through its effect on HPA function leading to secondary hypoadrenocorticism and directly by impairment of hepatic gluconeogenesis.

The exact mechanism by which chronic alcohol abuse affects HPA function is still not known. There is, however, evidence from our own laboratory (Wright *et al.*, 1966) and elsewhere of other defects of hypothalamic-pituitary function amongst chronic alcoholics. Some of these abnormalities may contribute to the development of alcohol-induced hypoglycaemia.

It is well recognised that growth hormone deficiency, like adrenocortical deficiency, not only causes fasting hypoglycaemia in its own right, but contributes to its development from other causes. It is of interest, therefore, that Andreani and his colleagues (1976) observed a profound and apparently isolated failure of growth hormone secretion in a chronic alcoholic subject who had been admitted for investigation of alcohol-induced hypoglycaemia. In this patient all evidence of impaired growth hormone release had disappeared when he was re-examined eight to nine months later having abstained from alcohol in the meantime. Further evidence of interference by acute and chronic alcohol use with growth hormone secretion has been adduced from clinical and experimental observations in man (Priem *et al.*, 1976), despite the fact that under certain circumstances acute alcohol ingestion can, by acting as a stressor, stimulate growth hormone secretion (Bellett *et al.*, 1971) seemingly in exactly the same way as it stimulates ACTH and cortisol secretion. But whilst, in rare cases, adrenocortical hyperfunction of sufficient severity to be confused with Cushing's syndrome can be induced by chronic alcohol abuse (unpublished observations) there is no evidence of acromegaly ever being produced this way. Why some individuals should manifest evidence of hyperadrenocorticalism as a result of chronic alcohol abuse whilst others show just the reverse is unknown. It is, however, no more surprising than that some individuals should develop 'diabetes' as a result of alcohol abuse (Lundquist, 1965; Phillips and Safrit, 1971) whilst others become hypoglycaemic.

Finally, there is good evidence that chronic alcohol abuse leads to abnormalities of hypothalamic-pituitary-gonadal function but how far this represents a direct effect upon the hypothalamus (Symons & Marks, 1975; Wright *et al.*, 1976) and how much it reflects metabolic disturbances secondary to liver damage (Editorial, 1966) is the subject of intense investigation at the present moment.

Reactive Hypoglycaemia

The possibility that alcohol might contribute to the development of reactive hypoglycaemia – that is, hypoglycaemia occurring in response to, and as a result of, hyperglycaemia following the ingestion of carbohydrate-containing food, has received scant attention in the past. There is, however, reason to believe that it might not only be much commoner than (fasting) alcohol-induced hypoglycaemia, but also an important and unrecognised cause of alcohol-associated morbidity.

Existing literature on the subject is both confusing and misleading. In the first place insufficient distinction has been made between the effects of alcohol itself upon oral glucose metabolism and those resulting from chronic alcohol abuse and which may be secondary to alcohol-induced damage to other organs; notably the liver, pancreas, gut and hypothalamic-pituitary axis. Secondly, the metabolic effects of alcohol are heavily dose dependent as well as varying according to whether the subject is alcohol habituated or naïve. Glucose intolerance is commonly observed in chronic alcoholics (Lundquist, 1965) but is only very rarely associated with overt clinical diabetes. A slight but nevertheless definite impairment of glucose tolerance was observed by Dornhorst and Ouyang (1971), in acute studies on alcohol-naïve healthy subjects who ingested alcohol simultaneously with glucose. Their observations were not confirmed by Nikkilä and Taskinen (1975) who found no difference in glucose tolerance between alcohol-treated and non-alcohol-treated subjects.

In contrast to its known ability to lower plasma insulin levels when given to fasting subjects, several workers have reported that under experimental conditions alcohol increases plasma insulin secretion in response to glucose-induced hyperglycaemia in man and improves peripheral glucose utilisation (Metz *et al.*, 1969; Friedenberg *et al.*, 1971; Nikkilä & Taskinen, 1975). These are the very conditions that predispose to the development of reactive hypoglycaemia. Indeed, this was observed in some of the subjects studied by Nikkilä and Taskinen (1975).

Farmer *et al.* (1971) reported that insulin secretion was increased and that reactive hypoglycaemia was a frequent occurrence during prolonged oral glucose tests in alcoholic subjects although in a subsequent study only four out of twenty-one subjects tested had a three-hour blood glucose nadir below 50mg/100 ml (2.8 mmol/1). In a personal unpublished series, four of seven unselected actively-drinking chronic alcoholic patients investigated by means of a 100 g glucose load after an overnight fast developed a blood glucose concentration less than 45 mg/100 ml (2.5 mmol/1) on at least one occasion during the first three hours. In three of the patients blood glucose values below 35 mg/100 ml (1.9 mmol/1) were recorded (Figure 1). In none of the four 'hypoglycaemic' subjects did plasma cortisol rise in response to the reactive hypoglycaemia in contrast to what is usually seen.

Investigations currently under way in my laboratory suggest that reactive hypoglycaemia, which may or may not be accompanied by symptomatic neuroglycopenia, can often be induced in normal volunteers three to five hours later by persuading them to take three double gin and tonics, containing roughly 50 g of carbohydrate as sucrose and 40-50 ml of ethanol, instead of a more nutritious lunch at about midday. How relevant these observations are to everyday life is open to question; nevertheless, they add to the growing evidence that alcohol, whether consumed chronically or only at the same time as a readily assimilable form of carbohydrate, may cause symptomatic reactive hypoglycaemia which may itself be responsible for some of the symptomatology normally attributed to the cerebral effects of alcohol.

It might be supposed that the incidence of reactive hypogylcaemia following the ingestion of alcoholic drinks could be reduced by the

Figure 1 Reactive Hypoglycaemia in an Alcoholic. Venous blood glucose
response in a 54-year old 'actively drinking' male chronic alcoholic subject
given 100 g glucose by mouth after an overnight fast. The mean response
± 1 SD in 50 unselected non-alcoholic, non-diabetic outpatients is shown
for comparison.

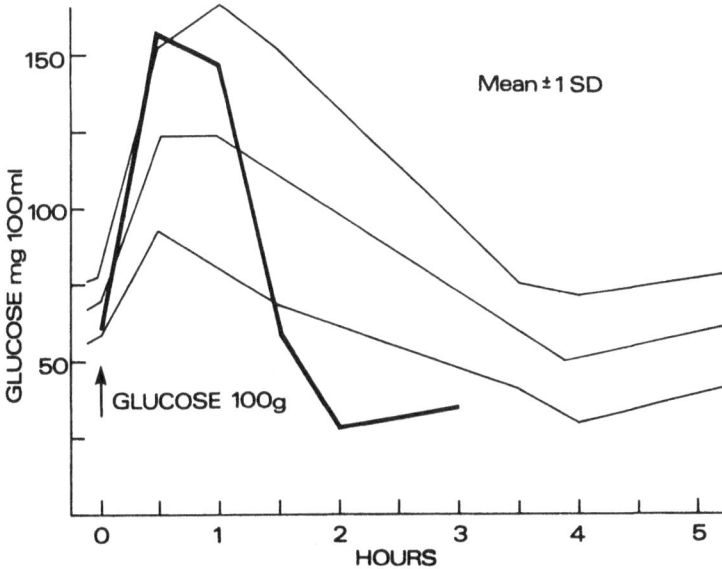

use of non-calorigenic sweeteners (such as saccharin), or non-insulin
stimulating sugars (such as fructose), instead of sucrose in soft drinks
used as dilutants for spirits and this is currently being investigated.

Hypoglycaemia in Diabetics

Two other situations should be noted in which the hypoglycaemic
effect of alcohol is particularly important. First is the particularly
malign effect of alcohol in insulin and/or sulphonylurea treated
diabetics in whom it may predispose to the development of
irreversible hypoglycaemic, coma and death (Arky *et al.*, 1968). The
mechanism is still unknown, but even in normal subjects alcohol can
delay recovery from insulin-induced hypoglycaemia. The second is
the production of hypoglycaemia in athletes as a result of the
combination of ingestion of alcohol and severe exercise (Haight &
Keatinge, 1973).

References

Andreani, D., Tamburrano, G., Javicoli, M. (1976). Alcohol hypoglycaemia: hormonal changes. In: Hypoglycaemia: Proceedings of the European Symposium, Rome 1974. D. Andreani, P. Lefebvre and V. Marks (eds.). Hormone and Metabolic Research Supplement Series, pp.99-105. Stuttgart: Georg Thieme Verlag.

Arky, R.A. and Freinkel, N. (1964). The response of plasma human growth hormone to insulin and ethanol-induced hypoglycaemia in two patients with 'isolated adrenocorticotropic defect'. Metabolism 13: 547-50.

Arky, R.A. and Freinkel, N. (1966). Alcohol hypoglycaemia: V. Alcohol infusion to test gluconeogenesis in starvation, with special reference to obesity. New Engl. J. Med. 274: 426-33.

Arky, R.A., Veverbrants, E. and Abramson, E.A. (1968). Irreversible hypoglycaemia: a complication of alcohol and insulin. J. Amer. Med. Assoc. 206: 575-8.

Bellet, S., Yoshimine, N., De Castro, O.A.P., Roman, L., Parmer, S.S. and Sandberg, H. (1971). Effects of alcohol ingestion on growth hormone levels: their relation to 11-hydroxycorticoid levels and serum FFA. Metabolism 20: 762-9.

Brown, T.M. and Harvey, A.M. (1941). Spontaneous hypoglycaemia in 'smoke' drinkers. J. Amer. Med. Assoc. 117: 12-22.

De Moura, M.C., Correia, J.P. and Maderia, F. (1967). Clinical alcohol hypoglycaemia. Ann. Intern. Med. 66: 893-905.

Dornhorst, A. and Ouyang, A. (1971). Effect of alcohol on glucose tolerance. Lancet ii: 957-9.

Editorial (1976). Feminisation in Liver Disease. Lancet ii: 408.

Farmer, R.W., Farnell, G., Pellizzari, E.D. and Fabre, L.F. (1971). Serum insulin levels during oral glucose tolerance tests in chronic alcoholics. Fed. Proc. 325: 250.

Farmer, R.W. and Fabre, L.F. (1975). Some endocrine aspects of alcoholism. In: Advances in Experimental Medicine and Biology. Vol.56: Biochemical Pharmacology of Ethanol, Majchrowicz (ed.). London: Plenum Press, pp.277-890.

Field, J.B., Williams, H.E. and Mortimore, G.E. (1963). Studies on the mechanism of ethanol-induced hypoglycaemia. J. Clin. Invest. 42: 497-506.

Fredericks, E.J. and Lazor, Michael Z. (1963). Recurrent hypoglycaemia associated with acute alcoholism. Ann. Intern. Med. 59: 90-94.

Friedenberg, R., Metz, R., Mako, M. and Surmaczynska, B. (1971). Differential plasma insulin response to glucose and glucagon stimulation following ethanol priming. Diabetes 20: 397-403.

Freinkel, N., Singer, D.L., Arky, R.A., Bleicher, S.J. Anderson, J.B. and Silbert, C.K. (1963). Alcohol hypoglycaemia. I. Carbohydrate metabolism in patients with clinical alcohol hypoglycaemia and the experimental reproduction of the syndrome with pure ethanol. J. Clin. Invest. 42: 1112-33.

Freinkel, N. and Arky, R.A. (1966). Effects of alcohol on carbohydrate metabolism in man. Psychosom. Med. 28: 551-63.

Gadsden, R.H., Mellette, R.R. and Miller, W.C. (1958). Scrap iron intoxication. J. Amer. Med. Assoc. 168: 1220-24.

Haight, J.S.J. and Keatinge, W.R. (1973). Failure of thermoregulation in the cold during hypoglycaemia induced by exercise and alcohol. J. Physiol. 229: 87.

Kahil, M.E., Brown, H. and Dobson, H.L. (1964). Post-alcoholic hypoglycaemia versus islet cell tumor. Gastroenterology 46: 467-70.

Lovell, H.W. and Tintera, J.W. (1951). Hypoadrenocorticism in alcoholism and drug addiction. Geriatrics 6: 1-11.

Lundquist, G.A.R. (1965). Glucose tolerance in alcoholism. Br. J. Addict. 61: 51-5.

McLaughlan, J.M., Noel, F.J. and Moodie, C.A. (1973). Hypoglycaemia in humans induced by alcohol and a low carbohydrate diet. Nutritional Reports International 5: 331-6.

Madison, L.L. (1968). Ethanol-induced hypoglycaemia. Advances in Metabolic Disorders 3: 85-109.

Marks, V. and Chakraborty, J. (1973). The clinical endocrinology of alcoholism. J. Alcohol. 8: 94-103.

Marks, V. and Medd, W.E. (1964). Alcohol-induced hypoglycaemia. Brit. J. Psychiat. 110: 228-36.

Marks, V. and Rose, F.C. (1965). Morbid anatomy of the brain in hypoglycaemia. In: Hypoglycaemia. Marks and Roseare. Oxford: Blackwell, pp.317-19.

Merry, J. and Marks, V. (1973). Hypothalamic-pituitary-adrenal function in chronic alcoholics. In: Alcohol Intoxication and Withdrawal: Experimental Studies. M.M. Gross (ed.). Advances in Experimental Medicine and Biology, vol.35, pp.167-79. Plenum Press, London.

Metz, R., Berger, S. and Mako, M. (1969). Potentiation of the plasma insulin response to glucose by prior administration of alcohol. Diabetes 18: 517-22.

Nikkilä, E.A. and Taskinen, M.R. (1975). Ethanol-induced alterations of glucose tolerance, postglucose hypoglycaemia, and insulin secretion in normal, obese and diabetic subjects. Diabetes 24: 933-43.

Phillips, G.B. and Safrit, H.F. (1971). Alcoholic diabetes: induction of glucose intolerance with alcohol. J. Amer. Med. Assoc. 217: 217: 1513-19.

Priem, H.A., Shanley, B.C. and Malan, C. (1976). Effect of alcohol administration on plasma growth hormone response to insulin-induced hypoglycaemia. Metabolism 25: 397-403.

Steer, P., Marnell, R. and Werk, E.E. (1969). Clinical alcohol hypoglycaemia and isolated adrenocorticotrophic hormone deficiency. Ann. Intern. Med. 71: 343-8.

Symons, A.M. and Marks, V. (1975). The effects of alcohol on weight gain and the hypothalamic-pituitary-gonadotrophin axis in the maturing male rat. Biochem. Pharmac. 24: 955-8.

Tintera, J.W. and Lovell, H.W. (1949). Endocrine treatment of alcoholism. Geriatrics 4: 274-80.

Tucker, H.S.G. and Porter, W.B. (1942). Hypoglycaemia following alcoholic intoxication. Amer. J. Med. Sci. 204: 559-66.

Wright, J.W., Fry, D.E., Merry, J. and Marks, V. (1976). Abnormal hypothalamic-pituitary-gonadal function in chronic alcoholics. Br. J. Addict. 71: 1-5.

15 BLOOD DISORDERS DUE TO ALCOHOL

I. Chanarin

Descriptions of the blood changes in alcoholism and the mechanisms thought to operate in relation to the blood differ remarkably on the two sides of the Atlantic.

A series of studies from the USA have appeared in the last ten years (Sullivan and Herbert, 1964; Hines, 1969; Eichner and Hillman, 1971). These are based on observations in so-called 'skid row' alcoholics who are admitted to hospital in alcoholic coma over a weekend. The best known study is a case report (Sullivan and Herbert, 1964) of a sixty-one-year-old waitress, living alone, on a very poor diet largely devoid of meat, fruit or vegetables who had taken large quantities of wine and whiskey for twenty-two years. Her initial red cell count was 1.2 million, she was megaloblastic and she was transfused. The serum iron was high. Small doses of folic acid 25, then 50 and then 75 μg daily produced a suboptimal response with reticulocytes reaching 6.8 per cent. At this point whiskey and wine were given which depressed the reticulocytes. Withdrawal of the alcohol produced a marked reticulocytosis accompanied by a fall in the serum iron. This pattern was repeated on several occasions until with repletion of folate stores she became less susceptible to the effect of alcohol. This case thus illustrates the two facets of the effect of alcohol on blood, viz. folate deficiency which can give a severe megaloblastic anaemia as this lady showed on initial presentation, and the direct toxic action of alcohol.

The morphology of blood and marrow in the US alcoholics (and sometimes in British alcoholics) is as follows. Many of the red blood cell precursors are megaloblastic. Second, there is abnormal vacuolation in marrow cells, and third, there is an occasional failure of haemoglobin synthesis with accumulation of iron round the nucleus. These cells have been termed ringed sideroblasts (Waters, Morley and Rankin, 1966; Jarrold et al., 1967). Each of these manifestations are present after severe alcoholic intoxication in about 60 per cent of patients, and are only rarely seen in the UK type of alcoholic. These morphological changes are common to a variety of marrow toxins – the best known is chloramphenicol which at a dose level of 2 g/day produces indistinguishable changes.

218

Withdrawal of alcohol reverses many of these changes. There is reticulocytosis — an outpouring of new red cells into the blood and with it a rise in the haemoglobin level (Wintrobe and Shumacker, 1933). In some patients the platelet count may fall on alcohol ingestion and the platelet level rises on alcohol withdrawal (Eichner and Hillman, 1971). The morphological changes in the marrow return to normal in the next week. Because of the strong association between alcoholism and megaloblastic anaemia responsive to folic acid therapy, the American belief is that alcohol is acting on folic acid and damaging this enzyme directly.

In the UK we have studied a group of about eighty patients all taking more than 80 g ethanol daily (Wu *et al.,* 1975). Most of these were living with their families and holding down a job. Although some came to their doctor because of alcoholism, others came with other complaints, and excess alcohol intake only emerged after questioning. Most of our patients were eating relatively normal meals.

The haemoglobin level was generally normal and the single striking abnormal feature was the very large red cell size. The normal range for mean corpuscular volume (MCV) is 80 to 90. A small number of patients with non-alcoholic liver disease have an increased MCV but 85 per cent of the alcoholics have macrocytosis, the range being 92 to 125 fl.

The effect of alcohol on red cell size is becoming widely recognized. In the course of a survey of healthy staff in a large industrial concern Unger and Johnson (1974) found that 3 per cent had an elevated MCV. The majority were non-anaemic. Of seventeen consecutive such subjects, sixteen were taking excessive amounts of alcohol and eleven were heavy drinkers. A survey of the staff of a large food factory in London showed that those who indicated in a questionnaire that they took alcohol — quantity unspecified — had a higher mean MCV than those who did not take alcohol (Dr T. Meade, unpublished observations).

The American interpretation of this data is that alcohol made these people folate deficient. This led to a megaloblastic anaemia due to folate deficiency and this in turn led to a macrocytic anaemia. Our data however do not support this viewpoint. We measured folate levels in various tissues in this survey. Two-thirds of the subjects in the survey of Wu *et al.* (1975) had normal serum folate values. As 85 per cent were macrocytic the majority of these too have normal serum folates. Similarly red cell folate is normal in the majority. Most of these patients underwent a liver biopsy as part of their clinical work-up and a small portion of this sample was used to assay folate. This is compared with liver folate in a non-alcoholic group. These values are the same as we obtained from surgical biopsy samples some years ago (Chanarin *et al.*, 1966). Again the majority have normal liver folate levels. We concluded that neither macrocytosis, nor usually megaloblastosis, were related to folate deficiency but due to a direct toxic effect of alcohol.

In one third of the patients there was evidence of folate deficiency — that is, they had either low serum, red cell or liver folate. In most patients where this could be tested, macrocytosis disappeared only after alcohol withdrawal, but in the true folate deficient group folate was also needed. The development of folate deficiency was related both to the form of alcohol taken and to the adequacy of diet. Thus, where the dietary history showed a poor diet there was a significant reduction in the mean serum and red cell folate levels, but not in the liver folate levels. Similarly the spirit drinkers showed a higher frequency of folate deficiency than the beer drinkers. Beer contains significant amounts of folate (7-13 μg%).

In conclusion the great majority of alcoholic subjects show blood changes, the commonest of which is macrocytosis detected by modern blood counting machines. This is the consequence of a direct toxic effect of alcohol on haemopoietic cells. Other toxic effects are megaloblastosis, vacuolation and sideroblastic changes. All these disappear on alcohol withdrawal alone and are unaffected by folate medication. Superadded folate deficiency arises in about one third of UK alcoholics and almost all US alcoholics used in studies, due to dietary folate deficiency. The action of alcohol on haemopoiesis is not known. There is no evidence that it acts on folate coenzymes and attempts to show such an effect *in vitro* have been unsuccessful. To put it crudely, alcohol appears to pickle a large number of intracellular enzymes (Ali and Brain, 1974; Freedman *et al.*, 1975) including mitochondrial enzymes and some enzymes involved in the late stages of DNA synthesis. This latter finding by Tisman and Herbert (1973) will readily account for the megaloblastic transformation. Inhibition of haemoglobin synthesis as assessed by failure to incorporate ^{3}H-leucine into globin as well as the effect on mitochondrial enzymes will explain the sideroblast formation.

Finally, evidence deserves also to be noted for transient defects in intestinal absorption affecting folate as well as other nutrients, and which may contribute marginally to nutritional deficiency in these patients (Halstead, Robles and Mezey, 1971).

References

Ali, M.A.M. and Brain, M.C. (1974). Ethanol inhibition of haemoglobin synthesis: in vitro evidence for a haem correctable defect in normal subjects and in alcoholics. Brit. J. Haemat. 28: 311-16.

Chanarin, I., Hutchinson, K., McLean, A. and Moule, M. (1966). Hepatic folate in man. Brit. Med. J. 1: 396-9.

Eichner, E.R. and Hillman, R.S. (1971). The evolution of anaemia in alcoholic patients. Amer. J. Med. 50: 218-32.

Freedman, M.L., Cohen, H.S., Rosman, J. and Forte, F.J. (1975). Ethanol inhibition of reticulocyte protein synthesis: The role of Haem. Brit. J. Haemat. 30: 351-63.

Halsted, C.H. Robles, E.A. and Mezey, E. (1971). Decreased jejunal uptake of labelled folic acid (^{3}H-PGA) in alcoholic patients: roles of alcohol and nutrition. New Eng. J. Med. 285: 701-6.

Hines, J.D. (1969). Reversible megaloblastic and sideroblastic marrow abnormalities in alcoholic patients. Brit. J. Haemat. 16: 87-101.

Jarrold, T., Will, J.J. Davies, A.R., Duffey, F.H. and Bramschreiber, J.L. (1967). Bone marrow-erythroid in morphology in alcoholic patients. Amer. J. Clin. Nutr. 20: 716-22.

Sullivan, L.W. and Herbert, V. (1964). Suppression of haematopoiesis by ethanol. J. Clin. Invest. 43: 2048-62.

Tisman, C. and Herbert, G. (1973). In vitro myelosuppression and immunosuppression by Ethanol. J. Clin. Invest. 52: 1410-14.

Unger, K.W. and Johnson, D. Jr. (1974). Red cell mean corpuscular volume: a potential indicator of alcohol usage in a working population. Amer. J. Med. Sci. 267: 281-9.

Waters, A.H., Morley, A.A. Rankin, J.G. (1966). Effect of alcohol on haemopoiesis. Brit. Med. J. 2: 1565-8.

Wintrobe, M.M. and Shumacker, H.S. (1933). The occurrence of macrocytic anaemia in association with disorder of the liver, together with a consideration of the relation of this anaemia to pernicious anaemia. Bull. Johns Hopkins Hosp. 52: 387-407.

Wu, A., Chanarin, I. Slavin, G. and Levi, A.J. (1975). Folate deficiency in the alcoholic – its relationship to clinical and haematological abnormalities, liver disease and folate stores. Brit. J. Haemat. 29: 469-78.

16 ALCOHOL AND SELF-POISONING

A.T. Proudfoot and J. Park

It has been appreciated for many years that people who poison themselves have frequently consumed alcohol before doing so and that many of them have a major problem in the use of alcohol. We estimated from their histories that 64 per cent of male admissions in 1968 had ingested alcohol before taking some poison and the proportion has not changed greatly since then (Holding *et al.*, 1977). In 1968 the proportion of female admissions who had been drinking before poisoning themselves was 25 per cent, and by 1975 it had risen to 43 per cent. As might be expected, alcohol consumption prior to taking drug overdose was most commonly found in those individuals admitted between 11 p.m. and the early hours of the morning.

The extent of alcohol use before poisoning cannot be reliably estimated from the patient's account alone, and at least two Scottish surveys had been carried out measuring blood alcohol concentrations in all patients admitted to hospital because of self-poisoning (Brown, 1970; Patel *et al.*, 1972). The distribution of blood alcohol concentrations in those found to be positive is shown in Table 1. It will be seen that the majority had levels exceeding the legal limit for driving and a substantial proportion were considerably higher.

Table 1 Distribution of blood alcohol concentrations in those found alcohol positive on admission after self-poisoning

Blood alcohol concentration (mg/100ml)	Edinburgh* n=67 (%)	Glasgow** n=169 (%)
<80	26	26
80 — 160	40	46
161 — 240	20	16
241 — 320	10	12
321 — 400	4	1

*   Derived from S.S. Brown (1970).

** Derived from A.R. Patel *et al.* (1972).

We have also found that 45 per cent of all males on their first admission in 1975 had an alcohol problem, including 7 per cent who had physical consequences of chronic alcoholism, 16 per cent who were dependent to the extent that they suffered symptoms on withdrawal, and 22 per cent who were considered to be excessive drinkers. In contrast, only 14 per cent of women on their first admission that year were thought to have an alcohol problem. Self-poisoning related to alcohol abuse, however, is not confined to the individual with the problem, but may occur in his relatives. Almost one third of married women living with their husbands who are admitted because of a drug overdose, have some complaint about their spouses' drinking habits.

Despite the magnitude of the alcohol problem in the population that poisons itself and the continuing steep rise in the incidence of self-poisoning, very little attention has been given to how alcohol may modify the physical response to the poison. There are various reasons for this. Patients with self-poisoning are not usually treated in special units, nor is there much sympathy or interest in this important aspect of medicine. Many poison themselves with more than one drug as well as alcohol and it is frequently impossible, even with the results of the most sophisticated analyses, to assess the contribution of each to the individual's physical state. Hard-pressed health service laboratories may have problems enough trying to assay the plasma concentration of the principal poison without bothering about secondary ones. Perhaps the most important reason is that clinical experience suggests that provided the patient reaches hospital alive, whether or not he has an alcohol problem does not seem to have a striking influence on morbidity or mortality. This in turn may be due to the fact that it is relatively fit alcoholics who take overdoses. We rarely find individuals with severe hepatic impairment doing so.

To clarify some of these matters, the physical consequences of poisoning in 273 admissions of individuals with alcohol problems were compared with those in 599 admissions of adults without alcohol problems. Both groups were admitted in the first six months of 1976. As would be expected, many fewer patients with alcohol problems were aged between twelve and twenty, and more were in the forty to sixty age category. The female:male ratio was 0.6 in the alcohol group, and 3.0 in the non-alcohol group.

The principal poisons ingested by patients in both groups were very similar and are listed in Table 2. It will be noted that they are usually ethical drug preparations. It is extremely uncommon to find an

Table 2 Principal drugs taken in overdosage by patients with and
without an alcohol problem

Principal drug	With problem (%) n=273	Without problem (%) n=599
Benzodiazepine	31	32
Tricyclic antidepressant	11	14
Barbiturate hypnotic	7	6
Other hypnotic	8	4
Phenobarbitone	4	4
Salicylate	5	13
Paracetamol	8	8
Other	26	19

individual taking poisons such as methanol or carbon tetrachloride
as a substitute for acceptable forms of ethanol. One might also expect
that interactions between ethanol and drugs such as disulfiram would
be a common problem but this is not the case. Benzodiazepines were
taken by about one third of patients in each group and together with
tricyclic antidepressants, phenobarbitone, barbiturates and other
hypnotics, comprise about 60 per cent of principal drugs in the groups.

The sources of these drugs in the groups were again comparable
(Table 3), about 60 per cent having been prescribed for individuals
taking the overdose, 20 per cent belonging to relatives and friends,
the remainder being bought. Patients with alcohol problems were more
likely to take drugs bought on the black market – most probably
obtained in pubs.

Following overdosage fifty-three patients with alcohol problems
(20 per cent) and eighty-four without (15 per cent), were unconscious
and were compared separately. The distribution of depth of coma in
the two groups was similar (Table 4), but other indices of the severity
of poisoning, including the need for endotracheal intubation and
assisted ventilation, were less in the group with alcohol problems and
they also had a lower incidence of hypotension (Table 5). The most
striking feature was that only 11 per cent of those with an alcohol
problem were unconscious for more than twelve hours, compared with
45 per cent of those without a problem. This finding may be explained
in one of two ways. It is possible that coma was mainly due to alcohol

Table 3 Source of main drug in patients with and without an alcohol
problem

Source	With problem (%)	Without problem (%)
Prescribed	57	56
Chemist/supermarket	10	14
Black market	8	3
Relative	13	17
Friend	6	6

Table 4 Depth of coma following overdosage in patients with and
without an alcohol problem

Depth of coma	With problem (%)	Without problem (%)
Conscious	80	85
Responsive to minimal pain	10	8
Responsive to maximal pain	6	3
Unresponsive to pain	4	4

Table 5 Indices of severity of poisoning in unconscious patients with
and without an alcohol problem

Index of severity	With problem n=53 (%)	Without problem n=84 (%)
Need for endotracheal intubation	23	30
Need for assisted ventilation	2	13
Hypotension	11	19
Hypothermia ($<35^{o}C$)	2	4
Coma $>$ 12 hours	11	45

rather than drugs in the problem group, while in the other it was due to drugs alone. Alternatively, liver microsomal enzyme induction may have enabled the individuals in the alcohol group to metabolise the poison much more rapidly. On balance, the former seems the more likely explanation for the difference in duration of coma, though increased metabolic rates may be important, particularly if barbiturates are involved. A precise answer awaits more detailed study. Perhaps the introduction into clinical practice of alcohol meters based on analysis of expired air, will offer a simple and inexpensive way round at least one of the difficulties.

Liver microsomal enzyme induction may on occasion, however, be a positive disadvantage when the metabolite produced is toxic. Alcoholics have long been recognised to be at particular risk from carbon tetrachloride poisoning but today this is rare. More important is paracetamol overdosage, a problem which has only become prominent in the last few years. Therapeutic doses of paracetamol are metabolised in the liver to sulphate and glucuronide conjugates, but when a large overdose is taken these pathways are rapidly saturated and increasing quantities of cysteine and mercapturic acid conjugates appear in the urine. The latter are formed via a chemically reactive metabolite which immediately complexes with glutathione and is thereby rendered non-toxic. There is evidence to suggest that the rate of formation of the reactive metabolite is increased when microsomal enzymes are induced by alcohol or barbiturates. On the other hand hepatic stores of glutathione are not increased and indeed are quickly exhausted when a large overdose of paracetamol is taken. Free metabolite may then attach itself to macromolecules in the cell and produce necrosis. A little evidence has been presented to show that chronic abusers of alcohol are at greater risk from paracetamol poisoning but this is not yet sufficiently common to cause anxiety.

Finally, individuals with alcohol problems are at risk of developing withdrawal symptoms if they are admitted to hospital with self-poisoning. This is particularly likely if decisions about discharge are delayed.

Conclusions

When patients with alcohol problems who poison themselves are compared with patients without alcohol problems who indulge in the same behaviour it is found that they ingest the same drugs in overdosage, obtain them from the same variety of sources and are equally likely to be unconscious as a result. Those with alcohol problems however tend

to be less severely ill in other respects and significantly fewer are
unconscious more than twelve hours. The precise reason for this
difference is not known.

It is uncommon for patients with alcohol problems to ingest toxic
alcohol substitutes, to suffer serious reactions because of consuming
alcohol on top of drugs such as disulfiram or to develop hepatic
necrosis after taking paracetamol despite being more vulnerable
because of hepatic enzyme induction resulting from chronic alcohol
abuse. Alcohol withdrawal symptoms are a greater risk after admission
for self-poisoning, particularly if discharge decisions are delayed.

References

Brown, S.S. (1970). Blood alcohol in poisoned patients. Journal European de
Toxicologie 6: 349-51.
Holding, T., Buglass, D., Duffy, J.H.C. and Kreitman, N. (1977). Parasuicide
in Edinburgh: A seven-year review. Brit. J. Psych. (in press).
Patel, A.R., Roy, M. and Wilson, G.M. (1972). Self-poisoning and alcohol.
Lancet 2: 1099-102.

17 HEAD INJURIES AND ALCOHOL
W.R. Murray

In Glasgow one of the main ways in which the abuse of alcohol can become a problem for the general surgeon and neurosurgeon is through its apparent relationship with head injuries. The problem is particularly prevalent in Glasgow, but also exists in other major industrial cities in Great Britain.

The Western Infirmary is a large teaching hospital near the centre of Glasgow, taking patients from one sector of the city. Although it deals with a cross-section of the population, it is situated in a high density tenement area with numerous public houses. It is one of five teaching hospitals, having the second busiest casualty department. During a recent three month period at the Western Infirmary, head injuries accounted for 27 per cent of acute male surgical admissions, constituting by far the largest individual diagnostic group. This figure only included those patients admitted to the wards of the hospital for observation, mainly due to brief periods of unconsciousness, and the total number of head injuries attending the casualty department of the hospital was probably three to four times this figure. Figure 1 shows the increase in head injury admissions between the years 1963-73. At present the incidence of head injury admissions to the Western Infirmary is approaching 1,000 cases per year. When the case records of a sample of patients admitted to the hospital with a diagnosis of head injury were examined in a pilot study, it was found that almost 50 per cent of the head injuries had resulted from assaults or falls under the influence of alcohol. Road traffic accidents only accounted for 27 per cent of the head injuries. This incidence of road traffic accident causation is low compared to most other series available in which the incidence is around 50 per cent (Rowbotham et al., 1954; Barr and Ralston, 1964; Kerr et al., 1971).

A Prospective Study

A prospective study, over a one year period, of all patients admitted to the Western Infirmary with a diagnosis of head injury was then carried out (Galbraith et al., 1976). The aims of the study were to examine any relationship between alcohol and head injury and secondly

Figure 1 Head Injury Blood Alcohol Level

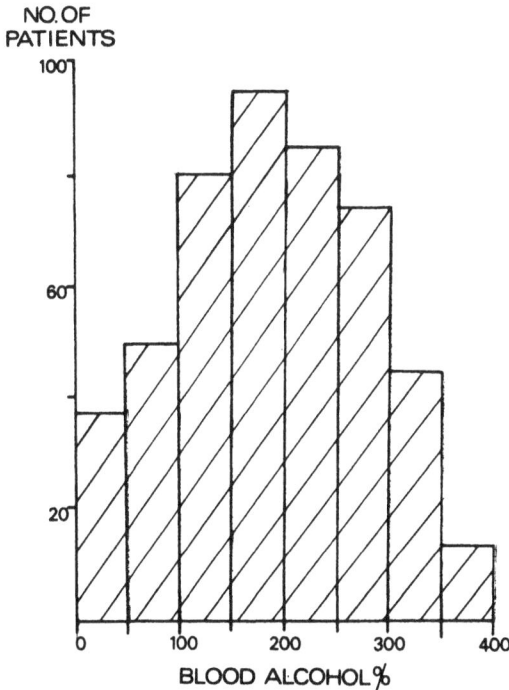

to study the effect of alcohol on the conscious level. All the patients
in the study were examined and interviewed by one of two doctors,
samples taken for blood alcohol estimation within one hour of
admission, and assessment and recordings noted over the admission
period. Over a one year period, 918 patients were admitted to this
study. It was found that 42 per cent of the patients were admitted
between 9 p.m. and 5 a.m. This finding relates well to evening drinking
in public houses, which is often continued elsewhere after closing time.
It was also found that 47 per cent of the patients were admitted on
Fridays and Saturdays, commonly the days when heaviest alcohol
consumption takes place in Glasgow. Since nearly three quarters of
these patients arrive at the hospital after 5 p.m. and nearly half on
Friday and Saturday, a particularly heavy burden is imposed at times
when staffing is difficult, especially in the accident and emergency
department.

Of the 918 consecutive head injury admissions, 658 were men and
260 were women. Figure 2 shows the age and sex distribution of this

Figure 2 Head Injury: Prospective Study: 1973-74. Age and sex breakdown

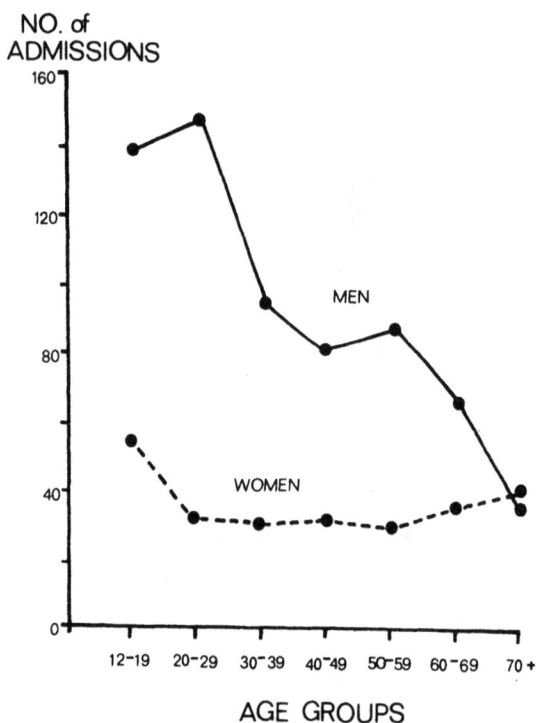

group of patients and it is clear from this graph that men between the ages of sixteen and forty made up a large part of the study group. This finding is in keeping with an association between alcohol and head injury, since the greatest alcohol intake in men occurs in this age range. Of all males admitted to this study, 62 per cent had alcohol detected in their blood. The mean blood alcohol for those men that had consumed alcohol was 193 mgs %. Only 27 per cent of the females admitted to the study had a detectable blood alcohol level. Their mean blood alcohol value was 165 mgs %.

The mode of injury in this large study bore out the findings of the smaller pilot study referred to above. Of the males, 56 per cent received their head injuries as a result of either assault or a fall under the influence of alcohol compared with 32 per cent of the females. Only 23 per cent and 28 per cent respectively had been involved in road traffic accidents of one kind or another. When the modes of injury were compared, it was found that both men and women admitted having fallen under the influence of alcohol, had a statistically higher blood alcohol level than those admitted following an assault. There appeared, however, to be some difference between the sexes regarding sensitivity to alcohol since the absolute values for women were found to be lower than for men. It therefore appears that in Glasgow a moderate elevation in blood alcohol may result in a fight and assault, while a greater blood alcohol level results in a person falling over and injuring the head. The patients not placed in either of these two categories of mode of injury had a mean blood alcohol level of only 30 mgs %.

This work has illustrated that in Glasgow at least, there appears to be a definite relationship between alcohol and head injuries. This relationship is borne out by the time and day of admission, the age and sex distribution of the patients, and the mode of injury of many of the patients described above. Almost one quarter of the cases fell under the influence of alcohol, and here alcohol was certainly the precipitating cause for the head injury. These patients, who are often obstreperous on admission, create a demanding work load for the hospitals. As already mentioned, this work load falls heaviest on the accident and emergency departments where the patients are initially received. At this level the number mentioned in the study may be quadrupled since not all cases of this type require admission to a hospital bed. On weekend evenings, therefore, the accident and emergency department may be heavily committed to dealing with head injuries, and accordingly some delays can occur in treating patients with potentially more serious illnesses.

The Diagnostic Problem

The majority of these head injuries were minor: 85 per cent of the patients were discharged within forty-eight hours, only 1 per cent had multiple injuries and only 3 per cent required transfer for definitive neurosurgical care. This fact, however, must not lead to any sense of complacency. As long ago as 1879, Sir William McEwan pointed out that mistakes were being made in determining the causation of unconsciousness. Patients were being labelled as being unconscious due to alcohol whereas they were really suffering from intracranial damage in one form or another. This problem is undoubtedly still with us, and is accentuated when large numbers of head injuries have to be handled. When head injury observations are being made on a number of patients at one time mistakes can be made. Changes in conscious level and the development of localising neurological signs can be missed due to pressure of work.

Figure 3 shows the range of blood alcohol recorded in the 918 patients. A significant number of patients had blood alcohol levels over 200 mgs %. When the conscious level was studied three groups of patients could be identified; those fully conscious, those disorientated and those in coma. It was found that blood alcohol levels were significantly higher in those patients disorientated or in coma than those fully conscious. The mean blood alcohol level in the coma group was found to be 207 mgs % and in the disorientated group was 223 mgs %. There was, therefore, no significant difference between these two groups as regards blood alcohol itself. The important finding was, however, that 44 per cent of the patients in coma were found to have a concomitant serious head injury. This compares with only 14 per cent of patients in the disorientated group found to have a concomitant serious head injury. It is, therefore, dangerous to presuppose that a patient presenting in coma and smelling of alcohol is unconscious due to the alcohol alone. Patients have undoubtedly died due to the fact that their coma was ascribed to alcoholic stupor when in fact it was due to a treatable intracranial lesion. It is also known that an initial diagnosis of alcoholic coma has lead to delayed referrals to neurosurgical centres. In these cases suspcion is only aroused when the conscious level of the patient fails to show any signs of improvement after several hours in the hospital.

The masking of a serious head injury by apparent alcoholic stupor, therefore, remains a serious problem which must never be forgotten by doctors in contact with these patients. The measurement of blood alcohol levels may be a useful screening procedure since it is unlikely that a patient will be severely disorientated or in coma due to alcohol alone unless the blood alcohol level is over 200 mgs %. Even then patients in coma should always be observed closely for changes in neurological state, since a high blood alcohol level and a serious head injury not infrequently occur together.

Summary

Head injuries account for almost one third of acute male surgical admissions to the Western Infirmary, Glasgow. A prospective study of head injury patients has established that in Glasgow alcohol is a major associated factor, 62 per cent of males and 20 per cent of females having detectable levels in the blood. Assaults and 'falls under the influence' were common modes of injury, road traffic accidents only accounting for one quarter of the cases. Depression of the conscious

Figure 3 Head Injury Admissions 1963-73

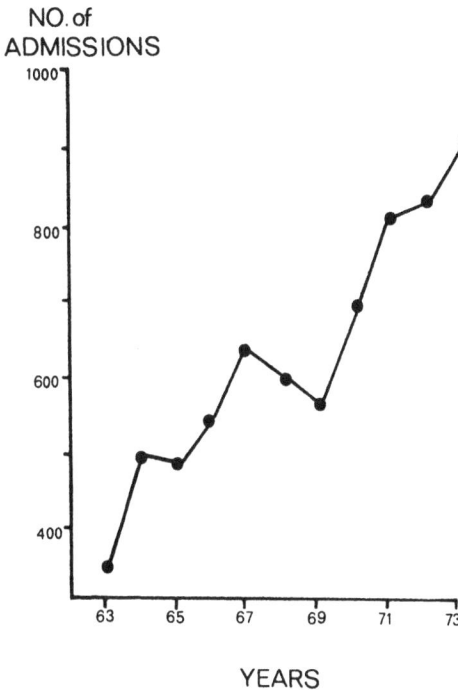

level occurred at blood alcohol levels around 200 mgs/100 ml, but a significant number of patients in coma had a serious head injury. The masking of a serious head injury by apparent alcoholic stupor remains a problem which must not be overlooked.

References

Barr, J.B. and Ralston, G.J. (1964). Head injuries in a peripheral hospital. Lancet 2: 519-22.

Galbraith, S., Murray, W.R., Patel, A.R. and Knill-Jones, R. (1976). The relationship between alcohol and head injury and its effect on the conscious level. Br. J. Surg. 63: 128-30.

Kerr, T.A., Kay, D.W.K. and Lassman, L.P. (1971). Characteristics of patients, type of accident, and mortality in a consecutive series of head injuries admitted to a neurosurgical unit. Br. J. Prev. Soc. Med. 25: 179-85.

Rowbotham, G.F., MacIver, I.M., Dickson, J. and Bousfield, M.E. (1954). Analysis of 1,400 cases of acute injury to the head. Brit. Med. J. 1: 726-30.

18 IMPACT OF ALCOHOLISM ON FAMILY AND HOME

Jim Orford

Essentially four points will be made in this chapter. Points (1) and (2) are central: (1) that alcoholism can constitute a major source of stress for family members; and (2) that this stress may produce a variety of harmful effects, both in the short term and perhaps also in the long term, on family members. Points (3) and (4) are qualifying: (3) that the circumstances of alcoholism in the family are going to be highly various, so that it is difficult to make any generalisations about the nature and degree of stress and the effects that this stress has; and 4) a qualifying point about the difficulty of attributing cause and effect in any social system as complex as a family. It is easily supposed that we are dealing with a simple matter of stress produced by a condition in one member of the family, which then produces effects upon everybody also. It will be argued that, in fact, a family is much more complicated than that, and it is not going to be such a simple matter to attribute cause in one place and effect in another.

Family Stress

Most of the research that has been done has been carried out on wives of men who are alcoholics; there is very little work on the complementary circumstances of husbands of women who are alcoholic. Also, although there has been a lot of speculation about what it is like to be a child living in a family where one of the parents is alcoholic, there has been relatively little good research on stress for children of alcoholics and the effect upon them.

It is frequently noted that the situation is a highly unpredictable one for the family, and that this itself is a source of confusion and stress. In the early days of the development of alcoholism in one family member, the family may go through a long period of indecision and confusion about, first, whether there is anything wrong at all, and second, having decided that there is definitely something wrong, what this something is and what it is to be called. Many people go through a long process of coming to the conclusion that there is a problem, that it is located in the husband or wife or in some other member, that it is to do with drinking rather than with anything else, and that, finally, it is something that can be called alcoholism, something that can be considered a disease, and something that requires outside assistance rather than unaided coping.

A second aspect that has often been mentioned is role rearrangement in a family or role transfer; the idea that functions normally carried out by the husband and father, for example, may have to be taken over by other members of the family. Incidentally, and to anticipate a later point, this is an example of how one might assume that the effects of alcoholism in a family are wholly bad when it might be possible that some of the effects are, for some people and to some extent, good. If, for instance, children have to take over family tasks at an earlier age than some other children, then this might in some cases stand children in good stead for the future rather than bad.

Social isolation and the shame attached to having an alcoholic in the family are further parts of the total stress. Some preliminary work which we have done in the Addiction Research Unit at the Institute of Psychiatry on children of alcoholics (Wilson and Orford, 1977) suggests that this may take a variety of subtle forms, some of which we could not easily have predicted. For example, one family told us that a source of difficulty for them was the husband/father's loud retching in the morning, which because of the circumstances in which they lived – a terraced house with relatively thin dividing walls – made them turn the radio up loud to cover the noise.

A lot of the children in the families that we have talked to mentioned something a little more general, of lower key, than some of the things one might expect to find in alcoholic families. They talked about a generally poor atmosphere and a lack of cohesiveness in the family, and in this respect they tended to compare their families with the families of friends. In the latter everybody seemed to be joking and laughing; a person would come in and immediately be asked what they had been doing, and the atmosphere would be friendly and warm and cohesive. They would contrast this with their own families where there was a great deal of silence, a great deal of tension, not much open communication and where people would tend to go to their own rooms rather than congregate in a family room. In other words this was nothing very dramatic but something to do with atmosphere, the feeling or climate in the home. It is difficult to know how important this is and what the effects of living in such a family over a long period of time would be.

Some of the researchers in the United States (e.g. Jackson and Kogan, 1963; Haberman, 1965) have run up indices of family hardship due to alcoholism. They have included items on financial hardship, items on the involvement of police, rowing, quarrelling, violence and infidelity. This last item comes up in most of these indices of hardship, and that illustrates another important point, namely that some of the sources of stress in these families are not going to be obviously linked to drinking. Now, it may be that in some way or other alcoholism and infidelity are linked, but it does seem to be the case that a lot of problems in these families may have pre-dated drinking problems, and may be just as important to family members as the drinking problems themselves. For example, we talked at great length to members of one family about the father's drinking and it slowly emerged that gambling, which the wife and children unhesitatingly described as compulsive gambling, was as much of a problem. They had really decided that they would settle for labelling the problem as alcoholism because they knew it was too much to ask that the father give up his drinking and his gambling at the same time. For the moment, at least, they would settle for him being called an alcoholic, hoping that he would at least give up his drinking.

A list of all the different sources of stress, minor and major, that can occur through a family having to live with alcoholism would be almost endless, and the above discussion has only hinted at a few of them.

Effects on Family Members

There have been various studies using psychological tests of one sort or another, with wives of men who are alcoholic. For example, a study by Kogan and her colleagues in the USA (1963), using the Minnesota Multiphasic Personality Inventory (MMPI), found that the wives of alcoholics had a generally heightened level of disturbance. Using the Eysenck Personality Inventory here, in a study which we carried out in the Addiction Research Unit, we found that 100 wives had abnormally raised neuroticism (anxiety) scores — not as highly raised as their alcoholic husbands but none the less significantly raised in comparison with the general population control sample (Orford, 1976a). The best research, by Margaret Bailey in the USA (1967), used the same scale of psycho-physiological symptoms that was used in the Manhattan Survey of Community Mental Health. The proportions of women who had scores indicating at least a moderate degree of disturbance were 66 per cent for wives still living with drinking alcoholic husbands, 43 per cent where the formerly alcoholic husbands were now abstinent, and roughly 33 per cent for control women in Manhattan. She also found that the time which had elapsed since the wife had been living with a drinking alcoholic was related to level of disturbance; the longer it was, the lower the level of disturbance.

As far as children are concerned, there have been a number of studies, all in some ways a bit weak because of the problems of sampling and the particular methods used. However, there is a certain consensus of opinion that children of alcoholics are more likely than others to display childhood psychiatric problems of the conduct or behaviour type rather than the neurotic type, if one can make that crude division of types of childhood problems. A study by Haberman (1966), finding that conduct problems and truancy were more common in children of alcoholics than in control children provides an example; and a study in Ireland by Keane and Roche (1974) found that temper tantrums, destructive behaviour and hyperactivity were the types of symptoms found most frequently in a sample of children of alcoholics. Chafetz and his colleagues (1971) found that child guidance children who had an alcoholic parent, compared with those who didn't have an alcoholic parent, were more likely to show symptoms that involved aggression in some way or other, rather than symptoms that involved disturbance of bodily states. In a study of Aronson and Gilbert (1963) teachers were asked to rate one child in their class who had been identified by the researchers as the child of an alcoholic parent, and also to rate three other control children who had been randomly picked from the same class, but who were not children of alcoholics. The teachers of course were blind to the fact that one of the children they were rating had been picked for special reasons, but it came out clearly that the children of alcoholics had relatively bad reputations with their teachers.

These studies – which suggest that the children of alcoholics are particularly likely to have conduct or behaviour problems – provide a provocative link with the work on intergenerational transmission of alcoholism. It is fairly well established that children of alcoholics are at relatively high risk of developing alcoholism or problem drinking themselves in the next generation. Findings on conduct or behaviour problems provide a possible explanation of how this might come about, for they tie in with some of the longitudinal prospective studies of personality and alcoholism (Lee Robins, 1966; the McCords, 1960; Jones, 1968), where it has been shown that exactly this type of childhood behaviour problem was predictive of later alcoholism. It begins to look as though children who themselves have an alcoholic parent are likely to display some of the very sorts of adolescent behaviour that we know tend to be predictive of alcoholism in later life.

Whether we are talking about types of personalities that are genetically linked in some way with susceptibility to problem drinking, or whether we are talking about environmental effects due to the stresses of living with alcoholic parents, is anybody's guess.

One of the aspects that impressed us in our preliminary studies of children of alcoholics and which has certainly impressed other people (Cork, 1969), is the question of friendship formation. Many people have said that the normal processes of friendship formation are disturbed in the children of alcoholics. Certainly, almost without exception, the children we talked to said that for various reasons they found it difficult to make friends. Sometimes this was because the alcoholic parent would not allow other children in the home, or the friend would be ordered out of the house in no time at all. But usually it was more subtle than that, and had to do with the child's feeling of reciprocity in friendship. If somebody invites you to his home, you normally want to invite him back, and many of these children simply did not feel that they were in a position to invite friends or potential friends back to their homes. This clearly links with the shame or embarrassment problems talked about earlier. There is little detailed research on this subject, but it clearly represents an important area of child and adolescent development that requires further attention.

Variations in Stress and Effects
It should be self-evident that drinking patterns vary enormously in the group of people whom we call, for want of a better word, alcoholics, and that therefore the degree of stress and the type of stress to which family members are exposed is going to vary enormously also. In the American studies, using indices of hardship, scores were found to vary greatly between families, and hardship was related to the extent to which the family sought outside help and also to the likelihood of the family breaking up (Jackson and Kogan, 1963).

It looks as if one of the key aspects of hardship is violence: this appears to be a factor that differentiates some alcoholic families from others, and within samples of alcoholic families is related to important other issues. In a study carried out in the Addiction Research Unit (Orford *et al.*, 1976b) we found that families could be arranged along a dimension that had to do with the degree of rowing, argumentativeness and violence within the family. Families varied greatly along this dimension, and the variation was related to the outcome of the drinking for the alcoholic husband over the subsequent year. When there was more violence, then the outcome tended to be worse for the husband.

There has been some American work on coping, which again showed that the general level of coping of wives was related to the amount of violence in the family (James and Goldman, 1971). It was when there was violence that the wives used all sorts of coping. They themselves were more quarrelsome, they felt angry, they felt helpless on other occasions, they adopted a strategy of withdrawing or avoiding the husband altogether, they had tried to get drunk themselves to show him what it was like, or they had locked the husband out of the house. Wives who had tried more coping tactics, were the wives who described violence in the family. The Irish study by Keane and Roche (1974) also suggested the importance of variations in violence in explaining differences in effects on children. They investigated forty-two families, and found that there had been violence in twenty of them, and that it was the children in the families where there had been violence who had the more symptoms. In those alcoholic families where there had not been violence, there was not that much difference in the amount of symptomatology in the children in comparison with control families. So violence seemed to be a key issue, indeed so much so that one might almost argue that it was violence rather than alcoholism *per se* which was the important stress and which produced effects upon the children.

That is one source of variation — variation in the severity or type of problem itself. Clearly an equally important, if not more important, source of variation, is variation in characteristics of the family members being affected: children vary in age when they are exposed to alcoholism, in sex and in temperament or personality. As is the case for any social psychological process, individual differences in reactions of the people exposed are going to make a great deal of difference. So much so, that one might even expect not just a difference in the degree of effect on a particular family member, but even a difference in direction of effect. It seems reasonable to suppose that some things that happen in alcoholic families might be bad for some types of children, or for children of a particular age or a particular sex, but might in some way actually be beneficial to a child with a different temperament or a child of a different age or of opposite sex. We should not expect easy generalisations.

Families as Complex Systems

Finally, the second qualifying point, about the direction of cause and effect. Much that has been said so far might be read as implying that the alcoholic was the villain; but there is a large theme in the literature on alcoholic families which puts a lot of the blame on to the wife or the spouse, emphasising the psychopathology or the psychopathological needs of wives married to alcoholics. There is wide discussion of complementary mate choice and about dominant, assertive wives choosing passive, weak males, of wives having a vested interest in the continued drinking of the husbands — so much so that they actually engineer their husbands' relapse. One frequently hears stories about wives greeting their husbands out of hospital with bottles of whisky, or in some more surreptitious way engineering their husbands' downfall. Then there is a part of this same literature which says that the wives themselves are particularly likely to break down when their husbands recover; that the husband's recovery throws out the complementary relationship of two personalities and the wife breaks down, not when her husband is drinking, but actually when he recovers from his alcoholism. And then it is sometimes said that daughters of alcoholics are particularly likely to marry alcoholics.

This sort of explanation ignores other types of explanation. Just to take the one point about breakdown following recovery: when one family member has a psychological illness, and another family member breaks down when that illness appears to recover, then one could explain this, not in terms of personality dynamics, but in terms of there being a limited amount of emotional room in the family (Hill, 1949). This is the idea that there is only room for one member of a family to be psychologically ill at a time and that, therefore, the wife's illness reaction is a delayed reaction to stress and comes to the surface when the other person recovers. Now that clearly is as speculative as the personality dynamic explanation but the point is that there are possible alternative explanations, and not just one.

Also, when one comes to look at the evidence for the wife's psychopathology type of explanation, there is relatively little evidence for it. One of the reasons that people have used the MMPI with wives of alcoholics, is to see whether they have special areas of psychopathology. In fact the finding seems to be rather that wives of alcoholics are mostly just generally and moderately disturbed. Then again, the work on wives breaking down when their husbands recover is largely based on just one piece of work by Macdonald (1956), in which he found a relatively small number of women in a mental hospital who had at some time in the past had a husband who drank heavily or was alcoholic. He asked them to recall the time of onset of their own illness and the ups and downs of their husbands' drinking — a retrospect sometimes of many years. The evidence in his data is in fact fairly weak.

However, having said that, there are some things about alcoholic families which are not easy to fit into a simple stress view. One is the fact that when you ask husbands and wives, as we did in our study (Orford *et al.*, 1976b) and as others have done in American studies, whether the alcoholic member was alcoholic when they first married, a very large number of people will say that there was at least a serious drinking problem at the time. In our study, roughly half gave a positive answer to this question. This percentage corresponds closely to that reported in an American study by Lemert (1962). We also asked families what the marital role arrangement was when they were first married: although the situation had got worse during the subsequent years, up until the year prior to coming into treatment, none the less the rate of wife domination of family tasks even in the first year of marriage was reported to be very much greater than the generally stated ideal.

In other words there is no simple answer to this question of how to attribute cause in one place and effect in another. There are a number of studies which demonstrate the complex interaction of variables, particularly a study by Kogan and Jackson (1965). In this study three variables were positively correlated with one another: what the wife said about her recent level of psychological disturbance, what she said about the recent level of stress to which she had been exposed in the family, and what she said about abnormalities of parenting in her own childhood. These intercorrelations leave one in no very good position to pull out simple cause and effect explanations or statements.

It is more valid to think of a family as a complex system of parts. In this connection recent work should be noted on observing different members of alcoholic families interacting while at least one of them if not more than one, is actually drinking — a study, for instance, of two brothers, both alcoholics. In practice one tended to drink while the other was not drinking, and there was an interesting complementary interaction of dominance and dependence behaviours (Steinglass *et al.*, 1971). This is interesting work which is now emerging and quite different from some of the traditional approaches.

High-Risk Families

What are the practical implications? Clearly children of alcoholics represent a high-risk group, and they are particularly at risk when alcoholism is accompanied by violence, and when children are already showing conduct or behaviour problems. There is a strong argument to be made for putting altogether more effort into the business of counselling or treatment in families of alcoholics, and the children in particular. Even if more facilities are not going to be available for the treatment of alcoholism in the near future, then efforts might be partially redirected towards treating families rather than focusing so much on the individual alcoholic. The treatment of the drinking of the alcoholic member of a family does not seem to be enormously successful. Some of our efforts might be redirected towards what might be a simpler activity, that of alleviating some of the distress of other family members. This could be done by professional help, or by mobilising self-help or non-professional help.

References

Aronson, H. and Gilbert, A. (1963). Pre-adolescent sons of male alcoholics: an experimental study of personality patterning. Arch. Gen. Psychiat. 8: 235-41.

Bailey, M. (1967). Psychophysiological impairment in wives of alcoholics as related to their husbands' drinking and sobriety. In: Alcoholism; Behavioural Research, Therapeutic Approaches, R. Fox (ed.). New York: Springer.

Chafetz, M.E. Blane, H.T. and Hill, M.J. (1971). Children of alcoholics: observations in the child-guidance clinic. Quart. J. Stud. Alc. 32: 687-98.

Cork, R.M. (1969). The Forgotten Children. Toronto: Addiction Research Foundation.

Haberman, P.W. (1965). Some characteristics of alcoholic marriages differentiated by level of deviance. J. of Marriage and the Family 27: 34-6.

Haberman, P.W. (1966). Childhood symptoms in children of alcoholics and comparison group parents. J. of Marriage and the Family 28: 152–54.

Hill, R. (1949). Families Under Stress: Adjustment to the Crisis of War Separation and Reunion. New York: Harper.

Jackson, J.K. and Kogan, K.L. (1963). The search for solutions: help-seeking patterns of families of active and inactive alcoholics. Quart. J. Stud. Alc. 24: 449-72.

James, J.E. and Goldman, M. (1971). Behaviour trends of wives of alcoholics. Quart. J. Stud. Alc. 32: 373-81.

Jones, M.C. (1968). Personality correlates and antecedents of drinking patterns in adult males. J. of Consul. and Clin. Psychol. 32: 2-12.

Keane, A. and Roche, D. (1974). Developmental disorders in the children of male alcoholics. Proceedings of the 20th International Institute on the Prevention and Treatment of Alcoholism, Manchester England.

Kogan, K.L., Fordyce, W.E. and Jackson, J.K. (1963). Personality disturbances of wives of alcoholics. Quart. J. Stud. Alc. 24: 227-38.

Kogan, K.L. and Jackson, J.K. (1965). Some concomitants of personal difficulties in wives of alcoholics and non-alcoholics. Quart. J. Stud. Alc. 26: 595-604.

Lemert, E.M. (1962). Dependency in married alcoholics. Quart. J. Stud. Alc. 23: 590-609.

Macdonald, D.E. (1956). Mental disorders in wives of alcoholics. Quart. J. Stud. Alc. 17: 282-7.

McCord, W. and McCord, J. (1960). The Origins of Alcoholism. Stanford: Stanford University Press.

Orford, J. (1976a). A study of the personalities of excessive drinkers and their wives, using the approaches of Leary and Eysenck. J. of Consult. and Clinc. Psychol. 44: 534-45.

Orford, J., Oppenheimer, E., Egert, S., Hensman, C. and Guthrie, S. (1976b). The cohesiveness of alcoholism-complicated marriages and its influence on treatment outcome. Brit. J. Psychiat. 128: 318-39.

Robins, L.N. (1966). Deviant Children Grown up: A Sociological and Psychiatric Study of Sociopathic Personality. Baltimore: Williams and Wilkins.

Steinglass, P. and Weiner, S. (1971). Familial interactions and determinants of drinking behaviour. In: Recent Advances in Studies of Alcoholism. An Interdisciplinary Symposium. Washington: NIMH and NIAAA, HSM, pp.687-705.

Wilson, C. and Orford, J. (1977). Children of alcoholics: report of a preliminary study, and comments on the literature. Unpublished manuscript, Institute of Psychiatry, London.

ALCOHOL AND ALCOHOLISM:
THE IMPACT ON WORK

B.D. Hore

The claim often made that alcoholism is a major problem to industry has produced little response; the situation is made more difficult by the unwillingness to allow investigators into individual industrial companies for fear of stigmatisation and industrial unrest. It is the purpose of this paper to examine three aspects of the problem of alcohol and work performance:

1. The effect of alcohol on physiological and psychological variables connected with work performance.

2. Work problems arising from alcohol abuse in industry.

3. The detection of alcohol abuse in industry and its management.

The Effect of Alcohol on Physiological and Psychological Variables

A variety of tests have been used to assess the effects of alcohol on relevant functions. *Motor function* has been investigated using such tests as body sway, finger coordination, reaction time, positional nystagmus and driving simulation. *Psychometric testing* has employed verbal and non-verbal assessments. *Sensory functioning* has been appraised by testing corneal sensitivity, flicker fusion threshold, visual acuity, judgement of distance, pain threshold and olfactory acuity. Comparing experimental subjects with controls, it was shown by Goldberg (1943) and others that there was impairment of function at surprisingly low blood alcohol levels; impairment began on average in the range of 0.31 to 0.65 mg/ml. It was noted that heavy drinkers were less influenced by the same dose of alcohol, and this was not accountable in terms of differences in rates of absorption of alcohol from the gastrointestinal tract nor from body distribution of alcohol, nor rate of disappearance from the blood stream. It was clear that this difference between the previous heavy drinkers and non-heavy drinkers was, in fact, due to a central brain effect and was an example of habituation. In other words, the degree of intoxication and performance impairment, besides being related to blood alcohol level, was affected by previous drinking habits. Besides habituation a number of other variables may also affect performances under alcohol. These include previous food ingestion, type of beverage, previous basal skill level and possibly aspects of personality. In addition at least in relation to skills such as driving (Matilla, 1976) coincidental tranquilliser medication may combine to produce a summated effect.

In a manner similar to that of hypoxia, with progressive intoxication due to alcohol there is a tendency for judgement to be impaired. The subject tends to over-rate the ability in relation to performance. Cohen and co-workers in 1958 showed this with driving skills, e.g. in tests which involved driving through increasingly narrow gaps of vehicles.

Work Problems Arising from Alcohol Abuse in Industry

The two major measures are absenteeism and industrial accidents. In general, both of these are increased in relation to alcohol abuse. One of the earlier studies was that of Stevenson (1942) in the USA in a steel mill, who found that 3 per cent of the male work force missed time through drinking. On average, 382 workers missed one to two days per year. The heavy drinking sample came from all work groups and was correlated with middle age and indices of social pathology, e.g. divorces, separation, etc. and also lower educational background. Glatt and Hills (1965) took a sample of 200 males attending an English Alcoholic Treatment Clinic and found that half of them had lost work during their early thirties, and over half had been sacked through drinking by their mid-thirties.

A study done in the 1960s by the Addiction Research Unit (Edwards *et al.*, 1967) found that 98 per cent of a sample from clients of alcoholism information centres had lost work due to alcoholism and, on average had lost eighty-six days during the previous year; 66 per cent of the sample were often late for work, and 61 per cent reported Monday morning absenteeism. In relation to bringing alcohol to work, 12 per cent admitted to doing this regularly, while 62 per cent admitted to doing so on occasion: 47 per cent had reduced their occupational status because of drinking. Saad and Madden (1976) in Manchester in a recent study have examined sickness certificates from Department of Health and Social Security records of patients attending an alcoholism treatment unit. They found that on average in the previous year, there had been seventy days loss of work if the patient was now in employment, and 208 days if the person was out of work when examined at the clinic. In 36 per cent of instances a psychiatric diagnosis was given on the certificate, 10 per cent mentioned accidents, 14 per cent digestive disorders and 14 per cent respiratory disorders. Only 3 per cent gave alcoholism as the diagnosis. Pell and D'Alonzo (1970) in the USA found accidents, muscular skeletal disorders and digestive troubles as the leading stated causes for absenteeism among alcoholics. A recent study in Sweden again showed high rates of absenteeism and poor productivity among alcoholics (Berglin and Rosengren, 1974):

> 868 patients attending seventeen alcoholism polyclinics in Western Sweden recorded how many months they had worked outside a hospital or other institution during 1970. On average, the 20-49 age-groups had worked during 50% of the year, while groups approaching pension age had worked only 25% of the year. A low production record (0-4 months) was reported by 40% of patients in the 20-49 age-groups and by 70% in the top age-groups. Premature pensions had been granted to some 20% of patients in the 50-59 age-group, and to some 50% in the 60-66 age-group.

It is of course more informative to compare rates of absenteeism among people with alcohol abuse against control groups, rather than just to record rates among alcohol abusers alone.

Observer and Maxwell (1959) in a study which examined medical records of 10,000 subjects found that the alcohol abuse group had 2.5 times the absenteeism rate due to illness of eight days duration or more, than controls. Pell and D'Alonzo (1970) found an absenteeism rate three times that of controls. Gautier (1965) in France, recorded blood alcohol levels and found that the accident rate was twice as high in those with raised blood alcohol than controls, and that most accidents occurred in the afternoon. Observer and Maxwell had found an accident rate three times higher in the alcohol abuse group than the control group: this was accounted for particularly by excess rates among older men who perhaps realise the danger or manage to avoid being detected. Alternatively, of course, it may be that if a man is more skilled at a task the impairment in performance is less marked as previously noted, and accident is then less likely.

An Australian study (Ferguson, 1973) found that there are other ways besides absenteeism and accident in which alcohol abuse can affect employment. For example, people who were heavy drinkers more often took on extra jobs outside their regular employment, were found to be more difficult for workmates to relate to and, generally, were more cantankerous and difficult as employees.

Detection of the Abnormal Drinker in the Work Place

Several workers such as Trice (1964) have suggested diagnostic criteria. The most thorough study, however, of clinical features which may identify the alcoholic employee would appear to be that of Maxwell in the United States (Maxwell, 1972). He examined data on 406 alcoholic employees who were in treatment. Although this study was a very detailed one of various areas of work pathology, in the absence of control data we do not of course know how often any of the reported features would occur among subjects who were not heavy drinkers. In Maxwell's study, 27 per cent of subjects had been away from work for a day or more at some time, due to drinking, and 26 per cent had left work early or temporarily, had taken longer lunch breaks or had been late to work – what was termed 'absenteeism on the job'. It should be noted as Maxwell pointed out that 32 per cent, however, had shown no evidence of absenteeism either on or off the job. Of his sample, 10 per cent reported accidents at work, which were thus in this study fairly infrequent.

In relation to physical changes, 64 per cent showed all or most of the following – redness of eyes, tremulousness of the hands and flushing of the face. Personality changes were an important feature and 54 per cent had shown between five and seven of the following – nervousness at work, edginess and irritability, sensitivity to others' opinions regarding drinking, resentment of questioning over drinking, intolerance of fellow workers, resentfulness of fellow workers, or generally more suspicious attitudes toward fellow workers.

In relation to work behaviour, 56 per cent of subjects in Maxwell's study had shown five or more of the following features – putting off things at work, more spasmodic work performance, avoiding boss or associates, neglecting details, lower quantity of work, making mistakes at work, lower quality of work. Serious hangovers were reported by 64 per cent. As for drinking on the job or during working hours, 37 per cent described drinking at lunch time, morning drinking, other drinking during working hours, or using breath purifiers.

Maxwell's conclusion was that 'important on the job changes produced by drinking problems, changes in addition to and often preceding stay-away absenteeism *are* present in most cases, and in spite of the great efforts which are generally made by alcoholics to conceal this, most fall, in fact, into the observable class'.

In summary, it is clear, therefore, that whilst absenteeism (due particularly to psychiatric disorders, digestive, respiratory, muscular skeletal disorders and accidents) is higher among alcohol abusers and should alert suspicion, other changes as described by Maxwell are frequently present in the employee with a drinking problem. Diagnosis, however, often requires more than knowledge. It requires an acceptance that alcohol abuse may be an illness and that the employer believes in treatment rather than punishment, and acceptance that reporting workmates is beneficial to them in the long term. Without a clear cut and preferably written company policy and an active rehabilitation programme, detection will not occur; indeed, there is no incentive for it to occur. As yet in the United Kingdom these two important planks are frequently absent. Without such policies, alcoholism remains, as always, the hidden disease.

Company managements and trade union organisations in Britain indeed behave over alcoholism in some ways rather like the alcoholic: because of the social and moral stigmata associated with alcoholism, they vigorously deny the problem and are reluctant to take corrective action. By 1972, thirty-nine of the 100 largest companies in the USA including Du Pont, Goodyear Rubber, US Steel, British American Oil Company (Von Weigand, 1972), had, or were in the process of developing alcoholism programmes. From 1966 to 1972 more alcoholism programmes were introduced there than in the previous twenty-five years. In Great Britain, apart from a handful of programmes, such programmes are generally non-existent. The usual approach in Great Britain is to ignore the problem until it becomes too serious, when dismissal is often then inevitable. The incidence of alcoholism in England is half that of the USA. In Scotland, it is at least as high.

Company Programmes

Von Weigand (1972) has given a detailed and persuasive analysis of the reasons why it is in the interests of both employer and employee that companies should set up rehabilitation programmes for people with drinking problems. He has provided tangible evidence for the cost-effectiveness of such policies. Production will be increased, cost of training new personnel avoided, and the bill for sick-pay curtailed. For instance, the US Post Office with 700,000 employees has projected a net benefit of $37 million annual saving from an energetic alcoholism programme. Industrial programmes can generally expect a 50 to 70 per cent success rate, and the person who is still in employment and socially stable is likely to be particularly well motivated for treatment.

Von Weigand believes that the cornerstone of any company policy must be the public declaration that alcoholism will be viewed as an illness, which will be handled in the same manner as any non-alcoholic disease. He outlines a number of practical steps for setting up a company alcohol programme – all instances of *unsatisfactory performance* should be documented in writing by the employee's supervisor, this written record will be the basis for review, discussion and counselling. Where corrective action is seen to be needed, and if problems in work performance continue and alcohol is deemed to be involved, then at a second interview the employee must be offered a number of clear choices. He may be offered leave of absence on condition that he is sober when he returns, or he may be offered treatment either of his own choice or within the company programme.

It is perfectly feasible to organise such programmes in Britain, and large companies should develop their own programmes. The major block is the recognition of need for such policies. Cooperation with organised labour should not be difficult, as labour usually reacts whole-heartedly when it is understood that the programme is in the employee's best interests, and that to permit him to operate comfortably in a job where his alcohol-related absenteeism and other violations are tolerated or excused is potentially to kill him with kindness, and to deny him the treatment which he is not able or not competent to seek for himself and which he so desperately needs.

References

Berglin, C.G. and Rosengren, E. (1974). The capacity for work and pensionability of 868 alcoholics. Swedish Med. Journal (in Swedish). Lakartidningen 71: 3520.

Cohen, J., Dearnley, E.J. and Hansell, C.E. (1958). The role taken in driving under the influence of alcohol. Brit. Med. J. 1: 1438.

Edwards, G., Kellog-Fisher, M., Hawker, A. and Hensman, C. (1967). Clients of alcoholism information centres. Brit. Med. J. 4: 346.

Ferguson, D. (1973). Smoking, drinking and non-narcotic analgesic habits in an occupational group. Med. J. of Australia 1: 1271.

Gautier, F. (1965). The industrial doctor's part in the control of alcoholism, the value of the ricossery test. (In French.) Rev. Alcoholism. 11: 312.

Glatt, M.M. and Hills, D.R. (1965). Occupational behaviour patterns in samples of English alcoholic employees. Brit. J. of Addict. 61: 71.

Goldberg, L. (1943). Quantitative studies of alcohol tolerance in man. Acta Physiol. Scand. Suppl. 16.

Maxwell, M.A. Alcoholic Employees, Behaviour Changes and Occupational Alcoholism Programme. Proceedings 30th int. Cong. on Alcoholism and Drug Dependence, Int. Council on Alcohol and Addictions, Case Postale 140, 1001 Lausanne.

Matilla, M. (ed.) (1976). Alcohol, drugs and driving. Modern Problems of Pharmacopsychiatry, vol.11, S. Karger.

Observer and Maxwell, M.A. (1957). A Study of absenteeism, accidents and sickness payments in problems drinkers in industry. Quart. J. Std. Alc. 20: 302.
Pell, S. and D'Alonzo, C.A. (1970). Sickness absenteeism and alcoholics. J. Occ. Med. 12: 198.
Saad E.S.N. and Madden J.S. (1976). Certified incapacity and unemployment in alcoholics. Br. J. Psych. 128: 340.
Stevenson, R.W. (1942). Absenteeism in an industrial plant due to alcoholism. Quart. J. Stud. ACC 2: 661.
Trice, H. (1964). New light on identifying the alcoholic employee. Personal, September/October.
Von Wiegand R.A. (1972). Alcoholism in industry. Bri. J. Add. 67: 181.

20 ALCOHOL AND ROAD ACCIDENTS
J.D.J. Havard

Introduction

Road accidents are the leading cause of death in European countries after the age of one year up to the age of about forty-five, and this disproportionate age distribution makes road accidents an important cause of loss of expectation of life, second only to malignant and cardiovascular disease. From Table 1 it can be seen that road accidents account for nearly one half of all male deaths in 15-24 age group. Furthermore, road accidents are a leading cause of permanent incapacity in the community, and again, as can be seen from Figure 1, the risk is highest in the 15-24 age group in the case of occupants of motor vehicles.

Research in Britain and other countries has shown that human factors are contributory in about 95 per cent of road accidents and that they are solely responsible for at least two thirds of all accidents. Most of the human factors which have been identified as increasing the risk of road accidents are either incapable of being quantified by existing techniques (e.g. fatigue), or are not amenable to modification (e.g. sex, age, years of completed education, etc.). The outstanding exception is ethyl alcohol. The combination of a drug which is accepted as a social habit and which is at the same time the most powerful depressant of the central nervous system to be freely available without the need for a medical prescription, is bound to create problems in connection with tasks such as driving in traffic which require a high level of perception and the ability to divide attention.

The Role of Alcohol in Road Accidents

Early studies on alcohol, based on simple reaction time and tests of concentrating attention, yielded equivocal results, as it was not appreciated that driving is a complex skill requiring appropriate distribution of attention and differential reactions. More recently case control studies have enabled us to identify the increased risk of accident involvement which occurs at various blood alcohol concentrations and Figure 2 sets out the results of one of the most important studies. As the blood alcohol concentration approaches 50 mg/100 ml the risk begins to increase. In between 50-80 mg/100 ml the extent of the

Table 1　Percentage of deaths among men due to motor vehicles in 1967, by country, for all ages combined and in age group 15-24

Country	Number of deaths due to motor vehicle accidents per 100 deaths from all causes	
	All ages	15-24 years
Germany, Federal Republic	3.6	50.2
Netherlands	3.8	47.3
Denmark	3.2	45.6
Belgium	2.9	44.2
France	3.6	43.8
Austria	3.7	43.3
England and Wales	1.8	41.9
Northern Ireland	2.2	41.0
Sweden	2.0	35.3
Switzerland	3.8	34.2
Scotland	1.8	33.2
Finland	3.3	32.5
Greece	2.3	28.8
Czechoslovakia	2.5	28.1
Ireland	1.7	28.0
Norway 1.8	1.8	27.2
Iceland	3.1	24.1
Portugal	2.6	21.6
Bulgaria	2.3	20.3
Poland	1.8	14.9
Hungary	1.3	14.4

Source: World Health Organisation (1970) World Health Statistics Annual 1967. WHO, Geneva.

increase in risk depends on the presence of absence of certain other factors which influence the risk of accident, e.g. age, sex, driving experience, years of completed schooling, marital status, alcohol habit, etc. By the time a concentration of 80 mg/100 ml is reached the effect of all these variable factors is ironed out and, in terms of the criminal law, it is possible to say beyond reasonable doubt that a driver with a blood alcohol concentration in excess of 80 mg/100 ml is more likely

Figure 1 Age Distribution of Road Accident Casualties — Drivers and passengers in four European countries

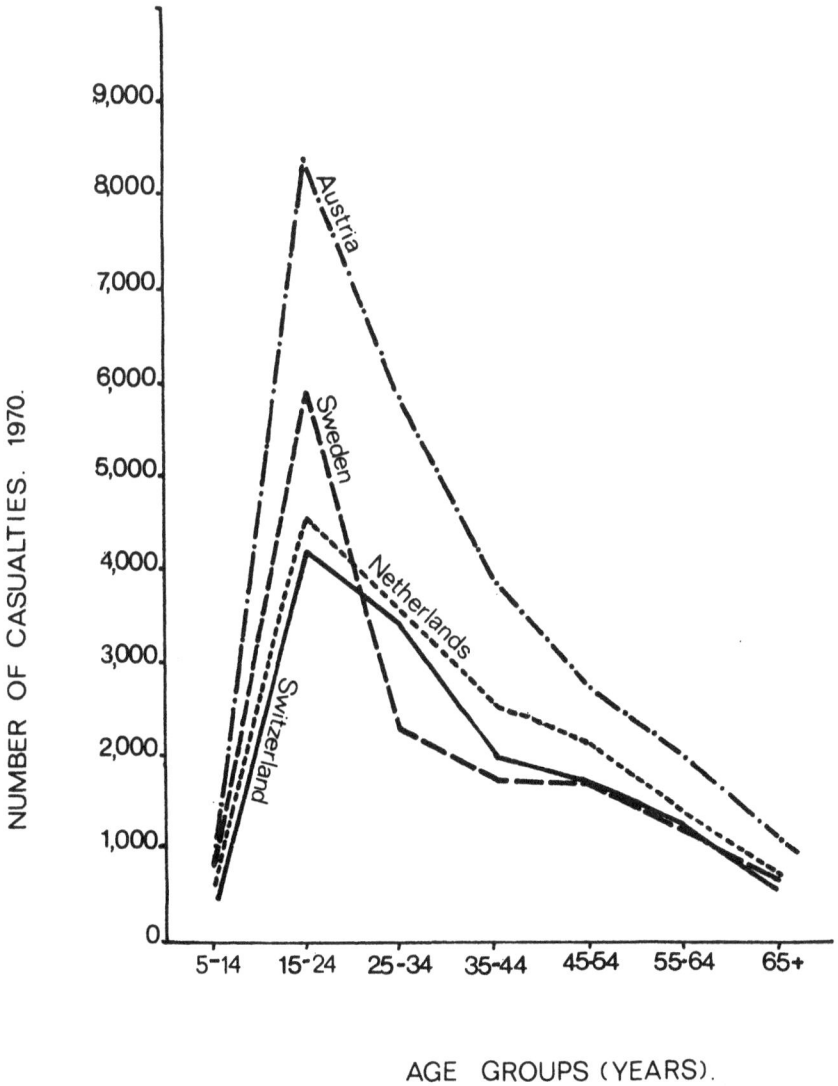

AGE   GROUPS (YEARS).

Source: Havard, J.D.J. (1973). Road Traffic Accidents. WHO Chronicle, vol.27, no.3, Fig.1, p.84.

to be involved in a road accident than if he had taken no alcohol or very little at all. This was the basis for the selection of 80 mg/100 ml as the limit for purposes of the new offence created by the Road Safety Act, 1967; the remainder of this chapter will concentrate on a discussion of the reasons why this act was not as successful as it might have been.

The Immediate Effect of the British Road Safety Act, 1967

The immediate results of this act were very satisfactory (Figure 3). On Saturday night and Sunday morning the casualty savings (estimated on the basis of the previous year's figures) were in the region of 40 per cent (Codling, 1975), a phenomenon which could not possibly be explained by the assumption that the Act has been totally successful in modifying the alcohol habit of drivers. My own interpretation of this bizarre result in the first year is that drivers knew that they could not be required under the Act to take a breath test unless they had been involved in an accident, in a moving traffic offence, or the police had reasonable grounds to believe they were intoxicated. Therefore drivers drove more carefully whether or not they had been drinking as they did not want to have to take the test.

The Failure to Maintain Casualty Savings

Figure 4 shows that the casualty savings were not maintained. The drop in 1974 is due largely to speed limits and other factors associated with the energy crisis which followed the Israeli war. In 1975 there was no further reduction and the most recent figures show a 5 per cent increase in casualties for the second quarter of 1976 as compared with the corresponding quarter of 1975. Perhaps the best way to discuss the reasons why the Act has lost much of its effect is by pointing out the measures which should have been taken in the years following 1967 in order to achieve the desired results. The need for these measures to be taken was in fact argued by me with the Director of Road Research in 1967, but the arguments were not accepted. As it happens the Blennerhassett Committee (Department of the Environment, 1976), has confirmed the view that these measures should have been taken.

Distribution Studies

The first need was to discover the distribution of alcohol in the driving population. Without this knowledge cost-effective screening (breath testing) procedures could not be carried out. Furthermore, it is an essential part of the process of evaluation of the effects of a counter-

Figure 2 Variation of Accident Risk with Blood Alcohol Content. These analyses
are based on a study by the Department of Police Administration, Indiana
University. A group of 5,935 drivers involved in accidents in the city of Grand
Rapids, Michigan, were compared with a control group of 7,590 drivers
selected from the city's traffic.
Borkenstein, R.F., Crowther, R.F., Shumate, R.P., Zill, W.B., and Zylam, R.
The role of the drinking driver in traffic accidents. Department of Police
Administration, Indiana University, Bloomington, Ind., 1964.

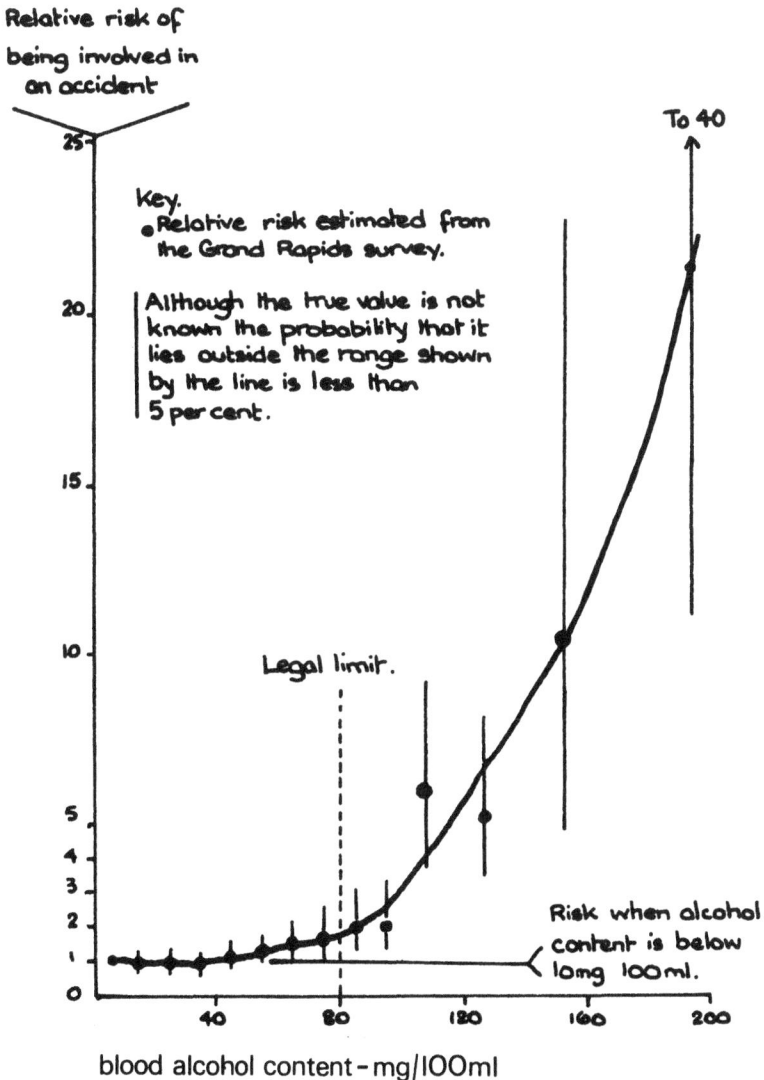

Figure 3 Trends in Car Driver Casualties In Fatal or Serious Accidents 1963-70.

▲ october 1966 -september 1967.   ▼october 1967 -september 1968.

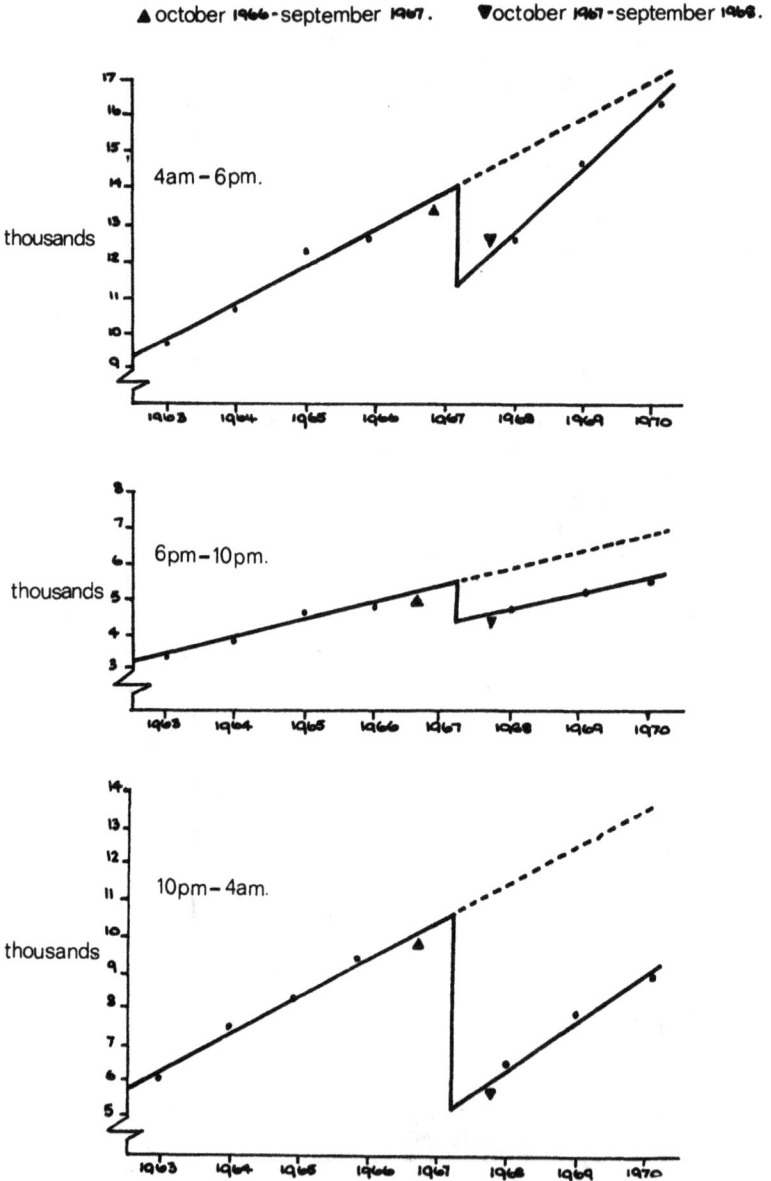

Source: Department of the Environment (1972). Road Accidents 1970.
(Great Britain.) London, HMSO.

Figure 4 Car Involvements in Fatal and Serious Accidents — 10 p.m.-4 a.m.

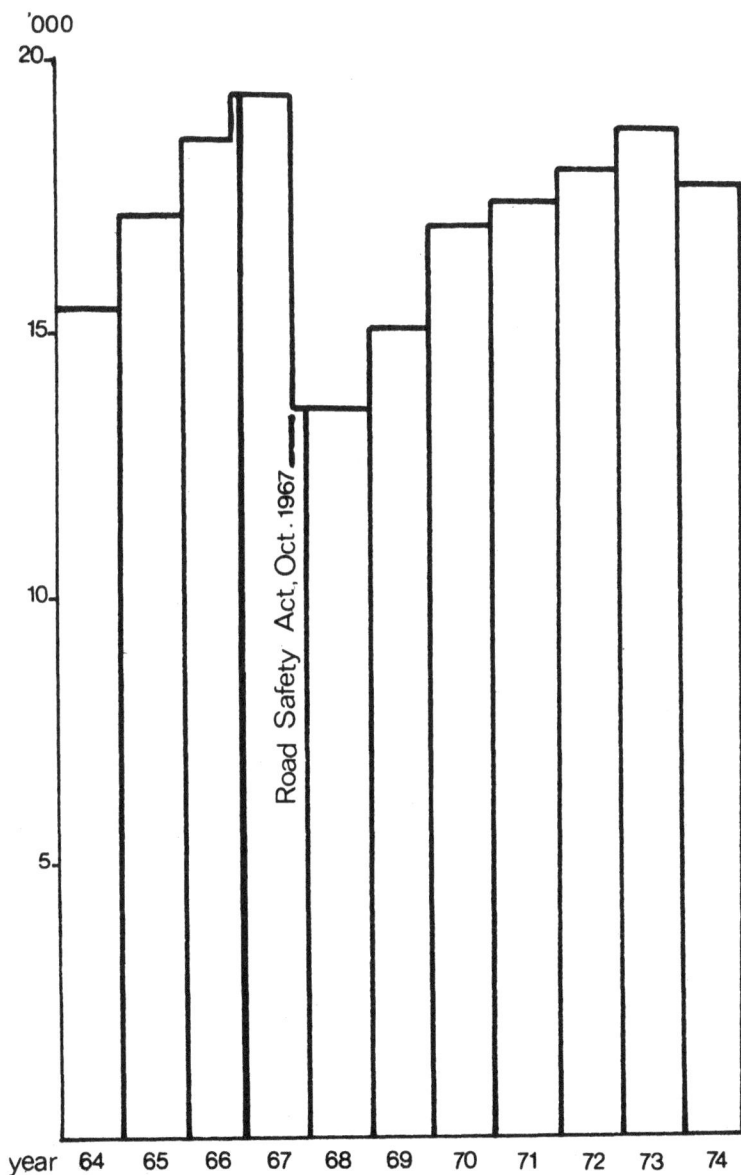

Source: Dept. of the Environment. 'Drinking and Driving'. Report of the departmental committee (Chairman: Blennerhassett), HMSO, 1976.

measure that changes in the distribution of alcohol in the driving population should be monitored. In the event the only studies which were carried out were into the post-mortem blood alcohol concentration of drivers killed in road accidents (Figure 5), and into the time distribution of drivers giving positive breath test (Figure 6). Neither of these groups can be regarded as representative of the driving population.

Figure 5 Drivers Killed in Accidents. Percentage over Legal Limit. (England and Wales.)

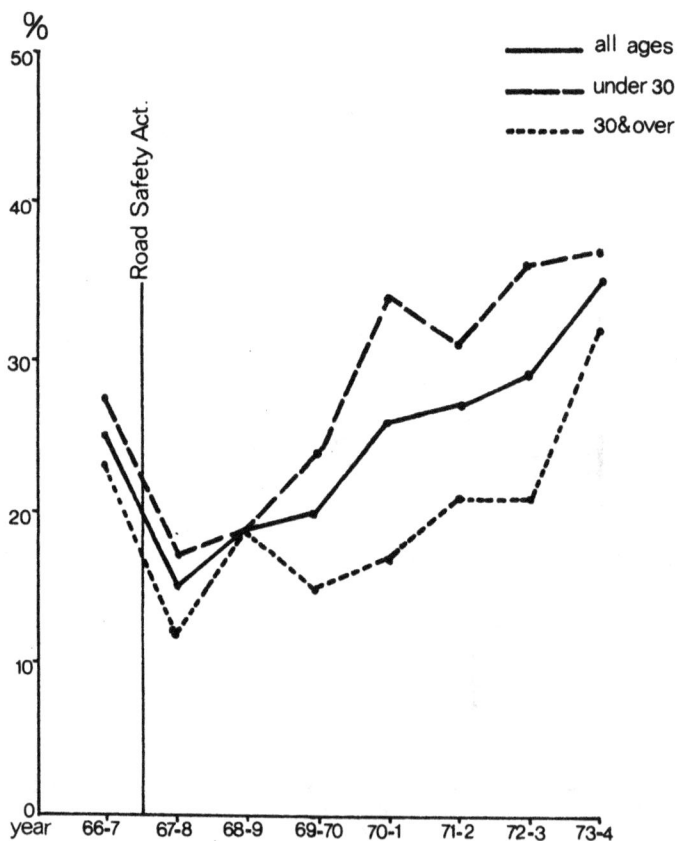

Source: Dept. of the Environment: 'Drinking and Driving'. Report of the departmental committee (Chairman: Blennerhassett), HMSO 1976.

Figure 6 Weekly cycle of Alcohol-Related Accidents in 1974. Positive breath
tests and refusals after accidents. (Great Britain 1974).

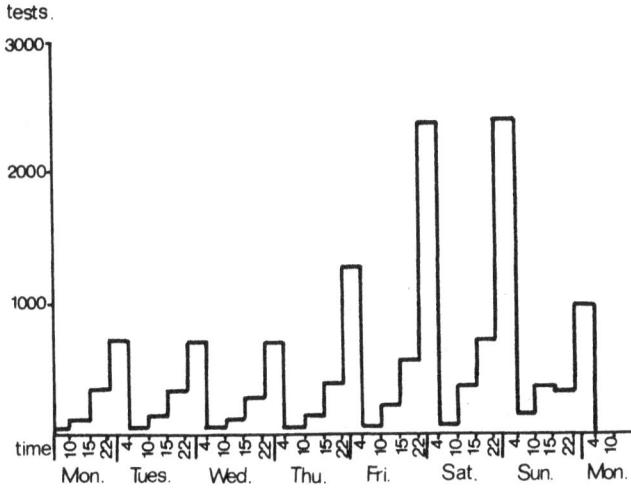

Source: Dept. of the Environment. 'Drinking and Driving'. Report of the
departmental committee (Chairman: Blennerhassett), HMSO 1976.

British Surveys

The British government has spent millions of pounds on campaigns
through mass media in attempts to modify the alcohol habit of drivers.
The most usual message is 'Don't drink and Drive' — a motivational type
of message which is known to be ineffective, and never so ineffective as
when it is directed to a compulsive drinker. It was already apparent in
1967 that there were at least three types of driver likely to exceed the
limit: problem drinkers and alcoholics; young drivers who are
inexperienced in drinking, inexperienced in driving and inexperienced
in driving after drinking; and experienced drivers who are accustomed
to alcohol. Propaganda — and particularly motivational messages —
which did not take into account the polyglot nature of the drinking
driving population was unlikely to succeed, and it did not.

There would have been a far better chance of success if steps had
been taken to ascertain the attitudes of drivers before attempts were
made to change them. A recent survey in France provides an excellent
illustration of this. In reply to the question as to what drivers thought
to be most important in avoiding an accident, the great majority of

drivers were found to be in favour of carrying a St Christopher badge or medallion (Giscard, 1967). This is, of course, the classical challenge to health education, and resembles the mythology which surrounded the causation of infectious diseases in the first part of the nineteenth century.

Studies of Characteristics of Offenders

As essential prerequisite to the success of the 1967 legislation was a study of the characteristics of offenders with a view to identifying the high risk groups, e.g. alcoholics, who are likely to repeat the offence. Unfortunately, these studies were never carried out, with the result that the courts did not exercise any informed discretion in sentencing (Havard, 1975). The futility of restoring a licence to drive at the end of the year to a florid alcoholic ought to have been obvious. The result has been that an increasing proportion of those drivers who are convicted repeat the offence.

Continuity of Education

Although the introduction of the 1967 Act was accompanied by a campaign which emphasised the dangers of driving under the influence of alcohol, no steps were taken to repeat it, notwithstanding the fact that each year new drivers would appear on the roads as they reached licensing age. The result has been that by 1976 none of the drivers in the high-risk age group of 18-24 had ever been exposed to the propaganda. The proportion of such drivers killed in road accidents with blood alcohol concentrations in excess of the limit has risen sharply and by 1974 had reached 45 per cent.

Deterrence

Whereas it is probable that nothing will deter a florid alcoholic from driving under the influence of alcohol — unless his licence is taken away (and even then he may continue to drive), there are two factors which detract from the deterrent effect of the 1967 Act. The first is that the prospects of being apprehended by the police when the limit has been exceeded are remote, provided the driver is not unlucky enough to have been involved in an accident or a moving traffic offence. The second is that even if the driver is caught, there is still a possibility that he may be acquitted on one of the technical defences based on the supposition that the police officer taking the breath test may not have followed the correct procedure. Recent cases have shown that drivers whose blood alcohol has been shown to be very high on analysis can be acquitted if the court is able to convince itself that the police officer did not have reasonable cause to suppose the driver was intoxicated when he requested the breath test. It would be interesting to see how the courts would react to a similar situation where a public health medical officer has taken a blood test from a suspected typhoid carrier working in the kitchen of a restaurant. It is difficult to imagine that no action would be taken if it could be shown that the medical officer had no reason to suppose that the worker was a typhoid carrier when the blood test was taken.

The Background of National Drinking

Driving whilst under the influence of alcohol is part of the larger problem of alcohol abuse and the availability of alcohol is therefore an important factor in prevention. Figure 7 suggests that the increase in British alcohol-related road accidents since 1967 has been closely paralleled by increased alcohol consumption. Therefore it is important that the authorities concerned with controlling the availability of alcohol should bear in mind the possible consequences to road safety of measures such as relaxing licensing hours, lowering the legal age for drinking or permitting the sale of alcohol on motorways. The experience of lowering the drinking age in Ontario was that a dramatic increase occurred in the road accident mortality and morbidity amongst the age group concerned (Interministerial Committee, 1974).

New Technology

A number of devices, notably alcohol-interlock-ignition systems, have been tried out in other countries with varying degrees of success. There are obvious disadvantages such as what might happen if the engine stalls at a busy intersection and the sober driver is too flustered to be able to solve the puzzle quickly enough to start his engine again.

Conclusion

Road accidents are a major and increasing cause of mortality and morbidity in the community and alcohol is a leading cause of road accidents. The *ad hoc* approach of road safety authorities to the problem is no longer acceptable. The problem must be tackled by means of proven epidemiological techniques and based on adequate information. The research necessary to provide this information has not yet been carried out in Britain.

Figure 7 Total National Alcohol Consumption (UK) (Beer, wines and spirits converted to equivalent pure alcohol. HM Customs & Excise.)

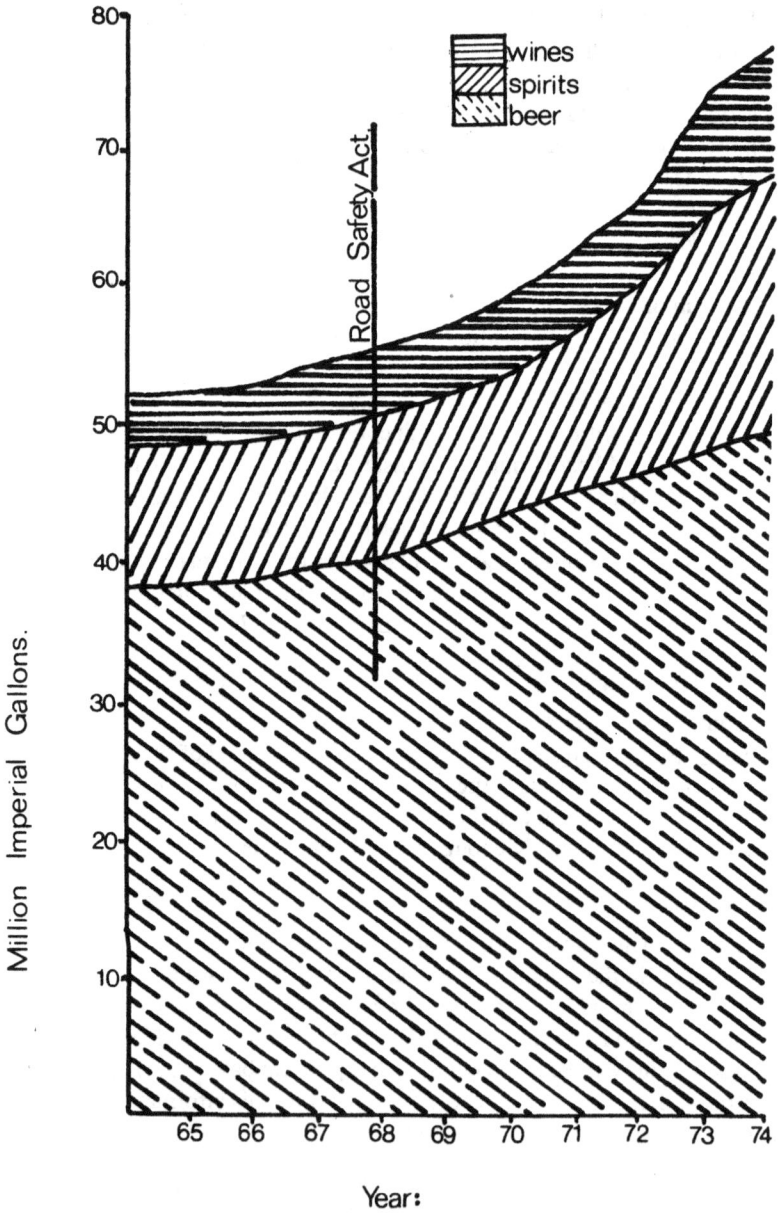

References

Codling, P.J. (1975). Road casualties since the 'drinking and driving' legislation. TRRL. Supplementary Report 134 UC.
Department of the Environment (1976). Drinking and Driving. Report of the Departmental Committee. London: HMSO.
Giscard, P.H. (1975). Conduite Automobile et Securite (Part 2). Paris: Cahiers d'Etudes, ONSER.
Havard, J.D.J. (1975). The drinking driver and the law. In Research Advances in Alcohol and Drug Problems, R.J. Gibbins, Y. Israel, H. Kalant, R.E. Popham, W. Schmidt, R.G. Smart (eds.). New York: John Wiley & Sons, vol.2.
Inter-Ministerial Committee on Drinking and Driving (1974). Drinking Driving in the Province of Ontario – A Report to the Provincial Secretary for Justice, p.13 (publisher not stated).

21 ALCOHOL AND CRIME

D.N. Hancock

In this paper I intend to describe the overlap between alcoholism and criminal behaviour, as necessary groundwork for the discussion which will then follow on the way in which society is at present responding to alcoholics who commit crimes. There is a conflict between society's normal response to crime as a danger which should be detected, controlled and punished, and society's desired response to alcoholism as a condition requiring treatment. How are these two responses reconciled for the person who is both an alcoholic and an offender? What happens at the contact points between the penal system and the medical services available for alcoholics? It is a discussion of these questions of social response which is the major focus and purpose of this paper.

The Flowerpot Lady

The flowerpot lady is a short-hand way of referring to an important judgement made earlier this year in the Appeal Court (R. v. Clarke, 1976). It is an encouraging judgement since it confronts one of the unspoken underlying principles of the relationship between treatment services and the penal system. That unspoken and often unchallenged principle is that the penal system takes over where treatment fails. This is what happened.

A young woman from a deprived background and with a history of violent offences had an eighteen-month prison sentence quashed and a £2 fine substituted. The woman had thrown some flowerpots at the police when they were called to a hospital because she refused to leave. The doctors said she had a gross personality defect but could not be treated in hospital. The probation service said it could not cope with her. The judge who gave her eighteen months said it was his duty to protect the public. It is worth quoting what the appeal court said in over-ruling the original sentence:

> There is some evidence that the attitude of the social services was, 'we cannot cope with this woman, let the courts cope with her'. The first thing to be said, and said very firmly indeed, is that Her Majesty's courts are not dustbins into which the social services can

sweep difficult members of the public. . .Sentences should fit crimes. The crime in this case was breaking a flowerpot in a fit of temper and doing damage to the extent of £1. One truth has been revealed by this distressing case. The national health service and the social services cannot cope with a woman of this type who does not require treatment (so it is said) but who cannot live in the community without disturbing others and being a source of danger to herself and to others. The welfare system makes no provision for dealing with that kind of case. This court has no intention of filling that gap by sending people to prison when a prison sentence is wholly inappropriate. We ask ourselves, what was the appropriate sentence for breaking a flowerpot? The answer is a fine of £2.

The fact that eighteen months was given in the first place strengthens the belief that many alcoholics find themselves in court and prison, not by virtue of gross criminality on their part, but as an expression of their alcoholism.

That public drunkenness is still an offence is an indication of this state of affairs. There are now over 100,000 convictions for drunkenness in England and Wales annually. This figure has been rising by about 4 per cent each year over the last decade. These convictions lead to about 3,000 prison sentences per year. A person is not actually sent to prison for being drunk but is usually fined; when however the fine is unpaid, that person can be sent to prison in default. Few of the drunks in court are casual roisterers (Gath *et al.*, 1968). Half show evidence of chemical dependence on alcohol as determined by morning shakes, morning relief drinking, amnesia, inability to stop drinking and hallucinatory experiences. Research findings tell us that there is an 86 per cent likelihood that a man who has had six or more arrests for drunkenness is chemically dependent upon alcohol.

The State of the Law

Alcohol is used to diminish inhibition by many people who commit offences, and a significant proportion of prisoners report being drunk at the time of the offence. This may or may not mean that they are alcoholics, but there is a real legal problem if the offender was so drunk at the time of committing the offence that he did not know what he was doing. What is the state of mind, and motivation, of someone who commits an offence at a time of alcoholic amnesia? Although intoxication or amnesia are in some cases only convenient excuses, in others the legal condition of *mens rea* or intention to do wrong is certainly absent. English law is here rather inconsistent, although in general the law states that drunkenness is no defence to liability in criminal law.

This position was underlined by a recent House of Lords judgement where it was found that intoxication could not be used as a defence against assault (R. v. Majewski, 1976). It was argued that the evidence for intention or *mens rea* was the intoxication itself; and that the recklessness involved in the act of getting drunk is equivalent to the wish to commit an offence. The only situation in which the law differs from that position is in cases of murder, where the charge can be reduced to manslaughter if the court is convinced that the murder was conceived and carried out in a state of excessive drunkenness. The present position does not seem altogether satisfactory. The Butler Report on Mentally Abnormal Offenders (1975) suggested that a new offence of 'dangerous intoxication' should be created, and perhaps this approach fits in better with our knowledge of alcoholism.

Prevalences

Many estimates of alcoholism prevalence amongst prisoners have been given, but here only a few of the more important studies will be quoted. The most thorough study was carried out by Bartholomew (1968) in Australia. This is probably the only investigation in which the researchers talked to family members to check what was said by the prisoner, while all other studies tend to take at face value what is reported by the man himself. Bartholomew found that 43 per cent of Australian recidivists were alcoholics. One of the most quoted studies carried out in Britain is by Gibbens and Silberman (1970). They excluded the 'drunks' – those serving sentences of under twenty-eight days – and took some trouble to ensure that the sample of men they studied was representative of the male prison population as a whole. Forty per cent of prisoners were found to be excessive drinkers. A study by Edwards, Hensman and Peto (1971), compared rates of alcoholism between different groups of prisoners. The greatest rate was, of course, amongst the short-term drunks. Other short-term prisoners, irrespective of types of offence, also showed high rates of alcoholism, whilst long-term prisoners demonstrated the least alcoholism. However, one must be careful not to generalise too much, for there is some conflict of evidence. Men serving life sentences certainly contain a high proportion of alcoholics.

The Handling of the Alcoholic Offender

Figure 1 attempts to display what may happen to the alcoholic offender in the penal system. He comes into the system at the top of the diagram when the police charge him with an offence and he goes to court. The possible sentences are indicated by three lines leading away from the court. The bottom of the diagram shows how these link up with the community resources.

Figure 1 The handling of the alcoholic offender

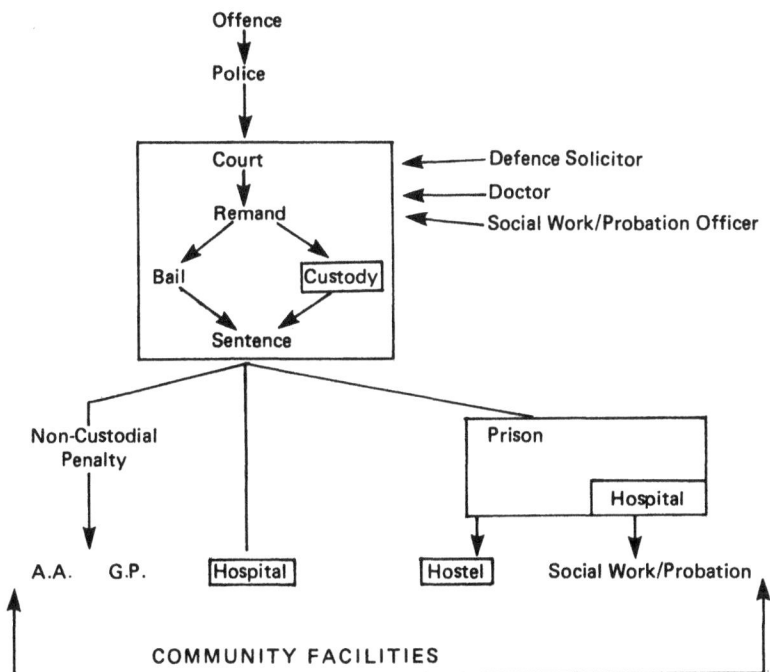

Alcoholism and the Processes of the Court

A number of points must be made about what happens in court. First there is the conflict which is often present between punishment and treatment. Very often courts are asked to strike a compromise between the treatment needs of the offender and the need of society to deter by imposing punishments. What is often confusing is that a court may wish to retain elements of both treatment and punishment within the decisions it makes. Sometimes this becomes a half-and-half approach and can be damaging, because the offender is not given the complete resources necessary for treatment; nor is it made clear to him that he is going to be punished, and that only when that is finished will something else be offered. If a bit is done under each heading, the message can be ambiguous, and the person continues in a state of mind where he is likely to commit offences, and reject treatment as it is offered in the context of punishment. Resolution of the court's conflict between punishment and treatment is one of the most important dilemmas that has now to be faced. Often the compromises achieved satisfy no one, produce ineffective treatment, together with a resentment in some quarters that the offender has 'got off' without punishment. The story of the flowerpot lady should help to clarify our thinking in this area, and give us greater confidence to keep separate the punishment necessary and the treatment required.

There is then a second aspect of what may happen to the alcoholic in court that has to be considered. In Figure 1 the arrows bearing in on the top box indicate the people who can influence the court: doctors can influence courts by making medical reports on offenders; social workers prepare social enquiry reports about the circumstances and situation of their clients; other people have the facility through the client's solicitor to influence the court. The decision of the court really is quite susceptible to being thus influenced, and often the court is more than willing to accept a recommendation which will prevent somebody going to prison. The important thing is for those giving advice to avoid contradicting each other. Examples can certainly be recalled where doctors have indicated that a particular offender has social problems, whilst the probation officer has said that the same problems are a medical responsibility.

There is then one final aspect of the court's functioning which deserves note, and which is often in fact crucial. If a person is remanded on bail, he is much more likely to receive a non-custodial sentence than if he is remanded in custody. Bail permits the maintenance of community ties during the remand period, and prevents a fundamental breakdown in the social position of someone who has already an insecure place within the community. Perhaps ways can be found to strengthen medical support during these remand periods on bail.

Alcoholism and the Prison System

Within a prison there may be a wide range of facilities in some way equipped to help the person with a drinking problem. There are one or two psychiatric units especially geared to treatment of alcoholism. Some prisons provide facilities for meetings of Alcoholics Anonymous. A visiting psychotherapist or a member of the prison medical service may take a special interest in alcoholism. In addition, most prisons have their own hospitals where treatment is available for straightforward medical or psychiatric problems. In a sense, the prison system has some of the same conflicts as the courts. It sometimes gives both punishment and treatment at the same time; and although much work is done by the prison system to try and rehabilitate people within it, usually such work is very frustrating and little is achieved.

Prison is in fact particularly inappropriate for someone with an alcohol problem. This does not imply that an alcoholic who commits a serious offence should not go to prison, but it does mean that it is a difficult environment in which to do anything constructive about the alcoholism. Being completely away from the temptation of drink, it is possible to live in a fairy-tale world. One of the big difficulties is therefore the denial of alcoholism, both amongst prisoners and by those responsible for running the prisons. It is fair to say that alcoholics often make model prisoners. In many ways they welcome their period of imprisonment as an opportunity to get back to good health, and to have the pressures of living outside removed.

Resettlement

Resettlement and after-care can be a different story. Release from prison is often traumatic; changes in accommodation, job, the use of money, the whole area of relationships and feelings have to be faced. Contact with welfare and medical services have to be established and managed. Often the energy and resources needed to overcome these changes defeat the man who is being released. It is a time of anxiety, and the period when a man is most likely to start drinking again, and the advantages of a man's body being completely free from alcohol can be wiped out within a few minutes or hours of his release. These difficulties are one of the worst aspects of the penal system. The problem is perpetuated, for it becomes more and more difficult to stay out of prison once the alcoholic has started to go there.

A Positive Future

Perhaps the negative aspects of the penal system may seem in this paper to have been stressed a little too much, and to redress this impression and end on a more positive note one must consider how in the future things might be managed rather better. There are many possible contacts between the penal system and welfare services, and we should look in detail at how these contacts can be more effectively used. On the basis of an analysis of how penal and treatment systems at present rather confusingly impinge, it should be possible to draw up a practical agenda for rationalising and improving their relationship. The interface is during the court processes, and after both custodial and non-custodial sentence. Perhaps the most neglected problem is the provision of social and psychiatric services for those released from prison, and here there are obvious constructive possibilities. More could be done to ensure the continuity of treatment for those released, and also to provide services to many alcoholics who find difficulty in adjusting to the community after a spell in prison. Work on this agenda should now be the positive concern of all those who deal with alcoholism so that a more effective caring system can be produced.

References

Bartholomew, A.A. (1968). Alcoholism and crime. Australian and New Zealand Journal of Criminology 1: 70-99.

Edwards, G., Hensman, C. and Peto, J. (1971). Drinking problems among recidivist prisoners. Psychological Medicine 5: 388-99.

Gath, D., Hensman, C., Hawker, A., Kelly, M. and Edwards, G. (1968). The drunk in court: a survey of drunkenness offenders from two London courts. Brit. Med. J. 4: 808-11.

Gibbens, T.C.N. and Silberman, M. (1970). Alcoholism among prisoners. Psychological Medicine 1: 73-8.

Mentally Abnormal Offenders, (1975). HMSO.

R. v. Clarke as reported in *Justice of the Peace* (1976), 140, 123-4.

R. v. Majewski as reported in *The Times*, 14 April 1976.

22 ALCOHOLISM AND SUICIDE

Bruce Ritson

Evidence for the Association

The association between alcoholism and suicide is well established. A recent review on this topic quoted sixteen reports observing this link (Goodwin, 1973). There have been two principal approaches to the analysis of this phenomenon. The first follows up a known population of alcoholics for variable periods of time and observes the incidence of suicide. Reports from different countries show that between 6 per cent and 20 per cent of alcoholics end their lives by suicide. This contrasts with a general frequency in the British population of 10 per 100,000. Schmidt and de Lint (1972) found an observed rate of suicide six times that expected in a matched sample study of mortality amongst more than 6,000 Canadian alcoholics. Probably the best known study of suicide amongst alcoholics was that of Kessel and Grossman (1961). They followed up two series of patients. The first consisted of 131 consecutive alcoholics discharged from the Maudsley Hospital and the other 87 discharged from an observation ward in a general hospital. The follow-up varied between one and eleven years, and in that time 8 per cent of the Maudsley series killed themselves, as did 7 per cent of those discharged from the observation ward. This was approximately eighty times the expected frequency of suicide for men of that age group.

A recent follow-up over at least ten years of 2,070 diagnosed alcoholics admitted to mental hospitals in England and Wales showed a greatly increased mortality risk, particularly amongst females. When the death certificates of those 794 who had died were studied, deaths where suicide was reported or seemed extremely likely were for men twenty-two times more common than expected. Amongst females the ratio was twenty-three (Adelstein and White, 1976). While it should be recognised that this sample was drawn entirely from a population of those who at one time had been inpatients in psychiatric hospitals, it is impressive evidence of the risk which the alcoholic runs.

The second approach takes a series of suicides and retrospectively seeks to trace how many were alcoholics. The evidence is equally striking. A review of eleven reports between 1825 and 1964 found 6 per cent to as many as 47 per cent alcoholics or heavy drinkers amongst suicides. The phrase 'or heavy drinker' is introduced at this

271

stage because the diagnosis of alcoholism which is often difficult or even arbitrary to assign to a patient in the consulting room becomes an even more dubious label when assigned on the basis of case records or reports by relatives concerning the former life-style of a successful suicide.

Nonetheless, and making allowance for all the methodological hazards, an association between alcoholism and suicide seems firmly established. This bleak association may only serve to reaffirm the prevailing pessimism which surrounds alcoholism and its treatment, unless a closer look at the evidence can provide clues towards the prevention of this tragic outcome.

There has been a tendency to view suicides as a uniform group on the grounds that they share a common terminal event, but Ovenstone and Kreitman (1974) have shown that this may be a dangerous oversimplification. They identified two distinct syndromes amongst those who kill themselves. The first are those where there is a long history of psychological problems, social deprivation, and previous para-suicide acts which culminate in a successful suicide. In the other group there is an acute decompensation, often in later life with no previous evidence of maladaptive behaviour. Alcohol contributes significantly to both groups, but in a very different way. Approximately two thirds of the para-suicides mentioned in the above study who subsequently killed themselves, were unusually heavy drinkers. This contrasted with one quarter of those whose suicide came at the end of a more acute and unanticipated decompensation. Table 1 describes the 'terminal phase' and alcoholic status of the two groups. Nonetheless, authors point out 'many of the depressive reactions occurring in non-alcoholics were associated with heavy drinking, although the drinking pattern was not that of recognisable alcoholism'.

Thus any consideration of alcoholism and suicide will have to take into account those who kill themselves after a protracted struggle to cope with their drinking problem and those who, overwhelmed by depression or some life crisis resort to alcohol in a desperate attempt to cope with their feeling of depression. A history of para-suicide is common in the life story of alcoholics. A study of 100 alcohol addicts attending a specialised unit for the treatment of alcoholism in Edinburgh found that 20 per cent had attempted suicide in the past (Ritson, 1967). A similar frequency has been observed in many other studies (Chandler *et al.,* 1971). Kessel (1965) in a review of admissions to the regional poisons centre in Edinburgh observed that 39 per cent of 151 men, and 8 per cent of the 314 women in the sample, were

Table 1 Terminal phase and alcoholic status of suicides reported by
Ovenstone and Kreitman (1974)

	No Formal Ilness	Depressive Reaction	Other	Total
Para-suicide group				
Alcoholic	2	20	1	23
Not alcoholic	1	23	3	27
Uncertain	—	—	—	—
Total	3	43	4	50
No para-suicide				
Alcoholic	—	6	—	6
Not alcoholic	2	39	5	46
Uncertain	—	2	—	2
Total	2	47	5	54

alcohol addicts. Batchelor (1954) found one third of the men and 12
per cent of the women who attempted suicide were alcoholic. He
further commented that the majority of these alcoholics came from
social class V and had unsatisfactory work records.

Predictors

If we accept that alcoholics are prone to think of suicide and at times
attempt to take their lives, are there any clues which might differentiate
those who are suicide prone from the general population of alcoholics?
The hunt for a pre-alcoholic personality type has proved fruitless, but
there is some evidence that the alcoholic suicide is more psychologically
disturbed than others. In one study mentioned above (Ritson, 1967)
there was a significant association between suicide attempts and severe
personality disorder as evidenced by life history, and supported by
personality testing using Fould's hostility scale. Chandler *et al.* (1971)
found a significant association between neuroticism and a history of
attempted suicide. These findings are hardly surprising, as para-suicide
is more likely to occur amongst those who are severely psychologically
disturbed, whether or not they are alcoholics.

The relationship between social class and alcoholism and a
propensity for suicide is not yet clear. It seems generally that reported
attempts are more common in alcoholics from social class III to V, but

this may reflect greater frankness in this group. Probably the greatest significance again is in the regularly observed fact that suicide attempts in general are inversely related to social class.

Casualty departments are familiar with the young man who is admitted late in the evening having consumed small quantity of drugs at the end of a weekend's heavy drinking. There seems to be a growing tendency towards simultaneous abuse of drugs and alcohol amongst a group of young men who often lead ill-organised lives with irregular, unskilled employment and many transient and unfulfilled relationships (Plant, 1976). It seems likely that a number of these young men will progress to established alcohol dependence and impulsive self-destruction. It is tempting to suggest that the alcoholic who has fewest social, economic and inter-personal resources to support him is most likely to call attention to his plight by suicide threats or attempts.

Those who take the view that suicide always occurs when the balance of the mind is disturbed might feel it self-evident that the suicide-prone alcoholic will be psychologically more disturbed than others, but psychotic depression, curiously, does not seem to figure prominently in the history of alcoholic suicides (Goodwin, 1973). This question should be studied more closely. Although there is no clear evidence that depressive illness as such is more common amongst alcoholics, it is significantly more common amongst female relatives of alcoholics, suggesting to some a unifying genetic association between the two conditions.

There is a recognisable but small number of alcoholics who suffer from depressive psychoses, and it is not uncommon to find a patient, often a female, who turns to alcohol late in life as a means of coping with depression, but they do not contribute significantly to the incidence of suicide amongst alcoholics. It has been remarked that women alcoholics commit suicide less often than men (Rushing, 1969). Again, we must recall that similar observation is true of all suicides.

Possible Dynamic Links

Some have adopted the view that identifiable forces within the personality contribute to both alcoholism and suicide. The best known proponent of this unitary concept was Menninger, who coined the phrase 'chronic suicide' to define the alcoholic's way of life. He stated:

> Alcohol addiction, then, can be considered a form of self-destruction used to avert greater self-destruction, deriving from elements of aggressiveness excited by thwarting ungratified eroticism and the

feeling of a need for punishment from a sense of guilt related to aggressiveness. Its further quality is that in a practical sense the self-destruction is accomplished *in spite of* and at the same time *by means of* the very device used by the sufferer to relieve his pain and avert his feared destruction.

While such an assertion fits some individual patients admirably, none would now feel that it could usefully be applied to all patients. Alcoholics may be encountered who find life unlivable without alcohol as a buffer between them and reality, and commit suicide when this comforter is removed. Such cases are uncommon.

Fenichel (1945) also suggested that addiction and depression were based on a *unifying* conflict. 'He goes through the world in a condition of perpetual greediness. If his narcissistic needs are not satisfied, his self-esteem diminishes to danger point.' Every clinician must have experienced patients who seem greedy for praise, love, affection and, of course, alcohol. Such hypothetical constructs are of value in helping make sense of certain patients' experience, but they rarely lend themselves to empirical study.

The characteristics of the first eight successful suicides occurring in a series of 300 alcoholics attending a specialised unit for the treatment of alcoholism have been examined (Ritson, 1968). Very detailed information had been prepared on each patient prior to death. There was a significant tendency for this small group to have been last born and to have more commonly reported idyllic, happy childhoods with intense affection for their mothers whom no one had ever replaced in their subsequent life. They appeared to have an insatiable need for selfless love and appreciation. Whatever the truth in their retrospective view of life, they felt it had never advanced on 'the pleasures of the nursery'. It is hard to know if such straws in the wind are of any real clinical help. They hint if anything at the presence of a dependent person, greedy for the esteem of others, who, when this support is not forthcoming, becomes suicidally depressed.

Other Explanations

The alcoholic with a history of para-suicide has a poor prognosis, and this may represent a further reflection of his impulsiveness and impaired capacity to cope with stress. He thus represents a particular challenge to conventional treatment methods.

The life of an alcoholic with its succession of hopes frustrated by failure with loss and recrimination would, in itself, readily explain recurrent feelings of failure, isolation, hopelessness and depression. There is evidence that suicide amongst alcoholics is particularly likely to occur shortly after experiencing loss – for instance of employment or a spouse, often by separation arising out of his drinking. Two thirds of these losses and crises had occurred within six weeks of the suicide of a series of alcoholics. This association is not so clearly observed in the suicide of primary depression (Murphy and Robins, 1967).

It is perhaps noteworthy that suicide most often occurs quite soon after a period of treatment (Dahlgren, 1945) and it is tempting to suggest that the pain of having 'failed again' contributes to the final decision that life is insupportable. It might be taken as a cue for those who advise us against promoting guilt in our patients by setting unattainable expectations for abstinence or social reform. Beck *et al.* (1976) have emphasised the over-riding importance of this sense of hopelessness even more than depression itself, in promoting suicide attempts. They point out: 'Many alcoholics are in a chronic state of hopelessness and have little orientation to the future. The more powerless an individual feels, the greater his tendency to act on impulse and seize his satisfaction in the present.' Hopelessness and powerlessness are common experiences for the alcoholic.

For some, death might seem a welcome relief if every morning starts with a hangover or severe withdrawal symptoms. And yet there is no study which links these experiences directly with suicide attempts. Indeed, hangover itself has been surprisingly little studied. Some have drawn attention to the depression which follows drinking in alcoholics and suggested that amine depletion might contribute to this mood change (Mayfield and Allen, 1967). This line of enquiry has not so far borne fruit, but certainly seems worth further exploration.

There are other ways in which alcohol itself contributes to the suicide act. We know that drunkenness is linked with many impulsive, ill-considered acts of a violent nature, whether these are undertaken in a motor car or in a pub brawl or domestic argument. It seems only reasonable that alcohol, which impairs judgement in these circumstances, also gives courage or takes away reason from the depressed man and facilitates self-poisoning. Further, the presence of alcohol in the system readily potentiates many of the commonest agents taken during suicidal attempts and may tilt the balance towards a fatal outcome. Thus, the fact of being drunk greatly heightens the danger attached to any kind of suicidal thinking. A report of the regional poisoning centre in Edinburgh revealed a growing number of males had taken alcohol at the time of the para-suicide – 53 per cent in 1970 and 62 per cent in 1973.

There was an even more rapid acceleration in this tendency amongst women, from 25 per cent to 38 per cent (Kreitman, 1976).

The Practical Message

In conclusion, it is clear that excessive drinking greatly increases the risk of suicide. However, the predictive factors which differentiate within a group of alcoholics are very much those which one could deduce from a study of the general population; social isolation, history of previous episodes of suicide attempt, previous psychiatric illness, social class. All are factors which need to be taken into consideration in predicting the likelihood of suicide, whether we are considering the alcoholic or the general population. What we are left with is the evidence that the male alcoholic who has these general 'at risk' factors and has recently completed a period of unsuccessful treatment (or treatment which he felt was unsuccessful), and has experienced recent loss is very much in danger. Even such sparse clues may be of some help in alerting the clinician to the possibility of suicide when he knows that a susceptible alcoholic has recently experienced a crisis in which some valued person or role has been lost.

References

Adelstein, A. and Graham-White, (1976). Alcoholism and Mortality. Population Trends 7.

Batchelor, I.R.C. (1954). Alcoholism and attempted suicide. J. Ment. Sci. 100: 451-61.

Beck, A.A., Weissman, A. and Kovacs, M. (1976). Alcoholism, hopelessness and suicidal behaviour. J. Stud. Alc. 37: 66-77.

Chandler, J., Hensman, C. and Edwards, G. (1971). Determinants of what happens to alcoholics. Quart. J. Stud. Alc. 32: 349-63.

Dahlgren, K.C. (1945). On Suicide and Attempted Suicide. Lund Lindstedts.

Fenichel, O. (1945). Psychoanalytic Theory of Neuroses. New York: Norton.

Goodwin, D.W. (1973). Alcohol in suicide and homicide. Quart. J. Stud. Alc. 34: 144-56.

Kessel, W.I.N., and Grossman, G. (1961). Suicide in alcoholics. Brit. Med. J. 2: 773-4.

Kessel, W.I.N. (1965). Self poisoning. Brit. Med. J. 2: 1265-70.

Kreitman, N. (1976). Personal communication.

Mayfield, D. and Allen, D. (1967). Alcohol and effect: a psychopharmacological study. Amer. J. Psychiat. 126: 1346-51.

Menninger, K.A. (1938). Man Against Himself. New York: Harcourt Brace.

Murphy, G.E. and Robins, E. (1967). Social factors in suicide. J. Amer. Med. Ass. 199: 303-8.

Ovenstone, I.M. and Kreitman, N. (1974). Two syndromes of suicide. Brit. J. Psychiat. 124: 336-45.

Plant, M. (1976). Young drug and alcohol casualties compared. Brit. J. Addict.

71: 31-43.

Ritson, B. (1967). A Unit for the Treatment of Alcoholism. MD Thesis, Edinburgh.

Ritson, B. (1968). Suicide amongst alcoholics. Brit. J. Med. Psychol. 41: 235-42.

Rushing, W.A. (1969). Suicide and the interaction of alcoholism with the social situation. Quart. J. Stud. Alc. 30: 93-103.

Schmidt, W. and de Lint, J. (1972). Causes of death of alcoholics. Quart. J. Stud. Alc. 33: 171-85.

SECTION III. TREATMENT AND EDUCATION

23 HOW GOOD IS TREATMENT?
Anthony W. Clare

Introduction

It is salutary to note that at a time when there is an increasing public awareness and concern with regard to the prevalence of alcohol abuse and its related problems, and a growing political involvement in discussions about how such problems might be controlled, there is a burgeoning literature which is questioning a number of the basic assumptions concerning the efficacy of alcoholism treatment.

The most widely used criterion of treatment success has been abstinence, but controversy has arisen over the wisdom of using abstinence as a singular outcome criterion. That the achievement of abstinence will necessarily produce an amelioration of the alcoholic's problems is being seriously challenged. Another fundamental assumption being examined is that treatment, whatever its kind or quality, is better than no treatment at all. The related assumption that not merely is treatment effective but the more intense, complex and lengthy the treatment the more effective it is likely to be, is likewise being contested. This paper will give a brief review of the current status of these assumptions.

Abstinence as an Outcome Measure

What constitutes recovery from alcoholism remains a vexed question. The most frequently used indicators of positive response to treatment include abstinence, consumption level, frequency of drinking, behaviour impairment, marital and family functioning and occupational status. The attrition rate from treatment and the degree of acceptance of treatment have also been used as measures of outcome. However, abstinence does appear to be the most popular outcome criterion.

Two distinct reservations have been expressed concerning this use of abstinence. The first doubts the wisdom of employing it as the sole outcome measure (Pattison, 1968). Indeed, data have been published disputing the assumption that the achievement of abstinence necessarily results in the amelioration of problems (Gerard *et al.*, 1962). In the

Gerard study, a large number of totally abstinent alcoholics were rated as overtly disturbed. The second reservation relates to the empirical evidence that a proportion of treated alcoholics are able to resume normal drinking while still maintaining stability in other adjustments (Davies, 1962; Pattison, 1968; Kendell, 1968).

In reaction to the reliance on abstinence as a sole success criterion some have advocated multidimensional measurement of treatment outcome (Foster *et al.*, 1972). The objective of treatment efforts then becomes a reduction of problem drinkers by successfully eliminating individuals from an identified cohort by remission of symptoms or cessation of *problem-related drinking*. The evaluation by Costello (1975a) of outcome results in treatment studies reported by other authors between 1951 and 1973 reveals the extent to which some form of multidimensional measurement tends to be employed even by those who appear to subscribe in theory to the idea that only the attainment of abstinence constitutes real success.

In all, fifty-eight studies reporting a one-year post-treatment outcome were reviewed by Costello. Four outcome indices were used to describe each of the studies; the methods of collating the material have been reported elsewhere (Costello *et al.*, 1973). A cluster analytic technique of hierarchical grouping was employed to develop groups of maximum multivariate similarity. A cohort of 11,022 alcoholics was tabulated over a one-year post-treatment period, and with a criterion of outcome which is flexible and allows not merely for abstinence but also for a 'controlled', or problem-free pattern of drinking, 25 per cent of the cohort were classified as improved, 53 per cent were still drinking with associated problems, 1 per cent were dead and 21 per cent lost to follow-up.

The results of twenty-three evaluations of alcoholism treatment during the period 1952-72 reporting outcome for 5,833 alcoholics over a two-year post-treatment period, employing the same four indices of response, were also analysed (Costello, 1975b). This shows that approximately 35 per cent of the cohort appear to show a significant improvement in their drinking status, 43 per cent were still drinking with associated problems, 3 per cent were dead and 19 per cent were lost to follow-up.

Although one must have reservations about the validity of pooling widely differing aggregates of alcoholics from different treatment situations in such a fashion, Costello's figures appear reasonable in the context of reports from other sources. In an analysis of 265 evaluation studies of psychologically oriented treatments for alcoholism, Emrick

(1974) found a two thirds improvement rate with about 50 per cent of those improved achieving total abstinence. In their detailed critique of evaluation research in this area, Hill and Blane (1967) argue that abstinence or improvement rates, bearing in mind methodological problems, are probably less than 50 per cent. Somewhat more optimistic recovery rates have been reported by Armor and his colleagues (1976) in their study of a proportion of the clients attending forty-four alcoholism treatment centres in the United States. In this study, the category 'Normal Drinking' includes only those clients who meet the following criteria: (i) daily consumption less than 3 ounces of ethanol; (ii) typical quantities on drinking days less than 5 ounces; (iii) no tremors reported; (iv) no serious symptoms. At six-month follow-up, 68 per cent of patients were in 'remission' — 18 per cent sober for the whole six months, 38 per cent sober for the previous one month and 12 per cent drinking 'normally'. The results at eighteen months were very similar.

These authors concede that there are inherent limitations in their definition of 'normal' drinking. Those who admit the possibility of a return to a normal pattern of drinking are usually at pains to point out that it is a realistic option for a minority of alcohol-dependent individuals only, and that total abstention is the only solution for the majority. But it is necessary to acknowledge the empirical finding in these and other follow-up studies of treated alcoholics that permanent abstention is adopted by only a small proportion of patients, while many others report drinking at levels similar to those observed in members of the general population.

Treatment versus No-Treatment

As Emerick (1975) points out in his detailed review of alcoholism treatment, evidence for the relative effectiveness of therapy must depend on an analysis comparing the drinking outcomes of treated and untreated alcoholics. Failure to take 'spontaneous remission' into account when assessing the worth of this or that particular therapeutic approach bedevils many reports of efficacious intervention in psychiatric research. Emrick analysed data from seven studies of alcoholics in receipt of no treatment whatsoever, and from a further seventeen studies in which alcoholics had some (but only minimal) formal therapy. Analysis revealed 13 per cent of non-treated alcoholics were abstinent and 41 per cent were at least somewhat improved; 21 per cent of minimally-treated alcoholics were abstinent and 43 per cent somewhat improved, the follow-up period in all cases being at least six months in duration. Emrick advises caution in view of the fact that such data are derived from so few studies, and patient variables were not controlled in making the no- versus minimal-treatment comparisons. Given such reservations, the results do suggest that many alcoholics can drink less or stop altogether with no or minimal treatment, and untreated alcoholics can change as much as those in receipt of minimal assistance.

In the Rand Corporation study (Armor *et al.*, 1976), clients with only a single contact with an alcohol treatment centre (ATC) had a remission rate of 53 per cent, compared with an overall remission rate of 68 per cent and a rate of 73 per cent for clients with high amounts of treatment. The suggestion that recovery may be relatively independent of treatment techniques is further supported by the remission rates for persons who received only AA assistance. AA attendance, provided it was regular, was almost as effective as ATC treatment. The view expressed by the authors to the effect that 'remission and eventual recovery depend to a major extent on characteristics and behaviour of the individual client rather than on characteristics of treatment' seems reasonable in the light of their evidence, but it is necessary to be somewhat cautious. The study involved data derived from the monitoring system employed by forty-four alcoholism treatment centres in the USA. However, the six-month follow-up sample and the eighteen-month follow-up sample surveyed in the study, represent only 21 per cent and 62 per cent of their full intake populations. Furthermore, the six-month follow-up sample represents all forty-four ATCs whereas the eighteen-month sample represents only eight ATCs. It is possible, therefore, that the two samples are biased with regard to the various outcome measures used, with those clients successfully followed up having higher remission rates. The authors are confident that the higher response rate for the eighteen-month study yields a better match with the full intake sample on most important characteristics and that since the eighteen-month follow-up sample has a response rate three times higher than the six-month sample, any serious bias due to non-response should result in less favourable outcomes for the eighteen-month follow-up. Since the eighteen-month follow-up is not less favourable, the authors conclude that their samples are not seriously biased with respect to remission rates.

However, given the size of the 'fall-out' in follow-up, reservations concerning the possibility of sample bias must remain alongside those concerning the adequacy of the data collection efforts and the accuracy of the self-reports relied upon in the study. Given such limitations, caution must be exercised in interpreting the apparent finding that minimal treatment can bring about beneficial results. The possibility that other factors unrelated or incidentally related to the treatment process may be of greater importance in determining post-treatment drinking patterns has not been sufficiently taken into account. Indeed, it remains to be established that minimal forms of treatment are any more effective in modifying alcoholic patterns of drinking than no treatment at all.

More Treatment versus Less Treatment

Comparing the efficacy of one treatment modality versus another is handicapped by all the problems inherent in the comparison of treatment with no treatment. Such comparisons depend on the criterion of successful outcome being employed, the manner in which the samples involved have been selected, the location of the treatment, its duration and the adequacy of the follow-up procedures. It has to be admitted, on reading the literature, that the lack of agreed criteria of treatment success, the variability of patient samples and the lack of information contained in so many reports concerning such vital factors as patient selection and randomisation, render any attempt to formulate generalisations even more than usually hazardous.

Such reservations have not inhibited attempts to pool data from a variety of treatment reports. Costello's one- and two-year collated reports have already been mentioned. Using cluster analytic techniques, he attempted to identify those factors which predisposed patients to do well in treatment and those which mitigated against a good outcome. The major features of his 'best outcome' group, which encompassed fifteen studies involving 1,544 cases, and of his 'poorest outcome' group, which encompassed seven studies, involving 3,447 cases, are shown in Table 1. On the basis of his findings, Costello (1975a) proposed baseline results or minimal standards of response to treatment of so-called 'good prognosis' and 'poor prognosis' alcoholics (Table 2). A similar approach was undertaken in Costello's collation of two-year follow-up studies (Costello, 1975b).

Costello observes that most studies in his 'best outcome' group employed client screening or selection procedures whereby 'high-risk' clients, such as vagrants, transients or clients with serious physical and/or mental illness were excluded. One example quoted of a study in this category, is that of Davies and his colleagues (1956), in which there was an initial inpatient phase of treatment, all the participating

Table 1   Characteristics of best and poorest outcome Sub-groups.
Adapted from Costello (1975a)

Best Outcome   15 Studies — 1,544 cases
   Active intense treatment orientation
   Inpatient stay of 1-40 weeks
   Considerable use of Antabuse
   Milieu ward orientation
   Social case-work with spouse, workmates, employers etc.
   Behaviour therapy
   Effective use of OP follow-up

Poorest Outcome   7 Studies — 3,447 cases
   No client selection employed
   Large numbers in treatment
   Poorly motivated clients
   Meagre treatment resources
   Reliance on superficial support and drugs
   Antabuse not emphasised as integral part of treatment

Table 2   Suggested baselines for treatment outcome. Adapted from
Costello (1975a)

Suggested baselines for 1-year follow-up of treatment of good prognosis alcoholics
   1% dead
   44% still drinking with associated problem(s)
   45% successful in moderating or stopping drinking
   10% lost to follow-up

Suggested baselines for 1-year follow-up of treatment of poor prognosis alcoholics
   0% dead
   60% still drinking with associated problem(s)
   12% successful in moderating or stopping drinking
   28% lost to follow-up

patients were voluntarily admitted, there was a firm doctor-patient relationship and the treatment programme was structured around the protective aspects of Antabuse, vocational retraining for vulnerable groups and an effective use of outpatient follow-up clinics. In contrast, most studies in the 'poorest outcome' group exercised no client selection, had large numbers in treatment, accepted poorly motivated clients and commanded meagre treatment resources. These studies tended to rely on superficial support and drug management although Antabuse was not emphasised as an integral part of treatment. One study, quoted as an example of those in this group (Rhodes and Hudson, 1969), is that of 'skid row' alcoholics in a TB sanatorium.

In addition to any shortcomings intrinsic to an approach which relies on a pooling of data derived from widely differing studies and a bewildering variety of patients, there are some fundamental limitations in the cluster analytic technique on which such collation studies are based. The technique is only as good as the basic variables fed into it. For example, one of Costello's findings is that inpatient treatment, lasting between one and forty weeks, correlates positively with good outcome. Such a finding may very well be an artefact of the approach. It seems reasonable to assume that those treatment programmes which involved carefully screened, small groups of voluntary patients would have been hospital-based, during the period surveyed by Costello. Likewise, programmes involving minimal resources, large numbers of poorly selected and motivated clients might have been unable to call upon hospital facilities except for short-term, drying-out care. The association, as a consequence, between inpatient treatment of a moderate duration and good outcome would be coincidental.

Evidence from other treatment studies strongly suggests that this is the case. Baekeland and his colleagues (1975) reviewed separately the outcomes of inpatient and outpatient treatments and did not find strong evidence to support the view that either setting is preferable. One of the few studies that was adequately controlled and that randomly assigned patients to either two months' inpatient or outpatient care reported insignificant between-group differences at six and twelve months from intake (Edwards and Guthrie, 1967). A more recent comparative trial of short-stay alcoholics revealed no difference in outcome in sixty-two patients (thirty-eight in the short-stay group), followed up two years after discharge (Willems *et al.*, 1973). The overall results were comparable with results obtained in other studies. This research suggested that low social class, greater social maladjustment and a history of delirium tremens are factors significantly related to a poor outcome.

There is some evidence that treatment duration is positively correlated to outcome in outpatient studies (Fox and Smith, 1959; Gerard and Saenger, 1966; Kissin *et al.*, 1968; Ritson, 1968). In both inpatient and outpatient studies, however, duration of treatment has been confounded with such factors as social background, motivation and other prognostic variables.

Emrick's review of some 384 studies of psychologically oriented treatment of alcoholism (1975) in order to assess the relative effectiveness of different treatment approaches, is the most comprehensive available. Only seventy-two studies used random assignment or matched treatment groups, thereby permitting a reliable assessment of treatment differences uncontaminated by patient characteristics. Only five studies were found that showed significant long-term differences between treatment groups. Ends and Page (1957) compared four treatment groups and found client-centred and psychoanalytic groups superior to a learning theory and social discussion group. However, only fifty-eight of an original ninety-six patients in this study were available to follow-up. Tomsovic and Edwards (1973) found superior outcomes for their lysergide-treated groups compared with two control groups. However, losses to one-year follow-up were 38 per cent, forty-two percent and 37 per cent for the respective groups. In a trial of electrical aversion treatment, Vogler *et al.* (1970) reported more contingently shocked patients were abstinent at eight-month follow-up than those in a sham conditioning group but randomisation in this trial was unsatisfactory and only 51 of 73 patients were followed up.

The fourth of Emrick's five positive studies, that by Pittman and Tate (1972), reported a positive finding after randomisation of men of low social stability between three to six weeks inpatient treatment followed by intensive follow-up care as opposed to ten days inpatient treatment followed by no aftercare. Improvement was greater at nine to thirty-two months follow-up in the first group. However, there was a remarkable similarity between the two groups for self-report for improvement of drinking (60 per cent and 55 per cent).

The fifth study is that by Sobell and Sobell (1973) which reports on the randomisation of seventy patients between four groups followed up for one year. Patients in the group receiving behaviour therapy with controlled drinking as the goal had more often 'functioned well' during most of the year than had those merely treated in the conventional programme with a goal of controlled drinking.

This study, in common with many others, lacks a double-blind control design, a shortcoming which, while it may be unavoidable, none the less is another good reason for exercising caution in drawing causal connections between specific forms of intervention and specific forms of outcome. Clearly it is essential that researchers assessing the efficacy of alcoholism treatment should be aware of these methodological shortcomings and should modify their therapeutic claims accordingly. Sadly, in alcoholism as in other areas of psychiatric research, such scepticism more often than not is lacking.

Summary

Any brief summary of a field as extensive as that of the treatment of alcoholism must of necessity be selective. Yet it is clear from those extensive reviews which have been published (Hill and Blane, 1966; Pattison, 1968; Costello, 1975a&b; Emrick, 1974, 1975; Baekeland *et al.*, 1975; Hamburg, 1975; Armor *et al.*, 1976) that most current assumptions concerning the treatment of alcoholism must be open to question. A number of conclusions seem reasonable:

1. A small proportion of alcoholics achieve abstinence within six and twelve months of receiving treatment, whatever the nature, intensity and duration of the treatment concerned.

2. A substantial number of studies consistently report a varying proportion of former alcoholics drinking at moderate levels without apparent difficulty.

3. The overall remission rate six months after the initiation of treatment appears to predict quite accurately the likely rate of remission at later periods of follow-up.

4. Few noteworthy differences among remission rates for various treatment methods have been reported. Regardless of the setting in which treatment occurs, remission appears uniform.

5. Those few studies which have attempted to analyse the outcome in minimally-treated or untreated alcoholics suggest a high rate of so-called 'spontaneous' remission, perhaps as high as 50 per cent in some cases.

6. There is little evidence that costly and intensive therapeutic interventions are more efficacious than more economic and simpler approaches in bringing about remission.

Such conclusions represent a somewhat meagre return for the exertions represented in clinical effort and research activity in the treatment of alcoholism over the past twenty years. They may strike some as unduly pessimistic. However, such pessimism would seem to be misplaced. What these conclusions appear to indicate is the need for more rigorous assessment of aspects of treatment coupled with a willingness to refrain from embarking on treatment programmes of unproven worth which are time-consuming, expensive and complex. Further work is needed to eliminate the bias due to non-response, to establish the validity of self-reports and to monitor the likely effects of more long-term follow-up. Given that some alcoholics do return to patterns of normal drinking, it becomes imperative to establish which alcoholics do achieve such a successful readjustment and which fail to do so. It is in these areas that further information is required if there are to be significant advances in the treatment of alcoholism during the coming decade. The case in favour of the significant effects of treatment in alcoholism remains to be conclusively established

References

Armor, D.J., Polich, J.M. and Stambul, H.B. (1976). Alcoholism and Treatment. National Institute of Alcohol Abuse and Alcoholism. The Rand Corporation. Santa Monica, California.

Baekeland, F., Lundwall, L. and Kissin, B. (1975). Methods for the treatment of chronic alcoholism: a critical appraisal. Research Advances in Alcohol and Drug Problems. In: R.J. Gibbins, Y. Israel, H. Kalant, R.E. Popham, W. Schmidt and R.G. Smart (eds.), vol.2. London: Wiley.

Costello, R.M. (1973a). Alcoholism treatment and evaluation: in search of methods. Int. J. Addict. 10(2): 251-75.

Costello, R.M. (1973b). Alcoholism treatment and evaluation: in search of methods. II Collation of two-year follow-up studies. Int. J. Addict. 10(5): 857-67.

Davies, D.L. (1962). Normal drinking in recovered alcohol addicts. Quart. J. Stud. Alc. 23: 94-104.

Davies, D.L. Shepherd, M. and Myers, E. (1956). The two-years prognosis of 50 alcohol addicts after treatment in hospital. Quart. J. Stud. Alc. 17: 485-502.

Edwards, G. and Guthrie, S. (1967). A controlled trial of inpatient and outpatient treatment of alcohol dependency. Lancet 1(1): 555-9.

Emrick, C.D. (1974). A review of psychologically oriented treatment of alcoholism: I. The use and interrelationship of outcome criteria and drinking behaviour following treatment. Quart. J. Stud. Alc. 35: 523-49.

Emrick, C.D. (1975). A review of psychologically oriented treatment of alcoholism: II. The relative effectiveness of different treatment approaches and the effectiveness of treatment versus no treatment. Quart. J. Stud. APC. vol.

Ends. E.J. and Page, C.W. (1957). A study of three types of group psychotherapy with hospitalised male inebriates. Quart. J. Stud. Alc. 18: 263-77.

Foster, F.M. Horn, J.L. and Wanberg, K.W. (1972). Dimensions of treatment outcome: a factor-analytic study of alcoholics' responses to a follow-up questionnaire. Quart. J. Stud. Alc. 33: 1079-98.

Fox, V. and Smith, M.A. (1959). Evaluation of a chemopsychotherapeutic program for the rehabilitation of alcoholics: observations over a two-year period. Quart. J. Stud. Alc. 20: 767-80.

Gerard, D.L. and Saenger, G. (1966). Out-Patient Treatment of Alcoholism: A Study of Outcome and its Determinants. Toronto: University of Toronto Press.

Gerard, D.L., Saenger, G. and Wile, R. (1962). The abstinent alcoholic. Arch. Gen. Psychiat. 6: 83-95.

Hamburg, S. (1975). Behaviour therapy in alcoholism: a critical review of broad-spectrum approaches. J. Stud. Alc. 36: 69-87.

Hill, M.J. and Blane, H.T. (1966). Evaluation of psychotherapy with alcoholics: a critical review. Quart. J. Stud. Alc. 27: 76-104.

Kendell, R.E. (1968). Normal Drinking by Former Alcohol Addicts. Quart. J. Stud. Alc. 24: 44-60.

Kissin, B., Rossenblatt, S.M. and Machover, S. (1968). Prognostic factors in alcoholism. Psychiatric Research Reports 24: 22-43.

Pattison, E.M. (1968). A critique of alcoholism treatment concepts: with special reference to abstinence. Quart. J. Stud. Alc. 27: 49-71.

Pittman, D.J. and Tate, R.L. (1972). A comparison of two treatment programs for alcoholics. Int. J. Social Psychology 18: 183-93.

Rhodes, R.J. and Hudson, R.M. (1969). A follow-up study of tuberculosis in skid row alcoholics: 1. Social adjustment and drinking behaviour. Quart. J. Stud. Alc. 30(1): 119-28.

Ritson, B. (1968). The prognosis of alcohol addicts treated by a specialized unit. Brit. J. Psychiat. 114: 1019-29.

Tomsovic, M. and Edwards, R.V. (1970). Lysergide treatment of schizophrenic and non-schizophrenic alcoholics: a controlled evaluation. Quart. J. Stud. Acl. 31: 932-49.

Willems, P.J.A., Letemendia, F.J.J. and Arroyave, F. (1973). A two-year follow-up study comparing short with long stay in-patient treatment of alcoholics. Brit. J. Psychiat. 122: 637-48.

Vogler, R.E. Lunde, S.E., Johnson, G.R. and Martin, P.L. (1970). Electrical aversion conditioning with chronic alcoholics. J. Cons. Clin. Psychol. 34: 302-7.

24 BEHAVIOUR THERAPY

Ray Hodgson

The behavioural approach to psychotherapy relies upon the concepts, discoveries and methodology of the behavioural sciences, especially psychology. (Rimm and Masters, 1974.) Within the context of social learning theory (e.g. Bandura, 1969), the behaviour therapist attempts to analyse behaviour by identifying the private and social events that are associated with the behaviour. What antecedent cues and reinforcing consequences influence the alcoholic's decision to be abstinent, to drink in a controlled way or to indulge in a drinking binge? This type of assessment is usually called a behavioural or a functional analysis (Ullman and Krasner, 1969; Sobell *et al.*, 1976). It could be argued that such an analysis may help but can never fully explain the alcoholic's behaviour since alcoholism is essentially an irreversible biological condition. This may be true, but Jellinek (1960) stressed that the 'disease model' is only a 'working hypothesis' to be modified or discarded if falsified by empirical evidence. Another working hypothesis considers excessive drinking to be a learned, compulsive habit which has a lot in common with other compulsive behaviours such as gambling and over-eating. If a social learning theory approach can explain the development and maintenance of the excessive drinking 'habit' at the biological, psychological and social level then the principles of learning and conditioning should suggest methods of extinguishing this habit. If there is an irreversible biological basis then the behavioural approach may still suggest ways of modifying drinking behaviour.

Before presenting a critical review of the behavioural approach to treatment it may be useful to describe the development of alcoholism in an individual case in order to clarify the possible relevance of learning and conditioning theories, a topic which has been discussed previously in many theoretical articles (e.g. Wikler, 1973; Conger, 1956).

Tom started drinking in his teens but began drinking excessively and habitually when he joined the Army. In many ways he was totally unsuited to Army life and found that only by drinking heavily could he feel that he was one of the lads. Drink reduced tensions and made him more gregarious. He also found that heavy drinking made him feel and appear more manly. Now it is a basic principle of a social learning approach that a compulsive habit can develop after many reinforced repetitions. Tom learned that without drink he was unsociable but that with drink he was one of the lads, and after using drink on many occasions he found that he experienced a compulsion to drink whenever he had to face social situations. At this stage he would be considered to be psychologically dependent, but during the next five years he regularly consumed a daily bottle of gin and began to experience withdrawal symptoms whenever he attempted to be abstinent. Tom was now physically dependent. The consequences of resisting drink were upsetting if not actually horrific. This state of physical dependence undoubtedly involved biological changes. Most theories of physical dependence suggest that alcohol influences neuronal functioning in such a way that withdrawal results in overstimulation (Kalant and Leblanc, 1971). However, we cannot ignore the very important conditioning experiences that a physically dependent alcoholic is subjected to. To give just one example, he associates stopping drinking with unpleasant consequences (e.g. tremor, tachycardia and nausea). When experiencing or expecting these unpleasant withdrawal symptoms he can escape from them or avoid them by taking a few drinks. This is a sequence of events which can hardly fail to reinforce a compulsive habit. Notice that two types of cues are hypothesised. First there are the social cues: Tom has a compulsion to drink whenever he has to face a group of people. Secondly there are cues elicited by drinking: Tom reported that drinking heavily after a period of abstinence, would probably make him feel off colour when he stopped and that these feelings would act as cues which could trigger a desire to drink. So, after a period of abstinence, Tom must face social cues which make him want to start drinking (stage 1 cues) and interoceptive cues which are elicited by drink and withdrawal which make it difficult to stop (stage 2 cues). To use the language of learning theory there are many discriminative stimuli which can trigger (or at least influence) the compulsion to drink. Abstinence is easier if these discriminative stimuli are absent (e.g. in hospital or prison), but anxiety or frustration is experienced if discriminative stimuli are present and drinking is resisted. The first aim of the behaviour therapist is to identify these cues.

If as a working hypothesis excessive drinking is considered to be a compulsive habit, then a number of methods of modifying the habit follow directly from a learning theory approach (Bandura, 1969; Rimm and Masters, 1974; Franks and Wilson, 1975). One is to develop *coping skills* so that an alcoholic can cope with stress and social anxieties without turning to drink. Secondly, an attempt can be made to change the reinforcement contingencies which are associated with drinking so that the alcoholic finds it easier to resist drink. This method is usually called *contingency management*. Finally, one method of reducing some types of compulsive behaviour involves prolonged exposure to the cues which trigger (or at least influence) the compulsion. If excessive drinking is at all analogous to other types of compulsive behaviour, then *cue exposure* may be the most direct method of extinguishing the compulsive habit. These three methods of modifying compulsive behaviour will be considered in some detail, followed by a discussion of the feasibility of a controlled drinking goal as an alternative to total abstinence.

Coping Skills

Marlatt (1973) found that in the months after treatment there were two major reasons for relapse. A large majority of his treated alcoholics started drinking again because they experienced frustration or anger, or because they could not resist the social pressure to drink. Miller *et al.* (1974) demonstrated experimentally that alcoholics tend to drink more when subjected to interpersonal stress. It appears that anxiety, anger or frustration, pressure from others and interpersonal stresses, are all cues which can trigger a compulsion to drink. Consequently one behavioural approach is to teach the alcoholic alternative ways of coping with these stressful events, thereby reducing their significance as cues for excessive drinking. *Anxiety management, assertive training* and *social skills training* are all examples of this approach.

Learning to cope with anxiety would be an appropriate approach to treatment if it could be shown that anxiety was a drinking cue. The theory that alcohol reduces tension and that tension can be a cue which triggers heavy drinking, is usually called the tension reduction theory. Recently this theory has been challenged on the grounds that much of the evidence from animal experimentation is inconclusive and contradictory (Cappell and Herman, 1972) and consequently a number of psychologists have questioned the relevance of anxiety management techniques. However, Hodgson *et al.* (1977) have argued that some animal analogues have been inappropriately used to test the tension reduction theory, and that if these particular analogues are ignored the hypothesis that alcohol reduces anxiety is actually strongly supported. Although the tension reduction theory is still the subject of debate it is probable that anxiety is just one of the many cues which can trigger a craving for alcohol. Recently behavioural techniques such as systematic desensitisation and flooding have been developed and used with reasonable success on a range of neurotic problems involving a well-defined anxiety-producing stimulus (Marks, 1975), and some successful results have also been reported with alcoholics (Storm and Cutler, 1968; Newton and Stein, 1974). If the locus of anxiety cannot be identified clients can be trained to cope with anxiety through progressive relaxation or other alternative coping strategies. Steffens (1974) reported that clients undergoing muscular biofeedback training showed much less muscle tension and lower blood alcohol levels than their control group counterparts who did not have biofeedback training. Steffens concludes that 'training in maintenance of relaxation could serve as an alternative response to drinking'.

Feelings of social inadequacy or inability to express emotions can contribute to frustration and thus serve as potent cues to drinking. Recently methods have been developed to enable people to overcome such problems by increasing their social skills and especially their assertiveness. Typically social skills training takes the following form. First, the client's specific problems are identified. It may be for example that the client is unable to resist or protest against unreasonable behaviour from his colleagues. The therapist in this case will then play the part of the colleague in acting out the situation with the client, often recording the scenario on video-tape. The therapist then plays the part of the client showing him how he should react to such provocation. He would concentrate not only on the content of the client's speech but also on eye contact, tone of voice, loudness of voice, body posture, etc. The client would then be encouraged to re-enact this more appropriate behaviour and would receive feedback from the therapist throughout. His performance may even be video-taped so that the client can see for himself the difference between pre- and post-training. After several such sessions the client is encouraged to practise his new skills in real life.

This technique is often used to modify marital interactions and in this context Eisler *et al.* (1974) used assertive training for an alcoholic husband. After observing the interaction of the client with his wife, four target behaviours were selected for modification in the assertive training session. These were (i) duration of looking, (ii) duration of speech, (iii) request for partner to change her behaviour, (iv) speed of responding. With a female therapist playing the part of the client's wife, ten marital encounters were simulated using material and situations that were troublesome in real life. Video-tapes were made of pre- and post-treatment marital interaction, and when these were analysed they showed that the husband had substantially increased his assertiveness and improved on all of the target behaviours. Not only did his assertiveness increase but the wife reduced the number of her own behavioural requests from a high to a more moderate rate.

Marlatt's finding – that a large proportion of his treated alcoholics gave as their reason for relapse the social pressure exerted by others to get them to take a drink – has stimulated a number of behaviour therapists to advocate that the alcoholic should be taught how to say 'no' effectively. One study by Foy *et al.* (1976) used social skills training techniques to help two alcoholics to cope with this specific situation. Actual incidents were recalled by each client in which social pressure to drink had been experienced and these were used in the role playing sessions, e.g. 'you're at your brother's house. It's a special occasion and your whole family and several friends are there. Your brother asks you to have a beer.' Two psychologists role-played the client's social acquaintances (pushers) and used a variety of arguments in an attempt to coerce him to take a drink, e.g. 'what kind of a man are you who won't drink with his friends?' or 'one drink won't hurt you.' The alcoholic practised looking straight at the pusher, varying voice and facial expression where appropriate and confidently articulating appropriate replies. The evidence presented indicates that the alcoholics were able to modify their habitual way of responding to social pressure, and reported both increased feelings of confidence and self-esteem after successfully refusing drinks with their newly learned skills.

Although teaching coping skills is one method of modifying behaviour (Bandura, 1970; Barber *et al.*, 1971), we must await rigorous treatment trials with meticulous follow-up assessment before we can accept that such an approach can help the alcoholic to inhibit his compulsive drinking in the long term.

Contingency Management

Contingency management is a term given to those procedures which help an individual to control his behaviour by altering the relationship between the behaviour and its consequences; a realistic approach to treatment should aim to change the contingencies that are operating in the alcoholic's environment. Hunt and Azrin (1973) argue that for the well-adjusted person excessive drinking interferes with vocational, marital, social and personal reinforcements. On the other hand an unemployed, lonely alcoholic with no spouse, few friends and no hope, has nothing to lose and a lot to gain from a heavy drinking binge, at least in the short term. The aim of Hunt and Azrin's 'Community

Reinforcement' approach is to increase social reinforcements so that, at the moment when an alcoholic is about to drink heavily, he is aware that he has a lot to lose. This programme aimed to help the alcoholic to obtain greater satisfaction from vocational, marital, social and recreational activities. The specific procedures were as follows:

Vocational Counselling

Patients without jobs were instructed to (i) prepare a resumé; (ii) read the pamphlet 'How to get the job' (Dreese, 1960); (iii) call all friends and relatives on the phone to inform them of the need for employment and ask them for job leads; (iv) call the major factories and plants in the area; (v) place a 'situations-wanted' advertisement in the local papers; (vi) rehearse the job interview; and (vii) place applications and interview for the jobs which are available. The counsellor stood by while phone calls were made, he role-played interviews with the client, arranged for letters to be typed and escorted the alcoholic to job interviews. As soon as the patient acquired a job he was released from hospital. This job finding counselling is described in more detail in a separate report (Azrin, Flores and Kaplan, 1975).

Marital and Family Counselling

Marital counselling attempted to (i) provide reinforcement for the alcoholic to be a functioning marital partner, (ii) provide reinforcement for the spouse for maintaining the marital relationship and (iii) to make the drinking of alcohol incompatible with this improved relationship. Twelve specific problem areas were discussed including money management, family relations, sex problems, children, social life, attention, neurotic tendencies, immaturity, grooming, ideological difficulties, general incompatibility and dominance. The husband and wife together constructed a list of specific activities that each would agree to perform in order to make the other spouse happy. This list typically included preparing meals, listening to the partner with undivided attention, picking up the children from school, redistributing the finances, engaging in sexual activities of a particular type or a minimal frequency, visiting relatives together and spending a night out together. Absolute sobriety was requested of the husbands by all of the wives as part of this agreement. This approach to marital counselling has been described in detail elsewhere (e.g. Stuart, 1969; Azrin, Naster and Jones, 1973). For unmarried patients living with their families similar procedures were used. For those patients living alone attempts were made to arrange a foster family who would regularly invite the patient to their house. Again, sobriety was made a condition for obtaining these family benefits.

Social Counselling

The social counselling procedures involved scheduling social interactions with non-drinking acquaintances and reducing interactions with friends who were known to have a drinking problem. Also a former tavern was converted into a self-supporting social club for the clients and provided a band, juke box, card games, dances, invited female companions, picnics, snacks, bingo games, films and other types of social activities. Alcoholic beverages were strictly forbidden at the club and any member who arrived at the club with any indication of drinking was turned away.

The counsellor made every effort to help his clients to gain satisfaction in the vocational, marital and social areas. For example a client might be encouraged to increase his social interactions by buying a car or having a telephone installed in his home. If necessary the counsellor arranged to pay the initial costs in order to prime the activity.

This community reinforcement programme was given to eight patients and a matched control group was given a traditional form of treatment. Both groups received the counselling and instruction which was part of the standard treatment package at the Anna State Hospital in Illinois. The counsellor visited all patients at least once a month during the six-month follow-up and obtained information about days unemployed, drinking days and days spent away from home. There was a correlation of 0.95 between the data collected by the counsellor and that collected by an independent assessor at the end of the six-month period. The results showed that patients who received the community reinforcement procedures drank less, worked more and spent more time with their families than did the control group. These changes were stable during the six-month follow-up period so that every month and for every measure there were significant differences between the groups.

Although these results are very encouraging we should be aware of a number of problems in interpreting them. The community reinforcement procedures are based upon the principle that the alcoholic with a good job and a satisfactory social life will remain abstinent in order to ensure that he does not lose his newly acquired satisfactions. However, it is also probable that the satisfied alcoholic is less prone to the anxiety, frustration, boredom and feelings of failure which can trigger compulsive drinking.

A more recent replication of these results (Hunt, 1976) using other counsellors and improved procedures, indicates that even though the treatment rationale may be uncertain we should nevertheless be giving very serious consideration to this approach. This study extended the previous one by: (i) the use of disulfiram to inhibit compulsive drinking; (ii) special motivational procedures for the continued usage of the disulfiram; (iii) the use of an early warning notification system to alert the counsellor that problems were developing; (iv) the use of a neighbourhood friend-adviser to continue social support of the client after professional counselling had been terminated; (v) group counselling procedures to reduce the amount of counselling time; and (vi) the use of different counsellors to determine the ability of different counsellors to use the new procedure. As in the previous study, the experimental design employed random assignment of one member of each matched pair of clients into a control group.

Several procedures were used to ensure that disulfiram would become a fully established habit: (i) a time for taking disulfiram was linked to an already well established habit or event such as meal time, brushing one's teeth, or arriving home from work; (ii) the spouse was involved in the administration of disulfiram each day so that she could remind the patient if he forgot, and if he should stop taking disulfiram she could notify the counsellor so that pre-crisis therapy could occur; (iii) since the disulfiram routine might be broken because circumstances such as vocations, weekends, sickness, running out of the drug supply, or deaths in the family, special counselling and rehearsal were given as to how to continue the disulfiram habit in spite of these potential interruptions; (iv) to assure that the client received social support he was to take the disulfiram only in the presence of his wife, peer adviser or counsellor; (v) to assure ease of obtaining and using disulfiram the counsellor referred the client to a knowledgeable and sympathetic physician.

The clients in the control group received housing and other hospital services from different counsellors and also received instructions regarding alcoholism and its dangers, individual and group counselling, advice to take disulfiram, and encouragement to join an Alcoholics Anonymous group.

As in the previous study the mean times spent drinking, unemployed, away from home and institutionalised during the first six months all differed significantly between the control and the community reinforcement group to the advantage of the latter. The improved procedures involved a mean of thirty hours of counselling per client compared with fifty hours per client for the previous procedures. The improved procedures resulted in clients drinking only 2 per cent of the time during the six-month follow-up compared with 14 per cent for previous procedures. Clients in the community reinforcement programme were followed up for two years and they continued to be mainly abstinent during this period.

The community reinforcement procedures which are based on a contingency management approach attempt to make drinking a less attractive alternative than abstinence. Another contingency management programme involving community services was conducted by Miller (1975). In this study ten chronic alcoholics 'were provided with required goods and services through skid-row community agencies *contingent on their sobriety'.* Ten similar chronic alcoholics acted as a control group. The experimental group members had blood alcohol levels tested once every five days. Subjects with blood alcohol levels of 10 mgs/100 ml or less were eligible for services and goods during the five-day block, and those above this level were denied them, as were subjects who were seen to be grossly intoxicated at any time during the five-day period by agency employees or personnel. Emergency services were never denied to any of the subjects. The control group received their services as usual, i.e. independent of their blood alcohol level. After two months the experimental group had achieved significant reductions in blood alcohol levels and arrests, and significant increases in hours of work per week. The controlled group showed no significant changes on these measures during the two-month period. Miller concludes that 'wide scale use of this procedure on the basis of this report would be premature but replication of these results in a longer term evaluative study appears warranted'.

It has often been suggested that aversion therapy is another method of reducing the relative attractiveness of drinking compared to sobriety and many people in the caring professions appear to equate behaviour therapy with aversion therapy. Nothing could be further from the truth. Many behaviour therapists who are involved in the treatment of alcoholism have lost interest in aversion therapy because there is not enough evidence. The aim of aversion therapy – to replace a positive craving for alcohol by a negative aversion – does not appear to be an unreasonable one. An attempt is made to pair the sight, smell and taste of alcohol with an unpleasant experience, and this is usually accomplished by using small or moderate electric shocks to the wrist, or by the use of a drug such as Emetine or Apomorphine to provoke feelings of nausea. These two techniques – electrical and chemical aversion – must be considered separately, since there is no reason to suppose that evidence which relates to the effectiveness of one technique is at all applicable to the other. In fact, there is some strong evidence from animal research that different laws apply to chemical and electrical aversion. For example, a taste aversion can easily be produced in a rat by pairing the taste with sickness, but not by pairing the taste with electric shock (Garcia and Koelling, 1966).

Electrical Aversion

First consider the following experiment from the Alcohol Behaviour Research Unit at Rutgers University (Wilson, Leith and Nathan, 1975). Six Gamma alcoholics were allowed to drink whisky or bourbon up to a maximum of between 18 and 30 one ounce drinks a day. Drinks were served at a simulated bar, or they were dispensed by a computer operated console in the alcoholic's bedroom, and throughout the experiment consumption was computer recorded. During the first four days the alcoholic's daily consumption was assessed and the aim of the experiment was to modify this baseline level. The experiment was designed to assess the effectiveness of electrical aversion therapy by comparing it with a control treatment. Electrical aversion involved the administration of shock when the alcoholic, following instructions, began to sip his alcoholic drink. Shock was terminated when, as instructed, he spat out the drink. In the control treatment a shock was administered *before* the alcoholic was instructed to sip his drink. It was predicted that if shock was administered *after* sipping alcohol then a conditioned aversion would develop, whereas no aversion would develop when the shock was administered *before* sipping alcohol. The results were quite conclusive. At the beginning of the experiment the alcoholics were consuming between 10 and 24 drinks per day and neither treatment was effective in reducing alcohol consumption below this baseline level.

The results of this experiment cast some doubt upon the effectiveness of electrical aversion and consequently, any clinical trial which reports that electrical aversion is more effective than other forms of treatment must be subjected to a very close and critical analysis.

Chemical Aversion

Although thousands of alcoholics have been treated by chemical aversion during the last twenty years we still do not know whether the technique is effective. Certainly a number of clinical reports suggest that chemical aversion may be an effective method of helping some alcoholics, but we are still awaiting the well-controlled clinical trial which will settle the issue.

In the late 1930s Lemere and Voegtlin, working at the Shadel Sanatorium in Seattle, developed an aversion technique in which Emetine is used to induce nausea and vomiting. Ingestion of alcohol is timed to precede this unpleasant state and hopefully a taste aversion is conditioned. In 1950, Lemere and Voegtlin reported their results after treating more than 4,000 patients. Overall 60 per cent of these patients were abstinent at one-year follow-up and about 50 per cent were abstinent after thirteen years.

Equally optimistic results have been reported by others (e.g. Thiman, 1949; Wiens, 1975). However, there are many reasons why we should not accept these figures until a well-controlled study has been completed. First, the patients were treated in private hospitals and tended to be of higher educational and socio-economic status than the average alcoholic. It is well known that this type of alcoholic has a better chance of doing well with most forms of treatment. Secondly, the patients were usually receiving other forms of treatment including group therapy and AA support. There is therefore no way of knowing whether chemical aversion therapy added anything to these traditional methods.

As noted earlier, at least in rats, a taste aversion can be easily established by pairing taste and sickness but not by pairing taste with an electric shock. This suggests that a similar phenomenon might occur in human aversive conditioning. Certainly, there is anecdotal evidence that we can develop strong taste aversions when a particular food is followed by nausea and vomiting. Seligman (1975), for example, described the development of an aversion to sauce Bernaise when he experienced nausea a few hours after his first taste. However, animal research suggests that this type of taste aversion is easy to establish only when both the taste and the sickness are unfamiliar (Revusky and Taukulis, 1975). Since both the taste of alcohol and feelings of nausea are familiar experiences for the alcoholic there is reason to believe that an aversion to the taste of alcohol might be difficult to condition. Even if a taste aversion can be conditioned a severely dependent alcoholic may still drink to achieve desirable consequences. Indeed many alcoholics report that they have frequently consumed foul-tasting liquids containing alcohol.

The fact that many thousands of patients have now been treated by this unpleasant technique although we still do not know whether it is effective, should convince the most unscientific layman, or therapist, that there is no substitute for a scientific experimental approach to the development of new treatment methods.

Cue Exposure

There are many similarities between the alcoholic and obsessive-compulsive disorders. Both addictive and compulsive behaviours can be triggered by cues, they are difficult to resist and once started they are difficult to stop. Recently a technique has been developed which considerably helps those suffering from obsessive-compulsive disorders (Hodgson *et al.*, 1972; Rachman *et al.*, 1971, 1973; Marks *et al.*, 1975).

The technique involves exposing the obsessional to those situations or cues which trigger his compulsion and then helping him to prevent his usual compulsive response. This is fairly easy to implement without physical coercion, is often self-paced and largely successful. Typically some discomfort is experienced initially but this dissipates over time, and dissipation becomes quicker as the experience is repeated across a number of sessions. The cue exposure approach has also been successfully applied to a case of compulsive masturbation (Hodgson and Rachman, 1976).

Applying a similar model to the problem of alcoholism the following programme emerges. Firstly the therapist identifies those events that act as signals or cues for the alcoholic to drink. These could be internal feelings, such as anxiety or depression, or external stimuli such as particular pubs or just the sight of a bottle of whisky. The model then dictates the second part of the programme, namely exposing the alcoholic to these cues and helping him to resist any subsequent urge to drink. Hodgson and Rankin (1976) report a case study in which a severe alcoholic received such treatment. A number of cues were related to his desire to drink but the most potent of these was the consumption of a moderate amount of alcohol (four vodkas). Once the patient had drunk four vodkas he experienced a very strong craving for more drink. As the model dictated, the therapists exposed the patient to this situation by giving him four vodkas and then giving support as he resisted continuing drinking. The results showed that although craving was initially moderately high it diminished over time and lessened at an increasing rate across sessions, so that at the end of the twelfth session virtually no craving was present immediately after the cue exposure (four vodka consumption).

It should be stressed that this method was not aimed at teaching controlled drinking. Indeed in the particular case cited the treatment goal was abstinence even though the *means* to that goal involved the consumption of alcohol. The ι,ypothesis is that by such a method one can extinguish craving and thus help the alcoholic to resist drinking excessively. Since the great majority of alcoholics on an abstinence régime will take a drink of alcohol within two years of hospital discharge (Orford and Edwards, 1977) such a technique, if effective, would be a useful adjunct to therapy.

Controlled Drinking as an Alternative to Abstinence

The most ambitious study of the use of the behavioural approach in attempting to achieve a controlled drinking goal was reported by Mark and Linda Sobell in 1973. They attempted to answer two questions. First, how does behaviour therapy compare with traditional treatment methods? Second, and more controversially, is it feasible to give the alcoholic the choice between abstinence and a controlled drinking goal? The seventy patients in this trial have now been followed up for two years (Sobell and Sobell, 1976) and the results can be summarised very briefly as follows. For patients who attempted to achieve a goal of total abstinence, behaviour therapy resulted in a better outcome one year after treatment but there was no significant difference after two years. On the other hand, where a controlled drinking goal was considered to be appropriate, behaviour therapy procedures were more effective than traditional methods at both the one-year and the two-year follow-up.

Since the major finding of this study was a successful treatment approach designed to establish moderate drinking, only this particular set of procedures will be described here:

1. The patients drank until quite intoxicated and then a few days later watched a video-taped replay. It was argued that the sight of their own mindless drunken behaviour, would increase their motivation to avoid excessive drinking.

2. Subjects were given a failure experience in which they attempted to complete a series of tasks which were, in fact, impossible. Maladaptive responses to this experience were then analysed and better ways of coping were discussed. Successfully coping with failure experiences could eliminate one important reason for drinking excessively.

3. The next ten sessions were devoted to practising drinking in a controlled way. Drinking was allowed in a simulated bar and cocktail

lounge and also in a simulated home environment. A large variety of confiscated alcoholic beverages were supplied by the California State Alcoholic Control Board. The alcoholic's aim during these sessions was simply to control his drinking. It is known that the alcoholic tends to gulp rather than to sip his drink, that he doesn't add a mixer but takes his drinks straight, and that, of course, he drinks to excess. Consequently, in these controlled drinking sessions, the alcoholic knew that he would receive a one-second shock whenever he gulped, ordered a straight drink, made a second order within twenty minutes of his previous order, or exceeded three drinks in any one session. Actually the maximum number of shocks received by any individual throughout the whole treatment period was six, and the majority of subjects received less than two. Most of the time drinking was completely controlled and the shocks were probably redundant. Furthermore, no subject found that he was compelled to leave hospital and go on a drinking binge.

4. A portion of each of the controlled drinking sessions was devoted to a discussion of the setting events which would result in excessive drinking (e.g. an argument with the wife). A series of alternative ways of responding to these setting events were then discussed and the consequences of each alternative were considered. In this way the alcoholic is trained to analyse the setting events or cues which influence his drinking and to work out an alternative way of coping. The Sobell's consider this aspect of treatment to be of crucial importance. As an example they described the way in which one alcoholic made use of this problem solving technique to deal with a strong desire to drink. He decided that he had a desire to drink because his brother was living in his house, sponging off him and attempting to seduce his wife. He then generated a number of possible responses to this situation including moving from California to Chicago. After considering the long-term consequences of each alternative he decided to ask his brother to leave. To his amazement this was a perfect solution, and thereafter there was a distinct improvement in his marital relationship and a reduction in his desire to drink.

5. Patients in the control group were considered to be appropriate candidates for a controlled drinking goal but they actually received traditional treatment which involved an abstinence goal.

This multifaceted approach was very successful for alcoholics with a controlled drinking goal. Of course the Sobell's approach embraces a large number of procedures and there is no way of knowing which ones are of crucial importance. All we can say is that the approach was successful.

This study demonstrated that a controlled drinking goal appears to be appropriate for some alcoholics, but it certainly cannot be claimed that controlled drinking is an appropriate goal for all alcoholics. Sobell and Sobell (1976) point out that:

> . . .legitimizing alternatives to abstinence as viable treatment objectives for some alcoholics does not imply that this is appropriate for all or even most alcoholics. Similarly, it should be recognized that not all or even most persons currently working in the alcoholism treatment field are presently skilled to pursue alternatives to abstinence with clients. As with any kind of therapeutic procedure, this treatment modality should only be used by trained individuals, aware of the methodology, benefits, dangers and limitations involved in such an approach. A further caveat is that just as the feasibility of this goal has been too easily dismissed by many of the past (Sobell and Sobell, 1975), so it is possible to erroneously accept a controlled drinking goal as a panacea.

It is now probable that Davies was correct when he noted in 1962 that some alcoholics do return to moderate drinking; there are now more than sixty references in the research literature that confirm his finding. It is certainly going against the evidence to suggest that 'there can be no relaxation for the stated position that no alcoholic may return with safety to any use of alcohol' (United States National Council on Alcoholism, 1974), or that research on controlled drinking 'might indeed expose them [alcoholics] to an inability to ever stop or to recover, and to eventual death or insanity.'(Mann, 1974).

If it is in fact beneficial for some alcoholics to practise drinking in a controlled way then it is unethical to deter research into such strategies, especially when it is remembered that the traditional abstinence approach is far from universally successful.

Conclusions

The behaviour therapy approach to the treatment of alcoholism is based on the assumption that drinking is influenced by antecedent cues and reinforcing consequences. If an alcoholic nearly always drinks after an argument with his wife (antecedent cues) in order to relax or to forget (reinforcing consequences) then a social learning theory approach leads to the hypothesis that he will be helped if he can be taught alternative ways of coping with his marital problem, if sobriety (or controlled drinking) is made more rewarding than uncontrolled drinking, and if the cues which trigger his drinking can be desensitised through cue exposure.

The decision to drink or not to drink is based upon learned expectancies. We must ask what the alcoholic expects to happen under certain conditions (discriminative stimuli or cues) if he drinks and if he does not drink. He will probably expect to feel anxious, frustrated or angry if he resists drink. His drinking decisions will be based upon these learned (often irrational) expectancies, as well as other factors such as his state of finance, availability of drink and expected feedback from family and friends. One result of successful treatment must be a modification of his expectancies especially as regards the negative consequences of resisting drink.

Most of the time behaviour therapy does not go against common sense and many psychologists, general practitioners and social workers could easily adjust their own treatment strategies to include a behavioural approach. Behaviour therapy is not a simple-minded approach which concentrates only on the presenting symptoms. Behaviour therapy is not inhumane; a treatment programme should always be devised by the patient and therapist together. Above all behaviour therapy is an applied science.

References

Azrin, N.H. Naster, B.J. and Jones, R. (1973). Reciprocity counselling: A rapid learning-based procedure for marital counseling. Behav. Res. & Ther. 11: 365-82.

Azrin, N.H., Flores, T. and Kaplan, S.J. (1975). Job-finding club: a group-assisted program for obtaining employment. Behav. Res. & Ther. 13: 17-27.

Azrin, N.H. (1976). Improvements in the community reinforcement approach to alcoholism. Behav. Res. & Ther. 14: 339-48.

Bandura, A. (1969). Principles of Behaviour Modification. New York: Holt.

Barber, T., Dicara, L.V., Kamiya, J. Miller, N.E., Shapiro, D. and Stovra, J. (eds.). (1971). Biofeedback and Self Control. New York: Aldine-Atherton.

Cappell, H. and Herman, C.P. (1972). Alcohol and tension reduction: a review. Quart. J. Stud. Alc. 33: 33.

Conger, J.J. (1956). Alcoholism: theory problem and challenge. II. Reinforcement theory and the dynamics of alcoholism. Quart. J. Stud. Alc. 17: 296.

Davies, D.L. (1962). Normal drinking in recovered alcohol addicts. Quart. J. Stud. Alc. 23: 94-104.

Dreese, M. (1960). How to get the job. (rev.edn.). Science Research Associates, Chicago.

Eisler, R.M. Miller, P.M. Hersen, M. and Alford, H. (1974). Effects of assertive training on marital interaction. Archives of General Psychiatry 30: 643-9.

Foy, D.W. Miller, P.M. Eisler, R.M. and O'Toole, D.H. (1976). Social skills training to teach alcoholics to refuse drinks effectively. J. Stud. Alc. 37: 1340-45.

Franks, C.M. and Wilson, T. (1975). Annual review of behaviour therapy: theory and practice. New York: Brunner-Mazell.

Garcia, J. and Koelling, R.A. (1966). Relation of cue to consequence in avoidance learning. Psychon. Sci. 4: 123-4.

Hodgson, R., Rachman, S. and Marks, I. (1972). The treatment of obsessive-compulsive neuroses; follow-up and further readings. Behav. Res. & Ther. 10: 181-9.

Hodgson, R. and Rachman, S. (1976). Modification of compulsive behaviour. In: Case Histories in Behaviour Therapy, H.J. Eysenck (ed.). London: Routledge and Kegan Paul.

Hodgson, R.J. and Rankin, H.J. (1976). Modification of excessive drinking by cue exposure. Behav. Res. & Ther. (in press).

Hodgson, R.J., Stockwell, T. and Rankin, H.J. (1977). Does alcohol reduce tension? Submitted to Behav. Res. & Ther.

Hunt, G.M. and Azrin, N.H. (1973). The community-reinforcement approach to alcoholism. Behav. Res. & Ther. 11: 91-104.

Jellinek, E.M. (1960). The Disease Concept of Alcoholism. New Haven: Hillhouse Press.

Kalant, H. and Leblanc, A.E..(1971). Tolerance to, and dependence on, ethanol. In: Biological Basis of Alcoholism, Y. Israel and J. Mardones (eds.). London: J. Wiley & Sons.

Lemere, F. and Voegtlin, W.L. (1950). An evaluation of the aversion treatment of alcoholism. Quart. J. Stud. Alc. 11: 199-204.

Mann, M. (1974). Presentation as part of a panel discussion on Human Subjects for alcoholism research: Ethical and Legal Considerations. 25th Annual Meeting of the Alcohol and Drug Problems Assoc., San Francisco, C.A.

Marks, I.M. (1975). Behavioural treatment of phobias and obsessive-compulsive disorders: a critical appraisal. In: Progress in Behaviour Modification. M. Herson, R.M. Eisler and P.M. Miller (eds). New York: Academic Press, vol.1, pp.66-158.

Marks, I.M., Hodgson, R., and Rachman, S. (1975). Treatment of chronic obsessive-compulsive neurosis by in-vivo exposure: a two-year follow-up and issues in treatment. Brit. J. Psychiat. 127: 349-64.

Marlatt, G.A. (1973). A comparison of aversive conditioning procedures in the treatment of alcoholism. Paper at Western Psychological Association, April 1973.

Miller, P.M., Hersen, M., Eisler, R. and Hilsman, G. (1974). Effects of social stress on operant drinking of alcoholics and social drinkers. Behav. Res. & Ther. 12: 67-72.

Miller, P.M. (1975). A behavioural intervention program for chronic public drunkenness offenders. Arch. of Gen. Psychiat. 32: 915-18.

Newton, J.R. and Stein, L.I. (1971). Implosive therapy, duration of hospitalization and degree of coordination of after-care services with alcoholics. In: US National Institute on Alcohol Abuse and Alcoholism. Proceedings, 1st Annual Alcoholism Conference, 25-26 June 1971.

Orford, J. and Edwards, J.G. (1977). Maudsley Monograph – accepted for publication, 1977.

Rachman, S., Hodgson, R. and Marks, I. (1971). Treatment of chronic obsessive-compulsive neurosis. Behav. Res. & Ther. 9: 237-47.

Rachman, S., Marks, I.M. and Hodgson, R. (1973). The treatment of obsessive-compulsive neurotics by modeling and flooding in vivo. Behav. Res. & Ther. 11: 463-72.

Revusky, S. and Taukulis, H. (1975). Effects of alcohol and lithium habituation on the development of alcohol aversions through contingent lithium injection. Behav. Res. & Ther. 13: 163-6.

Rimm, D.C. and Masters, J.C. (1974). Behavior Therapy: Techniques and Empirical Findings. New York: Academic Press.

Seligman, M.P. and Hager, J.L. (1972). Biological Boundaries of Learning. New York: Appleton-Century-Crofts.

Sobell, M.B. and Sobell, L.C. (1973b). Alcoholics treated by individualized behaviour therapy: one year treatment outcome. Behav. Res. & Ther. 11: 599-618.

Sobell, M.B. and Sobell, L.C. (1975). The need for realism, relevance and operational assumptions in the study of substance dependence. In: Proceedings of the International Symposia on Alcohol and Drug Problems, vol.6: Biological and Behavioural Approaches to Drug Dependence, H.D. Cappell and A.E. LeBlank (eds.). Toronto: Addiction Research Foundation.

Sobell, M.B., Sobell, L.C. and Sheahan, D.B. (1976). Functional analysis of drinking problems as an aid in developing individual treatment strategies. Addictive Behaviors.

Sobell, M.B. and Sobell, L.C. (1976). Second year treatment outcome of alcoholics treated by individualized behaviour therapy: results. Behav. Res. & Ther. 14: 195-215.

Steffen, J. (1974). Electromyographically induced relaxation in the treatment of Chronic Alcohol Abuse. Jour. of Consul. & Clin. Psych. 43(2): 275.

Storm, T. and Cutler, T. (1968). Systematic desensitization in the treatment of alcoholism: an experimental trial. Alcoholism Foundation of British Columbia.

Stuart, R.B. (1969). Token reinforcement in marital treatment. In: Advances in Behavior Therapy, R. Rubin and C.M. Frank (eds.). New York: Academic Press.

Thimann, J. (1949). Conditioned reflex treatment of alcoholism. II. The risk of its application, its indications, contraindications, and psychotherapeutic aspects. New England Jour. of Med. 241: 408-10.

Ullmann, L.P. and Krasner, L. (1969). A Psychological Approach to Abnormal Behavior. Englewood Cliffs, New Jersey: Prentice Hall.

Wiens, A.N. Montague, J.R., Manaugh, T.S. and English, C.J. (1975). Pharmacologic aversive counterconditioning to alcohol in a private hospital: one year follow-up. Unpublished manuscript, University of Oregon Medical School, 1975.

Wikler, A. (1973). Conditioning of successive adaptive responses to the initial effects of drugs. Conditional Reflex 8: 193-210.

Wilson, G.T., Leaf, R. and Nathan, P.E. (1975). The aversive control of excessive drinking by chronic alcoholics in the laboratory setting. Jour. of Applied Behav. Analysis 8: 13-26.

25 MAKING TREATMENT BETTER
Raj Rathod

Few would doubt that over the last two decades we have become more alert to the hazards of alcoholism and that we have a better understanding of the subject. We have available to us a wider range of therapeutic techniques and a greater range of facilities at our disposal, such as special units, hostels, information centres. However, there is no evidence to suggest that these developments have been translated into more effective management of patients. Most alcoholics still either go untreated or are treated inadequately. One of the stock solutions offered is to increase resources. Whilst this is a legitimate demand, it may be based on the assumption that the avilable resources are accessible to all the patients and are used to maximum effect. Such assumptions are ill-founded, for how else can one explain the fact that the number who are rejected or who drop out or who relapse after treatment exceed those who achieve or sustain the goal of treatment? Two popular alibis are used to excuse these shortcomings, one being the patient denying his illness and not being motivated for treatment, and the other being the relapsing nature of illness. While these may explain some failures, they cannot account for all.

Diagnosis

All therapeutic professions would agree that the earlier a problem is diagnosed the better are the chances of effective treatment and, furthermore, that the first requisite of diagnosis is to bear the possibility of a particular illness in mind. And yet it is strange that many alcoholics are misdiagnosed or missed during the early stages of their illness. It is understandable that a patient or his family may not be able to relate abnormal drinking to many of its symptoms. It is too much to expect an alcoholic to relate his insomnia to his drinking, or a family to attribute chhldren's behavioural disorders to the excessive drinking and related behaviour of the father or mother. Equally, the spouse of an alcoholic who suffers from depression may not be able to relate this disorder to the patient's drinking, although she might be able to relate it to things going wrong within their relationship. However, it is not acceptable that therapists should collude with this ignorance. Stories of alcoholic patients going to their doctors for insomnia, depression or anxiety states only to be prescribed symptomatic treatment are sadly quite often heard; thus not only is the real diagnosis missed and the chronicity of the illness perpetuated but, worse still, medications are prescribed which are dangerous when taken in conjunction with alcohol. Similar accounts are proferred about related physical disorders such as chronic gastritis or peptic ulcer. Surely the remedy is a simple one, and that is a greater awareness of the possibility of drinking as the cause of a wide variety of common symptomatic presentations. Education of therapists is needed to improve clinical acumen and achieve earlier diagnosis.

Limited Professional Perspectives

Constraints can arise from the hierarchical nature of the organisation of a treatment facility, the differing professional orientations of the therapists within such facilities, and the narrow range of treatment modalities that are offered. Even in the so-called multidisciplinary team it is usually the person in charge who dominates, if not dictates, all the decisions about a patient's treatment; others may be heard, but not necessarily listened to. Restricted professional training, over-valued beliefs in the contributions of that particular profession, and under-valuing of other professions' contributions, militate against free communication and constructive action.

Why otherwise, one may ask, does a physician who treats a patient with a peptic ulcer tell the patient to cut down his drinking but does not find it easy to refer for help from a psychiatrist; or why is a psychiatrist so preoccupied with the person that he may overlook the importance of physical, social or environmental factors; or why may a social worker labour the role of distorted interpersonal relationships at the expense of many other relevant and perhaps more important areas? Such happenings often reflect professional or status insecurity. One can sympathise with the patient and his family if in such circumstances they feel confused.

Restricted Facilities

Many treatment organisations over-emphasise the role of a particular facility — inpatient treatment for example — over all others, even though research might have shown that outpatient or day care facilities can be equally effective. The same applies to the treatment modalities used; group psychotherapy seems to stand supreme in the modes of treatment, even though it has never been proved or disproved that this necessarily is the best type of treatment to offer alcoholic patients. The practice seems to have been borrowed from Alcoholics Anonymous without questioning its validity. This is not to say that group therapy is unimportant, but just to make the point that the more or less universal favouring of group therapy should not be accepted uncritically: if offered as the main type of treatment, it can lead to a rejection of many patients. For example, a patient who has difficulty in verbalising, or who is a social isolate, would find it hard to assimilate himself in a programme in which group therapy is the principal mode of treatment, and such a patient would either be rejected by the staff from the outset, or may himself reject the treatment processes. The loser is the patient, not the professionals.

The same can be said about the goals of treatment. As far as drinking behaviour is concerned, total abstinence is appropriate for many alcoholics but not for all alcoholics. In a facility which adheres to total abstinence as the goal of treatment, a patient who does not accept this goal or submits to treatment with serious reservations and is unable or unwilling to work toward that goal, is likely to find himself rejected. Despite cliches like 'treatment must fit in with the needs of the patient', the organisation of the system is such that in practice it works the other way round. The patient always has to fit in with the system, and, if he does not, he finds himself deprived of the chance of having treatment and is labelled as uncooperative. Despite evidence pointing to the benefits of varying techniques and different goals of treatment, the therapists still cling to what they have learned from their personal experience and to self-fulfilling prophecies, rather than taking advantage of the evidence of research and the experiences of others.

Ethically, it should be incumbent on therapists to provide therapeutic facilities and modalities commensurate with clients' needs and goals. If they cannot provide these themselves, they should guide the patient toward the appropriate help.

The First Interview

The first interview is crucial in establishing a therapeutic relationship between the two parties. The alcoholic often presents himself as an irritable, irritating and rather aggressive person, and this can alienate even the most willing and patient therapist at times. One of the misconceptions in the first interview is to take the patient's behaviour at its face value and not to probe for the reasons behind it. Take for example the question of free choice. When a person comes to a therapist it is naïvely assumed that he has done so out of free choice. In many situations the patient has in fact little free choice, at least in a positive sense. He is forced into a situation where he has to choose the best of the various rather unpleasant alternatives. How else would one expect such a person – in a situation not primarily of his own choosing – to react except by being annoyed and feeling put upon and forced?

The therapist in turn might well be expected to be annoyed by this patient's negative behaviour and attitude towards the person who was supposedly there to help. In such a situation it is so easy for the client to reject the therapist or the therapist to reject the client and terminate the interview. A closer analysis should however give to the therapist an awareness that the client sees his situation quite differently from the way the therapist is seeing it, and hence the negative rapport. It is all too easy for the therapist and the patient not to appreciate each other's view, but such mutual understanding is necessary for any therapeutic progress to take place. The onus is more on the therapist than on the patient who is labouring under greater disadvantage.

Diagnostic Labels

Both the therapist and the client have their own perception – both at cognitive and emotive levels – of what is meant by words like 'alcoholic' and 'alcoholism', but the perception is usually not the same. Each has arrived at that perception through differing processes of learning, and has in mind differing connotations both for the here and now, and for the future.

To lay people, an alcoholic is one who is deviant in behaviour, has lost the capacity to regulate his alcohol consumption in the manner of 'normal' people, drinks excessively day in and day out and is often drunk, and who is a derelict with no claim ot self-respect, will-power or social acceptance. It is worse than having a cancer. Such a perception is misguided but very real. This reality has to be understood and respected. The situation is akin to what people may feel about a word like 'schizophrenia'.

To a clinician on the other hand the words 'alcoholic' and 'alcoholism' mean no more (hopefully) than a neutral clinical concept, both in terms of aetiology, signs and symptoms, and prognosis. A clinician who does not take the trouble to ask the patient or the client what they mean by the words 'alcoholic' or 'alcoholism' and, when asked 'What is wrong with me?' pronounces 'You are an alcoholic' or 'Your spouse is an alcoholic' can unwittingly cause distress to the recipient of this expert opinion. The recipient may not only reject the diagnosis but may opt out of any further therapeutic help.

The onus, therefore, of understanding what the patient feels about his problems, of persuading him to accept the therapist's opinion and of conveying this opinion in a manner that the client and his family can accept, is entirely on the therapist. This may sound very basic, but it is surprising how often these basic processes are ignored by the 'experts'. Lack of understanding of the other person's point of view is not a prerogative of the patient alone.

Next, the concept of illness. Here the patient finds himself in a double-bind. The therapist may call alcoholism an 'illness' to lessen the patient's guilt and shame. This the patient can accept for, as far as he is concerned, illness is something from which you suffer and in which you have relatively little or no active part to play. You take your illness to the expert whose job it is to take the whole responsibility for the cure. To tell the patient that he is ill, and at the same time to tell him that he has the responsibility of whether he will get better or not, is a contradiction in terms, so far as the patient is concerned. Either he is ill, and then the responsibility is that of the therapist, or he is not ill, and then the responsibility is that of the patient. Confusion is avoidable if enough care is taken to explain the nature of the illness, and the part the patient can and must play in promoting or hindering his own recovery.

The Need for Self-Questioning

We have little data on the natural history of alcoholism and insufficient facts to predict who will benefit from what treatment, where such treatment should take place and how long it should last. We do not always know what goals to set, and cannot, therefore, talk in terms of certainties but in terms only of possibilities. Our therapeutic efficacy would be enhanced if, instead of asserting our beliefs and practices, we are prepared to question them and experiment with new ideas. We may also benefit if we accept that the patient sometimes knows far more about his life situation and his goals for treatment than the therapist, and on this basis if we accord him and his family the status of members of the therapeutic team. It is unfortunate if the professionals become annoyed and respond only negatively when their practices and expertise are questioned, and label these seemingly rebellious or questioning patients as lacking in insight, uncooperative or unmotivated. As often, it is our own attitudes that have gone awry and need mending.

26 SETTING UP DETOXIFICATION CENTRES
B.D. Hore

Detoxification centres are a recent development in the United Kingdom. Britain has been late in this field, for such centres have been operating in Eastern Europe and North America for the last twenty years. Perhaps the fundamental aim of these centres, which deal with the chronic drunkenness offender, are best summed up in one of the earlier studies, that by Professor David Pittman (1958) entitled 'Revolving Door'.

He stated:

> a treatment centre should be created for the reception of the chronic drunkenness offender. This means that such offenders should be removed from the gaols and penal institutions, as the mentally ill in this country were removed from the gaols during the last century. Given the present state of knowledge concerning alcoholism, the time is right now for such a change. The present system is not only inefficient in terms of excessive cost of gaoling an offender thirty, forty or fifty times, but is a direct negation of this society's humanitarian philosophy towards people who are beset by social, mental and physical problems.

Drunken offences are very much on the increase in the United Kingdom. They have increased five times since the end of the Second World War. Currently, there are 100,000 cases per annum of drunken offence in England and Wales, and 50,000 in Scotland (this gives Scotland a rate five times higher than that of the rest of the United Kingdom). Studies in London and Edinburgh have shown that at least half of the drunken offenders are not casual roisterers but alcohol addicts by any definition. The reasons for the development of detoxification centres which were recommended in the Home Office Report on the Drunkenness Offender in 1971 included an acceptance of the futility of the 'Revolving Door' system, an awareness of the research evidence that many of these people are alcohol addicts, and the desire to propose a more rational system of handling which would constructively emphasise treatment and rehabilitation.

Two Models

The earliest detoxification centres were set up in Eastern Europe, particularly in Poland and Czechoslovakia. Much has been learnt, however, by experience in North America where there are two major models of detoxification centres. There are firstly the hospital-based centres such as those in St Louis, Missouri (which was set up in 1966) and secondly, non-hospital-based centres such as those set up in Ontario under the umbrella of the Addiction Research Foundation. Ontario indeed experimented with both approaches before making a choice. Both models were discussed at the European Institute on Alcoholism in Manchester in 1974 (Proceedings, 1974). The rationale behind these alternative approaches needs to be examined.

A hospital-based centre means of course that the centre is situated within a hospital, that it is directed by medical personnel although other personnel play an active role in the treatment programme, and that medical resources, including drugs, are used in the treatment. This model sees the clients as sick and therefore ethically insists that they deserve the best possible medical treatment. Intoxication and withdrawal are viewed as potentially serious conditions which demand investment of professional expertise in their care. Quick and energetic treatment is believed to be necessary if complications are to be aborted – at St Louis only 3 out of 10,000 admissions developed DTs.

The non-hospital-based model as developed say in Ontario, is founded on the following assumptions. Only a small percentage of the clients will require immediate medical attention (5 per cent in the Ontario experience). Routine medical examination is therefore viewed as unnecessary, and the operation is less expensive in time and costs. But it is important to realise that these centres are not necessarily entirely non-medical. Indeed, in Ontario they are frequently an integral part of a hospital complex in an administrative sense, although the building may be away from the hospital. This implies that the hospital and medical services cannot refuse to treat any of the centre's clients, should this be necessary. It is, however, the policy of such centres to use either no or minimal drugs, and to create an atmosphere where there is the least possible fuss and confrontation with the individual client. Counselling is the main form of treatment.

Pilot Experiments in the UK

As stated above, there is no doubt as to the increasing problem of drunken offenders in the United Kingdom. Studies such as those of

Hamilton (1976) in Edinburgh and Gath *et al.* (1968) in London, have shown that at least half these subjects are alcohol addicts who are not getting treatment. It has wisely been felt in the United Kingdom that we do not yet know enough about conditions in this country to develop a comprehensive service for the chronic drunkenness offender in terms of any one preconceived model, even if the financial resources were available. It is, therefore, planned to develop pilot schemes in this country. At present, there is only one such scheme in operation and that is at Leeds, which is based on the non-hospital model already mentioned. A second system is that developing in Manchester which will open in 1977. This is a hospital-based unit set in the grounds of a teaching hospital and part of a large complex, which includes a University Department of Psychiatry and an Alcoholism Treatment Unit. As could be expected, it has taken considerable persuasion for other specialties to agree the setting up of such a centre, and it cannot be stated that, as yet, the idea is fully accepted, although cooperation is likely. Referrals to this centre will be from police only, and the unit will have a high ratio of medical, nursing and social work personnel. It is, of course, essential that apart from detoxification and management of the alcohol withdrawal syndrome, there is careful social work assessment and follow-through to treatment for alcohol addiction in either hospital or non-hospital setting, such as hostel placement. The range of facilities in Manchester should enable such plans to be carried out, at least on a pilot basis. It must be re-emphasised that in both the Leeds and Manchester centres no attempt is being made to provide a comprehensive answer to the problem of the drunken offender in either city. Rather, these are pilot schemes which will probably be followed by other schemes, and eventually on the basis of the knowledge gained a coherent policy will be developed.

What the Detoxification Centre has to Manage

Before returning to the administrative aspects of such centres, it is necessary to examine, from the medical point of view, management of clients once they enter the centres. Management has to be of two problems, alcohol intoxication and the alcohol withdrawal syndrome, although treatment of the former may in fact prevent the development of the latter problem, as the St Louis experience shows. Alcohol intoxication is, of course, a well-known picture but Freeman (1964), writing in relation to the work of police surgeons (and before chemical estimations were readily available for blood alcohol), emphasised that with the exception of the smell of alcohol, the signs and symptoms can be mimicked by other conditions. Neither must it be forgotten (Lees, 1967), that depression of basal centres, although not common, can occur with alcohol intoxication, and sudden death can result, as well as collapse of basal centre function leading, for instance, to hypotensive collapse. In another paper in this volume (Hore, 1976), evidence has been reviewed that with relatively small levels of blood alcohol, there is impairment of sensory, motor and cognitive function, often beginning below 55 mg %.

The alcohol withdrawal syndrome is the name given to the condition which develops on withdrawal (either relative or absolute) from alcohol in the physically dependent subject. The syndrome has a variable range of features and may be variable in duration. American authors regard the syndrome as containing two major components, delirium tremens and alcohol hallucinosis. An important review is that of Gross, Lewis and Hasty (1973). English clinicians such as Letsom (1787), Pearson (1801) and Sutton (1815) gave careful clinical details of this picture, and Sutton referring to a syndrome of tremor, clouding of consciousness and visual hallucinations, introduced the term 'delirium tremens'. Bonhoeffer in 1901 described a variant of this stricture which was characterised by auditory hallucinations and minimal evidence of toxicity. This was acute alcoholic hallucinosis.

Taxonomy is confusing here. As has been stated, the majority of American authors consider this latter syndrome to be one of the two principal forms of the alcohol withdrawal syndrome. This nomenclature has not, however, been entirely accepted in the United Kingdom, where alcoholic hallucinosis is generally regarded as a syndrome due to the effect of alcohol on the brain but not necessarily a withdrawal reaction.

It has been shown that the frequency and severity of the alcohol withdrawal syndrome is affected not only by the type of alcohol available but also by socio-economic characteristics; clients in lower socio-economic groups have for instance more severe withdrawal experience. The features of the syndrome can be produced by experimental intoxication and withdrawal in non-addict subject (Isbell *et al.*,1955; Mendelson, 1964). The relationship between intoxication and withdrawal is further confusing in relation to symptomatology, in that Gross *et al.* (1973) have shown that some of the symptoms of the alcohol withdrawal syndrome are identical with those of alcohol intoxication. The features of the syndrome are well described by Victor (1970).

As yet, the causative features of the alcohol withdrawal state are

ill-understood, although the tremor and seizures in the first forty-eight
hours may be related to low serum magnesium levels accompanied by
respiratory alkalosis; there is then a withdrawal rebound of respiration
from the suppression of respiratory centres during intoxication. This
cannot, however, explain the features of delirium tremens, as the
serum magnesium and blood ph. have returned to normal by this point.
Hallucinations in alcohol withdrawal may be associated with the
alteration of sleep. Patients who are hallucinating generally have a large
increase in REM (Rapid Eye Movement) Stage 1 sleep, which again
may be a rebound phenomena, as alcohol reduces REM in normals and
chronic alcoholics; it must though be pointed out the REM suppression
in normals does not result in hallucinations when suppression is
released. Another factor may be the marked reduction in delta sleep
seen in withdrawal states. Gross and his colleagues (Gross *et al.*, 1973)
developed a reliable and valid method of measuring severity of the
alcohol withdrawal syndrome; in the UK their rating schedule is being
used in Cardiff and Manchester. They found that the features of the
syndrome can be factor analysed, with three factors accounting for 66
per cent of the variance. These they called the 'hallucinogenic',
'affective' and 'consciousness' factors. The names given to these factors
are to an extent self-explanatory: the hallucinogenic factor is loaded
highly on items which included hallucinatory experience and also
among others, nausea, tinnitus, insomnia and agitation; the affective
factor is loaded on depression/anxiety, and also tremor and sweating;
the consciousness factor includes gait disturbance and nystagmus, as well
as clouding of consciousness. These factors are relatively independent
so that in each patient, the clinical picture can involve an interaction
of different factors in varying amounts. As stated above, experiments
on alcohol intoxication and withdrawal have shown that the
symptomatology patterns are complex and often overlapping. Thus
factors one (hallucinogenic) and two (affective) also increase during
drinking experiments, a trend continued on alcohol withdrawal.
Conversely, factor three (consciousness) rose to a maximum during
intoxication, and then fell away. It is clear, therefore, that the
mechanisms behind intoxication and withdrawal are complex and
multifactorial.

   In relation to management of intoxication, the main aim is to
control disruptive behaviour and avoid possible complications, e.g.
injuries or inhalation of vomit. Experience in detoxification centres
has suggested that the level of disruptive behaviour can be altered by
environmental stimulation, and this is an important point. Recovery

seems to be relatively quick, perhaps within six hours. Probably chlordiazepoxide in doses of 100 mg intramuscularly or orally is a drug of choice (Kendis, 1964).

In relation to the withdrawal syndrome, the severity varies in different countries and even within the same country at different times (Salum, 1975). Important reviews of the treatment of this syndrome are those of Seixas (1973) and Gross *et al.* (1973). Basic steps in management include adequate sedation, preferably with drugs such as chlormethizole or chlordiazepoxide, as these seem to be most suited to reducing epileptic fits. Table 1 shows a suitable régime using chlormethizole.

Careful observation should be maintained particularly during the first forty-eight hours, and any necessary treatment instituted for complications or management of basic support systems. According to Tavel *et al.* (1961) fatalities usually result from hyperpyrexia, peripheral circulatory failure or status epilepticus. Some authors have recommended other measures such as the use of magnesium sulphate infusions, regular use of anticonvulsants, glucose injections to combat potential hyperglycaemia, or administration of multivitamin preparations. There is no definite evidence, however, of improved results with these adjuncts and generally they are not used in the United Kingdom. Finally, careful nursing is essential, preferably in a side room with minimum stimulation and with nurses familiar to the patient.

Table 1 Suggested dose of chlormethizole for use in treating the alcohol withdrawal syndrome

Day 1	500 mgms	x	3 t.d.s.
Day 2	500 mgms	x	3 t.d.s.
Day 3	500 mgms	x	3 t.d.s.
Day 4	500 mgms	x	2 t.d.s.
Day 5	500 mgms	x	2 t.d.s.
Day 6	500 mgms	x	2 t.d.s.
Day 7	500 mgms	x	t.d.s.
Day 8	500 mgms	x	t.d.s.
Day 9	500 mgms	x	t.d.s.

Implications for the British Experiments

Let us now return to the problems of organising such detoxification centres. Experience in North America has shown that to carry out a comprehensive programme of detoxification and subsequent treatment of alcohol addiction for the chronic drunkenness offender, is fraught with difficulties. Smart (1976) in a very important recent review has examined the effectiveness of the scheme in Ontario. His conclusions are surprisingly pessimistic. He found that a system which involves considerable cost has seemingly had little effect on drunkenness arrests; in fact, it has not replaced the revolving door. The system does not provide enough impetus for long-term referrals; only about 10 per cent of those admitted to the centres enter any sort of long-term care. Finally, and as would in consequence be expected, the results of treatment in terms of abstinence and recovery are very limited. The problem of the chronic drunkenness offender is probably larger in cities such as Toronto than in British cities. Examination of the Ontario system and other systems in North America have shown that when the aim is to set up a comprehensive service, rarely are there enough detoxification facilities; therefore, entry to specialised detoxification centres has not always been confined to police referrals, but other agencies have not been prepared to provide after-care for the type of client. Smart's timely paper warns us of the likely difficulties we shall experience in the UK and emphasises that to undertake anything more than a pilot scheme would involve considerable resources. Unless we are careful, we shall replace one 'revolving door' with another.

References

Bonhoeffer, K. (1901). Die akuten Geisterskrankheiten der Gewohnheit-strinker. Jena: Gustav Fischer.

Freeman, S. (1964). The drinking driver. Brit. Med. J. 2: 1634.

Gath, D., Hensman, C. and Hawker, A. (1968). The drunk in court. Brit. Med. J. 4: 808.

Gross, M.M., Lewis, E. and Hastey, J. (1973). Acute alcohol withdrawal syndrome. In: Biology of Alcoholism. B. Kissin and H. Bagleiter (eds.). New York: Plenum Press, vol.3, chap.3.

Hamilton, J.R. (1976). Helping the drunken offender. Health and Soc. Serv. Journal. P. 1550, 28 August 1976.

Hore, B.D. (1976). Alcohol and alcoholism: the impact on work.

Home Office (1971). Report on the Habitual Drunken Offenders. London: HMSO.

Isbell, M., Fraser, H.F., Wikler, A., Belleville, K.D. and Eisenman, A.J. (1955).

320   *Alcoholism: New Knowledge and New Responses*

An experimental study of 'rum fits' and delirium tremens. Quart. J. Stud. Alc. 16: 1.

Kendis, J. (1964). Treatment of the acute phase of alcoholism. In: Selected papers from 27th Int. Congress on Alcoholism and Addiction, vol.3, Frankfurt. (Obtainable from International Council on Alcohol and Addictions, Case Postale 140, 1001 Lausanne, Switzerland.)

Lees, F. (1967). Alcohol and the nervous system. Hosp. Med. 2: 267.

Letsom, J.C. (1787). Some remarks on the effects of lignus guassie amare. Mem. Med. Soc. 1: 151-65.

Mendelson, J.H. (1964). Experimentally induced chronic intoxication and withdrawal in alcoholics. Quart. J. Stud. Alc. Suppl. 2: 1-126.

Pearson, S.B. (1801). Observations on Brain Fever (private printing).

Pittman, D. and Gordon, C.W. (1958). Revolving Door. A Study of the Chronic Police Inebriate. New Brunswick, NJ: Rutgers Center for Alcohol Studies.

Proceedings of 20th. Int. Inst. of Prevention and Treatment of Alcoholism, Manchester (1974). p.8-16. International Council on Alcohol and Addictions, Case Postale 140, 1001 Lausanne, Switzerland.

Salum, I. (1975). Treatment of delirium tremens. Brit. J. Addict. 70: Suppl. 1: 75.

Seixas, F.A. (ed.) (1971). Treatment of the Alcohol Withdrawal Syndrome. National Council of Alcoholism.

Smart, R. (1976). The Ontario detoxification system – an evaluation of its effectiveness. Paper read at the 3rd Int. Conference on Alcohol and Drug Dependence, Liverpool, April 1976.

Sutton, T. (1813). Tracts on Delirium Tremens on Peritonitis and other Inflammatory Affections. London: Thomas Underwood.

Tavel, M.E., Davidson, W. and Batterton, T.D. (1961). A critical analysis of mortality associated with delirium tremens. Am. J. Med. Sc. 18: 242.

Victor, M. (1970). The alcohol withdrawal syndrome: theory and practice. Post. Grad. Med. 47: 68.

27 THE PRIMARY HEALTH CARE TEAM

D.I. Acres

Health care is becoming more and more a matter of interdisciplinary teamwork, both in hospital and in the community, and this has effected a considerable change in general practice during the past couple of decades. In the prevention and treatment of alcohol problems every member of the team has a part to play, but the principal participants are the family doctor, the health visitor and the practice nurse. Obviously, some of the treatment can only be undertaken by the medically qualified member of the team, but apart from that it is not useful to draw sharp lines of demarcation between their various roles, since so much depends upon personality and enthusiasm for the task. The work can best be carried out by the person who secures the confidence of each individual patient, but with adequate consultation with the other team members.

Both in prevention and treatment the family doctor, the practice nurse and the health visitor are in an especially favourable position, for the most part living within the community which they serve, generally working from the same premises, and often staying in a particular area for a considerable time, and building up, or at any rate having the opportunity of building up, a meaningful relationship with the patients.

From this standpoint the current trend towards group practice has both advantages and disadvantages. The main benefit stems from the greater possibility of attachment of a health visitor, and the feasibility of a practice nurse, together with the obvious advantage that within a group of GPs a degree of specialism is possible. Since problems relating to alcohol are not every doctor's cup of tea, it means that within the average-sized group it is usually possible to find one of the doctors who is sufficiently interested to make a study of the problem and to devote some time to its prevention and treatment. On the other hand, there is the difficulty that in a group practice where there is more or less random distribution of patients according to who happens to be taking surgery on that particular day, there is the inevitable loss of personal involvement, the reduced possibility of early diagnosis, and a smaller chance of developing the mutual understanding and trust which is essential for the effective treatment of alcohol-related problems.

After experimentation in our own group practice of six principals, we have come to the conclusion that the best compromise can be reached by dividing into pairs, so that every patient is seen (except for urgent visits after 10 a.m.) by not more than two doctors. At the same time, each of us have developed specialist interests and, although sometimes being asked to undertake a particular course of treatment for one of the others' patients, is normally involved in a consultant capacity.

Although we are not fortunate enough to have a health visitor based on the practice premises, we have a good liaison, and two of us have employed a half-time practice nurse who plays an important role in treatment and general support. Although we have a good working relationship with the social services department, especially where alcohol problems create anxiety about the welfare of a child, we do not have any significant involvement with them in relation to the treatment of alcoholism.

Education and Prevention at the Grass Roots

No hard and fast line can be drawn between prevention and early diagnosis, one merging into the other, but the primary health care team has a vital involvement in both these processes, both within the practice and in a wider sense in the surrounding district. Because of his or her standing in the community, the family doctor has an advantageous position as a health educator, and this position can be shared to a greater or lesser degree by other members of the team. Whilst realising that not all practitioners are keen on this type of involvement, it can be very rewarding indeed, both from the point of view of work within the practice and improving standards in the district.

A good deal of satisfaction can be gained from taking part in health education programmes in local schools and colleges. The involvement can be a direct one, actually joining in class teaching, taking part in health conferences, or on a more regular and formal basis, or it may be indirect, acting as a specialist adviser to individual teachers or groups of teachers. In either case, of course, it is vitally important that facts are presented completely honestly, in an unemotional way, and in a manner suited to the particular group concerned.

Two recent interesting projects may be mentioned, one in a comprehensive school and the other in a sixth form college. In the first instance the involvement has been in two ways: taking part in class teaching, and also in a two-way conference devoted to problems of personal relationships as well as mental health, alcohol and other drugs. Each aspect is introduced by a short talk or a film, and is

followed by group discussion led by experienced counsellors, and a
plenary session in which problems thrown up during the discussion are
posed to the speaker or to a small panel of 'experts'. We have found
these conferences, usually held during the fourth year, to be of
considerable benefit to the young people, who, sometimes several
years later, have expressed their appreciation. The other rather exciting
experiment took place in the local sixth form college towards the end
of the summer term, when many had completed examinations, and
took the form of a day seminar on alcoholism and violence in society.
The response was most encouraging, and the standard of discussion on
a good deal higher level than many adult groups, including the
magistracy!

This sort of involvement has a number of spin-offs and a few
difficulties. When one knows that one is to be exposed to very
searching questioning from a group of youngsters, it is an excellent
incentive to do one's own homework. Following some of these sessions
it is usual to be cornered by a youngster with a personal problem.
Sometimes this can be dealt with on the spot, or, in the case of a
patient within one's own group, by a subsequent appointment, or
where another practice is involved, by making the initial advance to
one's colleague on the enquirer's behalf.

There is a similar opportunity amongst adult groups, and whilst
talks to Women's Institutes, Young Wives' Groups, Men's Clubs,
Rotary Clubs and the like are scorned in some circles, they have in
fact an important educational function in the neighbourhood. After
some of these encounters it is common to have approaches from those
with a personal alcohol problem, or one within the family, and generally
speaking, it has been helpful to have demonstrated in advance a
compassion and understanding of their situation.

There is another special medium for education about alcoholism
and general health problems which can be developed — a weekly
column in the local evening newspaper. I have written such a column
for six years and have found it very useful in disseminating information.
This is not an opportunity which is open to every member of the
primary health care team, but it may be commended as a useful
addition to the educational armamentarium for those who are inclined
to make the initial approaches and are prepared to devote the regular
time to its preparation. It goes without saying that education in
relation to alcohol abuse can make up only a small proportion of the
total contribution.

Another useful contact is with the local probation service and with

the social services. Doctors who are willing to provide advice and
support are usually very warmly welcomed.

Early Diagnosis

The primary health care team has open to it unrivalled opportunities
for the early diagnosis of alcohol problems; like the problem of non-
accidental injury to children, a great deal depends upon one's level of
suspicion, but given a fairly high level the GP in particular has many
advantages. He has a long-standing and detailed knowledge of many
of his patients. Depending upon the mobility of the local population
(and in general the more mobile it is, the more alcohol-related problems
are likely to arise), he usually has contact with a good proportion of
his patients over a number of years. This enables him to be sensitive to
changes in a patient's behaviour and attitudes, and changes in his
attendance pattern. Several studies have shown how alcoholics tend to
visit their family doctors at least twice as often as others within the
same age and sex group, sometimes because of physical illness
associated with their excessive drinking, often though the problem may
be brought up on the 'while I am here' basis, or perhaps courage fails
at the last moment. We should be on the alert for this, and with other
indicators, such as occupation, obvious stresses, recurring dyspepsia
and persistent diarrhoea, and be ready to make the initial advance,
usually in a somewhat circuitous way so as to get around to the
subject of drinking habits.

Living in the community, members of the team have a splendid
opportunity of observing people shopping, in the pub, travelling on the
railway, and so on. Constantly going into patient's homes gives an
insight, especially if you pop in the back door without knocking.
Because of all these ties with the family, if the relationship is good, one
tends to be consulted. Over the years one gains an insight into different
individuals' reactions, and knows who one can directly approach, and
who needs the more subtle approach of 'You're looking a bit tired, I
think it might be worth doing a blood test.' Often this test will reveal
abnormal liver function, which can prompt the suggestion: 'Your liver
seems to be finding difficulty in coping with your alcohol intake.'

Against the advantages of the GP must be set definite problems.
Because of the very intimacy of the relationship with the patient, and
more especially with the whole family, some may not wish to confide,
and may open up better with a stranger. The family doctor may only
see a handful of patients with gonorrhoea each year, but he will not be
naïve enough to believe that that's all there are. They go to GU clinics

where there is greater anonymity and things are much more impersonal. Additionally, it must be admitted that all GPs are not highly motivated to deal with the problems of alcoholism. Some are like the little old Victorian lady, who, on hearing of Darwin's theory that we come from apes, declared, 'Pray God it be not true, but if it be true, that it be not widely known.' Being a family doctor, some alcoholics may have the suspicion, not always without foundation, that the welfare of other members of the family may be placed before the patient's own. It is important for one to view one's own reactions objectively, and to ensure a balanced approach, weighing carefully the welfare of the patient and that of other members of the household.

The Primary Health Care Team's Involvement in Treatment

Whilst there can be little doubt about the team's key role in the early diagnosis of alcohol problems, a greater area of disagreement exists about the treatment participation. One can find extremes of views amongst family doctors, ranging from those who invariably refer those patients whom they identify as having alcohol problems, to those who take an active interest and for the most part treat these patients themselves.

Naturally, this will depend upon the resources available in the district, and the personal interests of the individual doctor, together with his case-load, for there is no doubt that treatment can be very time-consuming. In any case good communications between the various members of the team is essential, and whilst this is a comparatively easy matter for those concerned with primary care, the liaison must spread much wider, involving detoxification facilities, local consultants, wardens of hostels, local Alcoholics Anonymous groups, the local Disablement Resettlement Officer and facilities in Government Training Centres and Industrial Rehabilitation Units. The causation of alcoholism is so multifactorial, that the involvement of all the available agencies is essential in the treatment as well as the identification of the problem.

GPs involvement in detoxification is likely to be small except in areas of high incidence, and for those who are concerned with detoxification units. For on-going treatment the fewer drugs that are used the better, it being so easy to switch from one form of dependence to another.

Personal experience leads to a reluctance to use disulfiram in general practice, except in those patients who have been introduced to it in hospital, and have experienced some of its alarming effects. On the other hand, vitamin injections may usefully be employed, partly for their pharmaceutical effects, and partly because this treatment affords an opportunity for continued contact with the patient. It can be a very face-saving manoeuvre from the patient's standpoint to have this definite reason for an appointment, and is a useful means of securing attendance. Obviously, the injection should be given on most occasions by the member of the team who is primarily involved in treatment, and this can either be the family doctor or the practice nurse, if she has an interest in the treatment.

In the early stages of treatment, fairly long appointments in a relaxed atmosphere are necessary, but as things progress it is quite possible to provide the necessary support at a normal appointment, reviewing progress and keeping the relationship alive. It is not always an easy task to give this support to the patient and to his family at the same time, for the reasons mentioned a little earlier, and this requires great tact and integrity. Often one has to resort to saying to the spouse, 'I must respect your husband's (or your wife's) confidences, as I respect yours, but this should not prevent your saying anything that you wish to me, giving me all the information which you think relevant. What I may not be able to do is to discuss all the aspects with you, but I will certainly consider everything you tell me.' This seems to get the best of both worlds, and usually is acceptable.

It goes without saying that it is of prime importance to adopt a neutral, non-judgemental attitude to both the patient and the family, and to maintain an atmosphere of confidence, warmly praising progress, but at the same time not be shocked or alarmed at the inevitable set-backs. Attainable objectives must be set, and for the most part the ultimate objective is likely to be total abstinence. Recent claims are interesting in that where the underlying personality problems can be resolved, it is possible to get patients back to social drinking. If this can be done it is obviously a major advance, as it will not present to alcoholics the problem of completely revising the life habits and their companions. However, a general practitioner is unlikely at present to have sufficient confidence in his therapeutic ability to make this the treatment goal, and will usually, at least for the time being, have to settle for the less attractive but more attainable goal of total abstinence.

The value of providing a ready opportunity for discussion with both patient and family cannot be over-emphasised. Families in particular often feel terribly socially isolated, and members of the primary health care team may be the only people in whom they feel able to confide. There is an important educational role here, for education plays almost as important a part in treatment as in prevention, and the family doctor and other members of the team can do much to help families to understand and cope with the problem of the alcoholic in their midst.

Whether the GP undertakes much of the treatment himself or enlists specialist help, his support will be needed on a long-term basis in after-care. For those without a supportive family, hostels may well be required, and the involved GP can have an important function in their day-to-day working. For those with the enthusiasm and opportunity there is the challenge of the army of homeless alcoholics to be found in most large conurbations, and who suffer considerable privations, not only from their alcohol-related problems, but from a wide range of physical disabilities. Few are able to get continuing treatment, and in common with seamen and others who are constantly on the move, are amongst the most underprivileged from the medical standpoint.

Not many will wish to be involved with such problems, nor be located so as to be able to be involved, and for the majority of family doctors their patients will be found amongst business executives, representatives, members of the licensed trade and bored housewives; this last group being the most rapidly growing one. Success is more common than many have been led to suppose, and at the present time 12 of the 15 alcoholics personally treated in a general practice are doing pretty well. Of course they have set-backs, and disappointments are all too frequent. It is essential to maintain interest, because most have a long experience of rejection, by friends, families and employers, and members of the health care team must not add to the list.

Despite occasional frustrations and the time-consuming nature of treatment, members of the primary health care team are likely to find a good deal of satisfaction in dealing with alcohol problems. Given a liking for involvement with people and certain basic skills, there is much that can be done.

28 A JOINT PSYCHIATRIC AND MEDICAL OUTPATIENT CLINIC FOR ALCOHOLICS

G.K. Shaw and A. Thomson

Although it is widely recognised that there are important medical psychiatric and social consequences of alcoholism it seems that in Britain it has not been usual to set up clinics competent to cope with the problem of the fundamental dependency and capable of assessing and dealing with the full range of these complications. All too often the medical experts and the psychiatric teams have functioned separately making it difficult to tackle the alcoholic as a whole.

Mindful of this a joint medical and psychiatric clinic for alcoholics was set up a little over a year ago in a district general hospital. The distinctive feature of this clinic is that each new patient is seen by a member of a medical team headed by a consultant physician, and by a member of a psychiatric team headed by a consultant psychiatrist. The medical team consists of three or four doctors, under the control of a consultant physician with beds in the district general hospital. The psychiatric team consists of two or more doctors, a social worker skilled in the alcohol field, and either a nurse-therapist who has undergone training in alcoholism or a trained psychologist. The psychiatric team are based on the local alcohol treatment unit and have access to eight detoxification beds and seventeen treatment beds in that alcohol treatment unit. It is important that the teams have this ready access to beds of all kinds so that a full range of outpatient and inpatient facilities can be offered as required. It will no doubt be readily appreciated that there are formidable organisational problems to be overcome. It is necessary to ensure that each patient is in fact seen by both teams, that they are not exasperated beyond endurance by being asked the same questions by both teams, and that they are not offered conflicting advice and, equally important, that they are not offered incompatible follow-up appointments. An agreed schedule for history-taking and skilled reception staff do much to alleviate these problems.

When the clinic was set up we had initially four aims in mind:

1. That the mingling of medical and psychiatric teams would be stimulating to both, and would help to promote a better

understanding between medical and psychiatric teams of what they might reasonably expect from each other.

2. That a joint clinic of this kind in a district general hospital would be attractive to referring agents, so that cases might be referred at an early stage of their illness. It is of course accepted that the best results can be expected in those early cases.

3. That physical and psychological change be detected as early as possible. Although our knowledge of the pathogenesis of physical and psychological change in the alcoholic is limited it is generally agreed that early recognition of change is desirable if treatment is to reduce the increasing morbidity and mortality from alcoholism (Popper *et al.*, 1969).

4. Given that a proportion of referrals would not accept or achieve a goal of abstinence it was hoped that regular contact, offering prophylactic or treatment measures when necessary, and monitoring of damage, might none the less result in reduction of morbidity.

We are satisfied that the first of these aims has been achieved and that the clinic has been stimulating for the team members.

An analysis of the characteristics of sixty new referrals shows that the mean age was 44.5 years and that the male:female ratio was 3:1. Class distribution showed social class I, II, 45 per cent; III, 18.3 per cent; IV, V, 29.9 per cent; not known 7.1 per cent. There was thus an over-representation of higher social classes. As for domicile, 78.3 per cent were living with family, 8.3 per cent in good quality hostels, and 3.3 per cent in poor quality hostels (10 per cent unknown). Fifty-five per cent of subjects were in steady employment (three or more years), 4.9 per cent in casual work, 3.3 per cent housewives, 15 per cent unemployed and 10 per cent retired (11.6 per cent not known).

If one adds to this the information that 37 per cent of the referrals claimed to drink less than the equivalent of half a bottle of spirits daily it would appear that the second of our aims has been met and that we are seeing a sample of alcoholics at an early stage of their illness.

With regard to our third aim, despite the fact that we are seeing an early sample of alcoholics, evidence of physical injury was frequently found. Sixty-nine per cent have abnormally high gama-glutamyl transpeptidase levels and 40.3 per cent show elevated aspartate transaminase levels. Conventional liver function tests, however, are insensitive indicators of early liver injury and provide limited information on the activity or severity of liver disease (Leevy, 1967).

Failure to find elevated serum pyruvic transaminase activity may be due to concomitant vitamin B_6 deficiency (Leevy *et al.*, 1970). Clinical recognition of liver disease has been facilitated by the use of objective criteria for the measurement of liver size (Leevy, 1974) and the wide use of percutaneous liver biopsy. An adequate biopsy specimen allows detection of liver disease, evaluation of its activity (Popper & Schaffner, 1963) and investigation of its ability to regenerate (Leevy, 1966). Approximately 50 per cent of the clinic patients are biopsied and the characteristics of the first sixty biopsies are shown in Figure 1. The histological profile resembles the findings in randomly selected alcoholic patients admitted to a large municipal hospital in the United States because of withdrawal symptoms or intercurrent illness. There, 31 per cent showed normal liver by light microscopy and 40 per cent fatty liver, but there was a higher incidence (29 per cent of cirrhosis) (Cherrick & Leevy, 1965). For comparison, the non-clinic patients biopsied in all departments of Greenwich Hospital are also shown in Figure 1.

Figure 2 lists the associated clinical features and emphasises the patient's multisystem involvement. Adequate recognition and treatment of nutritional deficiency, associated hepatic, pancreatic, cardiac and

Figure 1 Histological Findings in 60 Biopsies in Clinic Patients, Compared with Non-Clinic Patients from all Hospital Departments

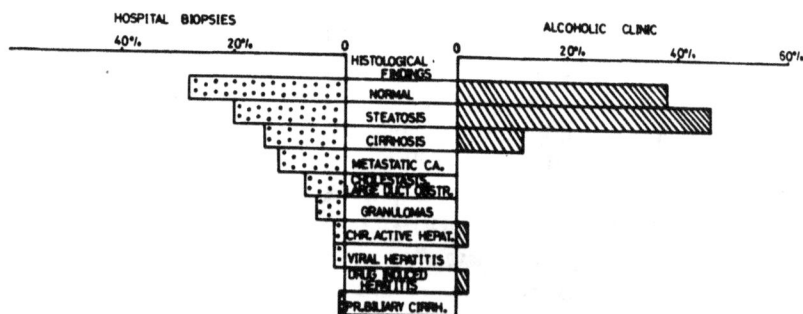

Figure 2 Signs and Symptoms in the Clinic Population

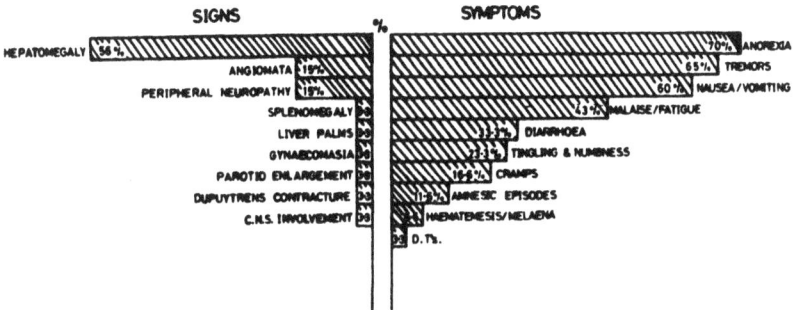

SIGNS % SYMPTOMS

HEPATOMEGALY 56%
ANGIOMATA 19%
PERIPHERAL NEUROPATHY 18%
SPLENOMEGALY
LIVER PALMS
GYNAECOMASIA
PAROTID ENLARGEMENT
DUPUYTRENS CONTRACTURE
C.N.S. INVOLVEMENT

70% ANOREXIA
65% TREMORS
60% NAUSEA/VOMITING
43% MALAISE/FATIGUE
DIARRHOEA
TINGLING & NUMBNESS
CRAMPS
AMNESIC EPISODES
HAEMATEMESIS/MELAENA
D.T's.

neurological disease is facilitated by the presence of medical specialists in the clinic. Hepatic disease is often accompanied by vitamin deficiency since it gives rise to an increased need for vitamins in the face of a decreased intake (Leevy *et al.*, 1965). Although deficiency among alcoholic patients has been studied in other countries (Leevy *et al.*, 1965), the extent of the problem in Britain is unknown. Figure 3 shows the results of vitamin B complex estimations on patients admitted to the detoxification unit at Bexley Hospital. Many patients have elevated vitamin B_{12} levels suggesting release secondary to hepatic necrosis (Rachmilewitz *et al.*, 1958). Fifty-six per cent of patients show biochemical evidence of thiamine (vitamin B_1) deficiency determined by the erythrocyte transketolase (ETK) activation test (Heller *et al.*, 1974a) and 54.7 per cent a deficient riboflavin status (vitamin B_2) by the erythrocyte glutathione reductase (EGR) activation test (Heller *et al.*, 1974b). Estimation of vitamin B_6 levels by the erythrocyte glutamate oxaloacetate transaminase (EGOT) test fails to demonstrate any abnormality. However, more recent estimations of the pyridoxal-5-phosphate (PLP) levels suggest pronounced vitamin B_6 deficiency among outpatients. Vitamin deficiency in the alcoholic may result from inadequate intake, intestinal malabsorption (Thomson *et al.*,

Figure 3 Vitamin Status of Patients Admitted to the Detoxification Unit at Bexley Hospital

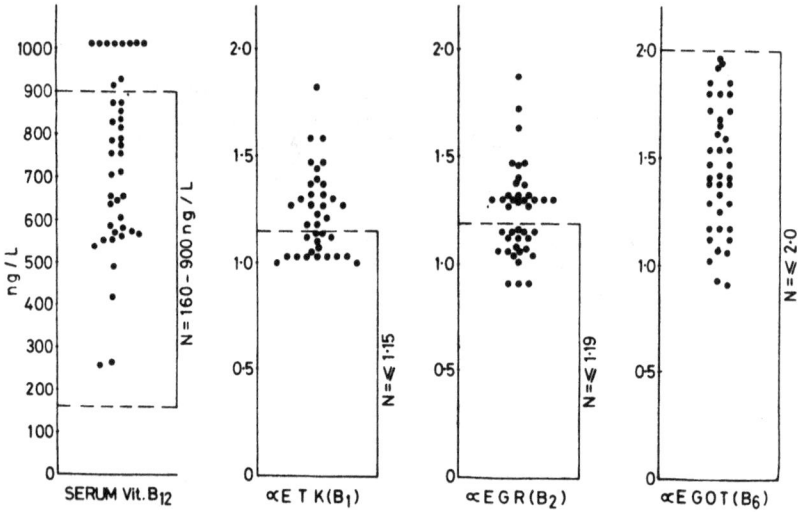

1970; Thomson and Leevy, 1972), reduced hepatic storage capacity (Cherrick *et al.*, 1965) or failure to convert the vitamins into metabolically active forms (Fennelly *et al.*, 1967). Appropriate administration of vitamins is required to meet the need for increased nucleic acid synthesis and liver regeneration. The absorption of orally administered ^{35}S-thiamine hydrochloride is often however markedly reduced in the malnourished alcoholic or by the presence of circulating ethanol (Thomson, 1969). This block may be bypassed by using a different molecular form of thiamine — thiamine propyl disulfide (Thomson *et al.*, 1971), and previous work has shown the effectiveness of thiamine propyl disulfide in treating a patient with Wernicke's encephalopathy.

The 45 minute BSP test frequently fails to detect sub-clinical liver disease and cannot be used to quantify the degree of injury in severe liver damage because of extrahepatic removal of the dye (Leevy *et al.*, 1963). The introduction of the ear densitometer allows early detection of liver injury in the clinic by measurement of the clearance of indocyanine green (1CG) (Leevy *et al.*, 1967). Preliminary data in our laboratory indicate that Naftidrofuryl (praxilene) which is known to improve cerebral function by increasing glucose uptake, will significantly increase the rate of ICG clearance in patients with alcoholic liver injury (Figure 4). A trial on the combined effects on the psychological and physical aspects of treatment is in progress.

With regard to our fourth aim a careful clinical study will be required to determine whether early intervention and monitoring thereafter will enable a clinic such as ours to make a significant impact on the long-term morbidity of the alcoholic process. Hopefully the clinic is so constructed as to facilitate collection of the necessary data.

Figure 4 The Effect of Intramuscular Naftidrofuryl on the Half-Life and Percentage Disappearance Rate (PDR) of Indocyanine Green in Alcoholics and Control Subjects 24 hours after Administration

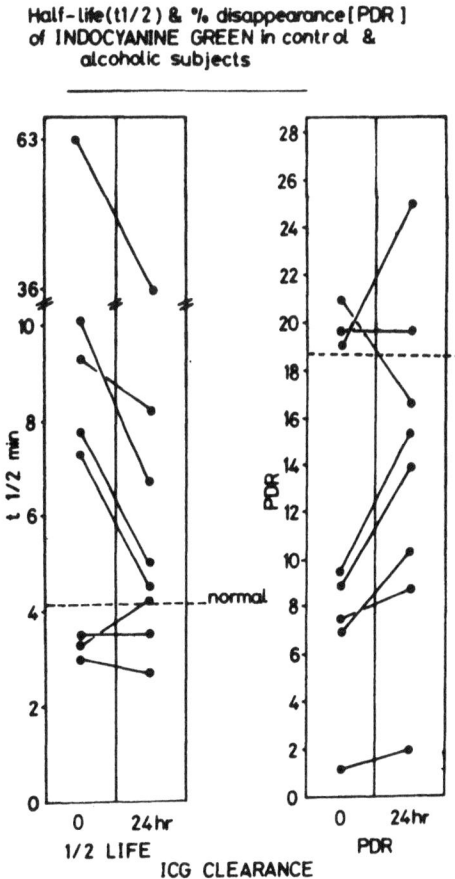

Half-life(t1/2) & % disappearance [PDR] of INDOCYANINE GREEN in control & alcoholic subjects

334   *Alcoholism: New Knowledge and New Responses*

References

Cherrick, G.R., Baker, H., Frank, O. and Leevy, C.M. (1965). Observations on hepatic avidity for folate in laennec's cirrhosis. J. Lab. and Clin. Med. 66: 446.

Cherrick, G.R. and Leevy, C.H. (1965). Effects of ethanol metabolism on levels of oxidised and reduced nicotinamide – adenine dinucleotide in liver, kidney and heart. Biochim. Biophys. Acta 107: 29-37.

Fennelly, J., Frank, O., Baker, H. and Leevy, C.M. (1967). Red blood cells transketolase activity in malnourished alcoholics with cirrhosis. Amer. J. Clin. Nutr. 20: 946-9.

Heller, S., Salkeid, R.M. and Korner, W.F. (1974a). Vitamin B1 status in pregnancy. Amer. J. Clin. Nutr. 27: 1221-4.

Heller, S., Salkeld, R.M. and Korner, W.F. (1974b). Riboflavin status in pregnancy. Amer. J. Clin. Nutr. 27: 1225-30.

Leevy, C.M. (1966). Abnormalities of hepatic DNA synthesis in man. Medicine 4: 423-33.

Leevy, C.M. (1967). Clinical diagnosis, evaluation and treatment of liver disease in alcoholics. Fed. Proc. 26: 1474-81.

Leevy, C.M. (1974). Evaluation of Liver Function in Clinical Practice. Indianapolis, Ind.: Lilly Research Laboratories.

Leevy, C.M. Bender, J., Silverberg, M. and Naylor, J. (1963). Physiology of dye extraction by the liver: comparative studies of sulfobromophthalein and indocyanine green. Ann N.Y. Acad Sci. 111: 161-76.

Leevy, C.M., Cardi, L., Frank, O.. Gellene, R. and Baker, H. (1965). Incidence and significance of hypovitamineaemia in a randomly selected municipal hospital population. Amer. J. Clin. Nutr. 17: 259-71.

Leevy, C.M., Smith, F., Longueville, J., Paumgartner, G. and Howard, M.M. (1967). Indocyanine green clearance as a test for hepatic function. (Evaluation by dichromatic ear densitometry). J. Amer. Med. Assoc. 200: 236-40.

Leevy, C.M., Thomson, A. and Baker, H. (1970). Vitamins and liver injury. Amer. J. Clin. Nutr. 23: 493-8.

Popper, H., Davidson, C.S., Leevy, C.M. and Schaffner, F. (1969). The social impact of liver disease. New Eng. J. Med. 281: 1455-8.

Popper, H. and Schaffner, F. (1963). Fine structural changes of the liver. Ann. Internal. Med. 59: 674-91.

Rachmilewitz, M., Aronovitch, J. and Crossowicz, N. (1958). The clinical significance of serum cyanocobalamin (Vitamin B12) in liver disease. Arch. Internal Med. 101: 1118.

Thomson, A.D. (1969). Thiamine Absorption in Man. University of Edinburgh, PhD thesis.

Thomson, A.D., Baker, H. and Leevy, C.M. (1970). Patterns of S35-thiamine hydrochloride absorption in the malnourished alcoholic patient. J. Lab. & Clin. Med. 76: 34-45.

Thomson, A.D., Frank, O., Baker, H. and Leevy, C.M. (1971). Thiamine propyl disulfide: absorption and utilization. Ann. Int. Med. 74: 529-34.

Thomson, A.D. and Leevy, C.M. (1972). Observations on the mechanisms of thiamine hydrochloride absorption in man. Clin. Sci. 43: 153-63.

29 THE REALITY OF MEDICO-PSYCHIATRIC COOPERATION

N. Krasner

Introduction

> When ebriety has become so far habitual that some disease appears
> in consequence, the physician is for the first time called in and a
> task the most ungrateful devolves upon him.   Trotter (1810)

This statement from Thomas Trotter made over 160 years ago expresses
a frustration which holds good today, no less for the psychiatrist than
for the physician to whom it originally related. And yet this frustration
may often be generated by a lack of timely cooperation between
medical and psychiatric colleagues.

Alcoholism does not conform to the traditional model of a disease
and we have difficulty both in identifying the aetiology and in following
its natural history. The course of some of the somatic sequelae
however, is more predictable, and it is now beyond doubt that a
spectrum of liver disorders may result as a direct consequence of
chronic ethanol abuse. At the present time, liver disease is one of the
most prominent causes for incapacitating illness and premature death
in the alcoholic.

The list of agencies involved in the management of alcoholism is
extensive, but fragmentation of approach unfortunately is as much a
feature of medical management, in the broad sense, as of management
by non-medical groups, and although this brief paper refers to alcohol-
related liver disease, it might well apply to the many other facets of
alcoholism.

Extent of the Problem

In recent years, a steadily escalating trend in deaths from cirrhosis has
been noted, and these are mainly alcoholic in origin. The most recent
figures for the UK suggest a 12 per cent increase over the period 1969
to 1973, with 2,136 deaths recorded in 1973 (Annual Abstract of
Statistics, 1974). In a recent report from St Thomas' Hospital, London,
from a general unit, of all patients admitted with cirrhosis, 65 per cent
were deemed to be due to alcohol (Hodgson and Thompson, 1976).
However, although cirrhosis represents the most advanced form of

alcoholic liver disease, we should not divert all our attention to cirrhosis since other forms of liver disease also pose considerable problems, both numerically and in terms of management. The mortality figures for a series of 293 cases of histologically diagnosed alcoholic liver disease from the Liver Unit, King's College Hospital, London, from 1967 to 1974 are shown in Table 1.

Table 1   Mortality figures in alcoholic liver disease

Group	No.	Mortality % Within 8 years	% Within 3 Months
Fatty liver $\pm$ fibrosis	52	5.8	1.9
Acute alcoholic hepatitis	54	13.5	16.7
Cirrhosis	69	37.7	20.3
Cirrhosis + alcoholic hepatitis	104	43.3	27.9
Hepatoma + cirrhosis	14	100	100

Management of Alcoholic Liver Disease

On a theoretical basis, it is generally agreed that cooperation is essential in the overall management of the alcoholic patient, particularly with a somatic disturbance such as liver disease. Indeed, every new paper on the treatment of alcoholism stresses the need for management by a team. However, in the UK, apart from isolated instances in various parts of the country, this theory of cooperation has not been translated into working practice. It is worthwhile at this point to consider what traditional or projected roles are fulfilled by the physician and the psychiatrist in relation to alcohol-associated liver disease.

Role of the Physician

1. Diagnosis: The clinical discrimination of various forms of álcoholic liver disease may be difficult or impossible at the bedside and even a full range of biochemical function tests and a liver biopsy, which may be unrepresentative, may not provide a precise diagnosis. And yet, the diagnosis is important because of its bearing on morbidity and mortality.

2. Management: Although this is usually supportive and directed at improving the nutritional status of the patient or correcting

electrolyte imbalance and fluid retention, attention must be brought to bear on possible specific drug therapy; for instant, 'an anti-cirrhosis' drug or an agent to suppress an acute alcoholic hepatitis.

3. Prevention: The physician is probably best placed to find ways of minimising disturbances of structure and function, and closely allied to this is the need to define and examine more closely factors of host susceptibility. In particular, it would be worthwhile studying genetic influences and the role of immune responsiveness in the development and progression of alcoholic liver disease. The role of nutritional deprivation has still not been properly resolved.

4. Epidemiology: It has yet to be decided whether the main thrust in this field should be directed at the identification of the individual drinker or at assessing the problem in the community as a whole. In any event, this must obviously be a shared role and one in which the general practitioner (the primary care physician) has a vital part to play; it is he, after all, who in many cases identifies the patient and assumes a major responsibility in his after-care.

Role of the Psychiatrist

The control of alcoholic liver disease is essentially the control of alcohol abuse, and, as such, is predominantly a psycho-social problem. The interpretation of the role of the psychiatrist presented in this paper is a personal one, and is coloured by personal contacts, as a physician with an interest in alcoholic liver disease, with psychiatrist colleagues.

1. On the psychiatrist rests the major burden of assisting the patient in achieving abstinence, or at least in stopping him from drinking excessively.

2. He should be concerned with modifying the reaction of the drinker to his environment and immediate situation.

3. He should also, by manipulation of family relationships, work situation and leisure pursuits, try to construct an approach which may modify the reaction of the drinker's environment to the drinker himself.

4. Since the alcoholic without liver disease who stops drinking is less likely to develop this problem or once developed is less likely to progress to more severe forms of liver damage, a valuable facility can be offered through 'Drying Out' centres; at least a break in the drinking pattern might be offered with the hope of a halt, albeit

temporary, in the progression of hepatic dysfunction.

There is an additional challenge to physician and psychiatrist alike, and that is to act in the role of an educator as well as therapist. By providing information to the patient and public, and in particular to his medical colleagues, on the hazards of alcohol abuse, the doctor might hope to offer a significant contribution in the field of prevention.

The Reality of Cooperation

Although the remit of this paper is to discuss the reality of medico-psychiatric cooperation, there seems to be little to say on the subject, since within the National Health Service there is no unified approach, although guidelines have been suggested (Ministry of Health, 1968). Undoubtedly, there are groups in various parts of the country where combined clinics and treatment programmes have been initiated. The problems in establishing cooperative services are discussed elsewhere in this volume (Spratley *et al.*), and their experience in a joint clinic in Bexley and Greenwich Hospitals is discussed by Drs Shaw and Thomson.

Personal participation in the running of a combined psychiatric/ medical clinic for a trial of drug therapy in alcoholism (Krasner *et al.,* 1976) has left no doubts as to the value of such an exercise. It has also shown that the success rate, and this applies to the treatment of alcoholic liver disease as much as to the broader question of alcoholism, is at least to some extent proportional to the enthusiasm of the therapists.

Not every patient need be seen by the complete medical team so long as a comprehensive assessment is made of his state of health, and appropriate investigations and treatment instituted at the earliest juncture. Although only medical involvement has been discussed, success in management can only be achieved by making full use of ancillary help and voluntary agencies. Concrete attempts at widespread cooperative ventures are badly needed.

References

Annual Abstract of Statistics (1974). London: HMSO.
Hodgson, H.J.F. and Thompson, R.P.H. (1976). Cirrhosis in south London. Lancet 2: 118.
Ministry of Health, The treatment of alcoholism. Hospital Memoranda, 1968, HM (68), 37.
Krasner, N., Moore, M.R., Goldberg, A., Booth, J.L.D., Frame, A.H. and McLaren, A.D. (1976). A trial of fenfluramine in the treatment of the chronic alcoholic patient. Brit. J. Psych. 128: 346.

30 ALCOHOLISM: THE CHANGING ROLE OF THE PSYCHIATRIST

T.A. Spratley, A.K.J. Cartwright and S.J. Shaw

Background

For many decades alcoholism has been neglected by psychiatrists. It is interesting to note a recent finding (MacDonald & Patel, 1975), that alcoholism is still the least favoured of the organic and psychiatric illnesses amongst psychiatrists. In default of psychiatric care, voluntary effort within the community has provided most specialised care. Alcoholics Anonymous, hostels run by churches and counselling services run by local councils on Alcoholism, are examples of the non-psychiatric specialised services which are still in a process of expansion. In Britain, charitable bodies such as the Alcohol Education Centre, the National Council on Alcoholism and the Medical Council of Alcoholism have developed in order to remedy the deficiency of public and professional education in this field.

In 1962 the Ministry of Health's Memorandum on 'Hospital Treatment for Alcoholics' (MoH, 1962), recommended that the Regional Hospital Boards set up specialised alcoholism inpatient units to provide more effective treatment for alcoholics. This recommendation probably resulted from a widespread feeling that the care of alcoholics was being neglected by general psychiatrists. It encouraged some psychiatrists to specialise in the problem. The 1962 Memorandum was based upon a belief that alcoholism was a condition of a psychiatric nature which a person either had, or did not have, and for which he ought to have treatment. Furthermore, it was believed that the best treatment was inpatient psychiatric care based upon long-term group psychotherapy with similarly afflicted individuals. It was hoped that the units would not only act as models of treatment, but train interested staff who would generally raise standards of care.

About twenty such units are now functioning in England and Wales. However, the alcoholism problem has not been solved. If anything, there is even more widespread dissatisfaction with the services for alcoholics than before the units existed. Partly because of this the government has recently taken the step of establishing an Advisory Committee on Alcoholism to guide it in improving the situation.

The ideas for the future which are developed in this chapter borrow directly from the experience of the Maudsley Alcohol Pilot Project or MAPP (Cartwright *et al.,* 1975), which was specifically concerned to research how best the community's resources might be matched to the realities of the community's drinking problems.

Problems of the Present Situation

Practical experience in the field and recent research including our own study (MAPP Report, 1975) in a district served by a specialised alcoholism treatment service, indicates that there are major difficulties in the present pattern of care. Firstly, the vast majority of those with problems caused by alcohol abuse do not receive treatment by the specialist services, either as inpatients or outpatients. The reasons for this are many. In 1962 the magnitude of the prospective target population for the new units was not appreciated. Furthermore, since 1962 the size of the problem has undoubtedly increased. Our work showed that the size of the problem locally had increased by about one third in the last decade. It is therefore not surprising that there are usually very long waiting lists for inpatient care. These long waiting lists can cause much frustration and resentment amongst the referral agents, who are often faced with crises requiring immediate responses, or who are being pressurised by distressed families. Many referral agents criticise the inpatient units for their selectivity, which effectively excludes the majority of their clients. This is particularly true of social workers and probation officers, whose typical client is not suited to long-term group psychotherapy. These two factors of long waiting lists and selectivity, result sometimes in agents ceasing to refer altogether.

A further reason why a purely psychiatric alcoholism service will never treat a large proportion of the target population is that many of those individuals who admit that their drinking is causing them problems, do not see themselves as either alcoholics or in need of psychiatrists. This again is a cause of much frustration to referral agents who have often only with great difficulty recognised the problem, then to find that the patient refuses referral to a clinic or fails to keep his appointment.

Although alcohol abusers and their families use medical and social services more than the average person, there is usually a failure of the agent to recognise the underlying problem. This is sometimes due to active deception by the patient, but is frequently the fault of the agent concerned. There is a widespread ignorance amongst agents of the ways in which alcohol abusers can present to particular professions. Furthermore, many lack the skill to elicit the relevant history or to interpret it. Even when an agent recognises the problem, often no help ensues. Many agents are ignorant of the ways in which their profession can help the drinker. Some have an unduly pessimistic view of the value of treatment; some are too frightened physically by drinkers, whilst others fear their excessive demands. These factors, together with bad experience of referral, can result in collusion between drinker and agent so that the alcohol problem is denied by both parties. This denial rarely brings peace. If the underlying drinking goes on unchecked, problems recur and the agent becomes frustrated with his time-wasting failures. It is not surprising that some agents develop very hostile feelings to the whole subject of alcoholism.

A Plan for the Future and the Psychiatrist's Role

The services in a community should be so organised that treatment is available to all those harmed by their own drinking, or the drinking of someone close to them. The help should be forthcoming as early as possible in that person's drinking career. The responsibility for providing such help should not lie only with psychiatrists or even with the medical profession, but with a wide range of professional and voluntary helpers. The treatment response, wherever possible, should be 'community-based'. The term 'community-based' implies that the patient should be treated whilst continuing to live in his own home wherever possible; that it should involve his family; and that the treatment should always be given in conjunction with the primary level community agents — the GPs, social workers, community nurses and voluntary workers of the local community.

The agency which is most fundamental to the treatment is the primary health care team who have the best opportunity for initially recognising the problem, giving basic treatment for that condition, acting as the main focus and keeping in long-term contact with the patient and his family. A central recommendation which comes from the Maudsley Alcohol Pilot Project is then that the primary team and other community workers should be given the help and support of a district based specialist multidisciplinary team which is termed the Community Alcohol Team (CAT), and whose prime task will be to do such supportive work. The role of the primary health care team has been discussed elsewhere in this volume by Acres (chapter 27).

It is at this point that we should consider the future role of the psychiatrist. Although all general psychiatrists should assess the alcohol usage and abuse of every patient and if appropriate undertake initial therapy themselves, MAPP envisages that the size, importance and complexity of the alcohol problem requires that one psychiatrist in each district should take a special interest in the problem, and devote three or four sessions per week to it. It is then essential for the specialist psychiatrist to establish the multidisciplinary Community Alcohol Team. The other members of this team would be a social worker, a nurse and also, where available, an interested general physician, and a volunteer counsellor attached to the local Council on Alcoholism.

The CATs most important task would be not to provide specialised second level care to alcohol abusers, but to educate and support those general agents giving primary care. To change present practices requires that the skills and attitudes of community agents be improved. This can be done by small group sessions and also by personal contacts between specialist and general agents. It is a more valuable use of a specialist's time to spend an hour talking with the GP about an alcoholic patient, than to see that patient himself in an outpatient clinic. In the short term it is quicker to see the patient but in the long run, an informed, skilled and well motivated GP is more valuable. He will recognise alcohol abusers at an early stage in his practice, institute treatment and refer on cases for secondary level care only rarely. Pollak (1974), has demonstrated that a GP working this way can obtain good results.

It is important if primary level agents are to care for most of their alcohol abusers themselves, that they should have ready access for consultation to specialists they know and trust. If they feel adequately supported by specialists, many of these agents are prepared to care for difficult cases, and support by the specialist is usually welcomed. The CAT can congratulate themselves when the majority of contacts by primary level agents are in the form 'I would like to talk over with you how I can manage this patient', instead of 'Please see and treat. . .'.

Not all patients can be managed only at primary level. Not all primary agents will be willing or able to treat alcohol abusers, nor will certain patients be prepared to accept primary level care alone. Furthermore, the treatment of some patients requires highly specialised skills beyond the ability of the general agents or requires treatment in a specialised institution. Most specialised treatments such as individual counselling, group and family therapy, behaviour therapy, medication, educational and social retraining programmes, do not need inpatient care and can be given in a day-care setting. Ideally the CAT should be based in a specialised day-care setting.

The CAT will need access to residential provision. Although most patients can be safely detoxified at home or in the day-care setting, certain individuals will need detoxification in a hospital bed. Short-stay hostel and psychiatric beds will also be needed for acute social and psychiatric crises. There is little need for long-term psychiatric admissions for alcohol problems *per se.* Long-term residential treatment should preferably be given in a hostel with psychiatric support.

There are certain other forms of specialist care that the CAT should actively encourage and support. Alcoholics Anonymous together with Alanon and Alateen can give help to certain drinkers and their families. The CAT should know the quality of local groups and local sponsors. It is usually possible to establish excellent cooperative arrangements with them. Information and counselling centres run by Regional Councils are developing throughout the country. They provide a gateway to the services for some drinkers who initially do not wish to go to their GP. Their counselling services provide a good alternative to psychiatric outpatient clinics for many drinkers. If the specialist psychiatrist operates in the centre of a large city where there are many vagrant alcoholics, he will need to cooperate with other psychiatrists in providing and supporting special resources which are needed. These may include detoxification facilities, day shelters and a range of hostels capable of coping with homeless men.

Training the Psychiatrist Who Will Specialise in Alcoholism
The traditional training of the psychiatrist has taken place within psychiatric settings, where he has learned a way of thinking about the difficulties of his patients which prepares him for understanding their behaviour within those settings, and for discussing that behaviour with other psychiatrists. The language he has learned will often be more of a hindrance than a help in communicating about alcohol problems with general practitioners, and certainly with social workers, probation officers and voluntary workers.

In general, the specialist psychiatrist would be better prepared by a training which is more dynamically than phenomenologically orientated. Close supervision in individual, group and family therapy with alcohol abusers, will prove invaluable to his later work. Even if he has limited opportunity to practise these therapies later himself, the knowledge gained in his training will allow him to assess his cases more skilfully and support other workers more efficiently.

His experience in psychiatric settings will not alone be sufficient for him to function later as a specialist. Time spent in casualty departments, general medical wards, in health centres, social work area team offices, probation departments, hostels, day hospitals, marriage guidance clinics and reception centres would be valuable. The trainee will learn at first hand the multiplicity of problems caused by alcohol, but more importantly, he will learn early in his career to cooperate effectively with other disciplines. He will discover that members of these disciplines face practical difficulties in handling drinkers which are foreign to him as a psychiatrist, but which he must understand so that later he can provide meaningful consultation.

Traditionally medical training has been well served by the apprenticeship system, and without doubt the specialist ought to have a full-time apprenticeship to the kind of multidisciplinary community-based service described earlier. This local apprenticeship needs to be supplemented by the teaching materials and services provided by postgraduate courses such as are run in Britain by the Alcohol Education Centre, and which are increasingly available in many countries. The trainee must become aware of the full range of approaches available nationally, and indeed internationally.

References

Cartwright, A.K.J., Shaw, S.J. and Spratley, T.A. (1975). Designing a Comprehensive Community Response to Problems of Alcohol Abuse. Report by the Maudsley Alcohol Pilot Project to DHSS. September, 1975.
MacDonald, E.B. and Patel, A.R. (1975). Attitudes towards alcoholism. Brit. Med. J. 2: 430-31.
Ministry of Health. Hospital Treatment for Alcoholics. HM (62) 43.
Pollak, B. (1974). Clinics for alcoholics. Hospital Update, March 1974.

31 ALCOHOL EDUCATION

D.L. Davies

How one views alcoholism will determine what one teaches about it, and to whom.

The Concept of Alcoholism

The view adopted here is that alcoholism is the intermittent or continual ingestion of alcohol, leading to dependency or harm or both. Though not unimportant, drunkenness calls for separate consideration, and is acute intoxication, whereas the condition discussed here is chronic. Though some alcoholism is merely symptomatic of other readily and separately identifiable disorders — such as schizophrenia, dementia, manic depressive psychosis and personality disorders — by far the greatest part of those affected are initially normal people, who become alcoholic by drinking quantities of alcoholic beverage, and in such frequency, that they exceed the safe range which characterises all drugs of dependency (of which alcohol is just one).

The reasons for such excessive intake are now well understood. Life-style, which incorporates cultural, occupational, social and economic elements, is most important, especially in relation to availability of alcohol. Strictly personal factors, temperament, exposure to stress and the like, play a subsidiary role, possibly only in those who are otherwise biased towards the use of alcohol anyway, and who share a culturally determined attitude, favouring its increased use to induce a mood change.

It follows from all this that alcoholism presents sometimes as a medical problem, with complaint of ill-health, sometimes as a social problem, as when it leads to divorce or loss of job, and sometimes, when it consists simply of dependency, which, by definition, is harmless, it does not 'present' at all. Since, however, dependency for many is a potentially limited state, which can lead on to harm, not only by increased intake but also by a maintained steady intake over increasing periods of time, it is of the greatest significance when prevention is under discussion.

A statement of this kind would seem to be called for in somewhat explicit terms, before one can consider who are to be educated, and to what purpose, and what they are to be educated about. It is submitted that since alcoholism is a medico-social problem, it forms part of health education in the broadest sense. There is a public aspect, what the man in the street should know, to help him to avoid falling foul of alcohol. In that sense it belongs with personal hygiene, eating and drinking habits, recreation and the use of leisure, in short, with ordinary, everyday happenings, his awareness of these and his attitudes towards them.

Health education is the special business of various professional groups (medical and non-medical) as well as of government agencies. It is not proposed to dwell on this area here, except to say that in the case of prevention of alcoholism, the knowledge to be conveyed to the public is less easily summarised than, say, in the case of prevention of lung cancer and other disorders which attend cigarette smoking, and traditional techniques – films, posters, slogans and the like – have an even more limited role, and are less likely to convey what is a far from simple message.

It is very different with the education of professionals who, anyway, will encounter alcoholism in the course of their everyday work, whether they are physicians, dealing with physical ailments; psychiatrists with mental sequelae; social workers dealing with domestic, marital, occupational and economic problems; probation officers; health visitors; magistrates and many others, who all see the effects of excessive drinking in their day-to-day practice.

The Need for Prevention

They all require more knowledge of alcoholism than their professional training has provided hitherto. In saying this, one is inclined to assume that the purpose is to help them further to help their patients and clients. This is, of course, true, but it should be seen in perspective. The harm done by decades of excessive drinking (and that is the sort of time interval which precedes the presentation of alcoholic damage), is not lightly reversed. Curiously enough, those who survive the increased mortality from physical disease and suicide, which go with alcoholism, seem to make some sort of adjustment to their drinking with the passage of time, so that a 50 per cent remission rate couched in those terms may well represent the natural outcome. Sophisticated help, in one form or another, may raise this to 70 per cent, not a very striking increment, bearing in mind that the professionals involved see their role almost entirely as therapeutic.

To date, these efforts have not succeeded in stemming the tide – alcoholism everywhere seems to be on the increase, possibly doubling itself in this country every ten years at its present rate of progress, so that some rethinking of the role of these professionals, and the implication of such for education, is called for.

The position here is analogous to that in the case of smoking. Remedial measures for the heart, lung and other complications of smoking are losing the battle — whereas prevention by dealing with the antecedent habit has been clearly seen to work at least with one group able to appreciate the situation — doctors themselves.

It may well be, therefore, that with further education, which anyway is overdue, the present professionals might take on a role much more likely to reduce the harm wrought by alcohol, by a positive approach to prevention, long before alcoholism develops, certainly long before the harmful effects are seen. If it is true, as stated earlier, that the knowledge to be conveyed to the public is not easy to précis (if only because drinking is a deeply entrenched custom providing satisfaction to the majority who experience no harm), then a diffusion of such knowledge from well-educated professionals in the course of their everyday work, and at other times as responsible citizens, may achieve what is perhaps beyond the reach of the traditional vehicles of health education.

Content of Alcohol Education

So far, some hints have been given about the body of knowledge to be taught. In more detail, it will concern itself with learning theory; alcohol as a drug; the pressure to use it, which comes from the traditions of the social group concerned, peer and other pressures on the young; occupational, economic and legislative factors, bearing on individual intake; and the competition from other activities such as drug taking and gambling perhaps. So stated, it involves some study of psychology, pharmacology and sociology, areas of study which medical students share with science and arts students in their undergraduate years, and which are, or should be pursued in more depth after graduation, in accord with the now generally accepted view that professional education must continue throughout the practising life of the practitioner.

It is not possible in the space available here to particularise about what education is desirable for each professional group, either at the undergraduate or postgraduate stage (and for some groups, such as nurses and some social workers, these two terms are to be equated with the pre- and post-qualification stage). Nor is it possible to demarcate very closely education, on the one hand, which deals with habits of thought and judgement based on an understanding of principles, and training on the other hand, which is concerned with practice achieved largely by modelling of behaviour on that of experienced practitioners whilst carrying out the procedure involved. Both have an important part to play in producing the competent practitioner.

Medical Education

It might be appropriate, however, to look at one such group, the doctors, if only because of all those involved, it is the only one able to recognise and deal with the mental and physical complications of alcoholism, whilst traditionally heavily involved with social conditions, particularly where such bear on health (one thinks of pure water supply, nutrition, ventilation and other conditions of work, overcrowding and bad sanitation, in the long and creditable history of environmental health). This is in no sense in denying the role of non-medical people, either now or in the past. Indeed, some of the most important advances, particularly in the control of infectious disease, have come from non-medical men, like Pasteur and other chemists, whilst improvements in everyday living, with consequent benefits to health, have come from social workers, like the great reformers of the eighteenth and nineteenth centuries. (It might also be added that doctors have an increased propensity to develop alcoholism over the population at large, so that to focus on their education is additionally appropriate.)

Historically, alcoholism has featured very little in medical education at any level. Because alcohol is a drug, some mention of it occurs in the time devoted to pharmacology. Clinical alcoholism as encountered and recognised tends to be gross, and well advanced, whether it is in general medicine, neurology or psychiatry. The contribution of alcoholism to the work of doctors in general hospitals is insufficiently recognised though well documented, with perhaps one in seven patients in some general hospital beds falling into this category. In general practice, many alcoholics are missed even though they call on their doctors more than other patients. We know how such patients are overlooked — partly because an accurate (as far as it goes) diagnosis of, say, peptic ulcer or tuberculosis is made without further enquiry into the possible role of alcohol, and partly because of the persisting stereotype of the alcoholic as a down and out, so that such further enquiry is neglected in those who obviously are not.

Behind all this is the further difficulty that few of the pharmacologists and the physicians who are responsible for teaching the medical student are particularly interested in alcoholics, who are patients traditionally regarded (because of the stereotype) as largely beyond help, and anyway in disfavour because of the popular view (shared by many doctors) that they are constitutionally inferior, psychopathic or degenerate. Such terms comfortably remove the responsibility for monitoring his own drinking from all non-alcoholics (doctors and others alike).

Place in the Curriculum

If alcoholism is to be taught adequately at the undergraduate level, someone should accept the responsibility for seeing that through. That one person might be a coordinator of the teaching throughout the different departments of the medical school, or even of the university of which the medical school is a part, so that other professionals in training may receive, and contribute to, the multidisciplinary approach. There are cognate developments of this kind in the United States, which have relevance here.

Short of such revolutionary change, one department within the medical school should accept chief responsibility. The most likely would seem to be psychiatry or social medicine. The former since it usually has resources of one or more attached social workers and psychologists, would seem well placed, though the natural bias for such departments is towards therapy, and some may be hampered by an undue preoccupation with psychodynamics, which blurs the issue.

Social medicine departments, on the other hand, are more probably concerned with the understanding of conditions in which alcoholism arises, and are well placed to devote more attention to alcoholism on that account. It may well be that since tuberculosis is fast disappearing, they are already bereft of their model on which to teach the development of illness from social causes, overcrowding, malnutrition, dirty milk, spitting, poor work conditions and the like. If that is indeed so, then alcoholism might prove an even better model on which to teach principles of health, the virtues of multiprofessional collaboration, and prevention through the inculcation of understanding the role of quantity and frequency of drinking, and how drinking is promoted by customs, habits of thought, occupation and availability.

It might be as well, having regard to the on-going nature of medical education already referred to, if alcoholism were used as one model at least on which to teach basic principles of this kind in one department, and other principles, such as habit formation, in another, preferably by some agreement between these departments to prevent overlapping and to ensure economy. Perhaps at this point, the role of a coordinating person would seem especially appropriate.

More detailed teaching on this, as on other topics, should extend in the three years which follow basic qualification and lead to specialist qualification. Undoubtedly, general practice, general medicine and psychiatry more obviously call for consideration at this stage, though once again, community health should find its place among the leaders for reasons already given. At an even later stage, alcoholism should feature perhaps more than it does now, in the subject matter of the courses which are arranged in postgraduate medical centres and elsewhere as part of the programme of on-going professional education. It may be that in the course of time the evident reluctance of doctors to join with other professional workers in the kind of combined courses organised by the Alcohol Education Centre will diminish, as they see the problem as more and more social as well as medical, and appreciate that these other professions are involved with perhaps different problems of the same sufferers.

Education of Other Professionals

A point already made is that the basic knowledge about alcoholism needs to be given to all who work with alcoholics. Each kind of worker will apply this knowledge as seems relevant to his particular clients (whether they are people with family problems or on probation), and each group of workers will anyway have its own techniques, which broadly might be labelled casework for our purpose.

Since so many social workers are already possessed of casework techniques, their main need, before becoming more proficient in helping alcoholics, will be to inform themselves about alcoholism. Acquiring this knowledge in concert with their fellow social workers, nurses, health visitors and others, will be most economical if carried out through attendance at joint courses. An additional advantage of such an arrangement is the sharing of viewpoints and experiences which such joint courses engender. It would seem, therefore, that in alcohol education generally there is much to be said for some kind of central course, shared by different professional groups at corresponding stages of their studies, arranged on a faculty, or a university basis, and, in some cases, leading perhaps to a certificate in alcohol studies.

One recent development within a profession is worthy of note, the introduction in Britain by the Joint Board of Clinical Nursing Studies of a certificate in alcohol nursing. No doubt, social workers are considering the implications of this for their own work. More important, however, than increasing specialisation, is the need to introduce the study of alcoholism at greater length than at present into the syllabus of work for the main professional groups concerned, bearing in mind that alcoholism is so widespread, and increasing so rapidly, that willy-nilly it will force itself to their attention. If such teaching can be given, and especially if prevention at least equally with treatment is seen to be the role of these workers, then the prospect of stemming the tide of alcoholism becomes brighter (even without regard to the burgeoning knowledge which can be more effectively applied as it comes to hand), because the machinery for dissemination and implementation of knowledge has been created.

Some of those who accept the concept of alcoholism and its aetiology as outlined here, would place their emphasis in prevention on legislative action, and control of availability. The greater the progress along that road, the greater the reluctance of the public is likely to be, since all measures which restrict the liberty of the many for the sake of the few are unpopular and therefore politically unattractive. At some point, as with prohibition in the United States, control becomes unworkable.

Such measures are more likely to succeed if they proceed in pace with general enlightenment on the part of the public and changing habits however slowly evolving, towards restrained, rather than unfettered, drinking. Perhaps the success of environmental restraint is inextricably linked to personal restraint, and that, in turn, to education in the broadest sense. Professional workers are well placed to promote such change, but only if they themselves are educated to understand the nature of the problem, and see the logic in what they undertake in the course of their everyday work.

LIST OF CONTRIBUTORS

D. I. Acres is a General Practitioner in Benfleet, Essex.

I. S. Benjamin is a Lecturer in Surgery in the University Department of Surgery at the Royal Infirmary, Glasgow.

Howard Cappell is Head of Psychology and Psychological Studies at the Addiction Research Foundation, Toronto.

A. K. J. Cartwright is Research Director, Alcohol Pilot Project at Maudsley Hospital, London.

I. Chanarin is a Consultant Haematologist in the Department of Haematology, Northwich Park Hospital, Harrow.

Anthony W. Clare is a Lecturer in Psychiatry in the Institute of Psychiatry, London.

Christopher Clayson is former President of the Royal College of Physicians, Edinburgh, and former Chairman of the Scottish Council for Postgraduate Medical Education.

D. L. Davies is Medical Director, Alcohol Education Centre at Maudsley Hospital, London.

Michael Davis is Senior Lecturer and Hon. Consultant Physician in the Liver Unit at King's College Hospital, London.

Griffith Edwards is Hon. Director of the Addiction Research Unit at the Institute of Psychiatry, London.

Marcus Grant is Educational Director of the Alcohol Education Centre, London.

D. N. Hancock is Senior Probation Officer for the Inner London Probation and After-Care Service.

J. D. J. Havard is Deputy Secretary of the British Medical Association.

Ray Hodgson is Senior Lecturer, Addiction Research Unit at the Institute of Psychiatry, London.

B. D. Hore is Consultant in Charge of the Regional Alcoholism Treatment Unit at Withington Hospital, Manchester.

N. Krasner is Senior Registrar at the Gastrointestinal Centre of the Southern General Hospital, Glasgow.

Norman Kreitman is Director of the MRC Unit for Epidemiological Studies in Psychiatry at the University Department of Psychiatry, Royal Edinburgh Hospital.

J. M. Littleton is Reader in Pharmacology in the Department of Pharmacology at King's College, London.

Vincent Marks is Professor of Clinical Biochemistry at the University of Surrey.

C. D. Marsden is Professor of Neurology at the Institute of Psychiatry, London.

W. R. Murray is a Lecturer in Surgery in the Department of Surgery of the Western Infirmary, Glasgow.

Jim Orford is Principal Psychologist at Exevale Hospital, Exeter.

J. Park is at the Regional Poisoning Treatment Centre, The Royal Infirmary, Edinburgh.

A. T. Proudfoot is a Consultant at the Regional Poisoning Treatment Centre, The Royal Infirmary, Edinburgh.

Raj Rathod is a Consultant Psychiatrist at St Christopher's Day Hospital, Horsham.

Bruce Ritson is at the Andrew Duncan Clinic, Royal Edinburgh Hospital.

David Robinson is Senior Lecturer in Sociology at the Addiction Research Unit, Institute of Psychiatry, London.

Wolfgang Schmidt is Associate Director of Research at the Addiction Research Foundation, Toronto.

G. K. Shaw is a Consultant Psychiatrist at Bexley Hospital, Bexley, Kent.

S. J. Shaw is a Research Sociologist, Alcohol Pilot Project at Maudsley Hospital, London.

James Shields is Reader in Psychiatric Genetics at the Institute of Psychiatry, London.

T. A. Spratley is a Consultant Psychiatrist, Alcoholism Treatment Services at St Martin's Hospital Canterbury.

A. Thomson is a Consultant Physician at Greenwich General Hospital, London.

Roger Williams is Director of the Liver Unit, King's College Hospital, London.

INDEX

absenteeism 245-6
abstinence: as treatment goal 136,
  147, 310, 326; criterion of
  outcome success 279; effect on
  prognosis of liver disease 171-4;
  in non-treated alcoholics 281
acetaldehyde 109-10, 118, 164, 182
adoptee studies 122, 126-9
adrenal cortex: hypoadrenocorticism
  212-13; adrenocorticotrophic
  hormone (ACTH) 211
advertising: restrictions on advertising
  of alcohol 38; public health
  campaigns 69, 258, 346
aetiology of alcoholism: behavioural
  principles 104
affluence: effect on social drinking
  37, 43, 78, 82; increasing
  expenditure on drink 79
Alcoholics Anonymous (AA):
  conceptual stereotypes 56, 149;
  in prison populations 268; liaison
  with family doctors 325; supported
  by Community Alcohol team 343
alcoholism as a medical speciality
  71, 76, 88, 339
alcoholic beverage industry 38, 41-2
alcohol consumption distribution:
  acceptance of 35, 38; daily
  average 34; epidemiology 48-9,
  33, 50, 52, 151; related to
  excessive use 32-8, 42, 67-8, 157
alcohol dehydrogenase 118
alcoholic hallucinosis: genetic relationship to schizophrenia 120; related
  to delirium tremens 316; United
  States definition 316
alcohol-related problems :
  blood disorders 218-20
  endocrine disorders 208-15
  in outpatients 331
  liver disorders 158-61, 179-85
  neurological disorders 190
  pancreas disorders 198-201
  separated from dependence
    syndrome 140
amblyopia 193
amino acids 112

amnesic syndrome see Wernicke-
  Korsakoff psychosis
anaemia 218-19
'Antabuse' (Disulfiram) 285, 297, 325
antibody reactions 165-7, 170
anxiety: anxiolytic effect of alcohol
  62, 105, 292; in presence of
  drinking cues 291; role of
  neurotransmitters 111
ascites 160
assortative mating 124, 240
autoimmune reaction see antibody
  reactions
aversion treatment: chemical
  aversion 299-300; electrical
  aversion 286, 298-9

behavioural treatment of alcoholism
  community reinforcement 295-8
  controlled drinking goal 302-4
  day care setting 342
  development of coping skills 292-4
  operant learning techniques 88,
    101-3, 145
  response prevention 301
  see also aversion therapy
binge, alcoholic see bout drinking
blood disorders: macrocytosis 219;
  megaloblastic anaemia 219-20;
  morphology in acute intoxication
  218
blood groups 119
bone marrow morphology 218
bout drinking: genetic factors 129;
  liver disease in bout drinkers 162;
  pancreatitis associated with 204
Butler report 265

Canada 16-26 passim, 44, 51, 158
carbon tetrachloride poisoning 226
carcinoma, primary hepatocellular
  169-70
catecholamine metabolism 111
central pontine myelinosis see
  myelinosis
cerebellar syndrome 192
children of alcoholic parents see
  family studies

For Product Safety Concerns and Information please contact our EU
representative GPSR@taylorandfrancis.com
Taylor & Francis Verlag GmbH, Kaufingerstraße 24, 80331 München, Germany

www.ingramcontent.com/pod-product-compliance
Lightning Source LLC
Chambersburg PA
CBHW070547270326
41926CB00013B/2231